Acceptable Premise

An Epistemic Approach to an Informal Logic Problem

When, if ever, is one justified in accepting the basic premises of an argument? What is the proper criterion of premise acceptability? Can the criterion be theoretically or philosophically justified?

This is the first book to provide a comprehensive theory of premise acceptability and it answers these questions from an epistemological approach that the author calls commonsense foundationalism. It will be eagerly sought out not just by specialists in informal logic, critical thinking, and argumentation theory but also by a broader range of philosophers and those teaching rhetoric.

James B. Freeman is Professor of Philosophy at Hunter College of the City University of New York.

For the Hoffmans,
all of those who are with us,
and in memory of Don

Acceptable Premises

An Epistemic Approach to an Informal Logic Problem

JAMES B. FREEMAN

Hunter College of the City University of New York

CAMBRIDGE
UNIVERSITY PRESS

PUBLISHED BY THE PRESS SYNDICATE OF THE UNIVERSITY OF CAMBRIDGE
The Pitt Building, Trumpington Street, Cambridge, United Kingdom

CAMBRIDGE UNIVERSITY PRESS
The Edinburgh Building, Cambridge CB2 2RU, UK
40 West 20th Street, New York, NY 10011-4211, USA
477 Williamstown Road, Port Melbourne, VIC 3207, Australia
Ruiz de Alarcón 13, 28014 Madrid, Spain
Dock House, The Waterfront, Cape Town 8001, South Africa

http://www.cambridge.org

© James B. Freeman 2005

First published 2005

Printed in the United States of America

Typeface ITC New Baskerville 10/13 pt.   *System* LATEX 2$_\varepsilon$ [TB]

A catalog record for this book is available from the British Library.

Library of Congress Cataloging in Publication Data

Freeman, James B.
Acceptable premises : an epistemic approach to an informal logic problem /
James B. Freeman.
p. cm.
Includes bibliographical references (p.) and index.
ISBN 0-521-83301-9 – ISBN 0-521-54060-7 (pb.)
1. Logic.   I. Title.
BC71.F734   2005
160–dc22   2004045887

ISBN 0 521 83301 9 hardback
ISBN 0 521 54060 7 paperback

Contents

PART 3.   PRACTICE AND PERSPECTIVE

Preface

The project of this book is easily stated. Suppose a proponent puts forward some claim that is in some way doubtful or controversial. The proponent thus incurs a burden of proof. He may attempt to discharge this burden by presenting an argument for his claim. For simplicity's sake, let us assume that he puts forward a one-premise argument. But if that premise in turn is controversial, if by putting it forward the proponent incurs a further burden of proof, he will not have discharged his initial burden unless he discharges this further burden. By attempting to do that, the proponent may incur a further burden of proof because of the premise he puts forward to defend his controversial premise, and so on. Now the opposite of burden of proof is presumption. So if the proponent is proceeding in good faith, he is seeking a premise for which there is a presumption. Given a presumption, his premise should be acceptable. Now any noncircular argument will have basic premises, those not argued for in the course of that argument. So the proponent is seeking ultimately to ground his argument on basic premises for which there is a presumption. When is there a presumption for a premise and how do we recognize it? That is the project of this book, developed over Chapters 1 through 11.

Our conception of the problem of premise adequacy limits our investigation from being even more complex or drawn out. First, notice that our proponent is pictured as asserting each of the premises he puts forward. He has not supposed or asked his interlocutor to suppose some statement true for the sake of the argument. On our view, the question of premise adequacy or acceptability does not arise for supposed premises, such as those assumed in the course of a *reductio ad absurdum* or conditional argument. Such premises are not accept*ed*, at least in the contexts in which they are supposed, and thus the question of their acceptability does not arise in connection with their occurrences in those contexts.

There is another less trivial way in which the project of this essay is circumscribed. From our perspective, we turn to an argument to discover whether there is good reason to accept some claim. If we recognized that we were justified in believing the premises of an argument and that the argument transferred this justification to its conclusion, we would have a positive answer. Traditionally, logic has concerned itself with the connection of premises with conclusions, and thus with the issue of transferring justification. Informal logic's raising the question of premise acceptability, to our mind, raises the question of whether one is justified in believing or accepting the basic premises of an argument. But we may turn to arguments for other purposes. As Walton has pointed out on numerous occasions, arguments may occur in many types of dialogue. As Blair (1995) points out, this gives rise to different contexts of arguments raising different questions of premise adequacy. Whether or not one should argue for a premise may depend on whether the argument is occurring in the context of a quarrel, an attempt at rational persuasion, or an exchange involving hostile advocacy. But from our perspective here, growing out of the logico-epistemic evaluation of arguments especially as conceived by informal logic, we may set such issues aside. From our perspective, the issues of argument evaluation concern whether the conclusion is justified in light of the premises and whether those premises are justified. We address ourselves exclusively to premise adequacy in this sense in this essay.

To give just a hint of our answer, let us say here that premise acceptability is to be explicated in terms of presumption, which depends upon the source vouching for a statement. By a source, we do not mean simply some person or organization that might put forward that statement. If one believes some premise because one perceives that the state of affairs the premise alleges to hold actually does hold, one's own perception is the source (at least *a* source) vouching for that premise. What sources then may vouch for a premise? May we presume a particular source reliable in general or under certain circumstances? Because presumptions can be undercut or defeated, what factors defeat a presumption for a source's reliability? If we know how to answer these questions, we might very well be able to determine whether there is a presumption for a premise. But why should one worry about this question in the first place? Does the standard textbook account not tell us that an argument is good from the logical point of view just in case it has true premises which either deductively entail or give inductively strong support to the conclusion? Why is truth not the proper criterion for premise adequacy? That indeed would seem to be the first question. We turn to it in Chapter 1.

Acknowledgments

Some material prepared for this book has appeared in various previously published papers. Material from Chapter 1 appeared in "Why Classical Foundationalism Cannot Provide a Proper Account of Premise Acceptability," *Inquiry* (1996). Material from Chapter 2 was included in "A Dialectical Approach to Premise Acceptability," *Proceedings of the Second International Conference on Argumentation* (1991). Material from Chapter 3 appeared in "Consider the Source: One Step in Assessing Premise Acceptability," *Argumentation* 10 (1996), 453–60 (© 1996 Kluwer Academic Publishers). "Consider the Source" appeared earlier in *Analysis and Evaluation: Proceedings of the Third ISSA Conference on Argumentation* 2 (1995). Further material from Chapter 3 appeared in "The Pragmatic Dimension of Premise Acceptability," in *Anyone with a View: Theoretical Contributions to the Study of Argumentation,* 2003 (© 2003 Kluwer Academic Publishers). This paper also was included in the *Proceedings of the Fifth International Conference on Argumentation* (2003). Material from Chapter 4 was included in "Epistemic Justification and Premise Acceptability," *Argumentation* 10 (1996), 59–68 (© 1996 Kluwer Academic Publishers). Material from both Chapters 3 and 4 also appeared in "Premise Acceptability, Deontology, Internalism, Justification," *Informal Logic* (1995). Sections 1 and 2 of Chapter 5 are largely drawn from "What Types of Statements Are There?" *Argumentation* 14 (2000), 135–57 (© 2000 Kluwer Academic Publishers). An earlier version of this paper appears in *Argumentation & Rhetoric* (1998). Material from Chapter 8 is included in "Can Interpretations Ever Be Acceptable Basic Premises?" in *Argumentation and Its Applications: Proceedings of the Fourth OSSA Conference,* 2002. I hereby express my thanks to these publications and their editors for allowing me to use this material. In particular I note that material from the three articles in *Argumentation* and the article in *Anyone with a View* appears with kind permission of Kluwer Academic Publishers.

We wish to thank the editor of *The Monist* for permission to reprint selections from "Concepts of Epistemic Justification" by William P. Alston, Copyright © 1985, *THE MONIST: An International Quarterly Journal of General Philosophical Inquiry*, Peru, Illinois USA, 61354. Reprinted by permission. We wish to thank Dr. James Q. Wilson and The Free Press for permission to include quotations from *The Moral Sense* by James Q. Wilson. Copyright © 1993 by James Q. Wilson. Reprinted with permission of the author and The Free Press, a Division of Simon & Schuster. All rights reserved. Work on this book has occupied two sabbatical years, in 1994 and 2001, when I held Fellowship Leaves from Hunter College of The City University of New York. I hereby gratefully acknowledge Hunter College's granting me these leaves.

PART I

ACCEPTABILITY

Dialectical and Epistemological Considerations

1

Why do We Need a Theory of Acceptability?

When, if ever, is a premise – indeed a statement in general – acceptable? That is the central question of this book. Therefore, this is a normative investigation. This point needs to be underlined, as the very word "acceptability" contains an ambiguity. A statement's acceptability may mean its prospects for being accepted by a certain audience. This is not our meaning. We are not interested in the marketability of a statement but in whether the statement *should* be accepted. Is acceptance rationally justified for a particular audience? However, there are two preliminary issues we must address. Why is this book needed at all? Is there no simple, straightforward, and adequate answer available? The simplest way to address this question is to look at certain simple and straightforward answers and see that they either do not answer the question correctly or are fraught with problems. But first we should clarify what it means to accept a statement, and so by implication what "acceptability" means.

1.1 ACCEPTANCE – A BASIC DEFINITION

In (1992), L. Jonathan Cohen contrasts these two concepts: To believe a proposition that p is to be disposed to feel that p is true and that *not-p* is false, whether or not one is prepared to take that p as a premise for further belief or action. To accept that p is to take that p as a premise "for deciding what to do or think in a particular context, whether or not one feels it to be true that p" (1992, p. 4). Accepting a statement as a premise does not mean assuming it just for the sake of argument but unconditionally or categorically. We might talk of conditional acceptance or define assumption as conditional acceptance. But doing so would be confusing. Our ultimate interest is normative. We are concerned not just with what accepting that p means but with the conditions under which acceptance is justifiable. Such normative questions do not arise for premises taken conditionally. We can assume just about any statement we want.

Acceptance then is unconditional in the sense that accepting a statement means taking it categorically as a premise. But is acceptance categorical, unconditional in the further sense that proper, normatively correct acceptance is irrevocable? Are only statements that we could see not to be subject or open to defeat be properly acceptable? We should specifically address this major philosophical issue at the outset of our inquiry. On the one hand, there are intuitions indicating that we may quite properly accept a statement at one point in time fully acknowledging the possibility that at some future time we shall withdraw that acceptance in the light of further evidence. Acceptance, then, is not irrevocable commitment. We are not confronted with counterevidence now, else we could not accept the statement. But we may admit the possibility of such evidence. This is *not* to say that indefeasible statements are not accepted or that one never takes any statements he or she accepts as necessary or indefeasibly true. This also may happen. But, on this view, indefeasibility is not a necessary condition for acceptance.

On the other hand, there is a whole philosophical tradition that would see defeasibility as a bar to acceptance. In particular, indefeasibility is a necessary condition for the acceptability of basic premises. This is classical foundationalism, a position that we must address. Is certainty then a necessary condition for acceptability? This question raises the basic epistemological assumptions and approach of our inquiry. Our answer will determine the subsequent direction of our investigation and the extent to which it is philosophically undergirded. We turn directly to this issue in the next section.

1.2 ACCEPTABILITY, CERTAINTY, AND EPISTEMIC DUTY

That certainty is a sufficient condition for acceptability seems straightforward. If I am certain of a proposition p, what more reason could I need to take p as a premise for further deliberation or action? But what are we to say of the claim that certainty is a necessary condition for acceptability? On a foundationalist picture of knowledge, some beliefs will be basic, not accepted on the basis of propositions presented as evidence for them. Other beliefs will be accepted on the basis of propositional evidence.

This evidence will consist either of basic beliefs or of beliefs accepted on the basis of yet further propositional evidence. There are, however, no infinite regresses of support. Any chain of propositions $A_1, A_2, \ldots$ where A_1 is accepted on the basis of A_2, A_2 on A_3, A_3 on $A_4, \ldots$, will be finitely long and will ultimately end in basic propositions. This grounding relation also will not be circular. A_4 will not be accepted on the basis of A_1, for example.

For such a structure of beliefs to be knowledge, the basic propositions or beliefs must satisfy certain conditions. Some beliefs may typically be basic because it is hard to see how anyone would want evidence to support them or what propositions one would offer in their support. I seem to see a truck hurtling down the highway toward me or I seem to hear thunder (am appeared to thunderously). What evidence in the form of propositions would be needed or could be offered for such beliefs? Other beliefs are basic not because propositional evidence could not be given for them but because typically it would not be needed. I can just see that some simple *a priori* truths are true. Once I understand the concepts involved, do I need evidence for the laws of identity, noncontradiction, or excluded middle?

But not every proposition taken as basic need be properly basic. According to Plantinga, a belief is properly basic for me if it is basic for me, and also meets some other condition C, differing choices for C leading to different varieties of foundationalism (1993a, p. 70). Although classical foundationalists may themselves differ on the exact formulation of condition C, a belief satisfying C will be certain. For Descartes, C will be the condition that a belief be sufficiently clear and distinct. For Locke, "a belief . . . is properly basic for me only if it is either self-evident or appropriately about my own immediate experience" (Plantinga, 1993a, p. 71). But in either case, such beliefs will be certain. For Descartes, the only other beliefs that are acceptable besides basic beliefs are those deductively entailed by basic beliefs. For Locke, if a belief follows deductively or is sufficiently supported inductively ultimately by basic beliefs, it is acceptable. Classical foundationalism thus lends the weight of its influence to the view that certainty is a necessary condition for acceptability, at least for basic acceptability.

What is the rationale for this position? At the beginning of the First Meditation, Descartes says that "reason already convinces me that I should abstain from belief in things which are not entirely certain and indubitable no less carefully than from the belief in those which appear to me to be manifestly false" (1960, p. 75). Reason convinces Descartes of this because his goal is to achieve at least some "firm and constant knowledge in the sciences" (1960, p. 75). If that is one's goal, then one should abstain from accepting propositions that are less than certain, lest they render one's scientific opinions questionable.

In the Fourth Meditation, however, Descartes apparently goes further. We should unconditionally refrain from accepting what is not understood clearly and distinctly. Not to refrain is to use one's free will improperly, which may give assent only to what is seen with sufficient clarity and distinctness. (Compare Descartes 1960, p. 115.) Otherwise, one risks falling into error, misusing the will. It is our epistemic duty then to avoid error and this requires accepting nothing except what is seen clearly and distinctly.

John Locke also enunciates this same theme of epistemic duty. However, while Descartes enjoins accepting nothing but what is perceived with sufficient clarity and distinctness, Locke endorses accepting nothing except on good reason. "Faith is nothing but a firm assent of the mind: which if it be regulated, *as is our duty*, cannot be afforded to anything, but upon good reason" (quoted in Plantinga 1993a, p. 13, italics added). For Locke, certainty is a necessary condition for basic acceptability, for the acceptability of basic premises.[1] To simply accept a proposition that is not certain, without adequate reason, would violate epistemic duty for Locke.

What are we to say to the view that the only basically acceptable propositions, acceptable in themselves without argument, are those that are certain? What propositions are certain? Clearly, besides truths of reason they are propositions about our experience in the sense of how we are appeared to or about the immediate contents of our minds. Should I perceive a tree in front of me, the proposition that there is a tree in front of me is not certain, for this may be a skillful illusion. What *is* certain is that I am now appeared to treely. Truths of formal logic and mathematics, together with semantic truths, statements true by virtue of the very meaning of the nonlogical constants they contain, are certain. These are the traditional truths of reason. But clearly, not every such truth is acceptable as a basic premise. For a mathematical truth may be certain, yet require much ingenuity to show it certain. But surely there are some truths of reason whose status or certainty can be immediately recognized. These propositions are self-evident. What then may we say to the claim that only propositions that concern one's immediate experience or are self-evident truths of reason, the properly basic propositions of classical foundationalism, are acceptable as basic premises?

We argue that this view (1) has unacceptable consequences for ordinary deliberation and action; (2) has unacceptable consequences for argumentation; and (3) is neither self-evident in itself nor provided with sufficient argument. Concerning (1), should only propositions concerning one's immediate experience or stating self-evident truths of reason be basically acceptable, I could not accept that there is a tree in front of me without evidence in the form of propositions supporting that claim. What would that argument be like? Can I show that there is a tree in front of me from propositions about how I am appeared to treely? Is any statement then reporting what we are now perceiving ever acceptable? But if I am looking at the tree in good light, with normal perceptual abilities, what reason have I for doubting that the color, shape, size I perceive are veridical? Is the fact that my senses have been occasionally deceived strong enough reason for doubt here, *pace* Descartes?

On this view, I could never accept anyone's testimony without evidence in the form of argument. Accepting what someone says as to time of day, direction to my destination, indeed answers to just about any question I might ask is not proper. Not only would personal testimony not yield any statements acceptable in themselves, neither would expert opinion nor so-called common knowledge. I cannot accept without evidence my doctor's diagnosis or commonly acknowledged reports about the past or commonly agreed to moral judgments. None of these statements may I take as basic premises for further deliberation or action. But unless I have reason to think these sources mistaken or deceiving, why should I not accept personal testimony or that of experts or "common knowledge"? If I do not, how could I get around in the world? What would I have to reason from?

Concerning (2), that this view would have unacceptable consequences for argumentation, it would seem that in attempting to convince others of some claim by argumentation, our stock of basic premises would be even more limited. For if I am genuinely trying to get my audience to accept some claim, the premises of my argument should be statements my audience already accepts. Can I in the course of this argument appeal to a basic premise about *my* experience? Are such claims certain for both speaker and audience when used as premises in arguments? It may be certain to Descartes that he thinks, but should he offer that proposition as a premise in an argument, it will not be certain to his audience that Descartes thinks. Likewise, it seems that incorrigible propositions are self-evident only to persons who report about their own current perceptions, what each is perceiving right now. But although "The fire seems hot to me now" may be certain for Descartes, should he offer it as a premise, it will not be certain for his audience that the fire feels hot to Descartes. Does this mean that these types of propositions which are certain are available only in arguments with oneself? That would be too hasty a conclusion.

Descartes could phrase his premise this way: "Consider what you are doing when you entertain this premise. Isn't it evident that you are now thinking?" If the addressee admits yes, she has admitted that she herself, not Descartes, thinks – a proposition apparently certain to her. Should Descartes say "Look at and feel this. Isn't it evident that it looks blue and feels hard?" Again, if the addressee admits yes, she has admitted that this looks blue and feels hard to her, not Descartes. In this way, Descartes could build an argument on premises certain for his audience. But there is something very anomalous here. These premises may be certain to the audience, but not to Descartes himself. Should one accept without argument only those propositions that are certain, then Descartes should not accept the basic premises of the very argument he is constructing (even though analogous statements are self-evident to him). But how can Descartes argue sincerely if he does not accept the very premises from which he argues?

We find the view that the properly basic propositions of classical foundationalism only are acceptable as basic premises is neither itself self-evident nor has it been properly supported by argument. We might think of taking a proposition as a basic premise as taking a risk. The classical foundationalist view then is tantamount to saying that the only acceptable risk is the null risk. Why is it unacceptable to take risks? Certainly that view is not self-evident as an investment strategy, and neither does it appear self-evident as an epistemic strategy. Have classical foundationalists presented compelling arguments for this requirement of certainty? As we noted earlier, Descartes may justify the claim conditionally. If our goal is to identify or reach sure knowledge in the sciences, then we should reject what is less than certain for our basic premises. But what if that is not one's goal, or not one's goal in all situations? Why then should one refuse to accept what is not certain?

To find arguments in Descartes, it seems we must reconstruct them. In (1971), Wellman ascribes two arguments to Descartes that reasoning must go back ultimately to self-evident or indubitable premises, and he rebuts each.[2]

> (1) Knowledge is distinguished from mere belief by its certainty. Any
>   conclusion based upon premises that could possibly be doubted

> is itself subject to doubt. Therefore one can claim to know that a
> conclusion is true only if it is derived from indubitable premises.
> (Wellman 1971, p. 145)

The problem with this argument, as Wellman points out, is the first
premise. Why should we understand knowledge this way? Furthermore,
the premise apparently involves a false dilemma. Are certain knowledge
and mere belief our only two alternatives? Is not rationally justified belief
a third? (Compare Wellman 1971, p. 146.)

> (2) There is always reason to doubt any conclusion based upon
> premises that are less than indubitable. So since one has reason
> to doubt such a conclusion, one is rationally unjustified in accept-
> ing it. (Wellman 1971, p. 146)

In (1), Wellman accepted the inference but rejected a premise. Here
Wellman accepts the premise but rejects the inference. Why, just because
there is reason to doubt a conclusion, are we rationally unjustified in accepting it? We would be rationally unjustified in accepting the conclusion
unconditionally, but not tentatively (Wellman 1971, pp. 146–47). So the
arguments for the classical foundationalist strictures are not sound.

But we may bring an even more devastating criticism against classical
foundationalism. Following Plantinga, we may claim that many forms
of this view are self-referentially incoherent. What of the claim C that a
statement is acceptable if and only if it is either self-evident, concerns my
immediate experience, or is supported ultimately by such statements? Is
C itself acceptable according to C? (Compare Plantinga 1993a, p. 85).

As we have pointed out, if our goal is certain knowledge, then only
what is clear and distinct is acceptable. But this leaves it open whether
there is not some wider sense of knowledge or justified belief, subject
to normative regulation, which need not be certain. Another remark of
Descartes is quite suggestive. He feels he cannot overdo his doubt, "since
it is not now a question of acting, but only of [meditating and] learning."
(1960, p. 80) Does this mean that when it is a question of acting, accepting noncertain propositions is appropriate besides accepting certain
propositions? Descartes does not address this question, but one wonders
why he would allude to this distinction if practical contexts did not allow
a wider field of acceptance. Hence the classical foundationalist demand
for certainty – of our basic premises at least – is not warranted, at least as
a general requirement on basic premises. If certainty is not required for
acceptability, then what is? What criteria adequately delimit acceptability?

We can readily think of a number of initially plausible answers, all ultimately problematic. We consider them in the next section.

1.3 "POPULAR" CRITERIA FOR ACCEPTABILITY

i. A Statement Is Acceptable If and Only If It is True

This is perhaps the simplest and most straightforward answer concerning acceptability. But we can readily see its inadequacy as others have amply shown. Being true is neither necessary nor sufficient for being acceptable. It is not necessary because the preponderance of evidence at one's disposal might favor some statement which is, in fact, false. That statement would then seem worthy of acceptance. It is not sufficient, for a statement may in fact be true, yet one might possess no evidence for it. Indeed, the preponderance of evidence one possesses might even be against it. In such cases, the statement would not be worthy of acceptance from one's point of view, even though true.

Blair raises an interesting objection to the claim that truth is not a necessary condition for statement acceptability in (1986). Some will claim that if statements are properly hedged then we can demand that they be true before accepting them. So, for example, where the preponderance of evidence supports "A is B" we should accept "A is probably B," unless the evidence actually entails that A is B. Fogelin points out in (1982) that there are two ways to hedge a premise or statement. Besides probabilistic qualifications, we can weaken the statement, replacing "all" by "most," "usually," "typically;" "most" by "many" or "some" (1982, p. 46). What may we say to this proposal? Will this hedging transformation always result in a true statement, allowing the critic to demand that only true statements be accepted? I believe the answer is negative for both types of hedging.

Suppose the preponderance of evidence is for Jones's guilt. Will I be assured of accepting a true statement if I accept not

(1) Jones is guilty

but

(2) Jones is probably guilty?

This move completely misconstrues the function of the modal word. In (2) and statements like it, there is tacit reference to the evidence supporting the claim of Jones's guilt. The modal word "probably" is really not part of the statement, but serves to make a claim about how strongly the evidence supports that statement. Although the conversational force of "probably" may be to indicate a weaker degree of commitment, literally we have not produced a weaker statement, but the same statement together with a comment on the weight of its supporting evidence.[3]

What about the nonmodal hedges? Now it is certainly true that on occasion, evidence will support a weaker, hedged version of a statement, but it is not at all obvious that it guarantees such a statement to be true. If every observed A is also a B,

(3) All A's are B's

may still be false. But are we guaranteed that

(4) Usually A's are B's

or

(5) Typically A's are B's

are true? Couldn't we have observed just atypical A's?
A critic might demand that we should hedge further. Surely our evidence does guarantee that

(6) Some A's are B's

is true. This is correct, but the demand that we accept only such severely hedged statements would render us incapable of cogently arguing on many occasions. For the statements available as acceptable premises would be simply too weak to support our desired conclusions. (Compare Blair 1986, pp. 15–16.) As with classical foundationalism, we may ask for the rationale for restricting acceptability to such statements and whether that rationale is justified. Given our understanding of what "acceptance" means, is this insistence that only true statements be accepted reasonable? To accept a statement is not to judge it indefeasible but simply to take it as a premise. It is simply understood that this taking may be withdrawn should rebutting evidence come to light. If that is what statement acceptance means, what is wrong then with accepting a statement for which there is a preponderance of evidence, even if that statement as a matter of fact is not true?

ii. A Statement Is Acceptable If and Only If It Is Known to be True

Surely, if a statement is known to be true, it is acceptable to those persons who know it to be true. What better reason could I have to take a statement as a premise? So being known true is a proper sufficient condition of acceptability. But is it a proper necessary condition? Understanding that knowing a statement to be true entails that it *is* true, one cannot know a statement which is false. But, as with truth as a necessary condition of acceptability, this criterion rules out the acceptability of a statement that all the available evidence favors but that is nonetheless false. Such a statement is not known to be true, but why in the light of such evidence, in particular evidence of significant weight, should that statement not be acceptable?

iii. A Statement Is Acceptable If and Only If It is Accepted

That this proposal is unacceptable should be obvious. Acceptability, as we have pointed out, is a normative concept. Whether or not a statement is accepted by some person or group of persons is an empirical not a normative question. Someone's accepting a claim is a separate question from his or her having appropriate justification to accept that claim. This definition baldly tries to define a normative concept in terms of an empirical concept.

Interestingly, this position is endorsed by C. L. Hamblin in (1970). For Hamblin, if, say, Alice is trying to convince Bertrand of some claim that he currently does not accept, and she presents him with an argument whose premises he does accept and from which the conclusion follows by an inferential step that he also accepts, then Alice has given Bertrand a good argument for that claim. (Compare Hamblin 1970, p. 245.) At least, Hamblin claims, it is good from Bertrand's point of view, from what will persuade him, and it is this sense of goodness that Hamblin takes as "the appropriate basis of a set of criteria" (1970, p. 242) for evaluating the goodness of arguments in practice. The issue here is whether the person or persons to whom an argument is addressed accept the premises. If, taking an adjudicative role, we say that the premises of the argument are true or its inferential move to the conclusion valid, we are changing the subject from what the audience accepts to what I accept. Of the logician as adjudicator Hamblin says

If he says "Smith's premises are true" or "Jones's argument is invalid" he is taking sides in the dialogue exactly as if he were a participant in it; . . . his formulation says no more nor less than the formulation "I accept Smith's premises" or "I disapprove of Jones's argument." . . . The logician does not stand above and outside practical argumentation or, necessarily, pass judgment on it. He is not a judge or a court of appeal, and there is no such judge or court: he is, at best, a trained advocate. It follows that it is not the logician's particular job to declare the truth of any statement, *or the validity of any argument.* (1970, p. 244, italics in original)

Hamblin here enunciates a position that rejects the common understanding of logical and epistemic evaluation. When logicians say that an argument is deductively invalid or inductively incorrect, they do not mean simply that they do not accept the inference but that it violates the objective canons of valid deductive argument or correct inductive inference. Likewise, to say that the premises of an argument are true signifies more than acceptance. It signifies that these premises satisfy some criterion of truth, for example, they square with the way the world is. Hamblin thus incurs a burden of proof to show that this understanding of logical and epistemic evaluation is faulty or wrongheaded. I do not see that he has discharged, or even really accepted, that burden of proof.

Furthermore, it is doubtful that Hamblin could discharge this burden of proof, even if he accepted it. For suppose Alice presents Bertrand with an argument containing as a basic premise a claim such as "Abortion is a form of premeditated murder," or "Capital punishment is nothing short of state-sanctioned murder," or "Racial minorities in America are and should recognize themselves to be in a state of war with the white majority." Suppose Bertrand accepts this premise. But surely these statements are controversial. If Bertrand wants to be rationally convinced of Alice's position, should he not demand evidence for this premise before he accepts it? If we agree that he does, then we have serious questions for Hamblin's analysis. How have we taken sides in this discussion between Alice and Bertrand by accepting this judgment? Whose side have we taken? We certainly have not taken Alice's side since she has put forward this premise. We have not taken Bertrand's side, as he accepts it. Does not the fact that we can make this judgment of the need for evidence show that an objective adjudicator's stance, external to the actual participants in a discussion, is possible? This adjudicator is making precisely the evaluative judgments required for argument evaluation that Hamblin says are not possible.

These considerations can be compounded. Suppose Alice presents Bertrand with a premise that is false, that she knows to be false, and that *we* know to be false. Would we not be objectively right in censuring Alice for using this premise, even if Bertrand accepted it? Could we not objectively judge this argument to be a bad or at least flawed argument, just because of this false premise? Suppose Bertrand was actually prepared to accept outright contradictory statements, to accept p and not-p, for some proposition p. And suppose Alice included p and not-p among her premises. Would we not then have objective grounds for criticizing Alice's argument? How would pointing out this logical contradiction somehow involve taking sides? Is it not an objective (and devastating) critique of her argument? Again, suppose Bertrand accepts a deductively invalid rule of inference and Alice's argument instantiates this rule and no valid rule. Is this invalidity not something that can be objectively shown? Are we not objectively criticizing this argument by pointing out this invalidity?[4]

iv. A Statement Is Acceptable When and Only When Accompanied by Argument

This also will not do, for pretty obvious and well-known reasons. Being defended by argument cannot be a sufficient condition of statement acceptability. For there can be very bad, fallacious arguments. How can a fallacy render its conclusion acceptable? Modifying this criterion to say that a statement is acceptable just when it is defended by cogent argument will ultimately not be satisfactory either. To be sure, if a statement were defended by an argument, and one could press no charges against the cogency of that argument, then that statement would be acceptable. So being defended by cogent argument is a sufficient condition for statement acceptability. But it is not a necessary condition. Some premises must be taken as basic in argument, used to justify some other claim but not themselves justified by argument. The attempt to justify every premise will land us either in circularity, vicious infinite regress, or both. For if *every* premise must be justified, then even when we have given reasons for a claim, we are nowhere near done. We must argue for each of those reasons. But this in turn will involve giving reasons for each of those reasons, which in turn will require further reasons, and so on. In this process, we shall either offer some claim in support of a premise ultimately used to justify that very claim – and so our reasoning will be circular or question begging – or we shall continually be giving further new reasons, each of which in turn demanding further new reasons – an infinite regress. The regress is vicious,[5] for if a premise, to be acceptable, needs to be justified, we shall never arrive at a bedrock of justified premises. Our arguments will never get off the ground. Rather, they will be mired ever more deeply in the ground. All this is straightforward, I can claim no originality for it. (Compare Govier 1985, pp. 79–80, Wellman 1971, pp. 144–5.) Hence we cannot require argument for every premise that we accept. Although some premises may be argued for in the context of a given argument, and some premises have been or may be argued for on other occasions, ultimately if we are to accept any statements at all, we must accept some statements without argument.

v. A Statement Is Acceptable If and Only If It Is Probable

Suppose there were significant evidence for a statement but that strictly speaking the statement was not known true. Would not that evidence make the statement probable? Why, in the light of that evidence, should the statement not be acceptable? Of course, known truth should be sufficient for acceptability. Let us understand this probability criterion, then, as counting a statement acceptable just when it is either known true or is probable. In (1991), Thomas accepts this definition. He advances that "for a step of reasoning to be sound and reliable, all relevant reasons . . . must receive a rating of 'Definitely true,' or at least 'Probably true'" (1991, p. 16). Here "definitely true" means "I know for a fact, with certainty, that this statement is true"; while "probably true" means "It is highly likely that this statement is true, but I do not know this with complete certainty" (Thomas 1991, p. 15).

Without doubt, Thomas's criterion is highly intuitive and may be very useful heuristically. But there is a distinct problem. The expression "highly likely" is vague. More fundamentally, what does it mean to say that a statement S is likely? Is this something that can be explicated through a probability value? Does it mean, for example, that $.r < \Pr(S) < 1$, where $0 < .r < 1$? Grennan in (1987) holds this view. According to him, if S is "likely true," $\frac{1}{2} < \Pr(S) \leq 2/3$. If S is "probably true," $2/3 < \Pr(S) \leq 5/6$. If $\Pr(S) > 5/6$, we may say that S is "'true,' provided we do not insist on equating 'true' with 'certain'" (1987, p. 21).[6] Grennan himself does not say that to be acceptable a premise must be either probably true or true. However, someone who adopted the probability criterion of acceptability would in effect be taking Thomas's criterion and connecting "likely" with a specific range of probability values. A statement S thus would be acceptable only if $2/3 < \Pr(S) \leq 1$. This provides a partial clarification of Thomas's "highly likely." But it is one which immediately raises further questions. When we say that $\Pr(S) = .r$, what does this mean? What sort of probability are we dealing with here and how may it be determined?

In (1984), Grennan proposes that we try to determine such probabilities by attempting to refute each premise. (Here the goal is discriminating between $\Pr(S) \geq .75$ (true), $.5 \leq \Pr(S) < .75$ (dubious), and $\Pr(S) < .5$ (false). Presumably, dubious or false premises would be unacceptable.) This involves consulting the experience we already have on the issue of each premise, seeking further personal observations if necessary, or checking the testimony of others, experts or eyewitnesses. The type of premise determines the specific information we seek. For example, if the premise is a categorical universal generalization, we seek a counterexample. Should the premise be a qualified or restricted universal (usually or typically S's are P's), we seek to show that a majority of S's fail to be P's.

Once we have focused on the type of information needed to refute a statement and have that information at hand, it should be intuitive whether the statement is true, dubious, or false as Grennan understands these terms. What is not at all obvious is what role the probability values play here. In a representative sample I find that almost all X's are Y's. That should make it likely that X's are Y's. But what work does the explication of "true," "dubious," "false" in terms of probability accomplish?[7] Our assessment of whether a claim is true, dubious, or false seems to proceed without the determination of probability values. Indeed, one could ask what Grennan's probability ascriptions actually mean.

Because we are examining the claim that a statement is acceptable just in case it is probable, the sense of probability here is monadic rather than binary. We are not talking about a statement's being probable relative to a set of premises. Rather, we are talking about a statement's being probable simpliciter. As Nolt points out in (1984), we may distinguish two senses of statement probability. Inherent or absolute probability is "the probability of a statement in and of itself" (Nolt 1984, p. 193).[8] Nolt points out that this sense of probability "can easily be defined in terms of possible worlds. The inherent probability of a statement is just the frequency among all possible worlds of the worlds in which it is true" (1984, p. 193).

Given this definition, it is easy to see that it is totally inappropriate to define acceptability in terms of inherent probability. For this definition will require us to count as unacceptable statements whose truth is manifest. For example, suppose you are 5′6″ tall and I can see that you are because you are standing next to a ruler painted on the wall. But, given all the heights you could possibly be, and given the contingency of your existence to begin with, in what proportion of worlds are you 5′6″ tall? Presumably, the proportion of such worlds is very small. So it is inherently improbable that you are 5′6″ tall – and consequently the claim that you are is not acceptable. In fact, because "in most worlds you don't even exist" (Nolt 1984, p. 193), it is inherently improbable that you do exist even when you are standing in front of me. I must find the claim that you exist unacceptable! But this is nonsense. Inherent probability is no criterion of acceptability.

We may contrast inherent probability with epistemic probability, the probability of a statement relative to all our relevant background knowledge. This is "the best estimate of the statement's truth, based on everything we know" (Nolt 1984, p. 193). Only when we have no evidence whatsoever bearing on a proposition is its epistemic probability the same as its inherent probability. (Compare Nolt 1984, p. 194.) Nolt points out, "In logic, the chief role of epistemic probability is in estimating the likelihood of basic premises. When we say that a premise seems 'implausible,' 'nearly certain,' 'doubtful,' or 'improbable,' it is epistemic probability we have in mind" (1984, p. 195). What shall we say to the thesis that a statement is acceptable just in case it is epistemically probable – that is, its epistemic probability is greater than some fixed quantity, for example, $\frac{1}{2}$, $2/3$, or $3/4$? Just what does this claim mean? Notice that epistemic probability is an indexed concept. Background knowledge varies from person to person and at each time for each person. Epistemic probability is then indexed to person and time. The epistemic probability of a statement would be the same as the inductive probability of the argument from premises expressing all the relevant background knowledge of some person at some time to the given statement as conclusion. We might then say that a statement is epistemically probable just in case we had an inductively good, correct, or strong argument here. But what does *that* mean?

In (1986), Skyrms gives this definition of inductive strength: "An argument is *inductively strong* if and only if it is *improbable* that its conclusion is false while [i.e., given that] its premises are true, and it is not deductively valid" (1986, p. 7). The problem with this definition, which Skyrms would readily admit, is that the key term "improbable" is intuitive and not defined. What do we mean by saying that it is improbable that the conclusion of an argument is false given that its premises are true? The response is that there is "no precise, uncontroversial definition" (Skyrms 1986, p. 20). What inductive probability is remains an outstanding problem of inductive logic (Skyrms 1986, p. 21). And this problem is foundational. Until we know what inductive probability means, we cannot measure it, in any exact way. Talk of arguments being strong or weak will again be intuitive. How would we tell whether an argument was inductively strong? Without some methodology, we have no way other than intuitive judgments to determine this. But without being able to determine the inductive probability of arguments, how can we determine the epistemic probability of statements?

It appears that the proposal to take probability as the criterion of acceptability is more an answer schema than an answer. An actual answer would connect the notion of acceptability with some systematic explication of inductive probability. This schema then has the obvious problem that it ties progress in understanding acceptability with progress in inductive logic, a notoriously thorny area. But even beyond this drawback, are there further problems with this approach? I believe there are. Skyrms points out, "Exactly how inductive logic gets us epistemic probabilities from a stock of knowledge depends on how we characterize a stock of knowledge" (1986, p. 18). Skyrms contrasts the certainty model with fallibility models. In the certainty model, we identify a stock of knowledge with a class of statements we regard as certain. This could be the observation reports that we take our actual observation to have rendered certain. Should we not be confident that our actual observation renders observation reports certain but rather only likely, then we would turn to a fallibility model. We would regard our observations as conferring a certain numerical probability on each observation report. (It is completely unclear what this probability is or means. Because epistemic probability is defined relative to a stock of knowledge, what does it mean to regard elements in that stock of knowledge as having a degree of probability?) Let us assume that in a given stock of knowledge, three observation reports are relevant to a given statement. To determine the epistemic probability of that statement on this stock of knowledge, we should need first to determine the inductive probability of $8 = 2^3$ arguments, where the various premise sets of these arguments reflect all the combinations of truth values that the observation reports can share. Once we have determined these inductive probabilities, "We will have to put together the inductive probabilities of these arguments in exactly the right way to get the epistemic probability of S" (Skyrms 1986, p. 19).

But is this procedure in any way reflective of the way we actually go about deciding whether or not to accept some claim, in particular in cases where no argument is presented to justify that claim? Consider: On September 1, 1983, the former Soviet Union shot down a Korean airliner that radar indicated had violated Soviet air space. Within a short period of time, news of this event was flashed around the world and millions came to believe and accept that this event had occurred because of what they heard on radio or television. Were they justified in accepting this claim? If they argued to some conclusion on the basis of premises that included this claim about the Soviet Union, would we calculate the epistemic probability of the claim as part of our evaluation of the argument, as part of our determining whether the argument had acceptable premises? What observation reports would constitute the relevant portion of the stock of background knowledge here? Or would the relevant background knowledge consist of some claim about the reliability of the news media? How would we assign a probability to that claim and its negation and how would these probabilities be combined? When hearing the report of this event on the radio, would we entertain any such process of reasoning before deciding to accept it? Surely we would not, and this strongly suggests that the whole project of approaching acceptability through epistemic probability is wrongheaded. Under what conditions then would we regard that report of the Korean airliner's being shot down as being acceptable?

1.4 CONDITIONS FOR ACCEPTABILITY

Of course, one condition making a premise acceptable would be its being adequately defended by cogent argument. But this obviously does not advance the situation very far in delineating the conditions for acceptability. If the defending argument is cogent, *its* premises must be acceptable and adequately connected to justify accepting the conclusion. Barring circularity, we must eventually come to basic premises, the starting points of reasoning. Under what circumstances, if any, are *these* premises acceptable without any further justificatory argument? Our task in this essay is to develop an account of acceptability for these basic undefended premises. Notice that if we had an account of basic premise acceptability *and* of connection adequacy, we would then have a sufficient condition for the acceptability of defended, nonbasic premises. The condition is sufficient, not necessary, because a defended premise might be acceptable in itself. The issue of argument cogency then divides into the question of basic premise acceptability and connection adequacy.

At first sight, the question of basic premise acceptability may appear quite paradoxical. How could we be justified in accepting a statement unless we had an argument for it? Would our very justifying reasons not constitute the premises of an argument for that claim? It is here that we must invoke a very fruitful distinction which Rescher makes in (1988) – that between discursive and presumptive justification. According to Rescher,

A belief is justified *discursively* when there is some other pre-established belief on whose basis this belief is evidentially grounded. . . . However, *presumptive* justification . . . does not proceed through the evidential mediation of previously justified grounds, but directly and immediately through the force of a "presumption." A belief is justified in this way when there is a *standing presumption* in its favour and no pre-established (rationally justified) reason that stands in the way of its acceptance. Presumption is the epistemic analogue of "innocent until proven guilty." (1988, pp. 49–50)[9]

Presumption, as we see it, is the hallmark of acceptability. A statement is acceptable if and only if there is a presumption in its favor. But when is there a presumption for a statement? Under what circumstances does this occur and how may these circumstances be recognized? Developing answers to these questions is the burden of the rest of this book. Spelling out exactly what this project involves is our task in the next chapter.

2

Acceptability and Presumption

At the end of the last chapter, we framed the following proposal:

> A statement is acceptable just when there is a presumption in its favor.

This proposal practically follows analytically from Cohen's characterization of a presumption as what we may take for granted absent reasons against doing so (1992, p. 4). But it holds out much further promise for clarifying just what acceptability means and how we may determine when statements are acceptable. The concept of presumption is used in various disciplines. Aspects of its various uses and various ways of determining presumption may guide us in constructing a concept of epistemic presumption suitable for explicating acceptability. To develop this proposal, we first look at just how the concept of presumption is treated in various contexts.

2.1 USES OF "PRESUMPTION"

"Presumption" is first of all a jurisprudential notion. A courtroom proceeding is typically a debate between two opposing sides before an adjudicative panel. Presumption and its cognate notion "burden of proof" are ways of determining which adversary must argue what before this tribunal. If there is a presumption in favor of the innocence of the accused, then the burden is on the prosecution to argue for the guilt of that person. At least initially, the defense need not argue for innocence. The adjudicative panel is enjoined to accept that claim (i.e., to "take it for granted") until and unless the prosecution successfully establishes guilt. This adversarial ancestry of presumption illustrates one component that we definitely wish to include in the concept that we are developing. If there is a presumption in favor of a premise, then the burden would be on the person who wishes to reject that premise to argue that it should be rejected or cast into doubt. A person who has no reasons or evidence to present against it may simply accept the statement, and could be expected to concede it.

Some familiar with the legal notion of presumption may question the appropriateness of applying it to basic premises. Some writers on jurisprudence speak of presumptions as inference rules, licenses, or directives. Given certain information, we are to draw certain conclusions. For example, Sir Courtnay Ilbert says

> A presumption in the ordinary sense is an inference.... It may be described ... as "a rule of law that courts and judges shall draw a particular inference from a particular fact, or from particular evidence, unless and until the truth" (perhaps it would be better to say "soundness") "of the inference is disproved." (Quoted in Rescher 1977a, p. 31)[1]

Again, we have this definition from a text on legal evidence: "A presumption may be defined to be an inference *required* by a rule of law drawn as to the existence of one fact from the existence of some other established basic facts" (Ullmann-Margalit 1983a, p. 145).[2] The inference rule understanding seems to be embedded in a number of familiar legal presumptions. A person unheard from for seven years, where there is no reasonable explanation for the silence, is presumed dead. Likewise, there is a presumption "that a marriage regularly solemnized is valid" (Ullmann-Margalit 1983a, p. 144). In both cases, we have, in effect, a (nondeductive, nonformal, material) inference rule that from certain premises we are to infer a certain conclusion, absent sufficient rebutting considerations. Our rules confer presumption status on their conclusions, which if used as premises are defended, not basic, premises.

Understanding presumptions exclusively as inference rules from sets of premises to conclusions would seem to rule out speaking of presumptions for basic premises. As they are not inferred, no rule confers presumption status on them. If the only premises for which there are presumptions are nonbasic premises, then how can we appeal to the concept of presumption for explicating the acceptability of basic premises? At this point, we must remind ourselves that there are initial presumptions in legal contexts. To speak of a presumption of innocence is not to say that given certain facts, we may take it that the accused is innocent. Rather, we presume the accused is innocent outright. There is an analogy here with the senses of burden of proof. As Rescher points out in (1977a), we may contrast an initiating burden of proof with an evidential burden of proof. At the beginning of a criminal proceeding, the *initiating* burden of proof lies with the prosecution. That side has the responsibility to argue for the guilt of the accused. Should this argument be successful, it will create a presumption of guilt. The *evidential* burden of proof will then be on the defense to attack this argument, to present counterconsiderations and counterevidence. Note the contrast here. The initiating burden of proof is not incumbent on the prosecution because of some proffered evidence. Rather the rules of legal procedure assign it to the prosecution outright. Evidential burdens of proof become incumbent on defense and prosecution given evidence presented. As there is an initial burden to show guilt, so there is an initial presumption of innocence. Not all burdens of proof then are evidential and not all presumptions come by inferential rules from previously accepted premises.

However, the legal concepts of presumption and burden of proof contain a component that we definitely do not wish to include in our concept of epistemic presumption. As is commonly acknowledged, legal presumptions and burdens of proof are distinctly stipulative. The presumption of innocence is laid down by judicial fiat in Anglo-American law, and other systems of jurisprudence may allocate the presumption differently.[3] But if presumption is to be the hallmark of acceptability and acceptability is to be normative, presumption must not be a matter of fiat. We cannot simply stipulate what premises are to be acceptable. Are there other senses of "presumption," then, which can be applied in situations outside formal legal proceedings, where "natural" or "rational" as opposed to arbitrary or stipulative presumptions may be identified?

Richard Whatley in his *Elements of Rhetoric* introduced "presumption" and "burden of proof" into rhetorical theory. According to Archbishop Whatley, "A 'Presumption' in favour of any supposition, means, not . . . a preponderance of probability in its favor, but, such a *preoccupation* of the ground, as implies that it must stand good till some sufficient reason is adduced against it; in short, that the *Burden of proof* lies on the side of him who would dispute it" (See Anderson and Dovre 1968, p. 26). But what does it mean to say that a supposition preoccupies the ground, and how is this recognized? Nothing here seems to require that such a preoccupation be a matter of fiat. What factors, for Whatley, would constitute this preoccupation of the ground?

In presenting his understanding of how Whatley's conception of presumption evolved, Sproule (1976) argues that Whatley's conception of "presumption" and "burden of proof" underwent an evolution over the course of the successive editions of the *Elements of Rhetoric*. Originally essentially legal notions, they developed into something determined by certain predispositions of the audience. Presumption and burden of proof were not assigned by rules of procedure. Rather, "The ultimate agency of assignment became . . . the audience whose recognition of a presumption was required for its successful application to a dispute" (Sproule 1976, p. 122). Certain audiences may be inclined to accept certain claims or arguments, or to find certain sources of information including certain persons credible or authoritative. Arguers, then, who utilize these claims and arguments in defense of some thesis or who can enlist authoritative sources in support of their arguments will have something of a presumption in favor of their cases.

Certainly we have here a nonstipulative view of presumption. That audiences are prepared to accept certain arguments and respect certain perceived authorities is a matter of empirical fact, determined by empirical investigation, and not of fiat, legal or otherwise. However, although this psychological notion of presumption is not stipulative, it is straightforward to see that it cannot do the *normative* work necessary for a proper explication of acceptability in terms of presumption. Our goal is not to provide an account of when statements are *accepted* but when they are *acceptable*. We are explicating an epistemically normative concept. Hence, we are not concerned with what sociopsychological factors foster audience predispositions to accept certain claims but, rather, what "logical" or logico-epistemic factors would justify acceptance.

In (1977a) and (1977b), Rescher seeks to introduce the concepts of presumption and burden of proof into epistemology. His development of these notions explicitly involves epistemological concepts. In (1977a), Rescher defines burden of proof this way: "To say that the burden of proof rests with a certain side is to say that it is up to that side to bring in the evidence to make its case" (1977a, p. 26). By contrast, when there is a presumption in favor of a statement, then in the absence of specific counterindications, the challenger may accept it (1977a, p. 30). Rescher points out that presumptions are not indefeasible statements constituting some apodictic epistemic foundation for the rest of knowledge (1977a, p. 33). Rather, they are "claims which are allowed at least *pro tem* to enter acceptably into the framework of argumentation" (1977a, p. 34). They are acceptable provisionally, deserving the "benefit of the doubt" (1977a, p. 34), until some refuting or rebutting evidence is presented. In the absence of such evidence, they are acceptable.

Rescher's calling presumptions "truth-candidates" is illuminating; they are plausible candidates for being truths. Not all candidates win elections and not all presumptions turn out true. To say that a presumption is a truth-candidate is to say that one should count it as true "*If one can,* that is, if doing so generates no difficulties or inconsistencies. A presumption is not *established* as true, it is backed only by a rationally warranted expectation that it may turn out true 'if all goes well'" (1977b, p. 115).

Rescher's speaking of presumptions as truth-candidates raises the question of whether at one and the same time there may be presumptions for several, incompatible statements. Can there not be several competing truth-candidates for each of which there is some presumption of some strength? This might seem distinctly possible. Suppose that a number of rival causal hypotheses were mooted to explain some event or regularity. Suppose that some of these hypotheses are so wildly implausible that they are "out of the running." But for some of the remaining plausible hypotheses, there may be varying amounts of evidence. Let us suppose, however, that in no case is the evidence decisive for one of these hypotheses over the others. Now it is certainly imaginable that one and the same person could possess all this evidence at the same time. From that person's perspective, then, would there not be a presumption for each of these rival hypotheses? Are they not all candidates in the running?

If so, our project of defining acceptability in terms of presumption would face a major difficulty. For according to our preliminary definition, that a statement is acceptable just in case there is a presumption in its favor, each rival hypothesis would be acceptable, no matter how strong or weak the presumption vis-à-vis its alternatives. It would be rationally appropriate to accept any one of them. But this is plainly counterintuitive. Why should it be rationally appropriate to accept one hypothesis in the face of a viable alternative for which there is a stronger presumption?

At this point, I believe we must make a distinction. "Presumption" and "truth-candidate" are not synonymous. All presumptions are truth-candidates, but not all truth-candidates are presumptions. As Rescher points out in (1977a): "Presumption favors the most *plausible* of rival alternatives – when indeed there is one" (1977a, p. 38). Our various plausible rival – causal hypotheses for which there is some evidence – are all truth-candidates, but only the most plausible of these may have the status of a presumption. Notice that given a field of truth-candidates, there is no guarantee that one of them will be the most plausible. Two or more alternatives might both be maximally plausible. In such cases, none of the alternatives would have the status of a presumption. However, should one of the alternatives be the most plausible, then it could have presumption status. How do we determine which candidate is most plausible? That in effect is to ask how we determine presumption. We develop our answer in Part II of this book. There we consider how to answer certain critical, presumption-determining questions, which we present in the next chapter. For now, it is sufficient to say that our conception of presumption is singulary.

But we are still faced with a problem. In the context of a given legal dispute, we may be able straightforwardly to determine which side has the presumption. In the light of certain evidence, we may be able to determine which alternative is the most plausible. But if the legal dispute had gone differently, if different considerations had been presented, the other side might hold the presumption. Likewise, in the light of different evidence, a different alternative would have the highest plausibility. But clearly, different persons will possess different sets of evidence, and so will be justified in making different assessments of presumption. Are we still faced with the problem of multiple presumptions? *Whose* presumption, presumption from whose perspective, shall we choose in defining acceptability? Or may anyone's presumption be taken? Is a statement acceptable just in case it has the status of a presumption for someone? But how could a statement be acceptable *for me* when from my perspective a contrary has a higher plausibility?

We may throw light on this problem by considering one more definition of "presumption." In (1984), Pinto presents this characterization: "A proposition or statement has the status of a *presumption* at a given juncture of an interchange if and only if at that juncture any party who refuses to concede it is obliged to present an argument against it – that is to say, is obliged either to concede it or to make a case against it" (1984, p. 17). This definition is illuminating for at least two reasons. First, it clearly indicates that "presumption" is a relational concept, not a unary attribute of statements. To speak of a statement in itself as being a presumption or having the status of a presumption is to speak elliptically. A statement is always a presumption relative to some juncture in some interchange. We shall see the significance of this relativizing shortly. A statement that lacked the status of a presumption at one stage of an interchange might gain that status at a later stage, given the argumentation presented for it. Conversely, a statement for which there was a presumption at a given stage of an interchange might lose that status in the light of some case made against it. "Presumption" relates a statement, on the one hand, and a state of an interchange, on the other.

We should emphasize that in defining "presumption" *relative* to a given point in an interchange, we are not committing ourselves to a *relativism.* In formal logic, whether or not a given statement is derivable in the sense that it may appear on the last line of a derivation will depend in general on what assumptions we have to derive it from. This depending on assumptions in no way indicates that the rules of derivation are somehow relative, or context dependent, or contingent on the perspectives or decisions of those constructing derivations. Likewise, that there may be a presumption at one point in an interchange for a claim and not at another or not in a different interchange does not indicate that the rules or principles by which presumptions are determined or allocated are somehow context dependent or peculiar to the participants of an interchange.[4]

Speaking of interchanges presents us with the second illuminating feature of Pinto's definition: "presumption" is basically a dialectical notion. To develop what we mean by this, we must develop what we mean by "dialectical." In particular, we must present our notion of a basic dialectical situation. We can then refine the notion of "presumption" in the light of these considerations on dialectic. This discussion will in turn pave the way for our refined definition of "acceptability" in terms of "presumption," which we present in Section 2.3. We proceed then to develop our understanding of "presumption" in the light of dialectic in Section 2.2.

2.2 PRESUMPTION AND DIALECTICS

A dialectical situation is a special type of dialogical situation. In a dialogical situation, principally two or more persons are discussing or debating some issue. Clearly, the participants may play a great variety of roles in this situation. Some may present claims or theses concerning the point at issue. Others may present counterclaims or countertheses. Some may attack various claims or argumentative moves that have been presented. Others may ask for evidence or justification for certain of these claims. Some may take the role of rational adjudicator, aiming to ascertain the merits of the various assertions presented and their justification. Clearly, these roles may overlap and the same person may play several in the same situation. We call such situations dialogical because there will (or should) be an exchange of ideas going on, a dialogue.[5]

Dialogical situations may clearly be unstructured and thus become undisciplined. One and the same person may both propose a thesis, attack other theses, and demand justification. There may be no agreed-upon way to proceed or advance the issue. Consequently, there may be no way to determine whether the issue has been advanced. By contrast, a *dialectical situation* is a dialogical situation governed by specific procedural rules. The participants will accept certain roles. These roles will circumscribe the types of contributions they may make to the exchange. In particular, one or more persons will be protagonists, putting forward initial theses, defending them, and presenting further justificatory claims when challenged. Other participants will be challengers, asking for justification and raising counterconsiderations. Still other participants will be rational adjudicators, determining just how good a case is developing for a given thesis. Of course, it is quite possible for one and the same person to play several roles in a dialectical situation. A challenger may have a thesis of his or her own to present and defend.

We call such situations dialectical because they display three salient features. First, they involve conflict or opposition. The challengers do not simply, passively accept what the proponents are saying. Second, the participants seek to critically resolve some issue. By raising and entertaining critical questions about the theses presented and their justification, by seeking the ruling of a rational adjudicator, the participants are putting these theses to a rational test. The aim is to come to a justified position concerning the issue of the dialectical exchange, justified at least until there is reason to continue the dialectic further. Third, we call these situations dialectical because the roles of the participants are circumscribed – in the first instance, the proponent and only the proponent makes the assertions and the challenger and only the challenger asks the questions – and there are recognized criteria for judging whether the dialectic is advancing.

We regard the *basic dialectical situation* as a model of how argumentation develops. There are just two participants, the proponent and the challenger. The proponent's role is simply to put forward some claim or thesis, and to answer the challenger's critical questions. The challenger's role is not to present and defend a counterthesis of her own, nor even to discredit or refute the proponent's thesis. Rather, acting as a constructive interlocutor, her role is simply to draw out from the proponent the best, most logically cogent argument for his claim of which he is capable. In this way, she acts as both questioner and rational adjudicator. The questions she asks are set by her perception of the logical and epistemic deficiencies of the proponent's argument as it has developed to that point in the dialectical situation. Her intention is to keep asking questions until she is satisfied that she has a cogent argument for the proponent's thesis.

Should the proponent answer all the challenger's questions, she would have such an argument. Should the proponent fail to answer a question, the challenger would have exposed a weakness, difficulty, or even fallacy in the argument.

How may this notion of a basic dialectical situation help to clarify the notion of a presumption? Modifying Pinto's definition, let us define "presumption" just with respect to those interchanges that are basic dialectical situations, or – more concisely – dialectical exchanges: *There is a presumption in favor of a statement at a given point in a dialectical exchange just when either the challenger must concede it or present a case against it.* As we see it, this definition characterizes presumption from the point of view of a rational adjudicator observing a dialectical exchange but not himself entering into it either by advocating or challenging theses. It is a definition of "third party" presumption. We could easily imagine that this adjudicator, at some point in the exchange, could say: "The proponent has made a good point here; the challenger must either grant his point or rebut it." Under these circumstances, the judge's verdict is that there is a presumption in favor of the proponent's claim. But we also can imagine the judge thinking to himself with justification, "If I were the challenger, I would proceed thus and so against the proponent's point."

This now raises a problem for our project of defining acceptability in terms of presumption. Should the judge find that statement acceptable at this point? If a statement is acceptable just in case there is a presumption for it, then it would seem the statement is acceptable. But how could it be proper for him to accept that statement in the light of this unmet challenge he sees to be justified? Notice that by entertaining this rebuttal, the adjudicator is in effect also playing the role of challenger. These considerations suggest that we should relativize the concept of a presumption not only to a given juncture in a dialectical exchange, but also to the two participants in that exchange. If our rational adjudicator could also play the role of challenger, he could present his challenge. At that point, there would no longer be a presumption for the claim from his perspective.

Given her role, whenever a challenger is aware of counterconsiderations, she is obligated to present them, thus undercutting the presumption for the proponent's thesis at that point in the exchange. Conversely, should she have no challenge to present, the presumption stands and she should recognize it. This motivates the following definition of challenger presumption – a ternary relation between a statement, a point in a dialectical exchange, and a challenger: *There is a presumption in favor of a statement S at a point **p** in a dialectical exchange for the challenger **C** of that* *exchange if and only if **C** is obliged to concede S at **p**.* That is, if proponent **P** has advanced a claim *S*, and the challenger recognizes that asking for justification for *S* would involve a burden on her to show why such justification is required in this context – not doing so would constitute a frivolous request for justification – and the challenger has no plausible justification for her request nor plausible counterconsiderations against *S*, then she is obliged to concede *S* at that point in the exchange. It is precisely at this point that we want to say there is a presumption for *S* from her point of view.

We may likewise define a notion of presumption from the proponent's point of view. Provisionally, let us consider the following definition: *There is a presumption in favor of a statement S at a point **p** in a dialectical exchange for the proponent **P** of that exchange if and only if **P** has answered all the challenges against S at **p**.* This will not quite do. Imagine a situation in which the proponent has compelling reasons to offer for his claim or compelling answers to the objections raised by the challenger, but has not yet presented these considerations at a given point in a dialectical situation. Because he can answer these challenges, is there not a presumption for his claim from his point of view?

Our definition, however, may be straightforwardly modified to accommodate this case. In modal logic, we speak of one world being accessible from another. Let us speak of a point **p′** in a dialectical exchange being accessible from **p** for the proponent just in case at **p** the proponent possesses the evidence to discharge the burdens of proof which are in fact discharged at **p′**. That is, at **p** the proponent sees how he can meet the challenges that have been raised against his claim and his meeting them will advance the dialectical situation to **p′**. We may now present this official definition: *There is a presumption in favor of a statement **S** at a point **p** in a dialectical exchange for the proponent **P** of that exchange if and only if there is a point **p′** of the exchange accessible from **p** for **P** and **P** has answered at **p′** all challenges raised at **p** against **S**.* Which (if any) of proponent, challenger (or adjudicator) presumption is appropriate for defining acceptability and why? These are the themes of the next section.

2.3 CHALLENGER PRESUMPTION AND ACCEPTABILITY

We think it obvious that the acceptability of a statement should be defined in terms of challenger presumption. To ask why a statement is acceptable – "Why should I accept that statement?" – is to take the challenger's stance. It is to enter, at least imaginatively, into a dialectical exchange with whomever has put forward that statement. A statement is acceptable, then, just when either that question has been satisfactorily answered or when raising or further pressing the question is unnecessary, even frivolous or otiose to begin with. Why should we think then that this condition has been satisfied just when there is a presumption for the statement from our perspective as challengers?

Suppose we found a presumption in favor of this statement. Given our definition of challenger presumption, this would mean that given what the proponent has said up to this point and given our background knowledge of the issues under discussion, we are obliged to concede the statement. Now we concede a point when we allow the person who has made it to reason from it, that is, to use it as a premise. When we are *obliged* to concede a point, then we are obliged to allow the person making the point to use it as a premise. But what is the nature of such obligation? By virtue of the structure of a dialectical exchange, the challenger is obliged to ask questions. Not questioning some assertion of the proponent is tantamount to conceding it. We as challengers then will be obliged to concede a statement when we have no further objections or questions to bring against it. But that would be precisely to find the statement acceptable from our point of view as challengers.

By contrast, suppose there was not a presumption for a statement from our point of view as challenger. This would mean that even in the light of the case the proponent has developed thus far and in light of our general evidential position, we would not be obliged to concede that statement. But this means we have an objection to bring against the statement – be it a legitimate request for evidence or some rebutting consideration. But under such circumstances, the statement would certainly not be acceptable from our perspective as challengers. So acceptability amounts to challenger presumption.[6] Hence, characterizing acceptability in terms of presumption is well motivated. Before we can present this characterization, however, we need to develop a further aspect of the concept of acceptability.

It is a commonplace that what is acceptable to one person may not be acceptable to another. Similarly, what may be acceptable at one time may not be acceptable at another. This means that acceptability is not a monadic property of statements, but a relation, in fact a ternary relation between a statement, a person, and a point in time. In defining acceptability in terms of presumption, then, we are defining one ternary relation in terms of another. As understanding presumption as a relational concept did not entail a relativism, neither does this relational concept of acceptability. That given different evidence and background beliefs, what is acceptable to one audience is not acceptable to another does not mean that acceptability is relative. We may admit that there are objective standards that justify judging that with respect to certain bodies of evidence and background beliefs, certain statements ought to be accepted, while, with respect to others, they ought not to be.[7]

How do we move from an acceptability situation, a situation in which we are confronted with the question of whether or not to accept a statement, to a basic dialectical situation in which we are playing the challenger role? Obviously, whenever we are confronted with a statement that is asserted, there is always someone who has propounded or asserted that statement, even if that person is unknown to us. Hence, we may imagine ourselves in a basic dialectical situation with that person as proponent and ourselves as the challenger. Furthermore, whenever the acceptability question arises for a given statement, we shall be able to identify a set of statements which we *do* currently accept, our stock of current commitments. When we imaginatively situate ourselves in dialogue with the proponent of an assertion, these commitments constitute a point in the dialectical exchange, at least from our perspective. Although these commitments may not have evolved through dialogue with the proponent, they constitute what in our minds has been established up to this point. It is in the light of these commitments that we must judge whether or not we are obliged to concede the statement. Accordingly, when the question of acceptability arises, we may straightforwardly identify statement, challenger, and point in a dialectical exchange, the three terms of the presumption relation. Given these considerations, we now offer this formal definition of acceptability: *A statement S is rationally acceptable for a person* **P** *at a time* **t** *if and only if given the commitments of* **P** *as a challenger at time* **t**, *Com(**P**, **t**), there is a presumption in favor of S for* **P** *as challenger at Com(**P**, **t**).* That is, acceptability amounts to challenger presumption.

One of the most significant benefits of connecting acceptability with presumption via this definition is that it allows us appeal to principles of presumption in determining or explaining whether or not a statement is acceptable. The acceptability problem is not just one of properly defining "acceptability," but of discovering how we may determine which claims are rationally acceptable or how we may justify judgments of acceptability. In Chapter 11, we call this the practice of epistemic casuistry. Our definition of acceptability will have practical value just to the extent that it connects up the concept of acceptability with a process of determining acceptability in particular cases. The definition we have presented will do this to the extent that we understand how presumptions are determined. In connection with his characterization of an epistemological sense of presumption, Rescher indicates that there are epistemic principles of presumption. For example, there is a presumption in favor of senses and memory, and being a matter of common knowledge is a presumption-making principle.

As we see it, the issue of whether there is a presumption for a statement in a given case can be determined by three presumption-determining questions:

1. What type of statement is it?
2. What source vouches for it?
3. Does this voucher create a presumption for the statement?

Answering the third question in particular involves appealing to principles of presumption. Our task in Part II of this book is to present a systematic account both of these presumption determining questions and these principles. However, there are some significant philosophical issues we must deal with first. We turn to those issues in the next two chapters. We want to conclude this chapter by comparing our criterion of acceptability in terms of presumption with two other recent accounts of acceptability, Blair and Johnson's analysis in terms of model interlocutors in (1987) and Wellman's account in (1971). The comparison with Wellman should have especial interest. In the light of our distinction between challenger presumption and proponent presumption, we read him as understanding acceptability in terms of proponent presumption or from the proponent's point of view.

2.4 COMPARISON WITH OTHER VIEWS

i. Blair and Johnson's Acceptability via Model Interlocutors

We may think of model interlocutors as a community of rational adjudicators. According to Blair and Johnson, they are characterized by various traits, which include first being *knowledgeable*. Given the question at issue, the community is aware of what already has been established on this subject, of what has not been established or what they do not know, and of how claims to knowledge can be checked. Members of the community are also *reflective*, "They have a well-established disposition to question, challenge, probe, and wonder" (1987, p. 51). The community is *open*, its members individually being relatively free of prejudices, which collectively cancel each other out, and the community collectively being prepared to revise opinions in the light of evidence. In addition, members of the community are *dialectically astute*, able to spot needs for evidence, problems of relevance, and objections. Blair and Johnson do not regard these four features as exhaustive but sufficient to suggest the character of the community.

How does the notion of basic premise acceptability get explicated through the notion of a community of model interlocutors? "In general . . . a premise in an argument is acceptable without defense just in case a person following the methods and embodying the traits of the pertinent community of ideal interlocutors would fail to raise a question or doubt about it" (Blair and Johnson 1987, p. 53). It should be clear that there is a very close connection between our notion of a challenger in a dialectical exchange and a person playing the challenger role with reference to a community of model interlocutors. We may characterize a challenger as a representative of the community of rational inquirers. Clearly this community is a community of model interlocutors. In seeking to extend current knowledge, the members are aware of the scope and limits of what is currently known, they have a disposition to question and challenge, are open to new evidence, and have a clear sense of when something is proven and when it is not. That is, a community of rational inquirers is knowledgeable, reflective, open, and dialectically astute. Conversely, any community of model interlocutors, by virtue of the fact that its members are reflective and open, is a community of rational inquirers. Indeed, we might take Blair and Johnson's characterization of a community of model interlocutors as a gloss on the notion of the community of rational inquirers. Hence, to describe a rational challenger as a representative of the community of rational inquirers or as proceeding with a community of model interlocutors as a regulative ideal amounts basically to the same thing.

Although Blair and Johnson do not index acceptability to a particular challenger at a particular time, such indexing is implicit in their discussion. As they point out, communities of model interlocutors are historically situated. They reflect what is commonly accepted at their time and they are not in any sense omniscient. Hence, to be acceptable to someone following the precepts of a community of model interlocutors is to be acceptable relative to the historical situation and current state of knowledge of that community, that is, relative to a certain point in time. And, because the pertinent community of rational inquirers is not omniscient and embodies a spectrum of points of view, we should expect that different rational challengers, proceeding according to the methods of this community, may differ on whether a claim should be challenged or not. So it is also in accord with the spirit of Blair and Johnson's characterization of acceptability to see it indexed to challengers as well as particular points in time. Finally, for a challenger proceeding according to the methods and traits of the pertinent community of rational inquirers to "fail to raise a question about" a certain claim would be for him or her to find a presumption in the claim's favor. Conversely, to find a presumption in its favor mandates failing to challenge it. Blair and Johnson's characterization of acceptability coincides with ours.

There is an important difference in our respective treatments, however. As Blair and Johnson admit, their "general theory of acceptability does not decide when a particular premise of a particular argument is acceptable or not..., [but] it provides a rationale for developing more specific and more immediate practical guidelines for the acceptability of premises" (1987, p. 53). By connecting acceptability with presumption, we are precisely in a position to develop such guidelines, given the principles of presumption we have alluded to earlier. It is a central thesis of this essay that these principles can be developed into wide-ranging guidelines for determining acceptability.

ii. Wellman's View of Premise Acceptability

Wellman makes this rather surprising assertion concerning the acceptability of basic premises: "It is quite proper to ask whether we are justified in accepting . . . first premises. My answer is that we are entirely justified in accepting them. But what is it that justifies our acceptance? It is the mere fact of acceptance itself" (1971, p. 153). Wellman immediately goes on to elaborate this claim: "We are justified in accepting these premises just because they are not challenged. . . . In the absence of any challenge, one need not give reasons to support his statement or beliefs" (1971, p. 153). Absence of challenge is a sufficient condition for proponent presumption. For a proponent finds a presumption for a statement at a point in a dialectical exchange just in case he can see how to meet all the challenges raised against the statement at that point. If there are no challenges outstanding, then vacuously the proponent has answered all the challenges at this point and finds a presumption in its favor. Wellman in effect is characterizing acceptability as proponent presumption.

We have argued that acceptability should be understood as challenger presumption. We see the nub of our disagreement with Wellman centering on this issue: Is the *contingent* fact that a statement has not been challenged (at a certain point in a dialectical exchange) sufficient to render that statement acceptable (at that point)? This, as I understand it, is Wellman's position. But critical questions for this position readily arise. When Wellman says "we are justified in accepting these premises just because they are not challenged," we may readily ask, "But are not there some premises which *should* be challenged? Should not any rational challenger demand evidence, justification, argument for certain premises under certain circumstances, and should we not refuse to grant acceptability to the premise until proper justification is presented?"

Wellman says, "We normally regard a person as having justified his conclusion when he supports it by appealing to generally accepted premises, whether or not these could have been challenged" (1971, p. 157). We may agree with Wellman that premises that are generally accepted (even though logically possible to challenge) are *prima facie* acceptable, such *general* acceptance constituting a reason for acceptability. That a claim is a matter of common knowledge creates a presumption for it, and what is a mark of common knowledge but general acceptance? But suppose a proponent appealed to a premise that was not a matter of common knowledge (and not a presumption on any other grounds), and suppose no one challenged it. Would that statement be acceptable? Does the mere contingent lack of a challenge render a statement acceptable?

Wellman addresses this point when he says,

Reflect for a moment on all the beliefs that you hold and that you feel rationally justified in continuing to hold. Now imagine yourself justifying them one by one by appealing to unchallengeable premises. . . . It is hard to imagine oneself fully justifying even a single interesting belief. At best, one's supply of indubitable premises is too small to justify one's conclusions. (1971, pp. 157–8)

But there is a false dichotomy here. In delimiting those premises that are properly rationally acceptable, we do not have to choose between those that are merely accepted although not challenged and those which are indubitable – beyond all challenge. It is at least logically possible that there is a third category – premises for which challenge is logically conceivable but that need not be challenged at the current point. And this is not simply a matter of challenger failure to put forward an objection. Challenges to these premises would, given the current evidential state, be otiose.

Interestingly, Wellman seems to suggest this position when he says, "The premises that are accepted without reasons because they have not been challenged have withstood the test of reasoning in one sense; they have presented themselves within reasoning and were thought not to need challenge" (1971, p. 160). But how do we determine which premises do not need challenge? Does the mere fact of nonchallenge mean there is no need to challenge? Again, Wellman suggests that his view of acceptability may be closer to ours when he says that merely accepted premises "have been accepted in the light of all the reasoning to date" (1971, p. 160). But is this true? If one were a rational challenger, one would bring forward all the challenges called for in the light of the reasoning to date. If those challenges were met, then the statement should be acceptable at that point. But will a challenger always be so ideal? Will the reasoning to date always have been carried out cogently and press all the challenges which should be pressed? If not, statements that should be challenged will go unchallenged. Why should they then be acceptable just because they have not been challenged? Yet, ultimately, it appears to be just this latter view that Wellman wants to defend. "Any statement constitutes a justifying reason as long as it remains unchallenged. At each moment the task is to meet the challenges that are being made at this time. Therefore, as long as some premise remains unchallenged it need not be justified" (1971, p. 164).

An unchallenged premise is acceptable until or unless it is challenged. We may agree that this is what acceptability means from the proponent's point of view. But when we ask whether a premise is acceptable, we are not in general asking that question of a premise in an argument we are putting forward. Rather, we are asking that of a premise in an argument with which we are confronted. This is a situation in which we are placed in the challenger or adjudicator role. Now the question of whether this premise *should* be challenged arises. When does a significant issue of burden of proof underwrite a demand for justification and when would such a demand be frivolous? The mere fact that we can make challenges, that conceiving of making challenges is logically possible, or the mere fact that no challenges have actually been tendered, does not give us any guidance here. But in judging whether the premises of an argument presented to us are acceptable, this is exactly the guidance we need. It is our contention that a system of principles of presumption together with the key presumption determining questions we have outlined will give us this guidance.

3

Factors Determining Presumption

Basic Considerations

We have given a definition of challenger presumption and indicated how challenger presumption may serve as a criterion of acceptability. As we noted at the end of the last chapter, if this is to advance our ability to determine when a statement is acceptable, we must be able to determine under what circumstances there is a presumption for a statement from a challenger's point of view. As Rescher points out in (1988), "The rational legitimation of a presumptively justified belief lies in the fact that some 'suitably favorable indication' speaks on its behalf, and no already justified counter-indication speaks against it" (1988, p. 50).[1] Our task now is to identify these suitably favorable indicators. Our first step will be to look at principles of presumption that have actually been advanced and accepted. We have already noted two, a presumption in favor of the senses and in favor of memory.

Before proceeding to our basic survey of the principles of presumption, we must develop a point implicit in the preceding paragraph. Rescher speaks of the rational legitimation of a presumptively justified belief. This suggests a distinction between presumptively justified beliefs, and establishing that there is a presumption for such beliefs. If there is a presumption for a belief for a particular person *qua* challenger, need she be aware of that presumption? Is there a presumption for her belief from her perspective only if she has determined that there is such a presumption by determining or recognizing that a suitably favorable indicator is present in these circumstances and no already-justified counterindicators are likewise present? On the one hand, this might seem quite legitimate. How can we say there is a presumption for a belief or claim from a challenger's point of view unless the challenger is aware of or sees that there is such a presumption? Does this not mean seeing that the factors determining presumption hold in this case? On the other hand, this clashes with what we apparently recognize concerning our accepting or assenting to many presumptively acceptable beliefs. Coming to believe and further accept a presumptively acceptable statement is frequently something immediate. Should I see a ten-ton tractor-trailer hurtling down the highway toward me on a collision course and take evasive action, my believing that this object was coming at me and my accepting that belief by using it as a premise for action are immediate. Consciously, at least, I consult no principles of presumption, I go through no reasoning process on the basis of which I accept my belief about the tractor-trailer. Notice, however, that we would not think my acceptance here inappropriate for lack of such a preceding discursive process.

Talk of immediately held presumptively justified beliefs suggests that one may have presumptively justified beliefs without having a rational legitimation or justification of them. Being a presumption does not entail having been determined to be a presumption. Basic beliefs may be presumptively acceptable. However, when the question arises of why these beliefs are presumptively acceptable, then discursive justification is called for. Although the basic belief that p may be presumptively acceptable, the claim that the belief that p is presumptively acceptable is not a basic belief. We thus propose distinguishing between the having and accepting of a presumptively justified belief and its rational legitimation. We need not be aware of the factors determining presumption for there to be a presumption for a statement from our point of view. Hence, in the sequel we may speak of there *being* a presumption from the challenger's point of view as opposed to the challenger *knowing* or recognizing or having determined that there is such a presumption.

However, this view has profound philosophical ramifications. To justify this dichotomy leads straight into issues connected with the debate between externalism and internalism. Seeing this will emerge during the course of this chapter. In the next chapter, we shall defend this dichotomy and situate our concept of presumption (and thus of acceptability) with respect to other central epistemological concepts such as justification and epistemic duty. But let us now begin at the beginning and proceed to survey principles of presumption that have already been recognized.

3.1 PRINCIPLES OF PRESUMPTION – A BASIC SURVEY

As we have noted, Rescher surveys certain standardly recognized presumption-making principles in (1977a). There is a presumption in favor of "common knowledge," and in favor of the testimony of suitable experts or authorities. There is also a presumption in favor of senses and memory (1977a, pp. 36–37). In (1988), Rescher expands this latter presumption to include the senses assisted "by established cognitive aids and instruments (telescopes, calculating machines, reference works, logarithmic tables, etc.)" (1988, p. 52).[2] Richard Whatley also in effect recognizes a presumption for common knowledge. He speaks of presumption against paradox. "There is a 'Presumption' against any thing *paradoxical*, i.e. contrary to the prevailing opinion: it may be true; but the Burden of proof lies with him who maintains it; since men are not to be expected to abandon the prevailing belief till some reason is shown" (1968, p. 28).

In (1969), Perelman and Olbrechts-Tyteca identify another standard presumption, that of trust. Unless we have evidence of dissembling, we may take what someone has said as reflecting what he or she sincerely accepts. The presumptions of trust and in favor of senses and memory jointly indicate that there is a presumption in favor of personal testimony, at least testimony concerning what has been seen or remembered. Persons making these claims do not incur a burden to establish their own veracity or the proper functioning of their perceptual and mnemonic mechanisms.

According to Rescher in (1977a), inductive considerations and desiderata play a role in determining presumptions (1977a, pp. 39–41). All things being equal, the best confirmed hypothesis receives presumption status. "The more simple, the more uniform, the more specific a thesis – either internally, of itself, or externally, in relation to some stipulated basis – the more emphatically this thesis is to count as plausible" (1977a, p. 39). In (1988), Rescher expands this to include a presumption for epistemic utility, analogy, and fit. Something has epistemic utility just in case it "would, if accepted, explain things that need explanation" (1988, p. 53). The analogy of something "with what has proved acceptable in other contexts" (1988, p. 53) and its fit or "coherence with other accepted theses" (1988, p. 53)[3] are also presumption-making factors. Analogy and fit are particular ways of identifying what is normal, and there is a standard, central presumption for what is normal, recognized by a number of authors. This is the survey we may glean from those authors who have specifically addressed the issue of presumption.

But this is just a survey. What we need is a systematic account of these principles.

3.2 PRESUMPTION AND BELIEF-GENERATING MECHANISMS

I believe that we can arrange the surveyed principles of presumption into three classes. Certain principles, such as the presumption for common knowledge, expert opinion, and trust concern external or interpersonal sources which may vouch for a claim. I may appropriate certain items of common knowledge. But the body of common knowledge is other than myself. If I consult an expert, I am consulting someone else. I may trust the word of others, again persons other than myself. The beliefs generated on the basis of what these interpersonal sources vouch for are not beliefs generated solely through my own cognitive faculties. The first class of principles of presumption then concern interpersonal belief-generating mechanisms.

Senses and memory by contrast are personal belief-generating mechanisms. They are my own cognitive faculties. I myself perceive objects in the external world and my perceptual cognitive faculty generates certain beliefs about them. In Chapter 1, we suggested that there was at least one other such personal mechanism which conferred presumption – reason. On many occasions, I can "see" that some tautology is self-evidently true. Accordingly, the second class of principles of presumption contains those concerning some personal belief-generating mechanism.

Finally, presumptions in favor of the normal, in favor of simplicity, uniformity, specificity, or any of the other inductive considerations, have to deal with plausibility. The question of plausibility arises in connection with one particular type of belief or claim, that of a hypothesis. As we shall develop in Chapter 8, hypotheses are generated by a further personal belief-generating mechanism, intuition. Questions of the connection between plausibility and presumption then arise in connection with whether under certain circumstances there is a presumption for intuition, that is, for the beliefs generated by this faculty.

Grouping the principles of presumption this way suggests how we may develop a systematic survey of the principles of presumption. What are the various interpersonal sources of belief we may identify? Do common knowledge, expert opinion, personal testimony constitute a complete list? Are sense, memory, reason, and intuition the only personal belief-generating mechanisms? In Chapters 6 through 10, we shall develop an account of the various sources, both personal and interpersonal, which

generate or furnish us with our basic beliefs and discuss which are presumption creating and under what circumstances.

We shall be arguing then that principles of presumption connect beliefs with the sources that generate those beliefs, as a prime factor in
determining whether there is a presumption in favor of a belief. "Consider the source" could be our motto for determining presumption. But
what exactly is it about a source that underlies a principle of presumption?
What conditions does the source satisfy? How, in particular, do we establish or argue for the proposition that a particular source generates beliefs
for which there is a presumption? These questions raise significant philosophical issues, issues that we can address in a general manner, and that
we must address for a philosophically adequate account of presumption.
Considering these issues will occupy us for much of the rest of this essay.

3.3 BELIEF-GENERATING MECHANISMS AND WARRANT

How does seeing presumption connected with belief-generating mechanisms advance our understanding of presumption or of the factors
which determine presumption? To answer this question we shall show
how belief-generating mechanisms are connected with a further notion,
developed at length by Plantinga in (1993a) and (1993b), that of warrant.

Plantinga's aim is to identify what distinguishes knowledge from true
belief, calling this condition warrant. According to Plantinga, warrant
involves four factors: the mechanisms producing the belief must be functioning properly; they must be operating in a cognitive environment for
which they are suited; they must be operating according to a design plan
or aspects of a design plan aimed at arriving at the truth; and the objective probability must be high that operating in this manner will reach
the truth. (Compare Plantinga 1993b, pp. viii–ix.) Let us look at each
of these conditions in some detail. Suppose I am confronted with the
appearance of a tree. I am appeared to treely, we may say, and on this
basis form the belief that there is a tree in front of me. Why or under
what circumstances should I be warranted in holding or accepting this
belief? We would certainly deny that the belief was warranted if we knew
that my visual perceptual mechanism was not working properly, if this
appearance of the tree were induced by some drug, hypnotic suggestion,
or neural malfunction. We would deny warrant, even if there were a tree
in front of me.

Being produced by a properly functioning cognitive or belief-
producing mechanism, although necessary, is not a sufficient condition

for warrant, as Plantinga develops (see 1993b, pp. 6–7). Suppose my vision is sound and proper. Suppose I am asked to observe some object which appears rectangular to me and I judge that it is a rectangularly shaped object. But suppose further that I am viewing the object through a series of distorting filters. The object is actually trapezoidal, not rectangular. We should not say that under those circumstances my belief had warrant, because the cognitive environment does not fit my cognitive faculties – they were not designed to compensate for such distortion.

As Plantinga points out, these conditions do not mean that our belief-generating mechanisms must be working *perfectly* or that the environment must be *exactly* of the type for which the relevant belief-generating mechanisms are designed. How properly functioning my belief-generating mechanisms must be or how free from distortion must be the environment is vague to some extent. My faculties must be functioning with sufficient propriety and the environment be sufficiently free from distortion or sufficiently similar to the environment for which my faculties were designed. This is not something that can be stated with total precision.

Proper function and appropriate environment are not jointly sufficient conditions for warrant. According to Plantinga, our cognitive faculties or belief-producing mechanisms may have several functions, only one of which is to get at the truth. We can no doubt think of many cases in which our holding certain beliefs, even with little or no evidence to support them, is necessary to our performing certain actions, actions that will have distinct positive value. Would political reformers risk reputation, comfort, fortune to correct some corrupt government organization or system if they did not believe that the organization or system could be corrected – that their efforts could be to some avail? But might they not believe this without hard evidence bearing on the issue? Their beliefs then would have distinct social utility but not warrant. Although they were generated independently of proper evidence to support them, our cognitive faculties may be designed to produce them anyway. For a belief to have warrant, then, it must be generated by a properly functioning belief-producing mechanism, operating in a proper cognitive environment, and engaged in or functioning to reach the truth.

Talk of faculties or mechanisms functioning to some purpose or goal leads Plantinga to introduce the notion of a *design plan* (which does not in itself imply a conscious, purposive, intelligent Designer). A design plan for an artifact, organ, or living organism specifies how it is "supposed" to function (1993b, p. 21). We may think of the design plan as a set of circumstance-response ordered pairs. Given a possible circumstance, the design plan specifies an appropriate response. The appropriateness of the response is determined by the overall purpose for which the artifact, organ, mechanism, or organism is designed (1993b, p. 22). The three necessary conditions on warrant that we have just presented are still not jointly sufficient. Being *aimed* at producing true beliefs is not the same as *successfully producing* true beliefs standardly, most of the time, or always. Our design plan may be seriously flawed, perhaps in some aspects. A belief, then, might be produced by a mechanism functioning properly according to aspects of the design plan aimed at producing true beliefs, in a proper cognitive environment, and yet those beliefs would lack warrant. What additional condition must be added for a belief to have warrant? According to Plantinga, "The module of the design plan governing its production must be such that it is objectively highly probable that a belief produced by cognitive faculties functioning properly according to that module (in a congenial environment) will be true or verisimilitudinous" (1993b, p. 17). As Plantinga points out, we ordinarily presuppose that this reliability condition holds, is satisfied. How high is highly probable? The concept is vague, but Plantinga feels that we presume the degree of probability varies with the degree of belief. The more firmly we hold a belief, the higher do we presume the reliability of the mechanism that produced it.

Four conditions then are individually necessary and jointly sufficient for warrant: (1) the belief-generating mechanisms must be functioning properly; (2) they must be operating in an environment or medium for which they were designed to operate or one similar to such an environment; (3) the segment of the design plan according to which they are operating must be aimed at the truth; and (4) they must be reliable, that is, the objective probability must be high that the beliefs they generate according to this segment of the design plan are true or have verisimilitude.

3.4 WARRANT AND THE FACTORS
DETERMINING PRESUMPTION

How may this exposition of the conditions of warrant advance our understanding of the factors determining presumption? Recall our definition of challenger presumption from Chapter 2. There is a presumption for a claim at a point in a dialectical exchange for the challenger of that exchange just in case she must concede that claim at that point. For convenience of expression, let us speak of there being a presumption for a statement from the challenger's point of view, meaning that were she participating as a challenger in an appropriate dialectical exchange, at that point there would be a presumption for that statement for her. Let us recall that to concede a proposition is to grant that it is acceptable. It is not to say that one must accept the proposition but that one is free to accept it, to use it as a premise for further deliberation or action. We have noted in Section 2 that the principles of presumption in our survey link presumption with belief-generating mechanisms. Plantinga's account of warrant identifies four features, conditions, states of belief-generating mechanisms under which the beliefs they form have warrant for the person who holds them. Suppose there were a presumption from the challenger's point of view that one or more of these four conditions held with respect to a given belief. Could that be a sufficient and necessary condition for saying that there was a presumption for that belief from her perspective? If so then our quest for conditions of presumption, factors determining presumption, would be advanced. We would then have a set of conditions under which there would be a presumption for a given belief.

Let us ask then first whether we can identify one or more conditions of the definition of warrant such that if from the challenger's point of view there is a presumption that these conditions hold of the mechanism generating a particular belief, there is a presumption for the belief itself. Let us consider reliability first. Is there being a presumption of reliability for the source of a belief or the mechanism generating it a sufficient condition for there being a presumption for the belief itself? Just what is involved in saying that there is a presumption that a source is reliable?

i. Does Presumption Amount to Presumption of Reliability?

What does saying that the objective probability is high that the beliefs a mechanism generates are true mean? Specifically, what does objective probability involve? It seems straightforward that for the concept of reliability, the objective probability involved is statistical. When I say that a belief-producing mechanism is reliable, I mean that the proportion or percentage of beliefs generated by that mechanism (given the mechanism is functioning properly, in a suitable cognitive environment, and aiming at the truth) that are true is high, given the total class of beliefs that mechanism generates.

Under what circumstances then will there be a presumption, from a challenger's point of view, that a mechanism is reliable? Surely she would be obliged to concede that belief-generating module **M** is reliable when she was in possession of evidence, say that the ratio of true beliefs **M** generates to total beliefs **M** generates is high. What would this evidence be? It would seem that our challenger would need to possess the results of a survey taking a fair, unbiased, or random sample of the beliefs generated by **M**, which indicated that a high proportion of the beliefs in that sample were true. Could the challenger ever be in such a position? Certainly on some occasions she might. Consider the module **M** producing a belief about the identity of someone on the basis of fingerprint identification, an instance of institutional testimony. At some point, humans discovered that fingerprints were unique – that the frequency of matching fingerprints among all the pairs of sets of fingerprints produced by two different persons is nil for all practical purposes. Hence, identifying who produced certain fingerprints by matching them against fingerprints whose producer's identity is known is a very reliable method of identification. That this source has been shown reliable creates a presumption for its reliability. But will we always be in such a situation for each one of our belief-generating mechanisms?

Consider perception. What the challenger apparently needs is evidence to the effect that the relative frequency of true perceptual judgments among all perceptual judgments is high. But how would she determine that a perceptual judgment is true? If truth for a perceptual judgment means correspondence, how will one compare one's perceptual judgment with the external situation? If one makes further observations and the resulting perceptual judgments all agree with one's given perceptual judgment, how will this constitute evidence for the truth or reliability of that judgment unless all these judgments are certified reliable? But the reliability of perceptual judgments is precisely the point at issue. If I agree that their reliability needs to be established, how may I proceed but to appeal to further perceptual judgments?

Suppose not only my own repeated observations but those of other witnesses all generate the same judgment that a car is maroon. Does this coherence or convergence establish reliability? (Let us ignore for the sake of this example the problems of how the laws of optics are shown true or verisimilitudinous in the absence of the reliability or even presumptive reliability of perception or how we establish that taking testimony from others about their perceptions, receiving their perceptual judgments through testimony is a reliable way of forming belief.) But this evidence is a collection of perceptual judgments whose reliability is at issue. Can we establish that perception is reliable on premises whose acceptability is in question? Suppose I and all the people I surveyed suffered from a curious epistemic or doxastic malady: When exposed to certain electromagnetic radiation, we hallucinated that there was a maroon car in front of us. Let us suppose that this source also generated tactile hallucinations so that we experienced feelings of resistance when our bodies were put in the spatial region where the car was supposed to be. Now suppose that our judgments that there is a maroon car in front of us arise under these circumstances. They would be coherent. But would the convergence or coherence of these unreliable perceptual judgments show perception reliable? Surely our belief-generating mechanism is not reliable in this case.

Unless I can find some perceptual judgments that are self-evidently certain, judgments that somehow carry unmistakable marks of their truth upon themselves, it seems that we are caught either in circularity or vicious infinite regress. But *perceptual* judgments are not certain in this way. Indeed, the academic skeptics argued specifically for this point against the Stoics. The Stoics believed that some impressions were "cataleptic." As Stough points out in (1969), such an impression "literally 'grasps' its object, resulting necessarily in knowledge of the object. Such an impression cannot be doubted. . . . [It] is so striking and clear as to compel assent" (1969, pp. 38, 39). Cataleptic impressions intrinsically come with a special mark of certainty. This mark "*authorizes* assent by the same fact that it *compels* assent. That is, a cataleptic impression 'generates' a proposition that is immediately evident and certain" (Stough 1969, p. 40). Against this, Carneades, an academic skeptic, points out: "For every true impression it is possible for a false impression to be indistinguishable from it" (Stough 1969, p. 42). If that were true, then there would be no cataleptic impressions, for such an impression is not only true but seen immediately that it must be true. Hence, if every true impression is possibly false, there are no cataleptic impressions.

To support this point, the academic skeptics ask us to look at various examples of impressions that compel assent and yet are false – hallucinations, dreams, illusions, errors due to the limitations of our sensory powers such as mistaking objects highly similar qualitatively (identical twins, two eggs, distinct wax impressions made by one seal) for each other (Stough 1969, p. 44). Such impressions can be just as convincing as true ones, yet they are false. But given an impression, even a true one, is it not possible that there could be a hallucinatory impression or one in a dream qualitatively indistinguishable from it? That there can always be perceptual error refutes the claim that some impressions show their truth by some qualitative difference. So it appears that far from being able to amass evidence that perception is reliable by showing somehow that perceptual judgments are preponderantly true, without the presumption of reliability it seems we cannot certify any perceptual judgment as true. But how then can we have a direct argument for the presumption that perception is reliable?

Is this whole approach wrongheaded – at least for perception? Although establishing that a source is reliable would show a presumption of reliability for that source, is this the only way to show that there is a *presumption* of reliability? Let us pose the question more generally and even more radically. Do we have to be in possession of evidence to justify a presumption? Certainly we do not in judicial contexts. At the initial stage of a trial, the defense attorney need not present any evidence for the innocence of the accused. The accused is presumed innocent. If someone asked us to justify this initial presumption of innocence, it is conceivable that we might proceed this way: We might attempt to produce a representative sample of cases of the persons charged with crimes, in which the majority were innocent of the crimes for which they were charged. But how could we secure our premises? Is it a matter of known fact that our law enforcement agencies and district attorneys do such a bad job that in most of the cases they bring to trial, the accused is, as a matter of fact, innocent of the crime of which he or she is charged? I think not.

Instead of appealing to inductive evidence to justify the presumption of innocence, I believe that we would appeal to certain broad social values. The presumption of innocence fosters the value of respect for the human individual. We are willing to tolerate the possibility that a guilty person will go unpunished rather than compromise the value of individuals and their rights. We could seek to foster other values. A presumption of guilt might very well foster the security of a society over respect for individuals and their rights. Under a presumption of guilt, more guilty persons might be punished for their crimes. We would tolerate the possibility that innocent persons would be unjustly punished in order to maximize the value of recompense to the guilty and the value of societal security which that fosters. We need not maintain that the choice between valuing individual rights over societal security is arbitrary. One might argue that a preference for individual rights accords better with the categorical imperative. The point is that the presumption of innocence, although open to justification, is not justified inductively, and the offering of such an argument would be wrongheaded.

It would be equally wrongheaded in certain cases to attempt to establish a presumption for the reliability of a cognitive module or belief generating mechanism **M** by arguing for the reliability of the mechanism through some relative frequency argument. This is not something that needs justification through argument, because there is already a presumption of reliability. That there is such a presumption is a basic truth and a properly basic truth, analogous to the judgments of immediate experience or *a priori* self-evident truths for the classical foundationalist. This is the approach of the commonsense school, stemming from Thomas Reid. How would a commonsense philosopher answer the question of why there is a presumption of reliability for perception?

Reid would respond that there is no need to defend the reliability of our cognitive faculties. Attempts to gather inductive evidence for their trustworthiness are attempts to justify something for which there is already a presumption. Reid makes two main points to support this contention. First, it is arbitrary to favor some faculties over others. Reid admits that we have a variety of faculties including perception, consciousness (introspection), and reason. The operation of these faculties is part of our constitution, as Reid calls it, our design plan in Plantinga's terminology. On the evidence of sense, on the basis of being appeared to through one or more of our five senses, we form perceptual beliefs automatically or immediately, given that our perceptual mechanism is functioning properly. That perceptual beliefs will be formed under conditions of sense appearance is a first principle of conception. That upon introspectively inspecting the contents of my consciousness, I form certain beliefs is a further first principle of conception. Recognizing relations between ideas, generating beliefs about those relations, is the province of reason. That upon certain presentations we shall form beliefs about such relations is an additional first principle of cognition.

For Reid, "the first principles of conception and belief are also the first principles of evidence" (Lehrer 1989, p. 17). For our purposes, we may take this to mean the following: Whenever a cognitive faculty is operating in accord with our constitution, how we are appeared to – more generally the presentations of which we are aware – constitute evidence – presumptively sufficient evidence – for the beliefs thus generated. Hume also would recognize perception, consciousness, and reason as cognitive faculties. But whereas Hume "assumed that the deliverances of consciousness and reasoning are trustworthy" (Lehrer 1989, p. 17), he was skeptical of perception. The situation is similar with Descartes. "I think" is an introspective judgment, which he took to be indubitable, and thus he accepted the trustworthiness or reliability of introspection, while subjecting perceptual judgments to Cartesian doubt. Reid's first main point is that this division of our cognitive faculties is arbitrary. "Hume can give no proof that these faculties are trustworthy and that perception, memory, and the other faculties are not" (Lehrer 1989, pp. 17–18). What gives any persons the right to pick and choose among their cognitive faculties, where is there any rationale for saying that one faculty is trustworthy, but not another? To be consistent, we must either trust all of our faculties or trust none.

A perceptual skeptic might reply to Reid along internalist lines. We are directly aware of internal states. Certain relations between ideas are immediately evident. Because of this direct awareness, the beliefs based on this evidence are certain. We have no special or internal access to the objects of perception. They are (allegedly) objects in the external world. The evidence for them consists of how we are appeared to through our senses, and the process or state of being appeared to in a certain way is not the same or identical with the external perceptual object that supposedly appears. Beliefs formed on this evidence are not certain. But regarding a faculty as trustworthy does not, for Reid, mean regarding it as infallible. "Our faculties are, Reid admits, fallible" (Lehrer 1989, p. 18). What does trusting an admittedly fallible faculty mean for Reid? It means that we should regard the beliefs these faculties generate "as epistemically justified or innocent until proven guilty" (Beanblossom 1983, p. xxx). That is, we are to accord a presumption for the beliefs generated by this cognitive faculty. They are acceptable until this presumption is defeated.

Hence, Reid could make the same reply to the skeptic of our "externally oriented" faculties that we made to the classical foundationalist in Section 1.2. The predilection for those faculties that generate beliefs that are certain is just that – a predilection or preference. That we may regard only those faculties as trustworthy is an assumption that has been taken as obvious but is not. Some faculties will generate beliefs that are certain. The presumption in their favor will be a limiting case of presumption, a presumption that cannot be undercut. But why should only such faculties be deemed trustworthy? This is the doxastic no-risk principle, a principle that is not obvious. In fact, Reid could go further. Not only is this assumption not obvious, it violates our constitution. "It is a first principle of our nature that we trust our faculties" (Lehrer 1989, p. 18).

The perceptual skeptic can still make a rejoinder along internalist lines. It is not because the beliefs generated by introspection or reason are certain whereas perceptual beliefs are not that we should trust the former but not the latter. It is that only because the former beliefs concern matters of which we are directly aware that we are in a position to say we have proper justificatory evidence for them. Only such beliefs can be justified beliefs. And surely being justified is a necessary, if not a necessary and sufficient, condition for being acceptable. This rejoinder raises significant epistemological issues. What is the relation between internalism, justification, and acceptability? We shall address this rejoinder fully in the next chapter, in which we situate acceptability vis-à-vis other central epistemological notions.

Reid's second main point for regarding as wrongheaded the attempt to *argue* that there is a presumption in favor of our faculties, is his claim that their trustworthiness is a matter of common sense. The trustworthiness of these faculties is not to be established *by* reasoning, but constitutes basic principles *from* which we reason. Because reason is the faculty of argument, to attempt to argue for the trustworthiness of a cognitive faculty is to assume that reason is trustworthy but to withhold that assumption from the faculty whose trustworthiness is allegedly being demonstrated. But this again is to make an arbitrary distinction among faculties. According to Reid, this is to confuse the provinces of reason and common sense. "The evidence of sense, the evidence of memory, and the evidence of the necessary relations of things, are all distinct and original kinds of evidence, equally grounded on our constitution.... To reason for them is absurd. They are first principles; and such fall not within the province of reason, but of common sense" (Beanblossom 1983, p. xxvii). For Reid, reason or philosophy has no jurisdiction over common sense. It can neither critique nor justify the principles of common sense. Again, Reid comments, "It is a bold philosophy that rejects, without ceremony, principles which irresistibly govern the belief and the conduct of all mankind in the common concerns of life.... Such principles are older, and of more authority, than Philosophy: she rests upon them as her basis, not they upon her" (Beanblossom and Lehrer 1983, p. 9). Reid says that first principles, matters of common sense, are self-evident. They may be illustrated, but they "do not admit of proof" (Beanblossom and Lehrer 1983, p. 152). Should a challenger question a first principle, the proponent's task is not to give evidence for the principle but to make its being evident manifest. A critical question arises at this point. Although one may be quite prepared, in the light of Reid's discussion, to concede that a presumption for the reliability of perception, introspection, and reason are first principles, is there a similar presumption for *every* belief-generating mechanism? Obviously, such a question can only be carried out in the light of a survey, as comprehensive as possible, of our belief-generating mechanisms, which we undertake in Part II. But surely to maintain that there is a presumption of reliability for some cognitive faculties does not mean that we must maintain that every faculty must be presumed trustworthy. We may have reason to believe that some of our faculties under some at least of their applications are unreliable. But in light of this question of the general reliability of belief-generating mechanisms, we can say that Reid has indicated how we may show or make manifest, at least in some cases, that there is a reliability for a source or belief-generating mechanism. All we need do is make manifest that trusting this cognitive faculty is a matter of common sense, that it would violate our design plan, indeed be absurd, not to grant this presumption.

Hence, the class of cognitive faculties or belief-generating mechanisms need not coincide with the class of presumptively reliable mechanisms, which may constitute just a proper subclass. It is important that we point this out, for the overall question that initiated this discussion is whether presumption amounts to presumption of reliability. Now any belief we have will have been generated by some mechanism. But if all belief-generating mechanisms are presumptively reliable and if being generated by a presumptively reliable mechanism is a sufficient condition for reliability, then there is a presumption for all beliefs. But this is obviously false.

One implication of this discussion of when there is a presumption of reliability for a belief-generating mechanism needs stressing. Earlier, we conjectured that we needed to clarify the nature of objective probability to be able to determine just when there would be a presumption of reliability for that mechanism. However, this is not right. We may recognize that there is a presumption of reliability for a belief-generating mechanism as a matter of common sense. The notion of probability, with all its complications and difficulties, need not enter into these considerations. A challenger can recognize a presumption for the reliability of a cognitive faculty without having any position on the nature of objective probability or even being aware of evidence supporting the proposition that the statistical frequency of true beliefs generated by this faculty is high.

What may we say then to the thesis that there is a presumption for a belief from the point of view of a challenger if and only if there is a presumption of reliability from her perspective for the mechanism that generated that belief? Clearly, presumption of reliability is a necessary condition of presumption. For how could a challenger be obliged to concede a belief if there were not a presumption, from her perspective, of the reliability of the mechanism generating that belief? Lack of presumption means that the challenger is aware of evidence against the reliability of the mechanism generating the belief. But under those circumstances she is certainly not obliged to concede the belief.

Clearly, however, presumption of reliability is not a sufficient condition. For although there may be a presumption of reliability for a cognitive faculty in general, in a particular application, with respect to a particular belief, there may be evidence that the challenger's belief generating mechanisms were not functioning properly or that the cognitive environment was not appropriate, or that in this particular instance, the module of the design plan operating to generate this belief was not aiming at the truth. Should a challenger be aware of any such evidence, the presumption for that belief would be undercut. Only a joint presumption for all four conditions of warrant possibly constitutes a sufficient condition for presumption. Before we can determine whether this is the case, we must ask what a presumption for the first three conditions of warrant amounts to.

ii. What Do Presumptions of Properly Functioning Belief-Generating Mechanism, Cognitively Appropriate Environment, and Truth-Oriented Design Plan Module Mean?

Taking for a moment the point of view of a rational adjudicator, a presumption of proper function would mean that it was incumbent upon anyone refusing to concede proper functioning in a particular case to show the belief-generating mechanism not functioning properly. From the point of view of the challenger, this means in addition that she has no rebutting argument to bring forward. Under what circumstances would a challenger be in such a position? Consider visual perception. Suppose I as challenger have formed the belief that there is a tree outside my office window on the basis of what I visually experience. When would I have grounds for not conceding that my visual perceptual mechanism was functioning properly? Suppose I were not appeared to in a treelike manner. Surely I would have evidence of distinct cognitive malfunction if upon inspecting my awareness, I could come across no treelike appearance and yet on the basis of being visually appeared to in *some* manner I formed the belief that there was a tree in front of me.[4] Being appeared to treely is having positive evidence for the claim that there is a tree in front of me.[5] For belief-generating mechanisms in general then, having evidence is a necessary condition for a presumption of proper cognitive function.

What is also necessary is absence of awareness of cognitive malfunction on any grounds besides forming a belief independent of evidence. If the appearance of the tree were outlined in bright red and blue colors, awareness of this appearance would undercut the presumption of proper function. Notice that there is a presumption of proper function from my point of view just when there is lack of awareness of defeating conditions. When I am aware of no evidence that my visual perceptual system has been tampered with to respond in an unusual, unorthodox manner, there is a presumption from my point of view that it is functioning properly.

We may similarly clarify what it means for there to be a presumption from the challenger's perspective for the cognitive environment to be appropriate. It means that she is aware of no information indicating that the environment is not appropriate. I perceive that tree. Why should I think that there is any reason to believe or even be concerned about whether the tree is an illusion produced by some evil genius, or that the appearance of the tree is caused by a holographic projection, or that some unusual and bizarre atmospheric occurrence has caused me to be appeared to treely when really there is not any tree there? What more is needed for there to be a presumption that my cognitive environment is appropriate than my not being aware of any evidence for such disturbing factors?

The issue of a presumption that the design plan module in accordance with which a belief was generated was truth-oriented raises two distinct philosophical questions. Does such a presumption presuppose that design plans are real in an ontological sense? Does it also presuppose that the design plan has been authored by a conscious designer? If so, this presumption apparently raises distinct burdens of proof. I argue that it does not. Clearly, in the light of current genetics, we understand living organisms including their cognitive mechanisms as developing according to a genetic code, which we may call a design plan. At least in the Western world, this conception is now common knowledge and thus there is a presumption for the existence of design plans in this sense. Apart from contemporary genetics, if in connection with design plans, we speak of organisms and their mechanisms as functioning to achieve certain ends according to certain specified – proper – patterns for functioning, which Plantinga's account of a design plan involves, we are making contact with a perennial concept, that of functional or teleological explanation. We may claim that talk of design plans conceptualizes a prominent feature of the world as we experience it. John Herman Randall points out that "Teleological relations, the relations between means and ends, or 'functional structures,' are an encountered fact" (1960, p. 229). For a given organ or organism, the notion of a design plan collects or sums up the manifold teleological or functional relations inherent in that organ or organism. Understood in this way, the claim that there are design plans would seem to be accorded near universal agreement. Again, there would be a presumption for it as common knowledge.

Notice that we say near universal, for there is skepticism over functional or teleological explanations. Many have objected to them on the ground that purpose presupposes a purposer, and so teleological explanations are anthropomorphic and not scientific. Our second critical question for warrant thus comes to the fore. To this objection we may reply that we may distinguish immanent from transcendent teleology. In discussing teleological explanation in Aristotle, Randall emphasizes that the final cause need not be the purpose of a conscious agent, a designer transcendent to what is designed, unless human agency is involved. Rather, as Aristotle puts it, "Whenever there is clearly some end towards which a motion goes forward unless something stands in its way, then we always say that the motion has the end as its For What" (Randall 1960, p. 231). If we say that a certain state or trait has positive value for an organism or species, we are making no explicit reference to any transcendent conscious agent. If we say that a functional advantage conferred by a trait is causally relevant to explain why an organism has that trait or why it has become fixed in the species to which the organism belongs, have we presupposed that the trait has been placed there by any conscious agency? Saying that being able to do something or do something better by virtue of having a certain trait produced a bias in terms of survival and reproductive ability for the organism which had that trait (compare Lennox 1992, p. 298) makes no reference to conscious agency of any sort. The functional advantage conferred by the trait explains why certain organisms have that trait. The causality is completely immanent. Admitting the legitimacy of teleological explanation does not commit one to anthropomorphism. Plantinga himself specifically asserts that his use of "design" in "design plan" does not commit us to there being a designer or author of the design plan.

Specific reference to design plan in the notion of warrant and presumption of warrant then does not make someone who would speak of warrant or presumption of warrant liable to a burden of proof either to show that there are design plans or that such plans are authored by conscious purposers. Talk of design plans is not talk of some obscure entities whose existence must be established by argument, and whose existence may very well presuppose transcendent agency. It is rather to make reference to a familiar feature of the world as commonly experienced. Thus, there is a presumption for seeing teleological and functional relations as features of the world and design plans as manifolds of such features. We can speak of there being a presumption that a segment of one's design plan is oriented toward the truth without incurring a burden of proof about philosophical issues associated with the concept of design plan.

In light of this discussion, then, under what conditions will there be a presumption from the challenger's point of view that the segment or module of her design plan in accordance with which a belief was generated was oriented toward the truth? She will have a presumption for this just in case she is aware of no evidence that her design plan was oriented toward some other value or goal. If she is aware of no evidence of wishful thinking, desire to maintain personal or species survival, to maintain commitments to other persons or institutions, that is, she is aware of no desire to reach any other value than the truth, she may presume that this particular module of her design plan that produced this particular belief was truth-oriented. But now to return to our simple tree example, we may ask – how is the simple belief that there is a tree in front of me connected with such ideals as personal survival or maintaining more commitments? Although such connections are possible in a broadly logical sense, they are rather unusual. Ordinarily believing simple descriptions about our circumstances is not connected with such goals. But this is precisely the point. Unless I am aware of evidence that my belief that there is a tree in front of me is connected with goals other than truth, there is a presumption that it has been generated solely by segments of the design plan aimed at the truth.

We have now discussed just what it means to say, for each of the four conditions of warrant, that there is a presumption from the challenger's point of view that the condition holds. We may now address the main question of this section. Is there a presumption for a belief if and only if there is a presumption of warrant for that belief?

iii. Is Presumption of Warrant a Necessary and Sufficient Condition For Presumption?

First, is presumption of warrant from the challenger's point of view for a belief a necessary condition for a presumption for that belief? Suppose there is a presumption for one of the beliefs of a challenger from her perspective. That is, she needs no evidence, or no further evidence, for the belief and she has no objections to bring against it. She must concede it. There will fail to be a presumption of warrant for this belief just in case there fails to be a presumption for one of the four conditions of warrant. But in each case, should there be such a failure, there will fail to be a presumption for the belief from the challenger's perspective. Suppose there is not a presumption that the belief-generating mechanism is functioning properly, as designed. That in itself would constitute an objection against the belief. Until this objection were somehow countered, there would not be a presumption for the belief. The same holds for each of the other three conditions for warrant. Failure of presumption that the environment is cognitively appropriate, that the design plan is aimed at the truth or that the belief-generating mechanism is a reliable generator of true beliefs, each constitutes an objection against the belief, one that would undercut the presumption in its favor.

What may we say to the converse? Is presumption of warrant a sufficient condition for presumption? Suppose then that a challenger finds herself in a position in which she has no reason to question, doubt, or rebut the claims that the mechanisms generating a belief were functioning properly, that they were functioning in an environment for which they were designed to function, that the segments of the design plan according to which they operated were aimed at the truth, and that regarding the mechanism producing the belief as reliable was a matter of common sense. Why, under these circumstances, should she not be required to concede the belief? Could she, in those circumstances, still have some objection to bring against the belief, some reason or argument to offer why it should not be accepted? Consider the following situation. Suppose Sue, while visiting her friend Bruce of unimpeachable honesty, asks him whether there are any tomatoes in the kitchen. Bruce says no. Suppose on going into the kitchen Sue apparently perceives a tomato on the windowsill – a fine, red tomato. Better, let us say she is appeared to red-tomatoly upon entering the kitchen. The tomato, however, is not real but artificial, albeit of striking realism. Under these circumstances, that is, of being appeared to red-tomatoly, Sue would be tempted to believe, and ordinarily would believe, that there is a red tomato on the windowsill. But is there a presumption for this belief from Sue's perspective in these circumstances, given what Bruce has just said and his reputation for veracity? It would seem not. Either Sue is deceived or her friend is mistaken. But it would seem that in light of her friend's statement and the recognized reliability of his testimony, the presumption for the perceptual claim that there is a red tomato on the windowsill is undercut. Sue should not accept or concede this perceptual judgment without further evidence.

But is there a presumption for each of the four conditions of warrant here? Sue has formed her belief on the basis of the red tomato experience and she is unaware of any condition causing her eyes to malfunction. Sue does not know that the tomato is artificial and there is nothing in the kitchen to indicate that it is artificial or that the cognitive environment is in any other way misleading. There is no indication of wishful thinking here or any other reason for Sue to think her belief-generating mechanism is operating to satisfy some other need than to get at the truth. Finally, that we may presume visual perception reliable is a matter of common sense. Also, Sue's eyes have always been reliable in the past. Sue has no reason to impugn *their* general reliability. Do we have, then, a counterexample to the claim that a presumption of warrant is a sufficient condition for a presumption in favor of a belief or claim?

This would be too hasty, but explaining why requires us to introduce a further feature of the design plan, its containing override mechanisms. If in these circumstances Sue formed the belief that there was a tomato on the windowsill and held that belief with the strength of conviction she would have held it should Bruce have said nothing about the absence of tomatoes in the kitchen, then her belief-forming mechanisms would not be functioning properly. Her belief-generating system would include what Plantinga calls *a defeater*, a specification that under certain circumstances the ordinary functioning of the belief-generating mechanisms be suspended, to which she would not be responding properly.

The design plan also specifies circumstances under which, even though you are appeared to redly, you won't or don't form that belief [that you see something red]. These circumstances would include, for example, your learning that the thing in question, despite appearances, is not red. . . . This defeater structure is to be found across the length and breadth of our cognitive structure, and nearly any belief is possibly subject to defeat. (1993b, p. 41)

So in these circumstances, where there would not be a presumption in favor of the claim that there was a red tomato on the windowsill from

Sue's perspective, she would not have formed the belief that there was, or at least would be confronted with evidence that her belief-generating mechanism was not functioning properly. Should she form the belief, she would not be responding properly to the defeater, and so there would not be a presumption of proper function from her point of view. There is thus no presumption of warrant for that belief. The counterexample fails when we take into account the presence of defeaters in the design plan.

Our counterexample will serve to make our point in general. A challenger would not be obliged to concede a statement *S* if more evidence were required before such a concession were proper or if she had some rebutting objection to bring against *S*. Suppose a challenger has an appropriate amount of evidence for *S*. Let *S* be the proposition that Jones stabbed Smith, and suppose ten witnesses have just independently testified that they saw Jones stab Smith. If in these circumstances our challenger refuses to concede *S*, she must either bring a legitimate objection against it – *she*, for example, must show that Jones was someplace else than at the scene of the crime when the stabbing took place, or she must raise significant questions about the reliability of the testimony. But should she raise an objection, then her belief-generating system – and the belief-generating system of anyone following the argument – would include a defeater. In such a circumstance, the claim that Jones stabbed Smith should not be generated as a belief. If it were, there would not be a presumption of proper function. Should our challenger raise legitimate questions about the reliability of the testimony, then should the belief that Jones stabbed Smith be formed, there would not be a presumption of reliability for the mechanisms that generated this belief.

But suppose that only one witness has testified that he saw Jones stab Smith and that Jones is on trial for capital murder. There is no reason to impugn the witness's reliability or trustworthiness. Should the challenger then believe that Jones stabbed Smith, she would have formed her belief on the basis of personal testimony. Anticipating our discussion in Chapter 10, it would seem in this situation that the conditions of presumption of warrant are satisfied. Without going into detail, let us assume that the challenger hears and understands what the witness says. There is thus a presumption of proper function and absence of environmental distortion. The challenger is seeking to determine the truth about Jones' guilt or innocence. The witness is giving personal testimony and receiving testimony is a presumptively reliable belief-generating mechanism. Hence, it seems that the four conditions for presumption of warrant are satisfied here. Yet, must the challenger concede the claim that Jones stabbed Smith? This brings us to the issue of the pragmatic dimension of presumption.

Why would one be reluctant to say that the challenger must concede that Jones stabbed Smith in this situation? Suppose she is a member of the jury. Her concession then could have very dire consequences for Jones. Indeed, should the other jurors concur and should the prosecutor's argument otherwise be in order, the consequence could be the termination of Jones's life! In this context, then, conceding the statement that Jones stabbed Smith has a very high cost. Given the cost, should the challenger concede the premise on the testimony of just one witness? She might be quite justified in believing the statement, that is, in *feeling* that it is true. But should she accept the statement as a premise for an argument whose conclusion could have such serious consequences?

We cannot properly answer this question until we define just what the cost of conceding a statement means. We approach this by asking first just what we mean by the cost of an action or state of affairs in general. Clarke in (1989) defines cost as a binary relation between an action, activity, or state of affairs and a person: *A has a cost for X if and only if X has an aversion to A.* (Compare 1989, p. 79.) Notice that X might have an aversion to A while Y does not. So A will have a cost for X but no cost for Y. If cost is understood in this relational way and cost of acceptance should be a factor in premise acceptability, then acceptability becomes relativized not just to the epistemic position of the challenger but to the challenger's desires and aversions. But is this consequence acceptable? Suppose X and Y are aware of the same evidence pertaining to a statement *p*. Should *p* be an acceptable premise for X but not for Y simply because X has no aversion to taking *p* as a premise or to the consequences that accepting *p* may bring about while Y has some such aversion? Should a premise be acceptable for one and not for the other on the same evidence?

We need not define cost in this relativizing way. Why should X have some aversion to *A*? Presumably, either X finds that *A* itself has intrinsic disvalue or leads to a state of affairs *B* that has intrinsic disvalue. But intuitionists such as Ross (1930) have shown that in virtue of possessing certain properties or features, states of affairs are objectively *prima facie* intrinsically good or bad. For Ross, involving pleasure, knowledge, virtue, or the apportionment of happiness to virtue are *prima facie* intrinsically good-making features of a state of affairs. The opposites make a state of affairs *prima facie* intrinsically bad. (See 1930, pp. 134–9.) These states of affairs may be constituents of complex facts or wholes, which may affect their actual intrinsic value. Pleasure may be *prima facie* intrinsically good but taking pleasure in the pain of others is not actually intrinsically good. When viewed in the light of the morally relevant wholes to which such states of affairs belong, we may speak of them as being objectively intrinsically good or bad *simpliciter*. Surely if a state of affairs A were intrinsically bad and X were cognizant of the badness, or of the factors on which that badness supervened, X should have an aversion to A. Hence, we may define cost objectively in terms of intrinsic disvalue.

Now, an action or state of affairs can either involve intrinsic disvalue in itself or lead to some further state of affairs B which has intrinsic disvalue. This motivates the following definition: *Where* **A** *is an action, activity, or state of affairs, by the* **cost of A**, *we mean the amount of intrinsic disvalue of* **A** *itself together with the intrinsic disvalue of any consequences* **B'** *of* **A**. We may analogously define the *benefit of A* objectively:[6] *Where* **A** *is an action, activity, or state of affairs, by the* **benefit of A** *we mean the amount of intrinsic value of* **A** *itself together with the intrinsic value of any consequences* **B'** *of* **A**. The intrinsic disvalue of A includes the intrinsic disvalue of the effort required to perform A together with the loss of intrinsic value of any benefits we forego in performing A.[7]

In the preceding definition, A ranges over actions or states of affairs in general. But we are interested in the cost of one type of action or activity, that of accepting a statement. Now it is easy to appreciate that the intrinsic disvalue of accepting a statement p may differ, depending on whether p is true or false. If it is true that Jones stabbed Smith, and should all the jurors accept that he did, a consequence could be their all voting to convict Jones of Smith's murder and Jones's facing a capital sentence. This obviously involves the intrinsic disvalue of significant pain (at least psychological) to Jones and the intrinsic disvalue of the termination of a human life. But if Jones is guilty, one could argue that the punishment is deserved, the pain is proportionate to the viciousness of his action. But it is intrinsically good that punishment be proportioned to vice. But now suppose that Jones did not stab Smith, even though the one witness testifies that he did. Suppose all the jurors again accept that Jones stabbed Smith on the basis of this testimony and vote to convict. Their acceptance now has the further intrinsic disvalue that Jones is about to be unjustly punished.

Because our concern is with premise acceptability, unless the evidence for a premise is something to which we have direct or internal access, the question arises of whether we should risk accepting the premise on the evidence before us even if it is false, or should seek further evidence bearing on the premise. Hence, we have two actions here whose costs can be weighed against each other – the cost of the action of accepting a premise when that premise is false or mistaken versus the cost of the action of seeking further evidence. Does the cost of obtaining testimony from a further witness or of obtaining other pertinent evidence outweigh the cost of accepting that Jones stabbed Smith should that statement be false?

This motivates what Clarke calls the pragmatic condition for premise acceptability. As a first approximation, we can say that if the cost of mistakenly accepting p outweighs the cost of obtaining further evidence, then p is not acceptable on the basis of the evidence e proffered at this point. Why should this condition be called "pragmatic"? For Clarke, pragmatism is "a theory that claims that the standards used in justifying acceptance of a proposition as rational must include reference to individual or community purposes" (1989, p. ix). Hence, pragmatism insists that "a necessary condition for the acceptance of p" involves "the fulfillment of interests and purposes to which this acceptance is related" (1989, p. 73). Although we are defining cost not with respect to aversion but intrinsic disvalue, as we shall develop in Chapter 9, the intrinsic badness or disvalue of a state of affairs is a reason for acting to avert the state of affairs coming about. Hence, by connecting acceptability with cost defined in terms of intrinsic disvalue, we are connecting acceptability with a reason for action and thus maintaining a connection with purpose.

The pragmatic criterion, as formulated, seems well motivated. It captures our intuitions, certainly in the case illustrating our discussion. Notice that if two independent witnesses both testified that they had seen Jones stab Smith, we might be far more inclined to say that the challenger must now concede that he did. The evidence of two witnesses covers risking the cost of mistakenly accepting that he did. However, there are cases where the pragmatic criterion does not capture our intuitions. As Clarke points out, the cost of checking to see that the ceiling above us will not collapse is small, while the cost of our being mistaken that the ceiling is sound, that it will not collapse, is significant. Yet, we do not check to see that the ceiling is sound and we regard that statement as acceptable. This is because we intuitively recognize that the probability of the ceiling's collapsing is low. This brings us to what Clarke identifies as the *expected cost* of an action or state of affairs. As the calculation of expected utility or expected value involves the product of the return of a given possible outcome with its probability, so expected cost is a function of the probability of the consequences of an action or state of affairs together with their intrinsic disvalue. (Compare Clarke 1989, p. 81.) We do not compare the simple cost of gathering additional evidence with the simple cost of mistakenly accepting a proposition but the expected costs. This motivates the refined formulation of the pragmatic condition: "X is justified in accepting a proposition *p* relative to evidence *e* as true only if the expected cost of acquiring additional relevant evidence *e'* is higher than the expected cost of acting on the basis of *p* which would be incurred if *p* were to later prove mistaken" (Clarke 1989, p 82). As Clarke points out, we shall ordinarily be quite certain that acquiring additional evidence will incur certain costs. Hence, in practice the cost of gathering further evidence does not differ much from the expected cost. By contrast, the probability that a mistake could occur could vary distinctly from case to case. In ordinary life, we estimate costs and probabilities intuitively. As Clarke puts it, "We rely on rough, intuitive judgments of our degrees of want or aversion towards consequences of our actions and rough estimates of the probabilities of these consequences coming about" (1989, p. 80). This is sufficient to apply the pragmatic criterion.[8]

Even given our refined pragmatic condition, our discussion still faces an objection. By supposing that our challenger were a member of the jury, we invested her accepting the witness's testimony with special consequences. Her accepting that Jones stabbed Smith can be a premise for her action to vote to convict, which will have such grave consequences for Jones if the other jurors concur. But what if our challenger were not a juror and could in no wise affect the outcome of this legal proceeding? How then could she act on her accepting that Jones stabbed Smith? Would this mean that the cost of her acceptance even if mistaken is nil and thus that she need not seek further evidence? Does this mean that in matters over which we have no control, the amount of evidence upon which to accept a premise is a matter of indifference, that we never need seek further evidence? This would seem distinctly counterintuitive.

We reply that intuitions may differ on this question. One might want to say, should the expected cost of X's accepting that *p* be significant but the expected cost of Y's accepting that *p* be minimal, then X has a greater responsibility to seek further evidence. Acceptability then is relevant not only to one's evidence but also to the expected costs for which one is personally responsible. By contrast, should not the gravity of the juror's mistakenly accepting that Jones stabbed Smith signal the seriousness of this issue for anyone, juror and nonjuror alike? That the consequences of the juror's mistaken acceptance have a certain expected cost is a factor in the expected cost for anyone in general. This point is reflected by the way the pragmatic condition is formulated. Notice that the criterion does not read that X is justified in accepting a proposition p on evidence e only if *X's* expected costs of acquiring additional information are greater than *X's* expected costs of mistakenly acting on p. Rather, it is *the* expected cost of acquiring additional information versus *the* expected cost of mistakenly acting on p. We are talking here about general expected costs, the expected costs of people in general either seeking further evidence or accepting that p. X's being justified in accepting that p on the basis of evidence e indicates general acceptability on e. Should the general population include jury members whose vote could convict Jones of a capital crime, the expected cost of their mistakenly voting to convict Jones is part of *the* expected cost of mistakenly proceeding on accepting that Jones stabbed Smith. In assessing the cost of accepting p on e, one could ask what would happen if everyone else did the same.[9]

So far, we have just considered assessing cost in connection with singular propositions. Some have questioned whether the concept of cost can be applied to accepting generalizations or hypotheses. "The end of such [theoretical] inquiry . . . is truth for its own sake, not specific applications, and the potential applications are so numerous and diverse as to make any evaluation of the cost of a mistake impossible" (Clarke 1989, p. 86). But, as Clarke points out, the concept of cost may be characterized for theoretical contexts also – even pure theory. First, even though specific applications of a hypothesis may not be identified, the range of potential applications may be anticipated. Is a particular drug being tested intended for use on humans or on animals? If on humans, the cost of mistakenly accepting the hypothesis that the drug is safe is a lot higher than the cost if the drug is to be administered only to animals. Furthermore, even in pure science, we know that discovering and accepting certain hypotheses have led to the devising of beneficial applications. If some mistaken hypothesis had been accepted instead, these benefits might not have come to light. That would be part of the opportunity cost of mistakenly accepting that hypothesis. "These costs cannot be calculated in terms of specific probabilities and utilities of outcomes. This does not prevent, however, their being compared with costs of evidence acquisition" (Clarke 1989, p. 87).

We may identify further costs. If a hypothesis is accepted, it may be used in testing further hypotheses. But if the hypothesis is mistaken, these tests may be fatally flawed and the effort expended in carrying them out wasted. Here assessing the cost involves assessing the centrality of the hypothesis in the body of scientific knowledge, should it be accepted.

If the hypothesis is central, such as a statement in theoretical physics, it may well guide research in a number of fields should it be accepted. Hence, if this hypothesis is mistaken, all these additional tests may be misconceived.

In light of these considerations, then, we propose that presumption of warrant and fulfillment of the pragmatic condition are jointly sufficient for there to be a presumption for a statement. For suppose a proponent has put forward a statement p. Suppose one of the challenger's belief-generating mechanisms is vouching for p. But suppose that in addition to there being an overall presumption for the reliability of this mechanism, the challenger is furthermore aware of no signs that her mechanism is not functioning properly in this situation, that the cognitive environment is deceptive, or that she is not on this occasion concerned to determine the truth concerning p. Suppose in addition that the expected cost of her obtaining further evidence for p would be higher than the expected cost of her proceeding on p, should p be false. Gathering additional information would be more trouble than it is worth. Why, under those circumstances, would the challenger not be obliged to concede p, to grant that p can be taken as a premise for further deliberation or action? Hence, presumption amounts to presumption of warrant together with satisfying the pragmatic condition.

Recall that we have proposed three questions to constitute a procedure for certifying whether a statement is acceptable from the challenger's point of view: What type of statement is it? – What source vouches for it? – Does this voucher create a presumption for the statement? Our considerations in this section concerning the relation between presumption, presumption of warrant, and the pragmatic condition indicate how we can break up the third question into three subquestions:

a. Is there a presumption that this source carries warrant for the statement from the challenger's point of view?
b. What is the cost of the statement?
c. Does the voucher cover the cost of the statement, that is, would the cost of seeking further additional sources to vouch for the statement be greater than the cost of accepting the statement, using it as a premise, should the statement be false or mistaken?

Should these questions determine an adequate procedure for certifying whether or not accepting a statement is proper, they indicate that most of the issues determining acceptability are local. Indeed, there is only one issue which is general, whether or not there is a presumption of overall reliability for a source, a presumption that where the other conditions of warrant are satisfied, the proportion of true beliefs the source generates is high. By contrast, one and the same source may function properly on some occasions and not others, may find itself in a suitable environment on some occasions but not others, may be oriented to the truth in certain of its employments but not others. The issue of cost is also local. Consider the claim that a gun belongs to me. If the owner is to receive a prize for owning and maintaining a fine antique weapon, then the cost will be that of giving the prize to the wrong person, should I not be the owner of the gun. By contrast, the cost could be the unjust loss of my freedom, should it rather be accepted that this gun has been used in an armed robbery.

That all but one issue determining acceptability is local has implications for how we should conduct our inquiry in this essay. Given the various types of sources that may vouch for a statement, we need to determine for each one the general question of whether it is presumptively reliable or under what circumstances we may presume its reliability. Determining this in a comprehensive way for the various belief-generating mechanisms – sources – which may vouch for a claim as a basic premise is our central aim in Part II. Once this is established we may present the specifics of our procedure for determining presumption – the practice of epistemic casuistry as we call it in Chapter 11.

Before we proceed to these issues, we must address the theoretical consideration raised at the beginning of this chapter. Must a challenger go through the procedure of epistemic casuistry to determine that a statement is acceptable for it to *be* acceptable from her point of view? We shall argue that this is *not* necessary. Say the challenger is appeared to in the manner of a white station wagon outside her window. On the basis of being thus appeared to, she forms the belief that there is a white station wagon outside her office window. Let us assume that she has no reason to question whether any of the four conditions of warrant hold in this particular case. But she may not be consciously aware that she has no awareness of any warrant defeating evidence. Hence, she may not be aware that there is a presumption of warrant, from her perspective, for this belief. Gaining further evidence would be otiose in this case, and our challenger feels no need to seek further evidence to corroborate that there is a white station wagon outside her window. But she may not be reflexively aware of this feeling.

Nonetheless, we claim that there *is* a presumption for that belief from her perspective. The belief is acceptable for her, even if she is not explicitly aware of the factors determining presumption and thus of its acceptability. There *being* a presumption does not entail *consciousness* or *awareness* of presumption. Arguing this claim involves looking at certain epistemological issues in some depth. We turn to these issues in the next chapter. But first we need to develop further how warrant and presumption of warrant are related and second the implications of this and the addition of the pragmatic condition for the notion of presumption.

3.5 WARRANT, PRESUMPTION OF WARRANT, AND PRESUMPTION

We must begin by observing that warrant and presumption of warrant are two different things. There may very well be a presumption of warrant for a belief and yet the belief itself not be warranted. We may see this readily by looking at Gettier's two counterexamples to the claim that knowledge is justified true belief. In the first, Smith and Jones have applied for a certain job. The president of the company has told Smith that Jones will get the job. In addition, Smith has counted the number of coins in Jones's pocket and found that there are ten. Smith then has strong evidence, surely evidence sufficient to justify belief, that *Jones is the man who will get the job, and Jones has ten coins in his pocket.* But, by the substitutivity of identity, this proposition entails *The man who will get the job has ten coins in his pocket.*

Assuming that Smith sees the entailment and accepts the conclusion on the grounds of the premise, his belief is justified. Gettier continues, "But imagine, further, that unknown to Smith, he himself, not Jones, will get the job. And also, unknown to Smith, he himself has ten coins in his pocket" (1963, p. 122). The conclusion is still true although inferred from a false premise. So here Smith has a justified true belief that is not knowledge.

Smith's belief is not warranted, for it fails the second and fourth conditions for warrant. The mechanism generating Smith's belief that Jones will get the job involves taking testimony from the company president, and this testimony proved unreliable. Now we may assume that in this case, Smith's hearing and his ability to understand spoken language were functioning properly, that the president spoke properly and was not speaking through a distorting medium such as a faulty telephone, and that Smith had no extraepistemic agenda impelling him toward belief that Jones would get the job. The problem is that the president's testimony was false and *this* constitutes a defect in the cognitive environment. Given this defect, the objective probability of coming to a true conclusion from this false premise is not high – certainly it is not high enough for warrant. As Plantinga analyses the situation, taking testimony as a belief-generating mechanism

> is designed to operate in the presence of a certain condition: that of our fellows knowing the truth and being both willing and able to communicate it. In the absence of that condition, if it produces a true belief, it is just by accident, by virtue of a piece of epistemic good luck: in which case the belief in question has little or nothing by way of warrant. (1993b, pp. 34–35)

But is there a presumption of warrant for the conclusion from Smith's point of view? It would certainly seem that in most cases there would be. For given that Smith has been appeared to in this auditory manner, why should he need any argument to convince him that his hearing and language understanding capacities are functioning properly, that the company president was speaking clearly through a nondistorting medium, that he had no extracognitive interest in this matter, and that the testimony of the company president speaking about company business is reliable? Smith would need arguments for any of these points only if he had objections to bring against them. But why should we suppose that he had? So while Smith's belief that Jones will get the job is not warranted, nor is his belief that the man who will get the job has ten coins in his pocket, we may take it that there is a presumption of warrant for the latter from Smith's point of view.

Gettier's second counterexample to the claim that knowledge is justified true belief also shows that warrant and presumption of warrant are distinct. Within Smith's memory, his friend Jones has always owned a Ford and Jones has just offered him a ride while driving a Ford. This constitutes strong evidence for the proposition that *Jones owns a Ford*. It also entails the proposition that *Jones owns a Ford or Brown is in Barcelona*, where Brown is another friend of Smith. Smith sees that entailment, and so he is justified in believing both premise and conclusion. Smith, however, does not know where Brown is. But now suppose Jones is driving a rented Ford and at present does not own one, and let us also suppose that Brown *is* in Barcelona. The conclusion is true, Smith believes it, and he is justified in believing it. But we would not say that he knows it. (See Gettier 1963, pp. 122–3.)

Smith does not have warrant for the conclusion because he has based it on and inferred it from the mistaken belief constituting the premise.

Again, we can say that there is a problem in the cognitive environment. The cars persons drive are ordinarily their own. To form the belief that someone who has owned cars in the past owns the car he is currently driving accords with a design plan aimed at generating true beliefs. When someone, then, drives a car not his own, we have a misleading or deviant (compare Plantinga 1993b, p. 35) factor in the cognitive environment leading to mistaken beliefs. Again, the objective probability is not high that mistaken beliefs will lead to the truth. The fourth condition of warrant also fails. But in most cases there will be a presumption of warrant for the conclusion from Smith's point of view. For what reason is there for Smith to think that his perception of the situation where Jones offers him a ride in the Ford is faulty or that his memory is defective? What reason is there for him to think that the environment is distorting his perception or that he forms or holds the belief that Jones owns a Ford to satisfy extraepistemic needs? Again, perception and memory when properly operating in nondistorting environments and in accordance with a design plan aimed at the truth are reliable and trusted as reliable. So there is a presumption of their reliability here. Hence, there is a presumption of warrant for the premise and also for the conclusion, even though neither of them are warranted.

Warrant, we should note and as Plantinga stresses in his account, is an externalist, not an internalist notion. We have no privileged access to the conditions of warrant the way we have privileged access to our own internal states, nor are these conditions of warrant, when they hold, self-evident to us in any other way. Suppose I am suffering from some brain disorder that causes me to feel acute panic whenever I see a dog and to form and hold the belief that the poor animal is the embodiment of an evil demon who intends harm to me and every human being in his way. I may be immediately aware of the panic reaction. I may be aware of my belief about the dog. But I am certainly not immediately aware of the disease or of the fact that my belief-generating mechanism is malfunctioning. By the same token, when my belief-generating mechanisms *are* functioning properly, am I immediately aware of that fact?

Whether or nor there are distorting factors in my cognitive environment causing me to form false beliefs is a matter for discovery, not immediate awareness. But likewise, that there are no such factors in my environment at present is something of which I am not immediately aware, a matter of something for which I have privileged access. Recognizing that I hold certain of my beliefs simply to hold myself together, that my design plan contains specifications for producing such beliefs to forestall psychic fragmentation given adverse conditions in my human environment, may be an achievement of insight oriented therapy. That my beliefs were thus formed, that my design plan contains such specifications is not a matter of my immediate awareness. Likewise, again, that some current belief is generated according to specifications in my design plan aimed at truth and not at some other purpose is not something of which I am immediately aware. Finally, how can I be immediately aware that my design plan or the aspects of it involved in generating a belief I currently hold is reliable in reaching truth, that the objective probability is high that these modules of the design plan will produce true beliefs? None of the four conditions of warrant are matters of immediate, internal, or privileged access. The notion is through and through an externalist concept.

What may we say then of the notion of presumption of warrant – is this internalist or externalist? Our discussion in the previous section has shown that there being a presumption of warrant from my point of view is a matter of my direct awareness – better for the most part of my direct "nonawareness." Suppose I have the perceptual belief that there is a tree in front of me outside my office window and there is a presumption of warrant for that belief. It follows that I am appeared to treely and that I am aware of no objection to the claim that my perceptual faculties are functioning properly or of any reason to question or demand evidence for their proper function. Even if the object of our consciousness is the tree as opposed to our being appeared to treely, we are conscious that we are appeared to treely and can turn our attention to being thus appeared to.[10] Likewise, it is a matter of my consciousness, that I lack awareness of factors calling the proper function of my perceptual mechanism into account and I can turn my awareness to such lack of awareness. So I may be directly aware of the factors determining presumption of proper function.

Likewise, given that I have a presumption of warrant for my belief, I am aware of no reason to think that the environment is distorting or misleading. Lack of such awareness is part of my consciousness and is something to which I have direct access. Again, although I might be quite surprised to find the tree outside my office window gone and indeed sorry that it was gone, I am conscious of no reason to think that its loss would cause me to have a nervous breakdown. But this betokens the fact that I am conscious of no reason to think that in forming the belief that there is a tree in front of me, my belief-generating mechanisms are operating according to specifications in my design plan aimed other than at the truth. Although this lack of awareness may not be the intensional object of my consciousness, as part of my consciousness, it is something to which I have direct access. Finally, my visual perception has been basically trustworthy in the past. I am conscious of no reason to think that my design plan when aiming at the truth through visual perception is unreliable. This again, as an aspect of my consciousness, is something to which I have direct access.

So I may have direct access to whether those conditions of presumption of warrant hold from my point of view. Presumption of warrant, then, as opposed to warrant is an internalist notion. Although I may not be explicitly aware of an existing presumption, the factors determining it are nonetheless open to my direct awareness. What may we say of the pragmatic condition? Is it an externalist or internalist notion? To satisfy the pragmatic condition, we must compare two estimated costs – that of acquiring further evidence versus accepting a certain proposition p even if p be false. We may argue that the notion of estimated cost, as we understand it, is an internal notion. First, consider the notion of the cost of an action. We understand cost as the intrinsic disvalue brought about by an action. Although we cannot present the argument here, in Section 9.3 we shall develop how our beliefs about what is intrinsically good or bad are generated by what we call the protomoral sense – for particular judgments of *prima facie* good or bad – and protomoral intuition – for general judgments of intrinsic value. But such judgments concern what is self-evident to us and thus that to which we have internal access. But recall that in estimating the cost, we rely on "rough estimates of the probabilities of these consequences coming about" (Clarke 1989, p. 80). Now on the frequency interpretation of probability, the objective probability of a consequence bearing disvalue coming about is an external notion. However, our *estimate* of that probability, our sense of how likely is that consequence is an internal notion. For practical purposes, an estimate that evidence is sufficient to cover cost may express itself as lack of awareness of any need to gather further evidence. If I am appeared to treely and have no awareness of any weighty consequence of my accepting that there is a tree in front of me requiring me to bolster the evidence of my own sense perception, I am aware that the pragmatic condition is satisfied in this case. The notion of estimated cost then is an internal notion and thus the conjunction of the pragmatic condition with presumption of warrant is internal.

By defining acceptability in terms of presumption and showing that presumption for a belief amounts to presumption of warrant for that belief together with the pragmatic condition, we have set forth an internalist account of acceptability. A belief is acceptable, from my point of view as challenger, just in case the belief is self-evident or I am both aware of warranting evidence, not aware of factors that would indicate that the belief is not warranted, and aware that the pragmatic condition is satisfied. Because warrant is an externalist notion while self-evidence together with consciousness of evidence and lack of consciousness of the factors spelling failure of warrant or failure to satisfy the pragmatic condition is a matter of internal, direct access, we may say that we are here presenting an externalist internalism.[11]

Can such a position provide a satisfactory account of acceptability? This leads us into central issues of epistemology. We must situate our notion of presumption and in particular presumption of warrant vis-à-vis certain very central epistemological concepts. These issues we address in the next chapter. But we can address one point here. Externalism seems to leave itself open to a rather obvious objection. Although some externalists may have a more sophisticated view, on a basic externalist account of justification, a belief is justified if it is produced by a reliable mechanism, if a person's holding that belief is a sufficient condition for the belief to be true. Notice one need have no knowledge of this connection for one's belief to be justified. Indeed one's belief will be justified even if one is aware of no reasons for the belief. But why should this be so? It seems quite unintuitive. Why should one's belief be justified if one has nothing resembling evidence or reasons for it; if, from one's perspective, as BonJour puts it, "it *is* an accident that the belief is true" (1985, p. 43)?

Our notion of presumption avoids this objection altogether. This is obvious from our argument that both presumption of warrant and the pragmatic condition are internalist notions. The believer has access to all four conditions for the presumption of warrant together with the pragmatic condition, and if these are all satisfied, surely the belief is not seriously unreasonable or unwarranted from his or her point of view. Intuitively, there being a presumption would seem to make accepting a statement eminently reasonable or justified. To show that this is sufficient, we need to meet other objections that can be raised along internalist lines. This is our concern in the next chapter.

4

Epistemological Considerations

Acceptability, Deontology, Internalism, Justification

Let us recall this point: Acceptability is a normative, not a descriptive notion. Acceptability does not amount to acceptance. It is no synonym for marketability. As we understand the notion, to say that a statement or claim (on our belief) is acceptable for a given person is to say that it is proper, correct for that person to accept it, that is, take it as a premise for further deliberation or action. One way to put this is to say that one is within one's epistemic or doxastic rights to accept that statement; one's acceptance violates no epistemic or doxastic duty. One is epistemically justified in accepting the statement.

In our explication of normativity in the last paragraph, we have made contact with other normative notions – epistemic rights and duties, being epistemically justified. These notions have received detailed development in epistemology. Has this development placed certain constraints on these notions and does our notion of presumption, that is, presumption of warrant together with satisfaction of the pragmatic condition, fall within those constraints? What does it mean to be within one's epistemic rights or to have done one's epistemic duty or to be epistemically justified, and *is* one within one's epistemic rights to accept a statement if there is a presumption of warrant in its favor and the pragmatic condition is satisfied? Must acceptability be connected with epistemic rights and duties to be a normative concept? Could it be connected simply with epistemic justification? Is it necessary to connect epistemic justification with epistemic obligation? Does a normative concept of epistemic justification presuppose talk of epistemic rights and duties? Alternatively, can an evaluative concept of epistemic justification be defined without appealing to the concept of epistemic rights and duties? Now rights and duties are deontological concepts. To explicate acceptability through such notions then is to present a deontological account of acceptability. Classical foundationalists have held a deontological account of epistemic justification. What then have they said about doxastic or epistemic obligation?

4.1 CLASSICAL FOUNDATIONALIST ACCOUNTS OF EPISTEMIC OBLIGATION

Let us begin by introducing a central distinction of which Plantinga reminds us in (1993a, pp. 15–25) between subjective and objective duties in ethics. An action is a subjective duty for a moral agent just in case that person believes that the action is morally required and has come to this belief in a conscientious and proper way. Such a belief is the judgment of a properly informed conscience – and the properly informed conscience is to be respected. But a proponent may have a sincere, conscientiously informed belief that he ought to do *A*, and a challenger have an equally sincere, conscientiously informed belief that the proponent should *not* do *A*. Now the challenger may concede that in doing *A*, the proponent fulfills his subjective duty. Her point is that his *objective* duty lies elsewhere.

The challenger may make such concessions in many cases, but not all. She is simply not prepared to concede that in these other cases the proponent could conscientiously hold that certain actions are morally required or permitted. If he does, he is not functioning properly. Stevenson gives us this memorable example:

A: It is by no means my duty to repay C.
B: Your moral feelings really torment you for not doing so, as you well know. You say you have no duty as a feeble effort to quiet your conscience, and free the expression of your crude selfishness. (1944, p. 116)

Although A may deny repaying C is his duty, B will not accept this as a conscientious judgment on A's part, that refraining from repaying C is subjectively permissible for A. B accuses A of insincerity. But if A convinced B that he was sincere in this, B would also believe either that A's faculties of moral cognition were not functioning properly or "that at some point he has culpably done something that has clouded his own moral vision" (Plantinga 1993a, p. 18). The moral we may draw from this is that subjective duty and objective duty coincide for a significant class of cases where we think to be mistaken about our objective duty is perverse, going against how a properly functioning human being would operate.

How may we apply this to epistemic duty? As Plantinga points out, for both Descartes and Locke, objective and subjective epistemic duty coincide for a significant number of cases, those where we can just see where our objective epistemic duty lies. For Descartes, it is our objective duty to accept nothing but what can be seen with sufficient clarity and distinctness. But if someone does transgress this objective duty, we would hold him blameworthy. Hence accepting only what can be seen with sufficient clarity and distinctness is also one's subjective duty. For Locke, it is one's objective epistemic duty to accept "only what is epistemically probable with respect to my total evidence" (Plantinga 1993a, p. 19), which evidence consists of immediately certain propositions. The question of epistemic duty does not arise for accepting immediately certain propositions, because they impress themselves upon us. Our acceptance is involuntary. By the same token, it contravenes neither an objective nor subjective epistemic duty. Presumably, recognizing when propositions that are certain give us good reason or proper support for further claims on our belief is also evident. Our subjective and objective duty vis-à-vis accepting these claims coincide. Being supported by total evidence makes an act of belief or acceptance objectively right. Accepting a belief on less than proper evidence, then, is objectively wrong. But such acceptance is also subjectively wrong, since we can "see" that we do *not* have proper evidence for these beliefs.

This coincidence of subjective and objective epistemic duty leads to internalism. These cases in which we can just see that accepting certain beliefs is objectively permissible epistemically are cases in which we have internal access to the conditions of objective epistemic permissibility. Certainty or self-evidence is something to which we have internal access. But this is the evidence on which properly basic judgments are founded. Again, being properly supported on the basis of propositions that are certain makes accepting the supported propositions objectively right. But proper support is something to which we also have internal access. It is because of this internal access that subjective and objective epistemic duty coincide on these cases.

The classical internalism stemming from Descartes and Locke goes beyond this internal access requirement to see two further implications of epistemic deontology, two further requirements. One holds that for basic judgments, our evidence completely determines the judgment, that is, the judgment is certain in light of this evidence. In the light of being appeared to redly, my judgment "I am appeared to redly" is completely determined, certain. In light of one concept's being included in another, my judgment that one is included in another is completely determined, certain. The other requirement we might call the meta-awareness requirement. I am not only internally aware *of* certain evidence, which would justify certain of my beliefs, I am aware *that* it justifies those beliefs. For Descartes, this would mean being aware *that* being clear and distinct or based on ideas that are clear and distinct makes a judgment acceptable, and being aware not only of clear and distinct ideas but *that* they are clear and distinct. For Locke, this would mean being aware *that* being properly based on total evidence, that is, certain knowledge constituting good reason, is what makes a judgment acceptable and being aware not only of good reason for a judgment but *that* it is good reason, that it makes the judgment probable. If we are within our epistemic rights, we are aware that we are within our epistemic rights.

We may now ask whether all three of these requirements of classical internalism are necessary for any adequate account of epistemic justification or acceptability. Notice that Locke accepts the second requirement only for basic or foundational beliefs. But why must the foundation be *certain?* In Chapter 1, we referred to this as the epistemic no-risk principle, and pointed out that it was neither self-evident nor argued for by Descartes or Locke (see pp. 8–9). Hence, we see no reason for insisting that we are within our epistemic rights regarding basic beliefs only if we accept those that are certain. What may be said for the meta-awareness requirement?

4.2 BONJOUR'S DEFENSE OF THE META-AWARENESS REQUIREMENT

In (1985), BonJour puts forward an internalist conception of epistemic justification that endorses the meta-awareness requirement. Our *cognitive* goal is to aim at or aim for the truth. Accordingly, we should accept only those beliefs we have good reason to think true and to accept a belief without good reason is to be epistemically irresponsible. "Being epistemically responsible . . . is the core of the notion of epistemic justification" (BonJour 1985, p. 8). For BonJour, a theory of knowledge is to provide criteria for recognizing good reasons. And this means showing that these criteria are "truth-conducive" (1985, p. 9), giving a *metajustification* (1985, p. 9) of the standards. The necessity of a metajustification has implications for epistemic justification. To be epistemically responsible in accepting a belief, one must not only recognize that one has reason good according to some theoretical criteria, but one must also have a metajustification of those criteria.

How can the fact that a belief meets those standards give that believer a reason for thinking that it is likely to be true . . . , unless he himself knows that beliefs satisfying those standards are likely to be true? Why should the fact that a meta-justification can be supplied from the outside . . . mean that his belief (as opposed to an analogous belief held by the outside observer) is justified? (1985, p. 10)

BonJour allows, however, that this awareness of the metajustification may be tacit or implicit.

We may draw an analogy between BonJour's picture of justification and formal derivations in symbolic logic. Recall that each derived line must be accompanied by a justification that cites the line or lines on which this derived line is based – the reason – together with the inference rule that licenses the inferential move – the criterion of why this reason is a good reason. But, for BonJour, citing lines and inference rule apparently would not be enough to justify accepting the derived line. One would need in addition a soundness argument for the inference rule to be justified in accepting the derived line. But is this metalogical requirement reasonable for justification? Suppose one's acceptance of the premises were justified and recognizing the validity of the inference rule were immediate. What more should be needed to justify acceptance of the derived line? Would I need reflective awareness *that* the inference rule was justified?

In his essay, BonJour develops a coherentist account of epistemic justification for empirical beliefs. Justification first presupposes membership in a coherent system. Second, the system "must contain laws attributing a high degree of reliability to a reasonable variety of cognitively spontaneous [i.e., basic] beliefs" (1985, p. 141). BonJour calls this the Observation Requirement. Third, the system of beliefs "must be coherent to a high degree and more coherent than any alternative which would also satisfy" the Observation Requirement (1985, p. 154). "Fourth, the person must have a reflective grasp of the fact that his system of beliefs satisfies the third condition, and this reflective grasp must be, ultimately but perhaps only very implicitly, *the* reason why he continues to accept the belief whose justification is in question" (1985, p. 154). Note that all these conditions accord with internalism. For will we not be introspectively and thus internally aware that we hold systems of belief? Again, that one's system of beliefs satisfies the Observation Requirement, is the most coherent of a set of alternative systems of belief with which one is confronted, and that one accepts a particular belief because it is a member of this system, all seem in principle open to internal awareness. This is because coherence for BonJour involves mutual support or inferability.

Is BonJour's criterion of justification necessary for acceptability? BonJour has set the price for accepting empirical beliefs about one's external world very high. Suppose I am appeared to treely and greenly, and that I am aware of no indication that my cognitive system is functioning improperly or that I need to receive further evidence. Under these circumstances, can I accept that there is a tree in full leaf outside my office window? For BonJour, this would not be sufficient. My system of beliefs must satisfy the Observation Requirement. That presumably would attribute a high degree of reliability to this belief. But my acceptance of it would still not be proper unless I recognized that the belief were a member of a system of beliefs satisfying the Observation Requirement and more consistent than any alternative system satisfying this requirement, and that I accepted the belief because it was a member of this system, and I recognized that accepting the belief for this reason was truth-conducive. To be sure, BonJour allows that some of these recognitions may be tacit. But what exactly does this mean in assessing whether one's accepting that p is epistemically responsible?

Surely it would seem on this account that the empirical beliefs of most persons are epistemically irresponsible. For to hold any belief with epistemic responsibility one must have seen that this coherence criterion is the way to best secure the epistemic goal of reaching the truth, that one's current set of beliefs is coherent, that it satisfies the Observation Requirement, that it is of alternative sets of beliefs satisfying the Observation Requirement the most coherent, and that one accepts the belief just because it is a member of this system. So, unless one can explain how tacit recognition can avoid this consequence, it would seem then that anyone who has not worked through the metajustification argument cannot hold *any* empirical belief with epistemic responsibility. The empirical beliefs of children then would certainly be epistemically irresponsible. The empirical beliefs of philosophically unreflective empirical or theoretical scientists would be epistemically irresponsible. Indeed, the empirical beliefs of just about everyone except certain philosophers who have worked through the metajustification argument would be epistemically irresponsible!

These considerations should be sufficient to show that BonJour has not given us a compelling defense of the classical internalist meta-awareness requirement. But we are still left with the internal access requirement – that when we are within our epistemic rights, we have internal access to the evidence. This requirement, however, seems intuitive. Can we talk of being within our epistemic rights in believing a statement that p if we do not have evidence that p? I believe we can concede that the requirement involves a necessary insight. But we can question whether the requirement formulates the insight in the only correct manner. Why must we use such a deontological concept as "being within our epistemic rights"? Does not such talk lead to maintaining the meta-awareness requirement? If to be within one's epistemic rights, one must have access to the evidence, why must one not also be aware that this evidence properly licenses one to make the claim one is making on its basis? Deontological talk leads to internalism. Can we then phrase this requirement without using deontological concepts? One may give a rough and ready restatement of the requirement by saying that one is epistemically justified in accepting a statement that p only if one has internal access to proper evidence for p. Now if one can give a nondeontological account of epistemic justification, our phrasing of the requirement need not be even implicitly deontological. But such accounts have already been given, as we proceed to see in the next section.

4.3 NONDEONTOLOGICAL CONCEPTIONS OF EPISTEMIC JUSTIFICATION

Several philosophers have given criteria for justification which do not involve such concepts as epistemic rights or duties. According to Firth, a belief is justified for a person just in case it "is based rationally on the evidence" (1978, p. 219). That is, the person has the evidence that properly warrants the belief and has arrived at that belief by seeing or recognizing the evidential relationship. According to Feldman and Conee, a belief that p is justified for S at t just in case believing that p "fits the evidence S has at t" (1985, p. 15). Conee continues that one "has a justified belief only if the person has reflective access to evidence that the belief is true. . . . Justifying evidence must be internally available" (1988, p. 398). Finally, Alston says that a belief is justified for a person S just in case it "was based on adequate grounds and S lacked sufficient overriding reasons to the contrary" (1985, p. 77).

I find two elements in these various accounts[1] of justification, although the second may only be implicit in some as stated. First, a belief's being justified presupposes that it is based on adequate or sufficient evidence.

Second, the evidence must be internally available. These accounts of epistemic justification then concede the internal access requirement. We have said that acceptability is a normative concept. Can the normativity of acceptability be spelled out via epistemic justification as characterized here in a nondeontological way?

Notice that there are areas of human activity in which an action may be normatively acceptable, right, and yet speaking of it as a duty or as being in accord with duty would be inapposite. Should one write or speak correctly according to the syntactical and grammatical rules of some language, the resulting discourse will conform to grammatical rules, the language use will be normatively correct and acceptable, but would it be right to say that the person was doing his linguistic duty or was within his linguistic rights in performing those actions which constitute his discourse? Does the question of duty even arise here? Although rules of grammar and syntax may be formulated for a language, we follow them not by conscious intention but by unreflective habit. Long after we learned to speak the language – and for the most part correctly – do we receive explicit instruction in its rules. To speak of accomplishing one's duty, do we not have to consciously apply some rule in an action? Is this not a necessary condition for subjective duty? Ideally, should not the aim be that "each moral agent should act self-consciously, aware of the grounds upon which he acts and prepared to defend those grounds" (Meilaender 1991, p. 5)?

Is there an analogy in the epistemic sphere? Could there be some instances in which unreflectively accepted beliefs were nonetheless acceptable, just as epistemically or doxastically acceptable as certain unreflective usages of language are grammatically or syntactically acceptable? Having separated justification from deontology, we have opened the door to this possibility. To show that it is an actuality, let us consider Alston's development of his nondeontological conception of epistemic justification in (1985).

4.4 ALSTON'S ACCOUNT OF EPISTEMIC JUSTIFICATION

For Alston, the epistemic point of view is "the aim at maximizing truth and minimizing falsity in a large body of beliefs" (1985, p. 59). In what then does goodness from the epistemic point of view consist? In asking whether "S's believing that p, as S does, is a good thing from the epistemic point of view...we want to know whether S had *adequate* grounds for believing that p, where *adequate* grounds are those sufficiently indicative to the truth of p" (1985, pp. 70, 71).

The concept of adequate grounds must be clarified. The grounds of a belief concern what it is based on. Hence, there are really three concepts to be clarified here – "based on," "ground," and "adequate." We may shed light on the "based on" relation and the concept of ground, what it is for a belief to be based on a ground, through some remarks Peirce makes in connection with his notion of a leading principle. For Peirce, when the human nervous system is stimulated, humans form habits as a result of what responses best remove the irritation. Some habits will convey us from one judgment[2] to another. These habits need not be conscious. Should we consciously formulate that habit in the form

From   P

We may take it that   C

we would have a rule of inference. If we formulated that rule as a proposition, presumably by taking its associated conditional or some suitable generalization of that conditional, then we would have what Peirce calls a leading principle (1955, pp. 130–1). Clearly, when a habit has conveyed us from one belief that p to another that q and we come to believe q in this manner, q is based on p and p is the ground of q. But, surely, habits may convey us from experiences to beliefs also. If I perceive a car outside the window and come to believe that there is a car outside my window on the basis of the perception, then that perceptual experience will be the ground of my belief, which is thus based on that experience. Notice that we would not speak of the perceptual experience as being the *premise* of the belief. Premises are statements that play a certain role in arguments. Perceptual experiences are not statements and we do not argue from them to beliefs or claims that we may accept.

Now for these grounds to constitute *adequate grounds* for the belief that p, the belief or experience must be strongly indicative of the truth of p. This means that "the *probability* of the belief's being true, given that ground, is very high" (Alston 1988, p. 269, italics in original). The probability here is objective. The ground must be a reliable indicator of the truth of the belief. Moreover, if the ground is a belief, that belief itself must be justified. But it is quite possible for some grounds to be strong indicators of the truth of p, yet the total relevant evidence at our disposal not to constitute a strong indicator. Other pieces of evidence may rebut the strength of our indicator. Our grounds then would be overridden. So for a belief to be properly justified, not only must there be adequate grounds but these grounds must *not* be overridden, at least in the perspective of the person holding the belief. Alston gives this official definition of his conception of justification J_{eg} ("e" for evaluative and "g" for grounds): "S is J_{eg} in believing that p *iff* S's believing that p, as S did, was a good thing from the epistemic point of view, in that S's belief that p was based on adequate grounds and S lacked sufficient overriding reasons to the contrary" (1985, p. 77).

Although reference to being good from the epistemic point of view makes this definition evaluative or normative, because the goodness supervenes upon the undefeated adequacy of the grounds, we can simplify this definition by taking just that clause as the definiens: S is J_{eg} in believing that p *iff* S's belief that p was based on adequate grounds and S lacked sufficient overriding reasons to the contrary. That S's belief that p was based on adequate grounds defines *prima facie* justification. Adding the clause that S lacks sufficient overriding reasons defines justification itself, or justification *simpliciter*, or as Alston refers to it, *ultima facie* justification (1988, p. 281).

Alston indicates that the criterion he is taking for adequacy of grounds is reliability of the mechanism generating (and sustaining) the belief. "To say that a belief was formed in a reliable way is, roughly, to say that it was formed in a way that can be depended on generally to form true rather than false beliefs, at least from inputs like the present one, and at least in the sorts of circumstances in which we normally find ourselves" (1985, p. 79). Making the criterion of adequacy the reliability of the mechanism that generated the belief commits Alston to a form of externalism. But by insisting that to be justified a belief must be based on adequate grounds, Alston is requiring that to have a justified belief, one must have, be aware of, adequate evidence for that belief. This introduces an internalist character into Alston's account of justification, for as he points out, "Grounds must be other psychological state(s) of the same subject..., which are 'internal' to the subject in an obvious sense" (1985, p. 78). This leads Alston to characterize his view as an internalist externalism.[3]

Alston sees his concept of epistemic justification as being free from objections brought against both externalist and internalist conceptions of justification. First, by insisting on justification presupposing adequate grounds, Alston avoids criticisms which are leveled against a straight externalist identification of justification with reliability. Our beliefs about some subject matter might be formed in a reliable way, yet they might just pop into our minds. We would neither have grounds nor base those beliefs on grounds, adequate or otherwise. Intuitively, we would not want to say that these beliefs were justified, and by Alston's definition, they are not.

J$_{\text{eg}}$ also avoids criticisms which can be brought against internalism. These involve the meta-awareness requirement. As we have seen, for the internalist not only must adequate grounds be accessible, the adequacy of the grounds must be accessible. But we have found no rationale for this stricture. On Alston's conception of justification, it does not apply. As he points out, J$_{\text{eg}}$ requires neither that S have a justified belief that proposition R is an adequate reason for *p*, where the belief that *p* is propositionally grounded, or that experience *e* is an adequate indication for *p*, where *p* is grounded on experience. Simply having adequate grounds puts one in a strong position epistemically. (Compare Alston 1985, p. 82.)

There is something extremely attractive in Alston's concept, which may be made more perspicuous if we draw an analogy with Toulmin's model of argumentation structure in (1958). For Toulmin, we should distinguish the grounds or data D offered for a claim C from the warrant W (not to be confused with Plantinga's notion of warrant upon which we have relied so heavily in Chapter 3), which explains why that data constitute grounds for the claim. Data are the premises of an argument. Although Toulmin's discussion may not always make this clear, warrants for him are inference rules, although not necessarily the formal inference rules of deductive logic. Keeping this in mind should help distinguish Toulmin's sense of "warrant" from Plantinga's. For Plantinga, warrant is the specific difference of knowledge, true belief being the genus. Knowledge is warranted true belief, the warrant being the satisfaction of the four conditions we have reviewed in Chapter 3. For Toulmin, the warrant in an argument explains how we get from data to claim. To ask why specifically given premises or data are relevant to the conclusion or claim they are alleged to support is to ask for the warrant of that inference. Toulmin's diagram of how these elements fit together highlights their distinct roles:

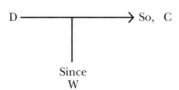

Using this terminology, Alston would say that one has a justified belief that C just in case one has a justified belief that D and the warrant W was reliable.

Notice that Alston would not require that one have a justified belief that the warrant W was reliable. Not requiring this seems straightforwardly appropriate. Although in a valid deductive argument we move from premises to conclusion via a valid inference rule, we do not state that rule in the course of stating the argument and may not even be aware of it or its validity. Yet, surely if one has a justified belief in the premises of an argument and one validly infers a conclusion from them, one has a justified belief in the conclusion, whether or not one recognizes the validity of one's inferential step.

Now a challenger can ask the proponent to make the warrant explicit. Once made explicit, the challenger can further ask why the warrant is reliable, why, to use Toulmin's terminology, it "should be accepted as having authority" (1958, p. 103). Such a warrant has to rest on something, what Toulmin calls its *backing*. The internalist in effect is saying that for one to have a justified belief that C, one must not only have a justified belief that D but also a justified belief in the reliability of the warrant W. But unless the reliability of the warrant were self-evident, foundationally properly basic, one would need both a justified belief that the backing B is the case and that backing properly authorizes the warrant, W. The latter claim in effect is a warrant in its own right, W'.

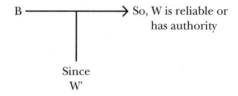

But what about the reliability of W'?

These reflections suggest a point that we have already made against the internalist: Internalism leads to skepticism. What reason is there to believe that we shall always reach self-evident warrants? In those cases in which we do not, we are in a vicious infinite regress. We can never have a justified belief that C because we can never ultimately justify the warrant. But would this not be the case with a vast majority of our everyday beliefs? If the demand for accessibility to the adequacy of grounds leads to skepticism, then why should we accede to that demand? Our representing the structure of the reasoning through Toulmin's model should heighten our perplexity over the demand. Why should we require a proponent to successfully defend his tacit warrant W, given that this request may in principle be impossible to fulfill, before we will grant that his belief that C is justified on the basis of D?

The internalist has a reply here. We need not require the proponent to have a justified belief in the reliability or authority of his implicit warrant W to have a justified belief in C on the basis of D. What we should require is less onerous: If the proponent is challenged to produce and back the warrant W, then only if the proponent can meet this challenge is his belief that C on grounds that D justified. We reply that as the justification itself has a warrant W', if W' is not self-evident or self-justifying, why should not the challenger challenge it? We are still potentially in danger of an infinite regress. The specter of skepticism is allayed but not banished. But besides this, do we want to hold that the proponent is not justified in believing C on the basis of a justified belief that D if he cannot produce a properly backed warrant? As we pointed out in examining BonJour's position, it seems that on this account children would not have justified beliefs. Are they conceptually sophisticated enough to produce the warrants for their beliefs? If we doubt this, how much more doubtful is their ability to show that these warrants are backed? Could persons in the street show that their adequately grounded beliefs are adequately grounded? Either they would have to see this *a priori* or they would have to back the adequacy of the ground. In a number of cases, that would involve an inductive argument to the reliability of the warrant and showing its inductive sufficiency. But as Alston points out, "many, or most, subjects are just not up to this" (1988, p. 278). So there is a very plausible rationale behind Alston's requiring awareness of adequate grounds for justified belief but not of their adequacy. The latter leads to skepticism.

What do we have then in J_{eg}? We have an evaluative yet nondeontological account of justification for beliefs, which does not involve us in internalism. Can this account of epistemic justification for beliefs be extended to acceptance? As we have already noted, reasons for belief are reasons for acceptance. Are good reasons for belief also good reasons for acceptance? If a belief is justified according to this criterion, is it also acceptable, as we have defined acceptability?

4.5 EPISTEMIC JUSTIFICATION AND ACCEPTANCE

Can one maintain that S is J_{eg} in believing that p *iff* p is acceptable for S? Is J_{eg} a proper criterion for both belief and acceptance? Surely if one's belief that p was based on adequate grounds and one lacked sufficient overriding reasons to the contrary, there would be a presumption for the belief from one's point of view as a challenger. Assume first that one's belief that p is based on adequate grounds. Then the mechanism whereby one is conveyed from the grounds to the belief is reliable. But then the belief-generating mechanism is presumptively reliable. Because one lacks sufficient overriding reasons to call one's belief that p into question in this case, then one has no reason to think that one's belief-generating mechanism is not functioning properly on this occasion, nor that the environment involves some anomaly, nor that one's belief-generating mechanism is not oriented to the truth. That is, there is a presumption of warrant for the belief-generating mechanism on this occasion. Furthermore, one would have no reason to think that conceding that p, if mistaken, had an expected cost which required corroboration from further grounds before one had adequate grounds. Otherwise, one would have an overriding reason, a pragmatic overriding reason, to the contrary. Thus, all the conditions for presumption would be satisfied and the statement that p would be acceptable.

It is straightforward to argue the converse, that if a belief is acceptable, it is justified according to J_{eg}. Let us assume that a statement p is acceptable for a challenger S at a given point in a dialectical exchange. Then by our definition of acceptability, there is a presumption that the belief-generating mechanism is reliable. But surely this should mean "that it is generally true that beliefs like that formed on grounds like that are true" (Alston 1985, p. 79). If this were not true, the presumption of reliability would have been undercut. That the pragmatic condition is satisfied should assure us that the extent of the grounds in this case is sufficient. S's belief that p then is based on adequate grounds. Furthermore, again, as p is acceptable, there is a presumption that p as a belief is generated by a belief-generating mechanism functioning properly in an appropriate environment and oriented toward generating true beliefs. Hence, S lacks sufficient reasons to override the adequacy of her grounds for p. Otherwise, one of these presumptions would have been undercut.[4] S is J_{eg} in believing that p.

There is a possible objection to this argument from acceptability to J_{eg}. In (1993a), Plantinga asks whether there are grounds for memory beliefs or for *a priori* beliefs. We similarly may ask whether there are grounds for introspective beliefs concerning current internal states of affairs of which we are directly conscious. He asks whether memory beliefs simply pop into our heads. Again, when we "see" that $2 + 3 = 5$ or any other self-evident truth of reason, what plays the role of the perceptual experience which grounds a perceptual belief or the premises that ground some inferred belief? (See 1993a, p. 190, n. 19.) Likewise, if I believe I feel a pain in my right leg, what is the ground of that belief?

The answer to this last question would seem obvious. The ground is my feeling of pain in my right leg. Why would one question that this is a ground? Notice that where my being appeared to treely is the ground of my believing that there is a tree in front of me, my ground is distinct from the fact which makes my belief true. But if I say that my ground for believing I feel a pain in my right leg is my feeling of pain in my right leg, it seems that the ground for my belief and the fact which makes my belief true are the same. But, as Alston replies, why cannot we allow this to be a limiting case of a ground? "In the first person belief about one's own conscious state the ground coincides with the fact that makes the belief true. Since the fact believed is itself an experience of the subject, there need be nothing 'between' the subject and the fact that serves as an indication of the latter's presence. The fact 'reveals itself' directly" (1985, p. 77). It would seem that the case of memory could be answered analogously. When I remember one event or having done something, do I not entertain some memory image? Is that not the ground on which my memory belief is based? This ground may not be produced directly by some external event, but it does constitute nonpropositional evidence for what is remembered having taken place and constitutes the ground for that belief.

As Alston points out, we can see the case of self-evident *a priori* propositions as another kind of limiting case, where the ground "is minimally distinguishable . . . from the belief it is grounding" (1985, p. 77). We can distinguish the proposition believed from the way that the proposition appears. Self-evident propositions will appear self-evident; obviousness in appearance is their ground. (Compare Alston 1985, p. 78.) Hence, we are satisfied that beliefs have grounds.

By showing that a belief is acceptable on our account – presumption of warrant together with satisfaction of the pragmatic criterion – if and only if that belief is J_{eg} justified, we have achieved the goal that motivated this chapter. We have shown that our account of acceptability can meet the criticisms that could be raised on internalist lines. Indeed, given our discussion in the last section of Chapter 3, our account meets criticisms that can be brought against both externalist and internalist positions. Absent further objections, our concept of premise acceptability is philosophically viable. We have established a presumption for it.

We are now ready to justify the distinction we made at the very beginning of Chapter 3 between there *being* a presumption for a claim from a challenger's point of view and the challenger recognizing, determining, or establishing that there is such a presumption. We allowed that there could *be* a presumption for a statement from the challenger's point of

view without the challenger being able to defend that there was such
a presumption or even being consciously aware of it. We can now see
why this is so and why this does not involve any anomaly. A deontological conception of justification requires that to hold a justified belief one
must have that belief not only on adequate grounds but be aware of the
adequacy of those grounds. But we have not seen reason to adopt this
stricture and have seen that ultimately it may lead to skepticism. Alston's
nondeontological conception of justification, J_{eg}, requires only that one
base one's beliefs on adequate grounds and not have sufficient reasons
that rebut those grounds. One need not be aware of or have access to
the adequacy of those grounds. Because our concept of acceptability is
equivalent to J_{eg}, as one did not have to be aware of the adequacy of one's
grounds for p for that belief to be justified according to J_{eg}, so one does
not have to be aware or recognize that certain features of one's cognitive
situation create a presumption for one's belief that p for there to be a
presumption for it or for the belief to be acceptable.

In discussing J_{eg}, Alston points out that, although knowledge or justified belief concerning the adequacy of the ground of a belief is not
required for that belief to be justified, such knowledge or justified belief
is "no doubt quite important and valuable for other purposes" (1985,
p. 82). Likewise, although one need not know or have a justified belief
that there is a presumption for a belief for there to *be* such a presumption
from one's point of view as challenger, knowledge of the conditions under which there is a presumption has distinct importance and value. The
proponent may want to explain the acceptability of some statement, in
particular, to meet a challenge to a claim he puts forward. Understanding the conditions of presumption may be necessary for showing that
there is a presumption for that claim. Some third party may want to be
able to explain why the statement is acceptable for the challenger. The
philosophical question still remains: *Why* in a given case or under certain
circumstances is a statement acceptable? We again may draw an analogy
with using language grammatically. Although we may be able standardly
to communicate using a natural language in accordance with its rules
of grammar without reflectively considering those rules, occasionally we
may be confronted with a hard case, where explicit, conscious appeal to
a rule is necessary to decide or justify a certain linguistic construction.
Again, in the moral sphere, although a virtuous person may ordinarily be
able to act as a matter of habit and thus unreflectively in accordance with
what is morally right, there may be moral hard cases involving explicit
appeal to rules. These are cases calling for casuistry. Hence, as moral

casuistry may be called for in some cases, so we may need on occasion to practice epistemic casuistry. Just what this practice involves we develop in Chapter 11. But one cannot practice epistemic casuistry without an understanding of the principles of presumption.

Understanding the conditions of presumption involves recognizing in a given case whether there is a presumption for a given statement and why. But this involves recognizing whether the belief-generating mechanism operating in that case is presumptively reliable and why. Hence, to determine under what conditions there is a presumption for a statement or belief, and thus when it is acceptable, we need to survey first just what are the belief-generating mechanisms. We then need to inquire just when there are presumptions for the beliefs generated by those mechanisms. But how are we to carry out our survey of belief-generating mechanisms? In Chapter 3, we indicated that the first question for determining whether a premise was acceptable was "What type of statement is it?" One might certainly expect that the beliefs expressed by different types of statements are generated by different mechanisms. Hence, if we first determined what types of statements there are, we could then determine what belief-generating mechanisms are associated with statements of that type. If our survey of the types of statements were comprehensive, so we expect would be our survey of the mechanisms. Once we had identified a mechanism, we could investigate whether or under what conditions it was presumptively reliable, the global condition for presumption of warrant. This will be our procedure in Part II.

PART II

STATEMENTS, BELIEF-GENERATING MECHANISMS, AND PRESUMPTIVE RELIABILITY

5

What Types of Statements Are There?

Determining the type of statement is relevant to determining whether the statement is acceptable. Suppose that in the course of a dialectical exchange, the proponent presents the following basic premise:

1. There was a red apple on the windowsill.

Suppose that the challenger may presume that the proponent has recently been in a position to observe the windowsill. Thus it is part of her evidential situation that the proponent's asserting statement (1) is a matter of personal testimony on his part. But the presumption for personal testimony renders (1) acceptable for the challenger at this point.

But now suppose the proponent puts forward

2. Horatio placed that red apple on the windowsill to show his love for Ophelia.

Prima facie, this case is quite different. Here, the proponent is not reporting what he has seen but explaining Horatio's overt act in terms of Horatio's dispositions and intentions. Now it may be that the proponent is an intimate of Horatio, and the challenger knows it. The proponent's asserting (2) constitutes in a sense expert testimony, for which there is also a presumption. In these circumstances, (2) is also acceptable from the challenger's point of view. But notice that this involves her being aware of the proponent's having expertise or at least special credentials concerning Horatio's intimate affairs. For his statement to be acceptable for her, she would need to possess such additional evidence, where she might be quite justified in simply presuming that (1) is an instance of personal testimony on the proponent's part.

But why can we judge (1) to be an example of personal testimony and (2) not? It is precisely here that the issue of type of statement comes to the fore. (1) predicates observable properties and relations – "x is red," "x is an apple," "y is a windowsill," "x is on y." All these observable properties require perception for their apprehension. But if one's word concerns what one has perceived, one is giving personal testimony. By contrast, although (2) does involve some observable predicates, its main point could be said to ascribe meaning by giving an explanation. But this meaning is not observable in at least two senses. Someone other than Horatio cannot directly observe Horatio's love for Ophelia, that which is meant. What can be perceived is overt behavior that is taken as a sign of that love.

But, further, the meaning connection, here one state of affairs being a sign of another, is not observable. We cannot perceive that a certain action, event, or state of affairs has a certain meaning, in particular, that two states of affairs are related as *explanans* and *explanandum*, the way we can perceive that the event or action has occurred. A different belief-generating mechanism is involved. We cannot claim a presumption for statement (2) on the basis of personal testimony, as we could for (1). This is not to say that our beliefs that meaning inheres in a given situation are not justifiable, that they are matters of mere opinion or taste. One may be able to give very cogent – logically cogent – reasons to defend a claim that a situation involves a certain meaning. Perhaps even in some circumstances meaning is immediately evident.

(1) and (2) are paradigm examples of what the rhetorician J. Michael Sproule classifies as descriptions and interpretations respectively. What our discussion thus far has shown is that in some instances at least recognizing that statements are descriptions or interpretations is germane to assessing whether a source's vouching for them creates a presumption from the challenger's point of view. We hold that this is true in general, but justifying this claim requires a typology of statements whose classification is relevant to this question of presumption or acceptability.

Rhetoricians have an obvious interest in classifying statements. Arguing persuasively for different statements may involve different strategies. If statements sharing certain features call for particular argument strategies, classifying these statements together as a type makes rhetorical sense. Rhetoricians have given us various typologies. Our contention is that distinctions some rhetoricians have drawn are highly suggestive and fertile for developing a classification of statements relevant to the issue of premise acceptability. Our goal is to develop such a typology. Our first order of business is to survey how some rhetoricians have classified statements.

5.1 RHETORICAL SYSTEMS OF STATEMENT CLASSIFICATION

Sproule offers a threefold classification of statements in (1980), descriptions, interpretations, and evaluations. He understands a description to involve an issue of fact, an issue concerning "the existence or objective correctness of something" (1980, p. 18). We might expect to get virtually universal agreement on an issue of fact from all rational judges (1980, p. 18). Furthermore, claims of fact are open to independent verification, being framed in observational language (1980, p. 18). Interpretations for Sproule raise primarily issues of definition; that is, interpretations place facts into categories, relate them, place them in perspective, give them a meaning. Giving something meaning, we add, should be understood as relating it in a nomic or lawlike way to a wider whole.[1] In an evaluation, the principal issue is a value of some sort. What is right or wrong, good or bad, preferable or not preferable, praiseworthy or blameworthy, virtuous or vicious?

Sproule's scheme stands within a long tradition, going back to the early Latin rhetoricians. As Kruger points out in (1975),

> They generally asked three questions about the subject of dispute:
>
> (1) *An sit* (whether a thing is) – a question of fact. For example, did Brutus, as has been alleged, kill Caesar? [Description]
> (2) *Quid sit* (what it is) – a question of definition. If it is granted that Brutus *did* kill Caesar, was the act murder or self-defense? Again, a question of definition. [Interpretation]
> (3) *Quale sit* (what kind it is) – a question of quality. If it was in fact murder, was Brutus justified in murdering Caesar? [Justification – Evaluation] (1975, p. 137)

In (1982), Fahnestock and Secor present a related classification of statements. They claim that we do not argue about matters of fact or taste. Rather, there are four basic questions arguments may address:

(1) What is it?
(2) How did it get that way?
(3) Is it good or bad?
(4) What should we do about it?

These questions then generate a typology of statements. Have Fahnestock and Secor identified any further types of statements that cannot be integrated into Sproule's classification scheme? Answers to the question "What is it?" are categorical propositions in the sense that a subject is related to a predicate. Although arguments for such claims may have distinctive procedures, the examples that Fahnestock and Secor give seem to fall each under one or the other of the description/interpretation/evaluation categories. They cite statements such as "That cat is gray," a clear description, "That cat is a nuisance," a clear evaluation, and "Representative government is time-consuming," an interpretation, all as instances of categorical propositions. All of their examples apparently can be included in Sproule's tripartite classification, although some may instance mixed statements. "Man is a beast to man" seems to be both an interpretation and an evaluation. We see no reason to count categorical propositions as an additional fourth type of statement.

Answers to the question "How did it get that way?" are causal statements. Sproule counts causal claims as one type of interpretation. So these statements are already accounted for on his scheme. Answers to the question "Is it good or bad?" obviously are evaluations. To say that we *should* perform some action or follow some policy is to evaluate that action or policy positively. So answers to the policy question are a subclass of evaluations and thus also accommodated on the tripartite scheme. To be sure, the questions "Is it good or bad?" and "What should we do about it?" are distinct, different questions. Arguing for a claim that something is good or bad might proceed rather differently from arguing for a claim that we should follow some course of action. If our goal is to examine what makes for persuasively effective argument, the goal for rhetoricians, it may make a great deal of sense to separate proposals from evaluations. But if our purpose is to distinguish basic types of statements with a view to assessing the epistemic value of the sources vouching for the statement, that we should include a specific category of proposals seems unnecessary in the light of our analysis.

By claiming that we do not argue for matters of fact, Fahnestock and Secor have not shown that the category of descriptions is not necessary. First of all, even if we do not argue *for* facts, we certainly argue *from* them in defending further claims. Fahnestock and Secor are trying to develop a classification scheme for arguable statements. Because we are concerned here with *premise* acceptability, we still may regard descriptions as a legitimate, distinct type of statement. But we can question Fahnestock and Secor's claim that we do not argue for descriptions. Suppose someone were accused of a crime. Then certain purely factual issues would be crucial to establishing guilt. The prosecution might expend great effort marshaling evidence to establish these facts. But would this not be to argue for those facts?[2] So nothing Fahnestock and Secor have said rules out descriptions as a legitimate class of statements.

In (1975), Kruger points out that modern textbooks retain descriptions and evaluations from the traditional classification but drop interpretations for policy claims (1975, pp. 137–8). He is dissatisfied with both traditional and current schemes. He complains that they leave many gaps, in particular ignoring the distinction between empirical and analytic statements (1975, p. 138). Kruger begins with that very distinction. For him, statements are analytic just in case "analyzing their form or meaning enables us to tell if they are true or false" (1975, p. 156, n. 6). Thus, not every analytic statement is self-evident for Kruger, for he counts analytically false or self-contradictory statements as analytic. Turning to nonanalytic statements, Kruger identifies two broad subtypes, factual and evaluative. He characterizes factual statements by giving examples of some representative types. These include descriptions, comprising not only perceptually verifiable claims but also ascriptions of personality traits and power. Factual statements also comprise correlations, claims that one condition is followed by or connected with another, causal explanations, and predictions. Evaluative statements may have a number of uses, including expressing approval or disapproval of something as a means to some end, asserting that some person or thing satisfies or fails to satisfy certain normative criteria, or judging the merits of some policy.

In analytic statements, Kruger has clearly identified a further type of statement beyond Sproule's three. These considerations suggest that we should adopt, at least as a working hypothesis, a fourfold classification. Is this typology viable? Can we, first of all, give definitions of these types which will allow us to distinguish them unambiguously? Can we see each statement as an instance of one or another of these categories or a mixture of them? Furthermore, does this typology enable us to classify statements in a way that illuminates the epistemic value of the sources vouching for them? Will identifying whether a statement is analytic or a description, interpretation, evaluation help determine whether the sources vouching for it thereby create a presumption for it? We turn to these issues in the next section.

5.2 A FOURFOLD TYPOLOGY OF STATEMENTS

Keeping our eye on the fourfold analytic/description/interpretation/ evaluation distinction, we shall develop a typology by proposing a series of dichotomous divisions of the class of statements. Clearly, we count such analytic statements as "All bachelors are unmarried," "If everything is conscious, then something is conscious," "Either it is raining or it is not raining" as necessary statements. Their negations, then, are necessarily false. Is the class of true analytic statements coextensive with the class of necessarily true statements and likewise does the class of analytically false statements amount to the class of necessarily false statements? We may argue that the class of necessarily true statements in the sense of broadly logically necessary is wider than the class of true analytic statements, and similarly for their false counterparts, as we shall see shortly. Hence, "necessarily true," "necessarily false" appear to indicate broader classes than "analytically true," "analytically false," although this might be contested by some philosophers. Broadly logically necessarily true statements and broadly logically necessarily false statements will be broadly logically determinate. This gives us our first division of statements: ***Broadly Logically Determinate versus Broadly Logically Indeterminate Statements.***

We hold that it is reason that recognizes broadly logically necessary statements, generating the beliefs of their truth and indeed necessary truth.[3] How might one argue that the class of truths of reason is wider than the class of true analytic statements? First of all, one may ask whether all mathematical statements are analytic. Although this has been and may continue to be the view of some philosophers, it meets with significant objections. Frege believed that all of mathematics could be reduced to logic, whose principles *are* analytic. But when Frege presented his reduction of mathematics to logic, it was to higher-order logic. This is obvious from the comprehension axiom which quantifies over properties:

$$(\forall F)(\exists x)(\forall y)[y \in x \equiv Fy]$$

Because, as is widely known, this comprehension axiom leads directly to Russell's paradox, Frege's project was not successful. Much work in modern mathematics has been devoted to reducing mathematics to set theory, variously axiomatized to avoid the paradoxes. Is set theory logic? Quine in (1970) points out a significant differentiating feature: "As soon as we admit '∈' as a genuine predicate, and classes as values of quantifiable variables, we are embarked on a substantive mathematical theory" (1970, p. 72). Thus, such basic axioms of set theory as

$(\exists y)(\forall x)(x \notin y)$ (null set axiom)

$(\forall x)(\forall y)(\exists z)(\forall w)(w \in z \equiv [w = x \lor w = y])$ (axiom of pairs)

quantifying over sets and asserting the existence of certain sets, do not count as analytic statements. Certainly we cannot determine their truth by reflecting on the meaning or truth-conditions of their component expressions as we could with the clear cut examples of analytic propositions we considered earlier. We recognized that those statements are true by recognizing the relations between "bachelor" and "unmarried" or the truth-conditions for "if-then," "every," "some," "or," "not." "Set" or "collection" are generally regarded as primitive, undefined notions in set theory. How can one maintain then that the notion of set implies the claim that there is a set with no elements or that for any two sets, there is a set that contains exactly the two of them? The issue of whether a certain set exists is not simply a matter of form or of analyzing meaning. These are substantive claims. We find this a telling reason for not regarding set theory as logic. Set theory, then, does not appear to be analytic, but it is to set theory that much of mathematics is reduced. But surely many of the propositions of mathematics intuitively have the necessity of the obviously analytic propositions we have considered. Hence, mathematical statements are necessary – at least broadly logically necessary, and are thus truths of reason.

There are further statements that are broadly logically necessary.

No physical object can be in two places at the same time.
No natural numbers are colored.
No object can have a property without existing. (I think, therefore I
  am.) (See Plantinga 1993b, p. 102.)

Here again, although these statements seem clearly broadly logically necessary, they do not appear to be analytic statements.

Why should we count these statements – and, indeed, true substantive mathematical statements – together with analytic statements as one category? Why should we first count analytic statements as a single category? As Kruger points out, analytic statements "literally contain their own evidence" (1975, p. 141). To come to believe that true analytic statements are true or false analytic statements are false, it is sufficient in many cases to analyze their logical form or the meaning of their component expressions. Although one may need experience to grasp the meaning of the concepts involved, once that meaning is grasped, and once the truth-conditions for the statement are grasped given its form, one may in many instances (those that are not too complex) see that the statement is true or false.

These features of analytic propositions are also true of the other statements we want to include in the category of broadly logically determinate statements. As Plantinga points out, for at least some statements in this category, we can come to *see* that they are true, where this involves forming the belief that the statement is not only true but necessarily true, and we can come to form this belief immediately and not merely on the basis of memory or testimony (Plantinga 1993b, pp. 105, 106). If one sees a proposition true in this manner, one believes it *a priori*. If one sees that a proposition follows (deductively) from a proposition one believes *a priori*, and on that basis comes to believe it, again one believes the proposition *a priori*. The key to the generalization is that all the statements in this category may be recognized true and indeed necessarily true *a priori*, or may be recognized false and indeed necessarily false *a priori*. The union of these two classes of statements constitutes the class of broadly logically determinate statements, as opposed to broadly logically indeterminate or contingent statements. Traditionally, one faculty was regarded as generating the beliefs that broadly logically necessarily true statements are true and broadly logically necessarily false statements are false, namely reason. Hence, it is appropriate to count broadly logically necessary statements together as one class of statement in an epistemic typology.

Turning to broadly logically indeterminate or contingent statements, it seems straightforward to divide them into evaluative and nonevaluative. There does not appear to be a convenient positive term to denominate the latter category. In (2000), we used "natural," but this term has restrictive connotations we wish to avoid. Consider the statement: "A transcendent God exists," in itself not an evaluative statement. If *pace* an Anselmian analysis, this is not an alethically necessary statement, it is still strange to classify it as a natural statement, because it makes a claim about that which is transcendent of nature. Again, as Searle points out in (1969, pp. 50–3) and as we shall develop in Chapter 8, statements such as "Jones scored the winning goal in the soccer match this afternoon" report institutional facts. Such statements presuppose the constitutive rules of soccer for their meaning. Predicates presupposing these rules are neither simply physical or psychological predicates. But Moore called nature "the subject matter of the natural sciences and also of psychology" (1903, p. 40), that is, what can be properly spoken about using physical or psychological predicates. If this be nature, can statements of institutional facts be natural statements? Hence, "natural" as synonymous with "nonevaluative" has undesirable connotations. The word "factual" is also a candidate, but it, too, makes suggestions we find unfortunate, as we shall discuss shortly. In the absence of a suitable positive term, we shall simply use "nonevaluative."

This gives us our second dichotomous division of statements, that is, of those that are contingent: ***Evaluative versus Nonevaluative Statements.*** This division is straightforward, because recognizing evaluations is straightforward. An evaluation characterizes something as either good or bad, better or worse, preferable or avoidable; an act as either right or wrong, obligatory, permissible, or forbidden; a person or character as praiseworthy or blameworthy; an action as morally good or morally bad. We recognize evaluative predicates straight off, and we can tell straightforwardly by inspection whether or not a statement predicates one of these attributes. Of course, one need not use the specific words "good," "bad," "right," "wrong," "should," should not" to assert evaluations. Merely by saying that something is a value or has positive or negative value we evaluate it. Again many words, especially those that are emotionally charged in some way, serve to express value judgments. This is not to say that every statement containing an evaluative predicate is thereby an evaluation.

> Testing nuclear weapons is right or testing nuclear weapons is not right.

is obviously an instance of the law of excluded middle and thus a logically determinate statement. It is not an evaluation, even though it contains the word "right." Is any act or policy said to be right or said not to be right by this statement? It makes no evaluative assertion. Given this caveat, our division of contingent statements into evaluative and nonevaluative is straightforward.[4]

Can the class of nonevaluative statements in turn be subdivided along the description/interpretation distinction? We believe this distinction is very important for an epistemic account of types of statement. Interpretations involve different belief-generating mechanisms from descriptions. Whether or under what circumstances these mechanisms create a presumption for the beliefs they generate is a distinct question from whether the mechanisms generating descriptive beliefs create a presumption for those beliefs. Thus, identifying whether a statement is a description or an interpretation is a significant first step in assessing whether there is a presumption for it.

However, we find one rhetorical differentiation of descriptions from interpretations – descriptions involving issues of fact, whereas interpretations involve issues of definition – to be problematic for a number of reasons. In neither case do we believe this gives an adequate definition.

Characterizing descriptions as statements dealing with issues of fact, although intuitively attractive, is philosophically problematic for at least two reasons. First, how does this distinguish descriptions from true statements in general? If I want to say that a statement S is true, cannot I say "It is a fact that S"? Is it wrong to say:

> It is a fact that cigarette smoking causes lung cancer.
> That stealing, except in very exceptional circumstances, is wrong is a fact?

If interpretations and evaluations are classes of statements distinct from descriptions, and descriptions concern issues of fact, then the above two statements are incorrect, or at best anomalous or misleading. But these statements are *not* anomalous or misleading. Unless one is to specify a meaning of "fact" under which causal statements and value judgments, even though true, will not deal with issues of fact, the definition is too broad. If descriptions be issues of fact, what is to prevent us from characterizing any true statement, or any statement about which we feel distinctly confident, as a description?

By contrast, if to be true and to state a fact are the same, at least for contingent statements, and only descriptions state facts, then neither interpretations nor evaluations are literally true. Because causal judgments are interpretations and moral judgments evaluations, it follows that neither are true or false – a highly controversial claim that should not be prejudged by a matter of terminology. This is the second reason why defining descriptions as those statements dealing with issues of fact is philosophically problematic. It suggests covertly endorsing a naive positivism. Hence we should regard the characterization of descriptions as statements drawing issues of fact as only a heuristic or programmatic suggestion. To develop an adequate characterization, we must go further.

Consider again Sproule's three criteria for facts – being capable of independent verification, description in observational language, and winning the agreement of all reasonable persons. These concern the reliability of the sources that vouch for statements said to report facts, more generally with the quality of evidence for these statements, and with the lack of controversiality about the issue when once all the evidence and testimony of the sources is in. Now, it is certainly true that many statements we intuitively want to count as descriptions state facts in this sense: "The living room rug is 9′ × 12′." We would obviously settle the question of whether this statement is true by measuring the rug. But any number of people may measure a rug. Its size is stated numerically according to a standard measure – certainly observationally. When once measured, what else would pertain to the question of its size? As Secor has pointed out, for the rhetorician "facts depend on a system of verification" (1998, paragraph 6). I believe this epitomizes the rhetorical understanding of 'fact.' If there is agreement about how a claim is verified, if it is agreed that certain evidence would establish that claim and such evidence is produced, then the claim is a fact. This relativizes the notion of fact to the verificational situation, an aspect of the overall dialogical situation. What may be a fact in one situation need not be a fact in another.

Even given these considerations, we still find defining descriptions with respect to this notion of fact problematic, even from the rhetorical point of view. First, such a definition would generate conflicting categorizations of statements. Consider: "The living room rug smothered the infant." This is a causal statement and so we would want to count it as an interpretation. But does it describe a fact? A number of persons could witness that the infant was found dead while covered by the rug. Several medical examiners could independently perform autopsies to ascertain the cause of death. The issue can be independently verified. Should the medical examiners' reports all concur, what more could a reasonable person ask for before giving his or her assent? There is an agreed-upon verification procedure here, in particular a procedure for determining when someone has been smothered. Is this casual statement a description, then, and not an interpretation? Is it both?

By contrast, consider the statement "An alien space ship passed over my house last night." Someone might present this as an eyewitness report. Intuitively, we want to count it as a description. It certainly does not seem to draw issues of definition or evaluation. Now although it was in principle open to independent verification last night, and is stated in observational language, is it capable of winning the agreement of all reasonable persons? Given that the subject of UFOs is highly controversial, this seems unlikely. The statement then fails to involve an issue of fact according to Sproule's criterion. What type of statement is it? Do we need a further category? If the issue of UFOs became established, would the statement then become a statement of fact? Hence, by defining descriptions as statements of fact, certain statements one does not want to count as descriptions will be so counted, and other statements one does want to count as descriptions will not count as such. Furthermore, in some cases whether a statement is a description depends in part on the controversiality of the statement. Some statements may become descriptions should they cease to be controversial, or cease to be descriptions, should they become controversial. This seems far from satisfactory.

These conflicting judgments reveal a deeper conflict in our approach to classifying statements. On the one hand, we categorize some statements based on certain features that they display in themselves. We judge statements such as:

> Exposure to radiation caused a significant increase in cancer in that population.
> Placing salt in the bunsen burner turns the flame yellow.

to be causal statements, based on their asserting that a certain type of relation holds, and independently of how well or how poorly verified these statements are or whether they can be verified in any way satisfying the criteria for being a description. But causal statements are a subclass of interpretation. So in these cases, statements are classified as interpretations, and thus not as descriptions, independently of whether they fail to satisfy the verifiability conditions for descriptions. Yet, on the other hand, as we have seen, these conditions apparently can be satisfied by some causal statements. Hence, we have a conflict. Again, some statements apparently report states of affairs and on this basis we tend to classify them as descriptions. The UFO claim is a clear example. But whether or not a statement reports the existence of some state of affairs is a feature of the statement, independent of whether what it reports satisfies the verifiability criteria for being a fact. Hence, we again have a conflict.

We recognize at least some broadly logically determinate statements through their self-evident truth or falsity. We recognize evaluative statements through their predicating some evaluative property or relation. In both cases, we identify a statement as being of a certain category based on some quality or feature of the statement in itself and independently of its mode of verification. Can this not also be done for descriptions and interpretations? To identify certain qualities of descriptions in terms of which we may define this class, let us begin by looking at some examples of statements that appear intuitively but straightforwardly to be descriptions.

1. A bus is passing my office window.
2. The house across the street is painted white.
3. Caesar crossed the Rubicon.
4. During the second week of January, thirty homeless persons were found dead on the streets of New York.

5. Fifty percent of the voters said they disapproved of the president's job performance.
6. All the subjects in the experiment displayed cold symptoms.
7. All swans are white (understood as asserting only that there are no swans which fail to be white).

We have a variety of statements here, illustrating the various types of descriptions. (1)–(3) make reports of events or conditions. (4) and (5) present summaries of reports, whereas (6) and (7) are accidental universal generalizations. They are accidental because there is no nomic ascription here. These generalizations merely assert constant conjunctions. They do not express a stronger or in some sense necessary connection between antecedent and consequent, in particular they are not understood to underlie or support subjunctive or contrary-to-fact conditionals. (6) does not support that "If John were a subject in the experiment, then he would display cold symptoms." But the accidental, non-nomic character of these universal generalizations is the clue to identifying the hallmark of descriptions.

All these statements are both contingent and have extensional truth-conditions. That is, in specifying the conditions under which these statements would be true, we would not make any reference to other possible worlds, as we would for modalized statements. This should be clear from the fact that all the predicates appearing in these examples are observational. I propose that we take this condition – truth-conditional extensionality – as the specific difference distinguishing descriptions from other contingent nonevaluative statements. Descriptions are extensional nonevaluative statements.

We propose to define interpretations, then, as intensional nonevaluative statements. We find this definition far more accurate than defining interpretations as statements raising issues of definition, which we also find problematic. Although in arguing for controversial claims that are interpretations, one may need to spell out the criteria for certain interpretive concepts to apply – just when is a deed an act of murder as opposed to self-defense? (compare Kruger 1975, p. 137) – this may simply be true of many interpretations, rather than being a defining condition of this type of statement. Simply saying interpretations deal with issues of definition is confusing on two grounds. First, why are not analytic statements (as a proper subclass of broadly logically determinate statements) interpretations according to this definition? "All bachelors are male." Is this statement not true by definition? Is not seeing that it is true primarily a matter of recognizing the definition of "bachelor"? Why is this statement then not an interpretation?

Again, one could ask whether statements involving technical terms, where one would have to know the definition of the terms before being able to understand the statement, are all interpretations on this definition. Do not these statements raise primarily issues of definition? But consider: "That berm is less than 5′ wide." Clearly, we cannot accept this statement until we know what "berm" means. But suppose we learn that "berm" means "the shoulder of a road" (see Beardsley 1975, p. 214). "The shoulder is less than 5′ wide" is clearly a description, not an interpretation.

We may go even further. Consider:

This is a triangle.
That is a piece of bronze.
The animal on the mat is a cat.

Do we not have to understand what the words "triangle," "bronze," "cat" mean to determine whether these statements are true or false? To determine whether any statement is true, do we not have to know first in some sense the definitions of the component terms? What statements, then, are not interpretations?

The error in this line of reasoning lies in confusing or conflating two senses of "meaning." We may distinguish on the one hand the meaning of a word or expression. This is the sort of meaning that is reported in dictionaries or proposed in coining new terms. In this sense, every statement involves an issue of meaning. By contrast, there is meaning that may be imported into, intuited, apprehended, or discovered in a situation. Interpretations are concerned with giving meaning in this sense. Recall that Sproule says that interpretations categorize facts, place them in perspective. Kruger proposed:

Brutus's killing Caesar was an act of murder
Brutus's killing Caesar was an act of self-defense

as involving questions of definition. Counting them as interpretations, we ask how does each put facts in perspective? Clearly, each statement claims that the overt fact of Brutus's killing Caesar is related to a system of intention. If the act were murder, Brutus's intentions would include goals of one sort. If it were an act of self-defense, he would have certain other goals. But, in either case, when once we see the act in the light of this interpretation, it becomes intelligible to us. We recognize a meaning that we did not before. This meaning consists in the act's being related nomically to this wider system of intention, which renders it explicable.

For an interpretive concept to be truly predicable, some explanation needs to be true. This is the hallmark of interpretive concepts. But explanations involve nomic generalizations of a universal or statistical sort. These nomic generalizations involve a nonalethic necessity. They are necessary, but not in the sense of broadly logical necessity, true in all possible worlds. For example, consider the causal generalization "Litmus paper always turns pink on being dipped in acid." Unlike the accidental universal generalizations that we have already cited as descriptions, our example claims that not only does any actual piece of litmus paper turn pink when dipped in acid but that in any physically or causally possible world, this happens (although we can imagine worlds where it does not). The statement then makes a claim about all possible worlds of some sort. It makes an assertion of causal necessity and could be expressed using a modality of causal necessity:

$$(\forall x) \boxed{c} ([Lx \And Dx] \supset Px)^5$$

We may likewise see that personal explanations involve a nonalethic necessity. Suppose an historian were to explain Henry VIII's seeking to annul his marriage to Catherine of Aragon by pointing out that he sought to remarry to obtain a male heir.[6] Getting a male heir through remarriage was his purpose and he believed the annulment was a necessary step in the optimal way to bring this about. The explanation presupposes this general principle:

> For any X, Y, and Z, if X has a conscious purpose to bring Y about and believes that doing Z is (part of) the (optimal) means to bring about Y, then X does Z.

But this general statement and various concretizations of it claim that there is a necessary connection, albeit not logical necessity, between conscious purpose or goal, belief, and action. Something more than constant conjunction is claimed here. We have a claim involving "personal necessity."

We may view causal necessity and personal necessity as species of nomic necessity, which we may denote with '$\boxed{N}$.' Let us delimit the class of interpretations as including statements predicating interpretative concepts, together with statements of nonalethic explanatory modality or generalizations of such statements.[7] We may contrast extensional and intensional statements by saying that extensional statements are those whose truth-conditions depend just on the states of affairs constituting the actual world, whereas the truth-conditions of intensional statements make reference to other possible worlds. Because interpretive concepts presuppose explanations, they are intensional concepts and the statements predicating them are intensional statements. Statements of nonalethic explanatory necessity and possibility are intensional. Descriptions then are contingent, nonevaluative extensional statements while interpretations are contingent, nonevaluative intensional statements. The description/interpretation distinction then comes down to distinguishing ***Extensional versus Intensional Nonevaluative Statements.***

Calling statements "interpretations" that either presuppose nomic statements or that assert such statements raises the question of whether we are significantly redefining that term from previous usage. We address this question specifically in Chapter 8. The fact that causal statements are a principal standardly recognized type of interpretation and that they assert nomic statements is positive evidence for our view.

Will every statement be unambiguously classifiable as one of the four types of statements that we have just characterized? Will there be borderline cases or instances in which a statement seems to be rightfully assigned to more than one category? This is certainly possible. Consider: "That project will be environmentally damaging." Is this an evaluation or an interpretation? To say that something is damaging, especially of something that has recognized positive value – the environment – is certainly to say that it is bad. So on these grounds, we want to classify the statement as an evaluation. But to say that something does damage is to attribute to it a power or causal efficacy, that is, to make an interpretation. Is the example then an evaluation or an interpretation? We may think of this statement as a conjunction, one conjunct being an interpretation – the policy has certain effects, the other being an evaluation – the consequences of these effects are deleterious to the environment, that is, bad. This conjunction is both an interpretation and an evaluation. It is a mixed statement. This means that we need not try to assign every statement to exactly one of our four categories. If a statement is mixed, it will be sufficient if we can categorize its various components. This holds true not just for statements that we may paraphrase as conjuncts but for explicitly truth-functional compound statements in general.

We have thus developed a typology of statements that honors the classical description/interpretation/evaluation distinction together with Kruger's amendment calling for a place for analytic statements. The rationale behind our distinction is semantic. Whether a statement is logically determinate or contingent is a semantic distinction. Whether or not it predicates an evaluation is a matter of what certain of its terms mean. Whether a nonevaluative contingent statement is extensional or intensional is a matter of its truth-conditions – again a semantic consideration. These semantic differences may mark epistemic differences. Different mechanisms may generate the beliefs expressed by different types of statements. We expect this is totally plausible and even commonplace. We come to hold logically determinate beliefs *a priori* or through reason. We hold contingent beliefs *a posteriori*, through experience. But what belief-generating mechanisms are connected with each type of statement? We believe it best not to try to answer that question all at once in this chapter but, rather, piecemeal in connection with examining each type of statement individually. This we proceed to do in the next four chapters. However, there are several points of clarification we want to emphasize and a heuristic suggestion concerning the relation between types of statements and belief-generating mechanisms we want to entertain. We close this chapter by considering these points.

5.3 BASIC BELIEFS, INFERRED BELIEFS, RECEIVED BELIEFS

As we made clear at the beginning of this essay, our concern is with basic acceptability, the acceptability of premises that have not been inferred. It is important that we reiterate this central focus of our inquiry at this point. For each type of statement in our typology, there may be a number of different mechanisms that generate beliefs expressed by statements of that type. For example, a description may express a perceptual belief. However, this descriptive belief could have been inferred from other beliefs, and so the proximate mechanism generating the belief will be some form of inference.

However, suppose we set aside inferred beliefs and deal just with basic beliefs. Can we, for each of the basic types of statement that we have identified in the last section, find a unique mechanism that generates beliefs of that type? Again, the answer is no. We may come to believe a description on the basis of perception or on the basis of testimony. Now, the receiving of testimony or more generally the taking of someone's word[8] is a basic belief-generating mechanism. To believe something on testimony or on someone's word is not to infer that belief from other premises. But this mechanism differs from our other basic belief-generating mechanisms in that it in a sense receives the belief ready-made. Its function is to make that belief our own, rather than to originate or initiate a belief. So we may distinguish personally initiated beliefs, those generated just by one's own belief-generating mechanisms, from received beliefs, those generated by taking the word of others.

We may thus speak of both personal and interpersonal sources of belief. In asking what source vouches for a belief, we must consider both types of sources. It is appropriate that we direct our attention to personal sources first. For, surely, if taking the proponent's word is to be a presumptively reliable interpersonal belief-generating mechanism on a given occasion for a challenger, we would expect the proponent's personal belief-generating mechanisms that generated his belief to be presumptively reliable also on that occasion. Hence, as we have identified four basic types of beliefs, we shall in the next four chapters consider what personal sources generate beliefs of each type and whether or under what conditions those sources are presumptively reliable. In Chapter 10, we shall consider the interpersonal source.

We can now pose the questions that will drive our inquiry over the next four chapters: For each type of statement that we have identified in the last section, is there a personal basic belief-generating mechanism or several personal belief-generating mechanisms that generate the beliefs expressible by statements of that type? If such a personal source vouches for such a belief, does that create a presumption for the statement? Before turning to those questions, however, there is a suggestion for correlating types of statements and belief-generating mechanisms that we want to consider. It may help motivate our ensuing discussion.

5.4 BASIC BELIEF-GENERATING MECHANISMS: A HEURISTIC SUGGESTION

There is a curious parallel between our logically determinate/ description/interpretation/evaluation distinction and Jung's theory of psychological types. According to Jung, there are four basic psychological functions – sensation, intuition, thinking, and feeling. The functions are completely distinct and not reducible to each other. However, according to Myers, we can group sensation and intuition together as modes of perception, and thought and feeling as modes of judgment. We may perceive either through our five senses or through intuition. "Your eyes and ears and other senses tell you what is actually there and actually happening. Sensing is especially useful for gathering the facts of a situation" (1980, p. 2).[9] The raw material here may come not just from the sense organs but from our sense of what is happening in our bodies. Intuition,

Myers tells us, "shows you meanings and relationships and possibilities that are beyond the reach of your senses" (1980, p. 2). In both sense perception and intuition, the contents are absolutely given, not arrived at through inference or reasoning. From our perspective, sense perception and intuition are both basic belief-generating mechanisms.

We may judge either by thinking or by feeling. One may argue that for Jung, thinking in general amounts to inferring, arriving at conclusions from premises. However, Myers emphasizes that thinking is especially concerned with inferring the causal consequences of possible actions preparatory to deciding whether to perform them. Thinking specifically as arriving at a judgment about what to do involves taking statements expressing causal regularities and the specifics of a proposed action as premises and inferring from them a prediction as to the causal consequences of that action. Feeling, as Jung puts it, "is primarily a process that takes place between the ego and a given content, a process, moreover, that imparts to the content a definite *value* in the sense of acceptance or rejection ('like' or 'dislike')" (1944, p. 543, italics in original). Rather than trying to arrive at a value judgment as conclusion by deriving it from premises, feeling "is solely concerned with the setting up of a subjective criterion of acceptance or rejection" (Jung 1944, p. 544). Perhaps this point could be made in our terminology by saying that feeling generates normative or value judgments as basic beliefs.

Jung's classification provides at least a suggestion for developing our inventory of basic belief-generating mechanisms. We may recognize in or associated with each of these modes of perception or judgment such a mechanism. Sensing is just sense perception. But we need to recognize what Jung and Myers call intuition also as a basic belief-generating mechanism. A paradigm example of intuition is the formation of explanatory hypotheses – the creative grasp or insight into connections or meanings not previously recognized. Indeed, we may intuit various alternative hypotheses that may explain some situation. Likewise, we may intuit various possible courses of action. The belief that these hypotheses are possible, that these courses of action are open alternatives has its source in intuition.

Thinking, as Jung has described it, is an inferential belief-generating mechanism. But surely this cognitive faculty has associated basic employments. In deductive logic, we not only identify arguments as valid, but statements as being logically true. Surely, in some cases, we may simply and directly apprehend that a statement is logically true. In analogous cases, we may directly apprehend that simple arithmetic truths or simple semantic truths are true. In all these cases, the cognitive faculty of thinking is generating basic beliefs. These beliefs are frequently called truths of reason, and it is better to refer to this faculty as reason rather than thinking. We may say we are engaging in thinking when we are engaging in reveries, remembering past events, imagining the goings-on in alternative possible worlds, or freely associating. These are not instances of thinking in Jung's sense, which we are considering here.

Finally, feeling discloses values. We shall develop this point in Chapter 9. If one had no feelings, could one have any values? If no state, real or imagined, ever occasioned in one any attraction or repulsion, any liking or disliking, could one ever value anything? Would not all be a matter of mere indifference? In some cases at least, on the basis of how we feel we form judgments directly as to what is good or bad. My belief that some state of affairs was good may derive from the feeling of satisfaction that state engenders. Likewise, my sense that a state of affairs was bad stems from my feeling of dissatisfaction or frustration that the action or state of affairs elicits.

The parallelism between this fourfold classification of cognitive faculties and our fourfold classification of statements is obvious. They are correlated one-one. Many descriptions express beliefs generated by sense perception. Interpretations involve intuition, while evaluations depend on feeling. Logically determinate statements are the product of reason. So it appears that we can have a very neat correlation between types of statements and basic belief-generating mechanisms. On the basis of the types of statements we may meet with, we may determine what personal mechanisms or sources generate basic beliefs expressing those statements and thus we have a systematic inventory of personal belief-generating mechanisms.

The problem is that for philosophical purposes, the correlation is too neat and can be easily questioned. Is sense perception the only basic belief-generating mechanism for descriptions? I sense a sharp pain in my left leg and form the belief that I have a pain in my leg. The statement expressing that belief is a description. Did perception generate this belief? Jung would answer affirmatively because he understood sensing to include our bodily sense. But we ordinarily understand perception to be outward-directed, concerned with the external world. What mechanism then generated this descriptive belief about what is internal to me? Philosophers have spoken of rational intuition and moral intuition. Can one speak simply of intuition? How is intuition related to reason as a basic belief-generating mechanism? Ross in (1930) holds that we come to recognize principles of *prima facie* duty as we come to recognize elementary arithmetical truths. But if reason is the mechanism generating the latter kind of belief, why is it not the mechanism generating the former? If feeling is the mechanism generating evaluations, are basic evaluations then simply subjective?

Despite the problems, we still feel that the correlation between types of statements and Jung's faculties has heuristic value. We have already indicated that reason is the faculty generating *a priori* beliefs. But what is logically determinate may be known *a priori*. Will not sense perception be a paradigm case of those mechanisms generating descriptions? If interpretations ascribe meanings to "facts" or relate them in a way that discloses meaning and intuition grasps meanings and relationships in a noninferential way, can we not expect that some form of intuition is a mechanism generating basic beliefs expressed through interpretations? Will not feeling have some role in the generation of evaluations as basic beliefs? We shall explore all these questions in the next four chapters as we consider successively each type of statement, the mechanisms that generate basic beliefs expressed by such statements, and the conditions under which there is a presumption for those mechanisms. There is good reason to treat types of statements in the order we have identified them. We hope this becomes apparent from our discussion. Hence, we turn to logically determinate statements and reason in the next chapter.

6

Necessary Statements and *A Priori* Intuition

In Chapter 5, we indicated that reason is a personal mechanism generating beliefs expressed by necessary statements. Are there any further personal mechanisms generating such beliefs? Let us ask first whether there are different types of logically determinate statements and then whether reason generates all the beliefs expressed by these statements.

6.1 WHAT TYPES OF NECESSARY STATEMENTS ARE THERE?

Let us reiterate that by necessary statements in this chapter we mean alethically or broadly logically necessary statements only. I believe we can identify five classes of necessary statements: formally true statements – statements true by virtue of their logical form, semantically true statements, conceptually true statements, mathematical statements, and metaphysical statements. To appreciate the comprehensiveness of these five categories, let us survey them in some detail.

Formally True Statements

This subclass includes first of all truth-functional tautologies and statements true by virtue of their first-order logical structure.

1. Either it is raining or it is not raining.
2. If everything is conscious, then something is conscious.

The class also includes higher-order quantificational truths, such as instances of the following schemata:

3. $(\forall p)\,([\,(\forall x)Fx \lor \sim(\forall x)Fx] \supset p) \supset ([\,(\forall x)Fx \lor \sim(\forall x)Fx] \supset (\exists x)Gx)$
4. $(\forall f)\,(\forall x)\,(fx \equiv Gx) \supset (\forall x)\,([Hx\ \&\ Kx] \equiv Gx)$

Truths of certain other branches of logic are standardly recognized as broadly logical. Chief here are the systems of alethic modal logic. Where "$\Box$" reads "it is necessarily the case that" and "$\Diamond$" reads "it is possible that," instances of

5. $\Box(P \supset Q) \supset (\Box P \supset \Box Q)$
6. $\Box P \supset P$
7. $P \supset \Diamond P$

all count as formally true. As is well known, there are many other modalities whose logics are recognized as genuine logic and thus constitute formally true statements. These include epistemic, deontic, and temporal logics. Thus, where "K_a" reads "a knows that," instances of

8. $K_a\,P \supset P$

are formal truths.

Semantically True Statements

Semantic truths are statements true not just by virtue of their logical form but by virtue of the meaning of certain nonlogical expressions they contain:

9. All bachelors are unmarried,

is the standard paradigm. Such semantic truths are not formally valid, but as is well recognized, they may be transformed into logical truths via semantic analysis of certain nonlogical terms occurring in them. Thus, we may transform (9) into the formal truth

10. All unmarried adult males are unmarried.[1]

Besides analyzing monadic concepts, we may recognize semantic truths by reflecting on the meaning of binary relations.

11. No one is taller than himself or herself.
12. If $\Delta A \simeq \Delta B$, then $\Delta B \simeq \Delta A$.
13. If $a \leq b$ and $b \leq c$, then $a \leq c$.

Metalinguistic statements indicating that certain formal or semantical truths are true, indeed logically or semantically true, can be classed under semantic truths.

14. "All politicians are motivated by self-interest and Jones is a politician" entails "Jones is motivated by self-interest."
15. All instances of "$(\forall x)Fx \lor (\exists x)\sim Fx$" are logically true.

Why may we count these statements as semantic truths? Consider their object language counterparts:

14'. If all politicians are motivated by self-interest and Jones is a politician, then Jones is motivated by self-interest.
15'. Either everything is conscious or something fails to be conscious.

One who can see that (14') and (15') are formally true, can see that (14) and (15) are true by virtue of those conditions and the meaning of "entails," "is logically true," and the device of quotation.

Conceptually True Statements

We may identify a number of other necessarily true statements whose truth depends not on a semantic analysis of nonlogical concepts but on other conceptual relations, in particular conceptual implications. We may call these conceptual truths. For example, from the fact that something is red, we may infer that it is colored. From the fact that something is an event, we may infer that it happened at some time or other. Hence,

16. Anything red is colored.
17. Any event occurred at some time or other.

are necessary truths. The first is true by virtue of a determinate/determinable implication; the second, by virtue of an implication between a category and its determinable essential properties.[2] But it is not obvious that the semantic analysis of concepts that "reduced" (9) to a formal logical truth is operative in recognizing these implications. Is "being colored" a conjunct of "being red," the way "being unmarried" is a conjunct of "being a bachelor"? Can "event" be semantically analyzed in a way to show that "occurring at some time or other" is a conjunct?

Mathematical Statements

In Chapter 5, we presented the null set axiom and the axiom of pairs, statements of mathematical constructibility, as examples of truths of reason that are not analytic statements. But although much of mathematics can be reduced to set theory, we would be remiss if we did not illustrate the class of mathematical statements with simple truths of arithmetic calculation such as:

18. $2 + 3 = 5$

or such truths of the class calculus as

19. $A \cap B = B \cap A.$

Metaphysical Statements

By recognizing statements of set-theoretic constructibility as truths of reason, we may gain insight into why at least certain metaphysical statements should count as truths of reason. Recall the examples

20. No natural numbers are colored.
21. No object can have a property without existing.

Part of learning a language is learning rules of syntax, or generative grammar in Chomsky's terminology, which are rules of construction. One may put the vocabulary of the language together in some, but only some, ways to construct complete well-formed sentences of that language. So knowledge of the generative rules, that is, principles of constructibility, allows us not only to generate sentences but to recognize constructions as either legitimate or illegitimate. Now consider (20). Clearly this reflects a principle of constructibility, better a prohibition on certain constructions. Color properties cannot be ascribed to natural numbers. Likewise, (21) indicates a prohibition on certain constructions. We cannot ascribe a property to what does not exist. Notice that both of these are statements of necessity. Having surveyed these subclasses of necessary statements, can we still maintain that reason is the personal source of our beliefs expressed by such statements? We turn to that question in the next section. We want to conclude this section by considering a possible objection to the classification we have just presented.

Quine's Objection to This Classification

Our discussion here and in Chapter 5 recognizes the analytic/synthetic distinction, something Quine inveighs against. We must consider and counter these objections. Quine has no problem identifying logical truths. These are the statements that remain true under all substitutions of their nonlogical components. But he finds what we have called semantic truths distinctly problematic.[3] Here truth is dependent not merely on form but on the meaning of certain nonlogical expressions. The thrust of Quine's critique is that we cannot make proper sense of the concept of meaning. If one says that semantic truths can be transformed into logical truths by replacing certain expressions with their synonyms, Quine replies that synonymy is distinctly problematic and philosophical attempts at explication all are wanting.

To those who would say that synonymy is a matter of definition, Quine would ask whence these definitions? "How do we find that 'bachelor' is defined as 'unmarried man'? Who defined it thus, and when?" (1961b, p. 24). We cannot appeal to dictionary definitions. The lexicographer is making an empirical report based on language usage. Presumably, his report records a relation of synonymy, and so "cannot be taken as the ground of the synonymy" (1961b, p. 24).

Another suggestion proposes that synonymy be understood in terms of interchangeability. If in all contexts, I can replace one expression by another *salva veritate*, then those two expressions are synonymous. But we cannot insist that two expressions be substitutable in *all* contexts *salva veritate*. Substitution of synonyms within quotation will in general fail. While "'Ewe' has three letters" is true, "'Female sheep' has three letters" certainly is not. But Quine admits that there is one apparent avenue of easy repair here. We can look at contexts of quotation as forming new, indivisible words. So the occurrence of "ewe" in "'ewe'" is fragmentary, and substitutivity *salva veritate* does not apply to word fragments. But, Quine objects, "Interchangeability *salva veritate* is meaningless until relativized to a language whose extent is specified in relevant respects" (1961b, p. 30). In a purely extensional language, two predicates with the same extension are interchangeable *salve veritate* but need not be cognitively synonymous. Substitutivity *salva veritate* then is not a sufficient condition for synonymy. Quine admits that substitutivity *salva veritate* relative to an intensional language, one that contains the modality "necessarily" at least, is a sufficient condition for synonymy. But, does not "necessarily *A*" mean that "*A*" is analytic? Our attempt to understand synonymy in terms of substitutivity *salva veritate* is circular. But we can clearly protest against Quine at this point. "Necessarily *A*" means that "'*A*' is true in all possible worlds." This characterization makes no reference to analyticity. So we find that Quine's charge here cannot be sustained.

We must ask a more fundamental question. Why do we need to explicate synonymy in other terms at all? Do we need such an explication to recognize synonymy? As Quinton points out, "'Synonymous' means the

same as 'means the same as' and the latter is no philosopher's techni-
cality but a perfectly familiar expression" (1967, p. 126). Do we not in
many cases have a firm grasp of the notion of synonymy and how to apply
it? Why cannot synonymy or sameness of meaning be taken as primitive,
cases of synonymy open to intuitive recognition? What considerations
so rebut the intelligibility of this notion that the burden of proof is on
those who claim its legitimacy to establish that it is intelligible? To say
that semantic truths are true by virtue of the meanings of their nonlogical expressions, that is, they can be transformed into logical truths by
replacing synonyms with synonyms, is not mysterious. Given this, we find
no problem with delineating the subclass of semantic truths in the class
of analytic truths in general. Objections to our classification on the basis
of questioning the analytic/synthetic distinction we find unconvincing,
for we find Quine's objections to synonymy not convincing.

6.2 NECESSARILY TRUE STATEMENTS AND REASON

The hallmark of coming to believe a statement *a priori* is coming to believe not only that the statement is true but necessarily true. (Compare
Plantinga 1993b, p. 106.) Now to come to believe a statement *a priori* is
to come to believe it through reason, as "Reason is the faculty whereby
we learn of what is possible and necessary" (Plantinga 1993b, p. 105).
As we noted in Section 5.4, reason can form both basic and inferred beliefs. Forming basic beliefs is an expression of *a priori* intuition. Forming
inferred beliefs is the operation of deduction. *A priori* intuition and deduction then can be seen as two subfaculties of reason (compare Plantinga
1993b, p. 107). Because we are concerned with basic premise acceptability and so basic beliefs, we can set aside deduction here.

Is *a priori* intuition then the personal mechanism that generates basic
beliefs expressed by the various types of necessary statements we have
identified? Let us review our catalogue. We need to show that someone
who comes to comprehend a necessarily true statement comes both to
believe it and to believe that it is necessarily true. Given how we have
framed the question, our answer is straightforward. To come to understand a truth-functional tautology, at least one not prohibitively complex,
one must come to understand both the truth-conditions of the truth-
functional connectives it contains and that these conditions determine
the truth of this particular tautology. But once one understands that,
one comes to believe both that the statement is true and that given any
combination of truth-values (i.e., given any possible world) the statement

will remain true, that is, that it is necessarily true. This reasoning can be repeated for the other types of formally true statements we have considered – first-order logical truths, higher-order logical truths, truths of modal logic of various sorts. Once one understands the truth-conditions of the logical expressions such statements contain and that the truth of the statements is determined by those conditions, one believes both that the statement is true and cannot be otherwise.

For semantically true statements, we need only add that coming to understand the statement involves not only coming to understand the truth-conditions of any logical expressions it may contain but also coming to understand the meaning of certain of its nonlogical expressions. Once one understands the logical form of "All bachelors are unmarried" and that "bachelor" means "unmarried adult male," one sees that the statement is true and *has* to be true. Likewise, once one understands the meaning of "strictly less than," one understands that the relation is irreflexive and thus that "No natural number is strictly less than itself" is both true and necessarily true (given that one understands the logical expressions in this statement). Likewise, for conceptual truths, part of understanding the meaning of a determinate concept is to understand that it falls under a certain determinable. Can one properly understand the meaning of "yellow" without understanding that yellow is a color? But once one understands this, one understands that anything which has the determinate property also has and must have the corresponding determinable.

Turning to mathematical statements, notice that once one understands the meaning of intersection, such statements as "$A \cap B = B \cap A$" reduce to semantic truths. What may we say of statements of arithmetic calculation, such as "$2 + 3 = 5$"? One may argue that one learns the meaning of arithmetic addition by abstraction from performing operations of physical addition. But once that meaning is learned, one sees that elementary statements of calculation are true and cannot be otherwise. Ross takes this view when he says, "We find by experience that this couple of matches and that couple make four matches, that this couple of balls on a wire and that couple make four balls: and by reflection on these and similar discoveries we come to see that it is of the nature of two and two to make four" (1930, pp. 32–33).[4]

What shall we say of such statements of mathematical constructibility as the null set axiom or the axiom of pairs – that there exists a set with no elements or that given any two elements, the set containing those two and just those two elements exists? Although "collection" is a mathematically primitive notion, through experiences of collecting one certainly comes to associate a meaning with this expression. Certainly a connotation of this meaning is that collections may be of different sizes. Now although this may require a refinement of our sense of the meaning of "collection," we may certainly allow that as a limiting case, we may have a collection with nothing in it. But once we see this, do we not see it true that there is at least one collection with no elements and that such a collection could be "formed" in any possible world? We see the truth, indeed the necessary truth, of the null set axiom. Likewise, when we understand that the mathematical notion of collection abstracts from physical limitations, we "see" that given any two things, we may collect them together, that is, we may form the collection consisting of the two of them, that is, we see that the axiom of pairs is true and we may see that its truth is not conditional upon any contingent fact. We come to believe the truth, indeed the necessary truth, of the set-theoretic axioms as principles of mathematical constructibility when once we understand, in a suitably abstract way, the meaning of "collection."

Finally, turning to those metaphysical statements that we count as broadly logically necessary, we have already pointed out that understanding such statements involves understanding principles of or restrictions on constructibility. To understand the concept of natural number and the concept of color is to understand that color concepts cannot be attributed to natural numbers, that is, that this is not *possible*. Likewise, to understand what it is to have a property is to understand that this presupposes existence. Again, once one understands the meaning of the concepts involved, which involves apprehending at some level the corresponding principles of constructibility, one comes to believe both the truth and the necessary truth of these metaphysical statements. Given our survey of the types of necessary statements, we have seen that in each case, when we come to believe them in a basic way through a personal source, that source is *a priori* intuition. Is this source presumptively reliable?

6.3 IS THERE A PRESUMPTION OF RELIABILITY FOR *A PRIORI* INTUITION?

Showing that there is a presumption of reliability for *a priori* intuition might seem totally straightforward. Indeed, there might hardly seem to be anything to show here. As we indicated in the last section, basic truths of reason have the feature that when we come to understand them, we come to believe not only that they are true but that they are necessarily true. By virtue of this recognition, we have internal access to these basic truths of reason. We can "see" their truth directly. Alternatively, we could say that these truths are *self-evident*. As Kruger points out, analytic statements in particular are called self-evident, "not because it would be difficult to disbelieve them but because they literally contain their own evidence" (1975, p. 141). He adds that statements are analytic because "analyzing their form or meaning enables us to tell if they are true or false" (1975, endnote 6). But if *a priori* intuition generates beliefs whose truth, indeed necessary truth, we can directly apprehend, then we need not justify that it is presumptively reliable. It *is* reliable, thus *a fortiori* presumptively reliable.

Our discussion in the last section has illustrated how *a priori* intuition generated self-evident beliefs. Surely claims such as

1. Everything is identical with itself.
2. Any proposition implies itself.
3. No proposition can be both true and false.
4. Either a proposition or its negation is true.

are self-evident. However, one may object that some apparently self-evident propositions turn out far from being necessarily true to be actually necessarily false. Frege's Comprehension Principle

5. For every property, there is a set that contains all and only those things of which the property is true.

is a prime example. It certainly seems intuitively obvious, self-evident that given any property, we can form the set of just those things having that property, of which the property is true. But should the property be "$x \notin x$" we may derive a contradiction straightforwardly, as Russell showed. So apparently *a priori* intuition is not totally reliable. In light of this, what may we say about its presumptive reliability?

We concede that *a priori* intuition is not totally reliable, but we do not concede that it fails to be presumptively reliable or that our considerations fail to show it presumptively reliable. A proposition like Frege's Comprehension Axiom that involves quantification over properties and asserts existence of sets is surely making a less self-evident claim than any proposition asserting elementary truths of arithmetic, simple tautologies, or straightforward semantic truths. Classically, Euclid's Fifth Postulate, making a claim that under certain conditions two straight lines will intersect if extended far enough, was thought less self-evident than the other four. Is it really self-evident that this intersection will occur? But if one *is* utterly convinced of the truth and necessity of a claim which one has apprehended through *a priori* intuition, if the claim indeed is self-evident, why should he question the reliability of his *a priori* intuition in the absence of specific evidence or argumentation that in this case his intuition was unreliable?

Indeed, this would seem to be the proper attitude in general to take toward the statements for which *a priori* intuition vouches, for such statements ordinarily come with some sense of conviction. As we indicated in Chapter 3, sense perception is one of our belief-generating mechanisms. Now there is a presumption for sense perception. This is not to say that perception is totally reliable. But that perception could on occasion generate mistaken beliefs does not undercut its general presumption of reliability. It does not mean that in general it fails to be trustworthy. So likewise, that *a priori* intuition may on occasion generate a belief in a proposition which is not self-evident and may even be false does not undercut the presumption in its favor, a presumption for which there is ample justification in the general self-evidence of the beliefs it generates.

7

Descriptions and Their Belief-Generating Mechanisms

Our goal in this chapter is first to identify the various personal mechanisms that generate basic beliefs that are descriptions and then to discuss whether and under what circumstances each of these mechanisms is presumptively reliable, and what grounds that presumption. Our first step again will be to determine what types of descriptions there are. For each type, we proceed to ask what personal mechanisms generate basic descriptive beliefs of that type. This is our project in the next section. In subsequent sections we shall discuss the presumptive reliability of each of the mechanisms identified.

7.1 WHAT TYPES OF DESCRIPTIONS ARE THERE?

Let us begin by looking at some intuitive examples of descriptions:

1. A bus is passing my office window.
2. The house across the street is painted white.
3. I have a pain in my right leg.
4. The last time my friends were over for dinner I served chicken.
5. I felt a curious sensation of warmth when the medication was injected.
6. The program will come on in a half-hour.
7. The sun will rise tomorrow.
8. During the second week of January, thirty homeless persons were found dead on the streets of New York.
9. Fifty percent of the voters polled said they disapproved of the president's job performance.

10. Fifty percent of the voting population disapproves of the president's job performance.
11. All swans are white.
12. None of the children in the room have brought their lunches.

These examples illustrate the various types of descriptions. The distinction of reports from generalizations dividing statements (1)–(8) from (9)–(12) is principal. Reports may concern particular events or conditions, either present, past, or future, witness (1)–(7). (8), by contrast, summarizes what could have been presented in a number of reports of particular events. It is a summary report. (9) and (10) both present statistical generalizations. Whereas (9) confines itself just to reporting the results of a poll, (10) extrapolates to the entire voting population. (11) and (12), by contrast, present universal generalizations. We understand (11) to present an accidental universal generalization concerning an open class, whereas (12) involves a finite, delimited class.

Seeing what mechanisms are requisite to generating beliefs expressed by these examples of reports is straightforward. Remember that we are concerned here just with personal basic belief-generating mechanisms. Statement (1) reports on a present event in the external world, whereas statement (2) reports on a present condition. We come to hold such beliefs through perception, being appeared to in a certain way through one or more of our five senses. By contrast, pain in my leg as reported in (3) is an event or condition internal to me. This difference is sometimes highlighted terminologically. Although descriptions of external events are called reports, descriptions of internal events or conditions are called avowals (see Coady 1992, pp. 63ff). If we understand sense perception to generate beliefs just about the external world, then beliefs expressed by avowals are generated by a further mechanism. Let us call it introspection. However, although introspection generates beliefs about what is internal to us, it does not follow that all such beliefs are generated through introspection. Not all beliefs about my self will be descriptions. Consider: "My need of the approval of others led me to forget completely the criticism I planned to make." As a statement of psychological causation, this statement is an interpretation, albeit an interpretation of some facts recognized introspectively rather than through perception.

Statements (4) and (5) introduce a further mechanism. When I recall what I served for dinner the last time my friends were over, I am not perceiving now what I served then nor am I introspecting my current internal states. I am remembering what I perceived earlier. Likewise, when I recall certain internal states that I have experienced, I am remembering what I introspected earlier. Thus, we need to admit memory as an additional belief-generating mechanism for descriptions.

There is still at least one class of reports for which we have not found a belief-generating mechanism – descriptions concerning the unobserved, in particular future events, such as (6) and (7). We follow Plantinga in saying that the belief-generating mechanism here is induction as a form of inference. Beliefs about unobserved events then are not basic. This is easy to appreciate with both our examples. How would I come to believe that a program would come on in a half hour, say at 7:00 P.M.? Presumably I already believe that 7:00 P.M. is the announced time of the program. Presumably I also believe, say through perceiving my watch, that the time is now approximately 6:30 P.M.. Putting these two pieces of information together clearly generates by inference my belief that the program will come on in a half-hour. Hence, we need not seek for a basic belief-generating mechanism for reports such as (6) or (7).

How might one come to believe the summary report (8) that during the second week of January, thirty homeless persons were found dead on the streets of New York? If one read such a report in the newspaper, one could form the belief as basic. But here the mechanism is interpersonal, taking the media's word. Is taking one's word necessary for generating any belief of a summary report? Consider:

13. Over the past two weeks, the cellar has been flooded six times.

As a report of what one has experienced recently, this belief could be the product of perception and memory.

14. The twenty-five rosebushes that received that fertilizer all bloomed extensively.

Certainly one could perceive giving fertilizer to a particular rosebush and remember that these twenty-five were the ones fertilized. One could perceive that each of these twenty-five bushes bloomed extensively, and one could combine these beliefs in memory. Although our examples involve just perception and memory, it is easy to see that introspection might be involved in the generation of certain summary reports. Summary reports, insofar as they involve just the personal belief-generating mechanisms, do not require us to introduce any further mechanism.

Turning from reports to generalizations, the contrast between (9) and (10) obviously marks the difference between a statistical summary of the results of a poll and a statistical extrapolation from those results. As an extrapolation, (10) then is an inferred, not a basic belief. How might one come to believe (9)? Clearly, perception, memory, and most likely taking one's word would be involved. But this presents us with no further belief-generating mechanisms. Because (11) ultimately rests also on an extrapolation from experience, it is an inferred belief. Because (12) concerns a finite and closed set, one comes to believe it as one comes to believe a summary report.

One might argue that we have ignored one descriptive belief-generating mechanism at this point. Consider the statements

15. Sofie feels very happy.
16. John was certainly angry last night.

Such statements make reports about external conditions or events, pertaining to the minds of others. What faculty generates our beliefs about the occurrent thoughts and feelings of other persons? Plantinga suggests an additional faculty called extrospection (see 1993b, p. 42). But do we need to recognize a *separate* faculty? How may we come to believe someone else has a certain feeling? We may be told so. But then our belief is generated through taking someone's word and is a received, not a personally initiated belief. Alternatively, we may observe certain behavioral signs of the feeling and infer from our belief that the persons is exhibiting those signs that the person is experiencing that particular feeling. But then the belief is inferred and not basic. But lastly, we may pass from observing these signs, from being appeared to in a certain signlike way, directly to the belief that the person has these feelings. The belief, then, is not inferred. I do not believe we need to recognize a faculty of extrospection that generates such beliefs, given a suitable understanding of perception. We shall argue for this claim explicitly in the next section, when we discuss perception and natural signs.

Hence, three personal mechanisms may be involved in generating basic descriptive beliefs, perception, introspection, and memory. In our unsystematic survey of belief-generating mechanisms in Chapter 3, we pointed out that presumptions for perception and memory were generally recognized. Introspection would seem to deal with matters with which we have internal and thus direct access. Are these three mechanisms then presumptively reliable and how may we assure ourselves of this? What may we say of perception?

7.2 PERCEPTION AND ITS PRESUMPTION

Because our preliminary survey of principles of presumption indicates that perception is presumptively reliable, the issue here is justifying that claim. As we saw in Chapter 3, Reid's commonsense philosophy indicates how we may proceed. His procedure involves treating the various senses separately beginning with smelling, perhaps the simplest to analyze. In smelling we are conscious of a sensation understood as a purely mental event or phenomenon. But by virtue of a power of our mind, an aspect of our constitution (an expression of our design plan, to use Plantinga's terminology), which Reid calls *suggestion*, this sensation refers beyond itself. It is a sign of something further which it suggests.

If we refer to the sensation as a smell or odor, we must be careful to keep in mind that we mean just that, not the external quality of a body. I believe we can give the following account of how Reid sees the two related and how by virtue of the sensation we may perceive the external body and its corresponding quality. When we become aware of a sensation, this change "suggests to us the notion of a cause, and compels our belief of its existence" (Beanblossom and Lehrer 1983, p. 25). We are not content simply with this suggestion. We find through experience that when a certain physical object is present, we experience this sensation. When the object is absent or removed, the sensation ceases. On the basis of this experience of constant conjunction, we identify the object as the cause of the sensation. Here Reid says, we are using the term cause "not in a strict and philosophical sense, as if the feeling were really effected or produced by that cause, but in a popular sense; for the mind is satisfied if there is a constant conjunction between them" (Beanblossom and Lehrer 1983, p. 27). But Reid indicates that we go further. "Without inquiring further, we attribute to the cause some vague and indistinct notion of power or virtue to produce the effect" (Beanblossom and Lehrer 1983, p. 27).

Reid is careful to point out that the sensation of smell and the power or virtue to which it corresponds are quite distinct. He denies that it is part of the commonsense notion that the qualities or features of the sensation of smell are likewise qualities or features of the virtue or power in the body producing the smell. This is significant for clarifying what the presumption for the reliability of sense perception involves or entails, not only for smelling but also for sense perception in general. Presumption of reliability does not entail a presumption that the features of how we are appeared to, of our sensations, are also features of the qualities, powers, or virtues that produce or occasion those sensations. Presumption of reliability does not entail a presumption of naive realism. We presume nothing about the nature of these external qualities in themselves but only that they exist and make us and other sentient beings feel or have the correlated sensations. By virtue of our constitution, the sensation – at least the sensation of smell – is a *natural sign* of this quality or power.

It is crucial for understanding the argument for the presumptive reliability of perception that we be clear about Reid's notion of a natural sign. Notice that according to Reid's conception, it is simply by virtue of our constitution that the sensation of smell is a sign of the cause having a power or quality to produce that sensation. This is not something we learn. Through experience, we may come to identify a certain body as that cause, but seeing the sensation as being a sign of a cause and its power is not learned. Nature has endowed us with the capacity to view the sensation with this significance just as nature by virtue of the quality has endowed the cause with the power to produce the sensation. The significance of the sign is a consequence of the natural endowment of our constitution. Suppose this sensation is the scent of a rose. As a natural sign, then, it is a sign just of the power that produces it. By virtue of this sensation, we come to have a perceptual belief that the body has this smell. Notice that just by virtue of this sensation we do *not* come to believe that the body is a rose, that is, an instance of that natural kind. Should the sensation, being appeared to rose-scent-ly, have this further significance, that would be by virtue of our having learned that it has this further significance. We would then have what Reid calls an acquired perception of the rose. We shall discuss acquired perception and its presumption after discussing the presumption for original perception. This analysis of smelling Reid applies to tasting and hearing also. Again in each we may distinguish the sensation, which is purely mental, from the quality, power, or virtue in the body that produces or occasions that sensation.

Two senses remain, touch and seeing. Of touch, Reid says, "we perceive not one quality only, but many, and those of very different kinds. The chief of them are heat and cold, hardness and softness, roughness and smoothness, figure, solidity, motion, and extension" (Beanblossom and Lehrer 1983, p. 35). Heat and cold are secondary qualities, and the same analysis for smelling applies here also. Hardness and softness are qualities actually in bodies. However, we may distinguish these qualities of bodies from the sensations they produce in the course of nature and that are their natural signs. Qualities and sensations do not resemble each other. "The firm cohesion of the parts of a body, is no more like that sensation by which I perceive it to be hard, than the vibration of a sonorous body is like the sound I hear" (Beanblossom and Lehrer 1983, p. 39). However, our constitution conveys us from the sensation of hardness to the corresponding quality in bodies. "The notion of hardness in bodies, as well as the belief of it, are got...by an original principle of our nature, annexed to that sensation which we have when we feel a hard body" (Beanblossom and Lehrer 1983, p 43–4). What Reid has said of hardness he believes can be repeated, *mutatis mutandis,* of softness, roughness, smoothness, figure, and motion (Beanblossom and Lehrer 1983, p. 46).

Finally, concerning seeing, Reid again indicates that we must distinguish the appearance or sensation from what, that is, the external quality, that sensation suggests. As touch reveals various kinds of qualities, so does seeing. Reid feels "we must distinguish the appearance of colour from the appearance of extension, figure, and motion" (Beanblossom and Lehrer 1983, p. 62). Color, for Reid, is a secondary quality and there is no intrinsic connection between the appearance of color and the quality in the body producing that appearance. Figure and extension, for Reid, are primary qualities. However, it would not be accurate to represent Reid as saying that certain features of visual sensations suggest or signify these primary qualities. For vision, the relation between how we are appeared to and these primary qualities is more complicated. Reid distinguishes between the tangible figure and the visible figure of an object. We might call the tangible figure the real figure. It is a property or feature of an external physical object. If an object is actually circular, its tangible figure is circular. But if a circular object is placed at an angle to the eye, it will appear as an ellipse. This is the visible figure and, as Reid points out, from the real figure and the angle, we can calculate mathematically the visible elliptical figure.

This visible figure is not a quality or property of a visual sensation, for Reid. It is what would appear on the surface of a hollow sphere with the eye at the center should there be a projection on that sphere of the real figure. It would be a two-dimensional representation or reflection of that object. See Figure 7.1. To clarify this notion further, Reid defines the notion of the position of an object (or of a point on that object) with respect to the eye. The position is determined by the angle formed by a straight line drawn from that object or point to the center of the eye. Taking a line drawn at a 0° angle from the center of the eye as a base, different objects or different points will have different positions depending on the different angles formed by lines drawn from those points to the eye and the base line. See Figure 7.1.

How then do we come to have beliefs about the figure and extension of objects, if our belief-generating mechanism does not take some feature of our sensations as input in producing such beliefs as output? Although

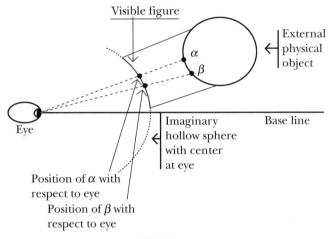

FIGURE 7.1

in Figure 7.1, the sphere on which the external object is projected is imaginary and so the visible figure itself is in a sense imaginary, there will be a projection on the retina. Reid calls this the *material impression* (Beanblossom and Lehrer 1983, p. 75). It is not a sensation or anything mental but an actual physical event or condition. According to Reid, this material impression suggests the color and position of some external object (Beanblossom and Lehrer 1983, p. 75). "I am not conscious of anything that can be called *sensation*, but the sensation of colour. The position of the coloured thing is no sensation; but it is by the laws of my constitution presented to the mind along with the colour, without any additional sensation" (Beanblossom and Lehrer 1983, p. 74, italics in original). It is this material impression, and not any sensation or mental impression, which suggests visible figure, and is thus the input in forming our beliefs about the figure and position of physical objects. It is by virtue of this material impression, then, that the mind is acquainted with visible figure even though there is no mental visual impression or sensation of visible figure. But visible figure in turn is "a sign of the tangible figure and situation of bodies" (Beanblossom and Lehrer 1983, p. 77). We do not attend to the visible figure but pass on directly to the tangible real figure, and that is what is intended in visual perception.

In all these cases of the various types of sensation, we have been discussing perceiving qualities or powers in objects in the external world by virtue of having sensations (or with visual perception material impressions), which by virtue simply of our constitution and not of what we have learned are signs of those qualities or powers. We have been dealing with what Reid calls natural signs and original perception. Why is original perception presumptively reliable? For Reid, it is by virtue "*of the original constitution of our minds*" (Beanblossom and Lehrer 1983, p. 41, italics added) that natural signs are signs of powers or qualities in the external world. As we have seen, reading the sensation as suggesting a cause in the external world is part of our constitution. We link that suggestion to an object through experience. But here, we meet with another principle of our constitution. When we have found things connected in the past, we believe they will continue to be connected. So if experience presents us with a constant conjunction between some object and a sensation, it accords with our constitution to believe that what the sensation signifies is that object. "It is by this general principle of our nature, that, when two things have been found connected in time past, the appearance of the one produces the belief of the other" (Beanblossom and Lehrer 1983, p. 99). Hence, to deny a presumption of reliability for original perception is to deny our common sense. It is to go against our constitution. From the epistemic perspective, there is no more need to argue that there is a presumption for the reliability of perception – original perception at least – than to argue that there is a presumption of innocence from the legal perspective. This is a basic or first principle.

Furthermore, consider the results of not affording a presumption to original perception. Then we would not regard our being appeared to in certain ways as evidence for the presence of an object with the power to cause such a sensation in us. Sensations of smell, sound, or color are not evidence of objects producing such sensations. Feelings of softness or hardness are not evidence of bodies with the corresponding qualities. But all of this seems manifestly absurd. To question the general evidential nature of such sensations is to reject common sense. We should be acting against our nature. Indeed, Reid feels this skepticism would be a rebellion impossible to carry out. "My belief is carried along by perception, as irresistibly as my body by the earth" (Beanblossom and Lehrer 1983, p. 85).

Should one still not be persuaded by this argument, considerations from Chapter 3[1] constitute further argumentation for the presumptive reliability of perception. Reid has argued that the skeptic's granting of reliability to introspection and reason but not perception is arbitrary. The internalist rejoinder that only introspection and reason but not perception generate beliefs that are certain confuses infallibility with reliability. Again, that we should trust only such faculties as introspection and reason and not perception because in only the former do we see that the evidence of which we are aware justifies the belief formed, that only here do we see the truth of the general principle that evidence of that sort justifies beliefs of a certain sort, what in Chapter 4 we called the meta-awareness requirement, is again to impose a requirement that cannot be properly justified.[2]

So far, we have discussed original perception only as generating beliefs about the physical world around us. At the end of Section 7.1, we indicated that we also could have perceptual beliefs about other minds, at least about certain of their occurrent states. Our discussion of natural signs has prepared us to understand why such beliefs are perceptual. For given our constitution, as certain sensations may be natural physical signs, so certain sensations may be natural signs of occurrent mental states in others. Reid identifies three basic kinds of natural signs: "modulations of the voice, gestures, and features" (Beanblossom and Lehrer 1983, p. 33). Notice that we perceive these as we would perceive other objects in the external world and their properties and relations. But modulations of the voice, gestures, and features can be quite revelatory of others' occurrent mental states. If we see someone with an angry countenance, is the physical countenance all that we see – or do we "see" that the person is angry? Surely, we may form beliefs about both countenance and mental state and surely also, ordinarily both of these beliefs are basic. We do not form a belief about the countenance and infer from that a belief about the mental state. But this indicates that our constitution contains principles for producing beliefs about the mental states of others on the basis of certain sense appearances. Notice also that we do not learn to interpret the appearance of someone's countenance as a sign of anger, as we learn the meaning of words. The interpretation is part of our constitution. "An infant may be put into a fright by an angry countenance, and soothed again by smiles and blandishments" (Beanblossom and Lehrer 1983, p. 43).

If we count descriptive beliefs about other minds grounded on natural signs as perceptual beliefs, can we still regard original perception as in general presumptively reliable? Surely we can. When we understand that perception produces beliefs about the occurrent states of other minds on the basis of being appeared to by natural signs of those mental states, we see that this employment of our perception is part of our basic constitution. These are basic beliefs from which we reason, and from which we may rightly reason until or unless we have reason to call into question this testimony of our perception.[3]

Besides original perception we also may have acquired or learned perception. This introduces what we may call the developmental nature of perception. Our perceptual belief-generating mechanism involves an interpretive component **IC** consisting of interpretive principles. **IC** is never empty – it will always contain natural principles by virtue of which certain sensations are natural signs. But through experience, **IC** develops to include more principles by virtue of which our sensations may become further signs. Our perceptual belief-generating mechanism does not contain a fixed and final set of principles. The results of these principles or the result of incorporating these principles is that certain ways of being appeared to become what Reid called acquired signs. Suppose I am appeared to rose-scent-ly and come to recognize through experience of constant conjunction that the quality of which this sensation is the natural sign resides in a particular object. Through experiencing the sensation, then, I perceive the object *qua* bearer of this quality or power. But I do not perceive the object as a *rose*, that is, as an instance of this natural kind. For that I would need experience of covariation – to use a concept that will figure prominently in Chapter 8. I would need to experience that a number of signs detected perhaps through various senses cluster together – and thus the qualities or properties they signify cluster together – this cluster of covariant properties or qualities constituting a natural kind given the name of rose in English.

We need to identify another type of acquired perception which Reid does not recognize. Searle argues persuasively in (1969) that besides brute facts (facts about the physical world and about minds – our own or others) we must recognize institutional facts. These are facts whose existence "presupposes the existence of certain human institutions" (1969, p. 51). For example, consider the report that the Metrostars scored three goals in the soccer game yesterday. This does not simply make a statement about certain physical occurrences. If it were not for the rules of soccer defining what constitutes scoring a goal, there could be no scoring of goals in a soccer game. By "institution" Searle understands a system of constitutive rules (1969, p. 51), soccer being a paradigm example. "Constitutive rules do not merely regulate, they create or define new forms of behavior" (1969, p. 33). The rules for a game not only regulate playing the game by indicating what moves are legal, they define what those moves are. Kicking the ball into the net counts as scoring a goal when kicked from within the field. If one is still not convinced that one must recognize institutional facts in addition to physical and personal facts, let one try to describe a soccer game, the behavior and acts of the persons on the field, without any reference to the rules of soccer. Then nothing that happens can be described as moves of soccer or interpreted or understood as such moves. Clearly this falls far short of describing what transpired as a game of soccer (compare Searle 1969, p. 52).

Clearly, just as Searle has shown that we must acknowledge institutional facts, so we must acknowledge institutional perception – a form of acquired perception. One who has learned (certain of) the rules of soccer can see in the basic way that a goal has just been scored. A system of certain sensations is the sign of the scoring of a goal, once the rules of soccer have been incorporated into one's interpretive component **IC**. Institutional perception differs from the acquired perception Reid discusses in that the interpretive principles acquired either are or are derived from the constitutive rules of human institutions, rather than being regularities of nature disclosed through experience.

Can we claim that there is a presumption for acquired perception as there is for original perception? Let us consider acquired physical perception first. Reid makes the following salient point: "The connection between the sign and the thing signified, *is established by nature*" (Beanblossom and Lehrer 1983, p. 91, italics added). We can draw a distinct analogy between original and acquired perception. In original perception, our constitution leads us to interpret our sensations as signs having reference in the external world and experience teaches us to what objects those sensations are connected. Nature has established the connection between sign and thing signified. In acquired perception, again through experience, either our sensations acquire a further significance or what they signify becomes a sign of something further. What we have originally perceived becomes itself a sign. What it has become a sign of may further become a sign. But in all this, the connection, like the connection between sensation and object signified in original perception, is established by experience, that is, by nature. But if there was a presumption for what nature teaches in original perception, why should there not be a presumption for what nature teaches in acquired perception?

I believe we can argue this further and straightforwardly on Reidian lines. Our constitution or design plan includes specifications whereby we expect nature to be uniform and specifications whereby we learn from encountered uniformity. Part of this learning, or the result of this experience, is to acquire further principles of perception. Our perceptual mechanisms contain not only a set of original specifications whereby we generate perceptual beliefs, but the capacity to supplement these specifications. Our perceptual belief-generating specifications may thus grow over time. But this capacity for expansion and the resultant belief-generating specifications are part of our design plan, our constitution. As such, then, there is a presumption of reliability in their favor. This is not to say that some principles of acquired perception cannot be mistaken. But as principles that have been incorporated into our constitution, as specifications that have become part of our perceptual belief-generating mechanism, there is a presumption of reliability in their favor, and thus a presumption for the beliefs perception generates in accord with them, until and unless that presumption is undercut.

In all these cases of acquired perception, it was nature working conjointly with our constitution that led to the development of our perceptual belief-generating mechanism beyond original perception. In institutional perception, by contrast, not nature but learned constitutive rules establish the connections by which one comes to have acquired perceptions. The question for institutional perception then is whether there is a presumption that we have learned the constitutive rules correctly. We should rephrase the question, for clearly we may have learned some constitutive rules quite well and others not at all. The question is when is there a presumption that we have learned a constitutive rule or a system of constitutive rules correctly. Clearly, there are two ways to learn such a rule or system: informally, through trial and error, by engaging in the practice they constitute, or explicitly by encountering some authoritative formulation. Of course, someone might learn a system of rules through a combination of these two approaches, and we expect this may be typical, but that does not raise any further epistemological issue. When will there be a presumption from our point of view that we have learned a constitutive rule or a system of constitutive rules?

Surely we shall recognize that presumption when we can enter into the practice constituted by the rules and our efforts are met with approval and not correction by those we deem competent if not authoritative in that practice. But we need not go this far. Even if we cannot successfully engage in the practice, when we can not only interpret the actions of others according to those rules but when our interpretations meet with general agreement from other competent observers, we may presume that we have learned the rules. If we interpret the trajectory of a soccer ball kicked by a Metrostars player as scoring a goal for the Metrostars and the fans erupt in cheering, we can be confident that we have learned, at least in part, the constitutive rules for scoring a goal in soccer. Certainly it would seem that the burden of proof would be on someone to show us that we did *not* understand the rules. But if there is a presumption that we have learned those constitutive rules, there will be a presumption for our institutional perception made according to those rules.

In this way, we may argue that presuming acquired perception reliable – including institutional as well as physical perception – is well placed. Together with our considerations on original perception, we have an argument for why there is a presumption for the reliability of sense perception in general, as long as, in the case of institutional perception, there is a presumption that we have learned the constitutive rules.

In addition to these "theoretical" considerations, we also may adduce practical or "pragmatic" considerations supporting a presumption for sense perception. We have already noted that Reid is profoundly skeptical that we could simply cast off our perceptual beliefs. They force themselves on us and we cannot choose to live in a state of perceptual agnosticism. But even if we could, what would be the consequence of taking this skeptical stance? It seems we would refuse to accept our perceptual judgments and thus not base our behavior on them. The consequence would be behavior regarded by others as insane. We would go around hurting ourselves until our friends properly put us in restraint! Can we be theoretical skeptics and practical believers? Reid replies, "If a man pretends to be a skeptic with regard to the informations of sense, and yet prudently keeps out of harm's way as other men do, he must excuse my suspicion, that he either acts the hypocrite, or imposes upon himself" (Beanblossom and Lehrer 1983, p. 86).

Cohen also presents a prudential argument in (1992). We should presume in favor of sense perception, we should accept what we perceive absent indications of illusion, and thus grant the presumptive reliability of sense perception, because such acceptance is necessary for us to get on with our lives and even to preserve our lives in some cases. If we perceive immanent danger and have no evidence of perceptual deception, we may need to take evasive action – fast – on this basis. Refusing to accept what is perceived in this situation could have disastrous consequences. So accepting a presumption in favor of perception is certainly prudentially justified.

A moment's reflection should convince us of how impoverished would be our resources for living did we not grant a presumption in favor of the reliability of sense perception. Simply, then, to get on in the world, to have sufficient premises from which to reason, and to pay heed to the "warnings" of our environment, we need to grant that sense perception is presumptively reliable. With this, we rest our case. We have explicated what it means to say that there is a presumption in favor of sense perception and have detailed how the popular recognition of this presumption accords with common sense. Indeed, with Reid, we could call it a first principle, a principle from which we reason but needing no defense.

7.3 THE PRESUMPTIVE RELIABILITY OF INTROSPECTION

There are two primary sorts of beliefs generated by introspection. The first consists of beliefs about the contents of one's mind; the second, beliefs about one's mental operations. Typical of the first kind are claims about how we are appeared to in sense perception – claims about our perceptual sensations – and about our internal feelings, the pleasures and pains we feel within our bodies. I am currently appeared to bluely, hotly, sweetly. Here we are not talking about the objects of perception, which allegedly cause these sensations or appearances, but about the sensations themselves. Likewise the feelings of pleasure or pain, as opposed to any bodily events allegedly causing them, are mental contents.

One might object to regarding pains as mental by pointing out that we frequently ascribe spatial locations to them. But spatial location is not a category of things mental. "I am currently having a pain in my left leg." *Prima facie*, this appears to be talking about something occurring in my body, located in a particular space, and not a content of my mind. But we can easily meet this objection, as Reid makes clear. He would counter that we are here combining in our thought the sensation with its cause. Distinguishing them dissolves the anomaly. The sensation is in the mind. The alleged cause is located in some area in the body. But one may object – I do not just feel pain but pain at a certain location. We reply that we may regard felt location, where the sensations are felt to be, as a property or feature of the sensation. So as one can speak of sharp pains or dull pains, so one can speak of in the left leg pains, in the right arm pains. Regarding these as qualities of sensations or feelings means that we do not assert any relation between the pain and some spatial region. To avoid the appearance of attributing spatial location, one might say instead of "I have a pain in my left leg," "I have a pain-in-my-left-leg." Here location is treated as a phenomenal feature of what is felt, not as a relatum to what is felt. "Pain-in-my-left-leg," "pain-in-my-right-arm" are two different but similar mental contents, not one content modified in different ways.

Besides beliefs about mental contents, we believe we think – perceive, remember, reason. These are active operations of the mind rather than ways in which we are appeared to. But we are conscious of these operations, just as we are conscious of mental contents, and our beliefs that we engage in these operations are also introspective beliefs.

Beliefs about mental contents and mental operations are the two primary types of introspective beliefs, as we have said. But what about an avowal of pain where I mean not just that I am experiencing a sensation qualified in certain ways, but that in addition the cause of this sensation, in some preanalyzed, intuitive sense of cause, is located in a certain region of my body? Is such a belief an introspective belief? Reid would regard the causal belief as a perceptual belief. Just as we perceive external objects, the causes of certain of our perceptual sensations, by means of those sensations, so we may perceive bodily events and conditions by means of bodily sensations. Through painful feelings we perceive disorders. Do we want to count such causal beliefs as perceptual beliefs? I believe that some terminological variation is possible here, but that all we propose is a terminological variation from Reid. Perception is ordinarily understood to be externally directed. We *perceive* objects and events in the external world. By contrast, we say we are *conscious* of things going on in our bodies or of our mental states; we introspect them. So it would make sense to count beliefs about the causes of our bodily sensations as introspective beliefs. All of the beliefs expressed by avowals then count as introspective beliefs for us. But we must remember that introspective beliefs then may concern more than mental contents and operations. Beliefs about bodily events that cause bodily sensations are not beliefs about mental events, but they count as an additional type of introspective belief.

Is introspection presumptively reliable? For beliefs about the contents of one's mind or beliefs about mental operations, this would seem indisputable. Indeed, this would seem to be a limiting case for presumption. For if, while being appeared to redly, I believe that I am now appeared to redly; if while experiencing a pain, I believe I am experiencing a pain; or if while thinking, I believe that I think; what more evidence could I ask for my beliefs and what evidence could possibly rebut them? It would seem that there is a presumption for these introspective beliefs that simply cannot be undercut. We not only believe these claims, we know them to be true. One would be hard put to find a less controversial philosophical thesis.

For Reid, it is a first principle that we should accept those beliefs about our mental contents and operations which introspection generates. We are conscious to some extent of the operations of our mind, and we can direct this consciousness to inspect mental contents and operations, to make them the object of our thought as opposed to the states of affairs they intend. This will heighten our awareness of these contents and operations. But if one doubts what this awareness or consciousness discloses, what can one say to him? "If a man should take it into his head to think or to say that his consciousness may deceive him, and to require proof that it cannot, I know of no proof that can be given him. . . . Every man finds himself under a necessity of believing what consciousness testifies" (Beanblossom and Lehrer 1983, p. 153). But this is to assert that the presumptive reliability of introspection, at least as it generates beliefs concerning mental contents and operations, is a first principle. Not to accept such beliefs would go against our constitution. We are designed to have such beliefs and they constitute basic evidence for us, beliefs from which we reason.

Is there a presumption of reliability for introspective beliefs about the causes of our bodily sensations? As Reid points out, in conceiving of such causes, ordinarily the idea of the sensation and the idea of the cause are welded into one. But then it would seem that we are just as much designed to form these introspective beliefs about the causes of these sensations as we are designed to form beliefs that perceptual sensations are caused by objects or events in the external world. To form these beliefs is a first principle of our constitution and they are therefore as presumptively reliable as perceptual beliefs. Hence, introspection in all its employments is presumptively reliable.

7.4 MEMORY AND ITS PRESUMPTION

The primary employment of memory is to generate beliefs about events or conditions in the past. More specifically, memory beliefs concern what we have witnessed in the past. We do not strictly speaking remember a fact which we did not witness, which we learned about through someone else's word (compare Plantinga 1993b, p. 59–60). To be sure, we may say we remember certain scientific or historical facts that we have not witnessed but have learned of somehow. But in these instances we are speaking of remembering in an extended sense. The question of presumption for the reliability of memory amounts to asking whether there is a presumption that the propositions expressing memory beliefs reliably describe events or conditions in the past, which we have witnessed.

Before addressing this question, we must consider a second type of belief generated by memory, belief in personal identity. Reid in particular stresses this aspect of memory. It might be more accurate to say that belief in a self, a something that experiences, thinks, and acts but is not identical with any experiencing, thinking, or acting (compare Beanblossom and Lehrer 1983, pp. 214–15), a self that persists through time, is jointly generated by introspection and memory. Reid points out that "Our sensations suggest to us a sentient being or mind to which they belong – a being which hath a permanent existence, although the sensations are transient and of short duration" (Beanblossom and Lehrer 1983, p. 43). There is no idea that we meet with which is of this self. It is as if the totality of what we introspect or remember is the trigger for generating this belief. Memory in particular contributes the factor of belief in the duration of self over time. Indeed, memory generates belief in temporal duration. We remember an event as past, that is, as there being some temporal interval between when the event happened and the present moment. But we not only remember the event as past but that *we* somehow witnessed it and thus *existed* at the time of its occurring. But, because my constitution does not generate a belief of me as an intermittently existing self, if I believe I existed *then* and I believe I exist *now*, I believe I persisted through the duration between these two points.

In Chapter 3, we noted that a presumption for memory was included in our unsystematic survey of principles of presumption. What may we say for the presumption of reliability for the mechanism which generates beliefs of these two sorts – beliefs concerning past events and beliefs concerning personal identity? Let us begin with beliefs about the past. Here again, we can argue that it is simply part of our constitution or design plan not only to form beliefs about the past but to accept at least those which are distinct or sufficiently vivid. As Reid puts it, "This belief, which we have from distinct memory, we account real knowledge, no less certain than if it was grounded on demonstration; no man in his wits calls it in question, or will hear any argument against it" (Beanblossom and Lehrer 1983, pp. 207–8). As long as a memory belief is distinct and not hazy, it needs no evidence for its justification, unless there is reason to question the proper functioning of memory on that occasion. That I remembered the past event that is the object of this belief is reason enough, barring evidence that our memory is unreliable in this case, for accepting that the event happened as remembered. In effect, the memory belief is its own justification. Reid sees no necessary connection between the past event remembered and a remembering of it. It is simply part of our constitution, a first principle, to remember and to rely on our memory.

What may we say then about the joint employment of introspection and memory in generating beliefs of personal identity? Is there a presumption for the reliability of these two mechanisms in this joint employment? Again, we can argue that there is such a presumption because to hold such beliefs is a first principle of our constitution. As Reid forcefully puts it:

> If any man should think fit to demand a proof that the thoughts he is successively conscious of, belong to one and the same thinking principle – if he should demand a proof that he is the same person today as he was yesterday, or a year ago – I know no proof that can be given him: he must be left to himself, either as a man that is lunatic, or as one who denies first principles, and is not to be reasoned with. (Beanblossom and Lehrer 1983, p. 154)

It is a necessity of our constitution or design plan to believe in our personal identity. Again, by the very nature of our constitution, there is a presumption of reliability for the mechanism producing beliefs in personal identity. That we are persons who persist through time as the subjects of our experiences, thinkings, and actions is a proposition we may reason from but not a proposition we can reason for or need reason for.

8

Interpretations and Their Modes of Intuition

In Chapter 5, we characterized interpretations as contingent nonevaluative intensional statements and developed their connection with explanations. An interpretation typically seeks to render events or conditions meaningful. This is done by somehow relating events nomically or indicating how some event or some condition is to be explained and thus related nomically to certain explanatory factors. In this chapter, we are attempting to determine, first, whether any interpretations are basic beliefs and, second, whether there is a presumption of reliability for the mechanism or mechanisms generating those basic interpretive beliefs. The connection between interpretations and explanations yields a strategy for proceeding. First, what sorts of explanations are presupposed by interpretations? Second, is there some core concept common to these explanations in terms of which the various types of interpretations can be explicated? Assuming this second question can be answered positively – and we shall argue that it can – we may then properly inquire about what mechanisms generate basic beliefs involving this core concept.

8.1 THREE TYPES OF EXPLANATIONS

As in Chapter 7 we distinguished physical, personal, and institutional perception, and correspondingly physical, personal, and institutional facts, so we may distinguish physical, personal, and institutional explanations. Physical explanations are a subclass of causal explanations. Some event or phenomenon in the physical world is explained in terms of some antecedent physical event or phenomenon and a covering generalization.

1. The match lit because it was struck.

This explanation explicitly appeals to the antecedent striking of the match to explain its lighting. But it appeals implicitly to a generalization that spells out certain conditions for the match to light:

2. If the match were struck with a force of a certain magnitude (or greater), in the presence of oxygen, the match being dry, then it would light.

That the other necessary conditions have also been satisfied is presumed here. We also may refer to physical explanation as inanimate explanation, because it makes no appeal to beliefs, intentions, or purposes of any conscious agent.

The class of physical explanations is wider than just those dealing with the subject matter of physics – mechanics, heat, electricity, light, sound – and includes explanations of features of the material world in general. Also, the generalizations may be statistical rather than universal. Physical regularities in turn may have physical explanations in terms of some wider physical regularity or a physical theory. Statements of these regularities might be included in the corpus of some physical science, although they could be expressed at the level of common sense.

By contrast, personal explanations appeal to the powers, beliefs, mental activities, desires, psychological dispositions, purposes, or intentions of conscious, personal agents (compare Swinburne 1996, pp. 21–22). As we are using the term, personal explanations include what Moore and Parker (1986, pp. 83–86) refer to as psychological explanations. Such explanations seek to explain some action by appealing to the motives or reasons of the agent. (Compare Moore and Parker 1986, p. 83.) Those dealing with motives are also causal explanations. If one said that

3. The accused murdered the victim out of a consuming anger brought about by years of taunting.

we are not explaining an action as intentionally chosen to accomplish some goal but, rather, as causally resulting from certain psychological "springs of action" (compare Nagel 1961, p. 19). We are dealing with motives rather than reasons. Such explanations also appeal at least implicitly to covering generalizations, albeit of a more statistical or probabilistic nature than those which may frequently appear in physical explanations.

The following might be an approximation:

4. In general, if one were to have been provoked to anger by the behavior of another individual, one would eventually react in violent retaliation against that individual.

To have a reason for some action is to have some justification for the action, either in itself or as instrumental to some further goal. To have reasons presupposes having intentions. For example,

5. King Henry VIII sought to annul his marriage to Catherine of Aragon in order to remarry and father a male heir. (Compare Nagel 1961, p. 19.)

This explanation is personal, attempting to render King Henry VIII's action understandable in light of his reasons for it, which involve goals he has consciously intended and chosen. Personal explanations appealing to reasons also invoke covering explanations, again of a statistical or probabilistic nature.

With these physical and personal explanations contrast

6. Jones received $10,000 because his late grandmother bequeathed him that amount of money in her will.

This appeals to the defeasible generalization:

7. If one were bequeathed a certain amount of money, one would receive that money upon the demise of the person making the bequest.

Unlike physical or personal explanations, this generalization is a matter of statute law. We have then a legal explanation.

The covering generalizations appealed to in legal explanations differ in one central respect from those in physical and personal explanations. They are not matters ultimately of empirical discovery but are rather given in or derivable from some body of statute law, an institution or a facet of an institution. One does not discover that signing a contract creates legal rights and obligations the way one discovers that signing the contract lowers the amount of ink left in the pen. One rather comes to understand that the law has certain provisions. We shall develop the epistemological import of this distinction in Section 8.5. Legal explanations are a paradigm of those appealing to institutional covering generalizations. There are others. A classification scheme for some branch of taxonomy is an institution. One could explain why an individual is of some genus by pointing out that the individual is a member of a species that the taxonomic scheme subsumes under the genus. This is explanation via classification.

Do we need to recognize a further type of explanation in terms of chance? We do not. To say that an event happened by chance is not to invoke some mysterious entity called "chance" whose unique powers somehow explain the event's occurrence. "Chance" has several senses. To say that an event happened by pure, ontological, or absolute chance is to say that it was completely undetermined causally and thus has no explanation. To speak of chance in an epistemological or relative sense is to claim that some event could not have been predicted, at least on the basis of the information available to us or to some other given party. A chance meeting of friends is not inexplicable in terms of physical and personal factors, but before the meeting neither friend could have predicted it upon the basis of his or her current information.[1] Hence, we need consider chance no further in connection with explanation.

Is there something common to physical, personal, and institutional explanations in terms of which we can explicate interpretations in a way which illumines the problem of whether any interpretations are ever properly basic beliefs under certain circumstances? We address that question in the next section.

8.2 EXPLANATIONS AND SUBJUNCTIVES

Each of the covering generalizations appealed to in our examples of explanations in Section 8.1 is a universally quantified subjunctive conditional. This is not peculiar to our examples but true of explanations in general in so far as they appeal to causal laws. This is standardly recognized. It is characteristic of causal laws, both physical and personal, to support subjunctive conditionals.[2]

As Burks indicates in (1951), the subjunctive conditionals appealed to in causal explanations may not be full statements of causal laws understood to assert that their antecedents are causally sufficient conditions for their consequents. Assertions of sufficient causal conditions claim a stronger connection between p and q than what an ordinary language subjunctive of the form "if it were the case that p, it would be the case that q" might be understood to assert. Thus, the subjunctive

1. If a beam of electrons were moving in a vacuum perpendicular to a magnetic field, then that beam would be deflected.

could be understood as asserting a defeasible connection between the antecedent and the consequent, one that could fail should the beam be subject to other forces. Burks introduces a binary connective "*c*" to represent causal implication. "*p c q*" asserts that *p* is a causally sufficient condition for *q*. He thus understands the symbolization

> 2. $(\forall x)(\text{E}x \, c \, \text{D}x)$

to represent

> 1'. If a beam of electrons were moving in a vacuum perpendicular to a magnetic field *and subject to no other forces*, than that beam would be deflected. (Compare 1951, pp. 367–8.)

This suitably qualified subjunctive is a causal law. But notice that this full causal law is also expressed by a subjunctive conditional, one whose antecedent is a conjunction. Notice also that in appealing to a subjunctive in a causal explanation that omits the qualification under which the subjunctive would state a causal law, we tacitly assume that these qualifications hold. Thus, if one were explaining why a particular beam of electrons had been deflected by pointing out that it had been moving in a vacuum perpendicular to a magnetic field, one would have assumed that no other forces were operating in this particular case. Hence, it is appropriate to refer to the subjunctives appealed to in causal explanations as causal subjunctives, whether or not they express causal laws without qualification.

As we suggested in Section 8.1, personal explanations that appeal to the consciously chosen goals or intentions of some agent may still involve covering laws expressible through subjunctives. We may not want to classify such subjunctives as causal propositions, at least on every occasion. Consider the following example based on material ultimately from Lewis Carroll.[3] Suppose the owner of a barbershop lays down certain rules:

> 3. If Carr and Allen are out, then Brown must be in.
> 4. If Allen goes out, Brown must accompany him.

Now, if Carr, Allen, and Brown all obey these rules, certain subjunctives will be true.

> 3'. If Carr and Allen were out, Brown would be in.
> 4'. If Allen were to go out, Brown would go out with him.

Clearly, we could invoke these subjunctives or universals that support these subjunctives in giving explanations. But assuming libertarian agency, an assumption we do not wish to foreclose to those who would give personal explanations, and thus allowing that Allen, Carr, and Brown's agency is presumptively free, it would seem odd to regard (3′) and (4′) as stating *causal* laws or causal subjunctives. Thus, when Burks says "If they do obey the rules, the barbers have certain causal dispositions – as is shown by the fact that counterfactual propositions may under appropriate circumstances be inferred" (1951, p. 378), we agree that the barbers have dispositions, but we question whether these dispositions should be denominated *causal* dispositions. (3′) and (4′) represent regularities based on the free decisions of Allen, Carr, and Brown. They are thus subjunctives of freedom. This should apply to personal explanations in terms of reasons in general, as long as the reasons were freely chosen. Given that *G* was a consciously and freely adopted goal of some agent *A*, we would expect that subjunctives of the following sorts would be true:

5. If *S* were a sufficient means for realizing *G* open to *A*, *A* would consider *S*.
6. If *A* were to believe that *N* was a necessary condition for obtaining *G*, then *A* would seek to realize *N*.

Although (5) and (6) can be generalized and thus express regularities, do they express causal laws or regularities as do the regularities appealed to in inanimate explanations? Although the causal structure of the world may determine whether *S* is a sufficient means for *G* or *N* is a necessary condition for *G*, these factors are not sufficient for the truth of (5) or (6). For that *A*'s free decision to seek goal *G* is necessary. (5) and (6) schematize subjunctives of freedom.

But does their being subjunctives of freedom make them any less subjunctives, or any less nomic than causal subjunctives? Consider Carr, Allen, and Brown again. Surely, the extent to which (3′) and (4′) express regularities concerning the behavior of these three men depends on how strong is their resolve to maintain their freely given commitment to abide by (3) and (4). To the extent that it is firm, (3′) and (4′) will express universal regularities. To the extent that there are regular exceptions under certain circumstances, (3′) and (4′) will be subject to qualifications. To the extent that Carr's, Allen's, or Brown's commitment wavers, the regularity will be statistical or probabilistic, rather than universal. But is this different from the situation with causal subjunctives? Some hold universally, expressing causal laws; others may need to be qualified; others express statistical regularities. Causal subjunctives and subjunctives of freedom have in common that they both express nomic connections.

We have already seen that legal explanations involve subjunctives:

7′. If one were to be bequeathed a certain amount of money, one would receive that money upon the demise of the person making the bequest.

Explanations via classification also obviously involve subjunctive conditionals.

8. That animal is a whale because it is a mammal.

Understanding in this case the sentence "A whale will be a mammal" to express not an analytic statement but one acceptable in virtue of some system of taxonomic classification ("A whale is classifiable as a mammal." – compare Toulmin 1958, pp. 103–4), the explanation obviously involves the subjunctive conditional

8′. If an animal were a whale, it would be a mammal.

If our argument here is cogent, we may ask whether the various types of interpretations that have been recognized may be seen as expressing subjunctives – in particular either causal subjunctives, subjunctives of freedom, or institutional subjunctives – which we have distinguished here. May some types of interpretations, even though they do not express such subjunctives, be nonetheless definable in terms of those subjunctives? Can some interpretations be seen as presupposing explanations involving such subjunctives? Can the classification of various sorts of interpretations be systematized in light of the subjunctives connected with explanations – be they physical, personal, or institutional? To answer that question, we must ask first: What types of interpretations are there, from a logical or semantic point of view? That is our subject in Section 8.4.

However, there is one issue we should address first. Some may question the value of our project of analyzing interpretations in terms of subjunctive conditionals, because they question the intelligibility of the subjunctive conditional. If one says that laws of nature support subjunctive conditionals, is one thereby committed to recognizing a mysterious nomic necessity? We shall return to this objection in Section 8.10. At this point, we reply that if we can give the notion of the subjunctive conditional a precise analysis in terms of intelligible concepts, then even if the notion should prove complex given that analysis, it will not be obscurantist. What could be more precise than a formal semantical analysis in a possible worlds framework? We present our candidate in Section 8.3. Our presentation in the next section is rather technical and may be skipped by those not interested in the details at this point.

8.3 AN ANALYSIS OF THE SUBJUNCTIVE CONDITIONAL

In (1980), with Daniels, we gave an analysis of the subjunctive conditional. We symbolized the subjunctive conditional connective by ">." However, we argued that ">" should be regarded as a ternary, rather than a binary connective, but also asserted that "$RP > Q$" should be read "If it were the case that P, then it would be the case that Q." What then does "R" represent? When one asserts "If it were the case that P, then it would be the case that Q, "one "assumes, if only tacitly, the truth of certain propositions" (Daniels and Freeman 1980, p. 640). Subjunctive conditionals are uttered against a background of interpretation. Consider, for example, "If you were to turn the key in the ignition, the car would start." This presupposes that the car is in proper working order, has some fuel in the tank, and that the laws of physics governing how the car's ignition mechanism brings about its starting remain the same. In all worlds where these conditions hold true, then if the ignition is activated, the car starts. We are not concerned with worlds where these conditions are somehow altered (compare Daniels and Freeman 1980, p. 640).

Although we believe that this ternary analysis has an important insight, we feel now that we can accommodate this insight without incorporating an unvoiced third component into the syntactic representation of the subjunctive conditional. Although "R" as a propositional variable imposes no restrictions on what might be tacitly assumed in asserting a subjunctive conditional, as our analysis in (1980) indicates, basically two sorts of suppositions might be made. First, one might assume certain causal laws when asserting "If P were the case, then Q would be the case." More generally, one might assume that the causal laws operative in the actual world also operate in those worlds where the antecedent 'P' also holds true. Because we also may assert subjunctives concerning human behavior involving presumptively free choice, we also should include here nomic regularities of freedom. Again, because we may assert institutional subjunctives based on certain constitutive rules, we should further include institutional regularities. So when we assert "if P were the case," we intend that P hold in just those cases, possible worlds, where all the laws of the actual world also hold. We could say that these worlds are nomically inclusive vis-à-vis the actual world or speak of them as being nomically uniform vis-à-vis the actual world. This does not rule out that there may be more laws holding in these possible worlds. These worlds may be nomically richer or more determinate than the actual world. The point is that they are not nomically weaker.

The second assumption concerns relevant variables. Whether or not a car is in proper working order or has fuel in the tank are variables causally relevant to whether the car will start upon turning the key in the ignition. Only if these variables have certain values, only if the car *is* in proper working order and at least some fuel *is* in the tank, will the car start upon the key's turning. So, in asserting "If you were to turn the key in the ignition, the car would start," one assumes that such values of the variables hold in the actual world and continue to hold in any situation in which one turns the key. More generally, then, in asserting a subjunctive conditional, "If P were the case, then Q would be the case," we assume that the relevant variables affecting whether or not Q holds, with the exception of P, have the same values as they do in the actual world in those worlds where P is the case.

We believe that both of these suppositions can be built into the formal semantics of the subjunctive conditional. Nomic uniformity can be handled through an accessibility relation R. To say of worlds w, w' that wRw' means that all the laws in w also hold in w'. R is clearly reflexive and transitive, but not symmetric. R thus is not a partition and we can make a clear distinction between truth in all worlds accessible to a given world w and truth in all possible worlds. The laws in the real world, although true in all accessible worlds, need not be true in all possible worlds. They need not be necessary in the alethic or broadly logical sense of necessity.

To accommodate what we might call variable uniformity or variable congruity, we need to give a formal account of a variable. A variable is a set of sentences. Such a set could be as simple as a pair, for example, {The car is in working order. The car is not in working order.} Typically, a variable might be a set of sentences in which for some predicate P and individual constants $c_1, c_2, \ldots, c_i, \ldots$, the set contains exactly the sentences $Pc_1, Pc_2, \ldots, Pc_i, \ldots$, that is, the set contains, for each value of the variable, the sentence stating that the particular value holds.

In (1980), we presented a propositional system S. The sentences of the system were generated from atomic sentence letters by means of the truth-functional connectives and the three-place sentence operator ">." Because causal laws and other nomic regularities might very well be expressed by generalized subjunctive conditionals, we understand the basic vocabulary of our language here to include predicate letters of any finite degree m, $m \geq 0$, individual constants, individual variables, the truth-functional connectives, the quantifier symbols "∀" and "∃", and the connective for the subjunctive conditional "□→." (We shall add an additional connective in the course of our discussion.)

An expression will be any sequence of these symbols. We may define a subclass of expressions that constitute the sentences of our language in the standard recursive way. An atomic sentence is an m-place predicate letter followed by m individual constants. (A zero-place predicate letter thus stands by itself as an atomic sentence.) We follow Leblanc and Wisdom (1976) in defining the recursive clause for quantification. Where $(\forall x)A$ is an expression, an instance is the result $A(c/x)$ of uniformly substituting some constant for every occurrence of x in A. Where an instance of $(\forall x)A$ is itself a sentence, $(\forall x)A$ is a sentence. (Compare Leblanc and Wisdom 1976, pp. 134–6.) We may thus think of $(\forall x)A$ as compounded from all its instances, which we refer to as subformulas of $(\forall x)A$, as sentential compounds are compounded from their components. We include these technicalities of the language because for convenience of exposition, it is useful to adopt a substitution interpretation of the quantifiers, which fits with such an understanding of statement composition.

Because in (1980) we were dealing with a propositional system, we defined a subjunctive-conditional-model, an S-model, as "a triple $<W, R, V)$, where W is a nonempty set of worlds, R is a binary reflexive relation on W, and V is a valuation" (Daniels and Freeman 1980, p. 642). That is, V incorporates a truth-value assignment such that for any statement A and world w, $V(A, w) = 1$ or $V(A, w) = 0$ depending on the value(s) of its components. We need to expand this definition. An S-model is a quintuple $<W, R, \nabla, V, \alpha>$, where W is a nonempty set of worlds, R is a binary reflexive and transitive relation on W, ∇ is a set of variables. We shall denote the members of ∇ by $\mathbf{v}_1, \mathbf{v}_2, \ldots, \mathbf{v}_j, \ldots$. Thus, each $\mathbf{v}_j$; is a set of sentences. V is a function mapping sentences to sets of variables, that is, where $\mathbf{S}$ denotes the sentences of a language generated by the above formation rules, V is a mapping from $\mathbf{S}$ into $\wp(\nabla)$. Intuitively, V associates with each sentence the set of those variables relevant to whether or not the sentence holds. α is a truth-value assignment relativized to worlds, that is, a mapping from pairs of atomic sentences and worlds into $\{T, F\}$. For a truth-functional compound C, the standard definition of truth on a truth-value assignment (relativized to a world) suffices. Given our substitution interpretation of the quantifiers, this may straightforwardly be extended to quantificational compounds. $(\forall x)A$ is true in w on α if and only if $A(c/x)$ is true in w on α for every constant c. Defining falsity at a world on a truth-value assignment is straightforward.

We may now give the following definition for the truth of a subjunctive conditional on a truth-value assignment α at a world w:

> For any sentences A, B, and $w \in W$, $A \;\Box\!\!\rightarrow\; B$ is true on α at w if and only if for all $w' \in W$ such that $w\,R\,w'$, and where $A \in \mathbf{v}$, $\mathbf{v} \in V(B)$, for all $\mathbf{v}' \in V(B) - \{\mathbf{v}\}$, where $C \in \mathbf{v}'$, $\alpha(C, w) = \mathrm{T}$ if and only if $\alpha(C, w') = \mathrm{T}$, then if $\alpha(A, w') = \mathrm{T}$, then $\alpha(B, w') = \mathrm{T}$.

Intuitively, a subjunctive conditional is true at a world w just in case at all those worlds that are nomically inclusive of w and where, in addition, the values of all the relevant variables affecting B except A are the same as in w, if A is true in such a world, then so is B.

Our analysis indicates that not every true subjunctive conditional states in its antecedent a causally (or more generally a nomically) sufficient condition for its consequent. Thus, consider Burks's example:

1. A beam of electrons moving in a vacuum perpendicular to a magnetic field is deflected. (1951, p. 367)

Moving in a vacuum perpendicular to a magnetic field does not guarantee that a beam of electrons will be deflected unless that beam is not subject to other forces (compare Burks 1951, p. 368). Hence, the subjunctive

2. $Ea \;\Box\!\!\rightarrow\; Da$[4]

will be true provided that a is not subject to other forces, but the universal generalization

3. $(\forall x)(Ex \;\Box\!\!\rightarrow\; Dx)$

will not state a causal law. For simplicity of exposition, let "Fx" symbolize "x is subject to forces other than being perpendicular to a magnetic field" – leaving aside how this predicate might be unpacked. "$Ex\, \&\, {\sim}Fx$" states a causally sufficient condition for "Dx." Hence,

4. $(\forall x)([Ex\, \&\, {\sim}Fx] \;\Box\!\!\rightarrow\; Dx)$

states a causal law.

What the instance "${\sim}Fa$" of "${\sim}Fx$" says in effect is that no relevant variables other than moving in a vacuum perpendicular to a magnetic field are operative here. Hence, in an *S*-model

5. $[Ea\, \&\, {\sim}Fa] \;\Box\!\!\rightarrow\; Da$

will be true at a world w if and only if given any accessible world w' where "$Ea\, \&\, {\sim}Fa$" is true, "Da" is true also. That is, we may disregard in this case the issue of whether the other relevant variables have the same values as in w, since no such variables are operative. "Ea & $\sim Fa$" states a causally sufficient condition for "Da."

Causal sufficiency claims a tighter connection between antecedent and consequent than what is claimed in a subjunctive, albeit it does not claim alethic necessity. To symbolize this stronger connection, we introduce the symbol "$\boxed{n}\!\!\rightarrow$". Here "n" stands for "nomic." "$A\boxed{n}\!\!\rightarrow B$" indicates that A is a nomically sufficient condition for B. Should the type of connection be causal, then A is a causally sufficient condition for B. But "$A\boxed{n}\!\!\rightarrow B$" might be true where "$A\,\square\!\!\rightarrow B$" expresses a subjunctive of freedom. The truth-condition for "$A\boxed{n}\!\!\rightarrow B$" is a straightforward simplification of the truth condition for "$A\,\square\!\!\rightarrow B$":

> $A\boxed{n}\!\!\rightarrow B$ is true on α at a world w if and only if for all w' such that $w\,R\,w'$, if A is true on α at w', then B is true on α at w'.

If "$(\forall x)(Fx\boxed{n}\!\!\rightarrow Gx)$" is true, then "$(\forall x)(Fx\,\square\!\!\rightarrow Gx)$" states a law – a causal law in the case of causal connection. Clearly, if "$A\boxed{n}\!\!\rightarrow B$" is true, so is "$A\,\square\!\!\rightarrow B$"; to say that A is a nomically sufficient condition for B implies that "if A were true, B would be true."

8.4 WHAT TYPES OF INTERPRETATIONS ARE THERE?

In Chapter 5, we indicated that those interpretations that assert interpretive concepts, such as "Brutus was guilty of murder" or "Brutus acted in self-defense" presuppose explanations. In the first two sections of this chapter, we developed how explanations appeal at least implicitly to nomic statements that involve or presuppose universally generalized subjunctive conditionals. Types of explanations correspond to types of subjunctives. These preliminary considerations already suggest the beginnings of a classification scheme for interpretations. We may first distinguish nomic statements from interpretive classifications. With nomic statements, we may then distinguish ways in which this nomic connection may be expressed, types of statements that may be paraphrased or explicated by explanatory subjunctives. For example, we might identify causal statements and attributions of sign and show how instances of each could be paraphrased as subjunctives presupposed in causal or personal explanations.

In light of discussions of interpretations in the literature, this procedure however seems daunting and may even be deeply flawed. Sproule (1980) has distinguished a number of types of interpretation – many, at least *prima facie*, seeming to have little to do with asserting subjunctives including comparison and minimization-maximization statements. But it is not at all obvious that a comparison statement such as "The terrain in Canada's Northwest Territories is like the terrain north of Alaska's Brooks Range" can be properly seen as involving a subjunctive. Nor is it at all obvious how a minimization-maximization statement such as "America's need for qualified, dedicated teachers in its public schools is far greater than its need to repair crumbling school buildings" is to be explicated in terms of subjunctives.

However, various considerations can help us put the task in a more positive light. First, recall that we are developing a logico-epistemological explication of the rhetorical notion of interpretation. The activity of explication, as Carnap indicates, involves replacing an intuitive or inexact concept by one more exact. The explicating concept need not have exactly the same meaning as the concept being explicated. Only sufficient correspondence, so that the new concept can replace the old, is required (compare Carnap 1947, p. 8). Thus, it should not be a mark against our analysis if certain statements rhetoricians might count as interpretations would not be interpretations on our account. Second, it is significant that in distinguishing interpretations, Sproule frequently speaks of arguments as opposed to statements. This reflects the different disciplinary perspective of rhetoric, being concerned with the persuasive effects of argumentation. There may be very good reasons to distinguish different persuasive strategies for certain statements, even if for logical or epistemological purposes the statements argued for can be seen as included in one category.

That many of the interpretations rhetoricians distinguish can be seen as interpretations on our account is evidence nonetheless that by identifying interpretations as a type of statement, we are carving nature at the joints. Let us proceed then to identify types of interpretations, turning first to those suggested by our classification of types of explanations. The question now is whether the various types of interpretations that have been identified can be understood in terms of the explanatory subjunctive or of concepts definable in terms of the explanatory subjunctive.

Modes of Expressing Nomic Connection

Causal Statements. We must begin with a clarification, because singular causal statements asserting that particular event or condition A caused particular event or condition B themselves assert explanations and thus presuppose nomic universals rather than simply asserting them. For example,

1. The meteor's hitting the earth caused a crater one mile in diameter to form.

Clearly (1) presupposes

1a. A meteor hit the earth at that location.
1b. A crater one mile in diameter was formed.
1c. If a meteor of the same size and mass moving at the same velocity were to collide with the earth at a point where the terrain were similar, then a crater one mile in diameter would be formed.

(1c) asserts the nomic connection and it is only causal statements of this sort, causal generalizations, with which we are concerned at the moment. What types of such causal statements may be identified and may they be paraphrased or explicated by explanatory subjunctives?

Causal generalizations assert either sufficient conditions, necessary conditions, or precipitating conditions. The difference is that statements of necessary or sufficient conditions do not admit of defeating conditions, while statements of precipitating conditions or causal influence do. This can be explicated most clearly through some examples:

2. Heating pure water to 100°C at air pressure of sea level causes it to boil.
3. Absence of oxygen at striking causes matches not to light.
4. Lightning bolts hitting forests in late summer cause forest fires.

(2) states a sufficient condition, (3) a necessary condition, and (4) a precipitating condition. Clearly, each may be paraphrased in a way that explicitly involves the subjunctive conditional.

2'. If pure water were to be heated to 100°C at air pressure of sea level, it would boil.
3'. If oxygen were not present at the striking of a match, that match would not light.
4'. If a lightning bolt were to strike in a forest in late summer, then there would be a forest fire.

Notice that if (2) genuinely asserts a sufficient condition, then if the antecedent of (2') were to be satisfied, so would be the consequent. There are no other relevant variables that could affect the outcome but here are presumed not to. Likewise, there are no relevant variables that could cause a match to light in the absence of oxygen and that are assumed not operating here. Where such relevant variables are present, we have claims of precipitating conditions, as in (4). If a summer had been atypically wet or if, by some singularity of nature all of the oxygen had been removed from the atmosphere surrounding the forest just before the bolt of lightning struck, there might not and in the latter case would not be a forest fire. Clearly, it would be appropriate to use our notation for causal sufficiency "$\boxed{n}\mapsto$" in formalizing both (2) and (3) and the "plain" subjunctive conditional "$\Box\mapsto$" in (4). All these various types of causal generalizations then can be paraphrased in terms of the explanatory subjunctive.

Dispositional Statements. As Burks points out, "Those symbolically simple predicates which designate 'dispositions', 'potentialities', or 'powers' contain causal implications implicitly" (1951, p. 367). In light of our discussion, we would say that they contain explanatory subjunctives implicitly, because not every dispositional predicate can be "unpacked" in terms of a physically causal as opposed to a noncausal personal or institutional explanatory subjunctive. To appreciate Burks's point, consider the following dispositional statements:

1. Sugar is soluble in water.
2. John is pugnacious.

Both of these statements may be straightforwardly paraphrased to make the implicit subjunctive explicit.

1'. If sugar were placed in water, it would dissolve.
2'. If John's anger were aroused, he would begin to fight.

(1') obviously involves a physical explanatory subjunctive. (2') links a psychological spring of action with overt behavioral response. It is a personal causal explanation.

Not all dispositional statements are of the simple "s is p" form of (1) and (2).

3. Adlai Stevenson would rather speak the truth than win an election. (Kruger 1975, p. 146)

This is clearly a dispositional statement. It also clearly supports an explanatory subjunctive conditional:

3'. If Adlai Stevenson were faced with the exclusive alternatives of speaking the truth or winning an election, he would speak the truth.

(3′) itself might be explained with reference to Stevenson's free decisions and commitments, and thus be a subjunctive of freedom.

Some dispositional statements support legal and thus institutional as opposed to physical or personal explanatory subjunctives. Consider

4. The contract between the author and publisher is in force.

Clearly (4) presupposes these subjunctives expressing legal necessity or lawlikeness:

4′a. If one party were to fulfill certain conditions, the other party would be mandated to satisfy certain reciprocal conditions.
4′b. If the other party were not to fulfill those conditions, avenues of redress and recourse would be open to the first party.

We have said that principally personal explanations appeal to the beliefs and desires or reasons of some agent in explaining some action. Personal explanations that are not simply causal but appeal to conscious goals and reasons will rely on a nomic connection between holding certain beliefs and intentions – consciously entertained goals if not freely chosen reasons – and performing certain acts. But we may see the ascription of beliefs and intentions as themselves interpretations analyzable as subjunctives.[5] The analysis of such dispositional statements involves such a detailed discussion that it deserves a special heading in its own right. As with Section 8.3, this discussion is technical and some readers may wish to skip details.

Ascriptions of Belief and Intention. What does it mean to say that "a believes that *p*"? Following Cohen, we understand a "belief that *p* [as] a disposition, when one is attending to the issues raised, or items referred to, by the proposition that *p*, normally to feel it true that *p* and false that *not-p*" (1992, p. 4). Belief statements, then, are dispositional statements. Thus the ascription of belief

1. Jones believed that igniting the fuse would bring about the bomb's exploding

is analyzed as

1′. If Jones were considering the issue of whether lighting the fuse would cause the fuse to light, he would feel that it is true that lighting the fuse would cause the fuse to light.

How may we understand the claim of goal, purpose, or intention in personal explanations? The paradigm way of expressing such claims is through "in order to" statements.

2. Jones ignited the fuse in order to explode the bomb.
3. Andy studied symbolic logic assiduously in order to increase his proficiency.

In analyzing "in order to" statements, Alston claims that they are equivalent to statements explaining some action in terms of some want.

2'. Jones ignited the fuse because he wanted the bomb to explode.
3'. Andy studied symbolic logic assiduously because he wanted to increase his proficiency.

Without further clarification, this is open to objection as an account of intentional explanation. Do (2'), (3') make the same assertions as

2''. Jones ignited the fuse because he had a goal that the bomb explode.
3''. Andy studied symbolic logic assiduously because he had a goal to increase his proficiency.

As we may distinguish between belief and acceptance, so we may distinguish between wants and goals. To have a goal that some state of affairs come about does not imply that one wants that state of affairs to come about, at least in one sense of "want." Jones may be repulsed by the prospect of the anticipated destruction from the explosion. But he may be under orders to bring about the explosion nonetheless. His intention is for the bomb to explode, although he does not *want* this result. We could clearly give many other examples to show that having a goal or intention that a given state of affairs come about does not imply that one *wants* that state of affairs to come about.

Our discussion presupposes a specific understanding of wanting or desiring. As Cohen puts it, "Desires...are dispositions to have certain feelable yearnings, cravings, wishes, likings, or hankerings" (1992, p. 43). As such, desires or wants, like beliefs, are involuntary. But just as beliefs have active counterparts in acceptances, "So, in normal people,... desires... have counterpart pro-attitudes that are as active and voluntary as acceptances. Among such active and voluntary counterparts of desires are the mental attitudes that consist in having such-or-such goals, aims, ends, objectives, plans, intentions, or policies" (1992, p. 44). Should "in order to" statements be explicated in terms of wants or goals? If our purpose is to explicate what is involved in personal explanations and ascriptions of agency, it would seem the answer is both. Surely, to say that Jones ignited the fuse because he believed it would cause an explosion and he wanted the explosion to come about is just as much to give a personal explanation of the fuse's igniting as would saying that Jones ignited the fuse because he believed it would cause the explosion and it was his purpose or goal for the explosion to come about. Considerations such as these led Alston to distinguish narrower and wider senses of "want." Cohen has explicated the narrower sense. The wider comprises that sense together with the active counterpart. In the wider sense, to have a goal to bring something about just *is* to want it to come about, even if one has no felt hankerings or tendency to feel hankerings for that state of affairs. It is with "want" in the wider sense that ascriptions of intention are to be understood.

What does it mean then to say that

4. Jones wanted the bomb to explode.
4′. Jones had the goal of exploding the bomb.

We explicate this through how wants or intentions are connected with action. As Alston puts it,

Wants give rise to actions by virtue of the fact that it is a lawful generalization that given a desire for S and a belief that doing A is (or will lead to) bringing about S, there will be a tendency to do A, whether or not the agent actually does A being further dependent on what other action tendencies simultaneously exist, as well as on whether factors which prevent any action at all are present. (1967, p. 406)

Thus, having the desire or want to S or the goal or purpose that S come about may be understood in the first instance as the disposition that were one to believe that doing A would itself be realizing S or would causally lead to S, and if it were possible to do A, one would tend to do A or that one's tendency to do A would increase (compare Alston 1967, p. 404, statement (26)). Here tendency is to be explicated through a frequency understanding of probability. Hence, asserting (4) or (4′) may be explicated as

4.1 For any action A, if Jones were to believe that doing A either itself would be bringing about the explosion or causally lead to bringing about the explosion, and Jones were able to do A, then Jones would tend to do A.

This, however, is only a first approximation. As Aune points out in dealing with actions that are means to some intended state, we must not only take into account a person's beliefs that these actions are causally efficacious in bringing about that state but also the agent's preferences (see Aune 1967, p. 199). There might be several actions *A, B, C*, each within Jones's ability, which would cause the explosion. Jones may prefer one of these actions to the others. Hence, where *B* is one of the non-preferred alternative actions, the fact that Jones believes doing *B* would causally lead to the explosion and Jones was able to do *B* would not mean that Jones would tend to do *B*. So we must add a clause that *A* is Jones's preferred means to bring about the explosion. Better we need to indicate that *A* is one of Jones's most preferred means, that is, that there is no means (at least in these circumstances), which Jones would prefer to *A*:

> 4.2 For any action *A*, if Jones were to believe that doing *A* would attain the explosion or causally lead to the explosion, Jones were able to do *A*, for any action *B* such that Jones believes that doing *B* would attain the explosion or causally lead to the explosion, and Jones were able to do *B*, Jones would not prefer *B* to *A*, then Jones would tend to do *A*.

But this is still not a complete analysis. The wanting to bring about the explosion has dropped out of the picture. Suppose it were true that whenever an action satisfied the antecedent of (4.2), Jones tended to do *A*. But Jones might still not want to bring about the explosion. His tending to bring it about or his tending to perform an action which he believed would bring it about could be a matter of some sort of compulsion to do *A*, not an intention to bring about the explosion. If Jones had a genuine intention to bring about the explosion, it would seem that he would have a disposition to think such thoughts as "I shall bring about that explosion." As Aune puts it, "A man who has a certain specific intention is also prone to think thoughts of the form 'I shall do *A* in *C*,' ... [i.e., to] have the disposition to think such thoughts, to think them, for instance, when he is deliberating about what to do at a certain time or under certain conditions" (1967, p. 200). We must incorporate this condition into our analysis. It states Jones's disposition, given appropriate circumstances, to think a statement of his intention to explode the bomb:

> 4.3 For any action *A*, if Jones were to believe that doing *A* would attain the explosion or causally lead to the explosion, Jones were able to do *A*, for any action *B* such that Jones believes that doing *B* would attain the explosion or causally lead to the explosion and Jones were able to do *B* Jones would not prefer *B* to *A*, and there are circumstances *C* such that if Jones were in *C*, he would think "I shall explode the bomb," then Jones would tend to do *A*.

(4.3) is again a dispositional statement, incorporating dispositional clauses in its antecedent. Not only is the belief clause dispositional together with the clause that for some circumstances *C*, if Jones were in *C* he would think a statement of his intention, but preference is also a dispositional concept. Surely, one prefers *A* to *B* if and only if were one given the choice between *A* and *B*, one would chose *A*. Although ascriptions of intention may be complex, they may nonetheless thus be analyzed through the explanatory subjunctive.

Attributions of sign. Statements of the form "*A* signifies *B*" or "*A* means *B*" may also be paraphrased as explanatory subjunctives. We are not of course here considering reports concerning word meaning, descriptions of linguistic behavior. Rather, to say that one event *A* is a sign of some further event, process, intention *B* is to assert that there is some lawlike connection between the two, from the occurrence of *A* we may infer the occurrence of *B*. This assertion however does not further assert the nature of that connection, for example, that it is causal. But this lawlike connection could either be appealed to in giving an explanation or follows from subjunctives that could be used in explanations. The lawlike connection, then, is an explanatory subjunctive. Some examples will illustrate this straightforwardly:

1. The smoke coming from the chimney means that the plant is operating again.
2. Frozen water in the gutter means the thermometer will read below 32°F.
3. That the peace negotiations have been proceeding for over two weeks behind closed doors is a sign that the negotiators are making progress toward some agreements.

Although in each of these cases, all that is asserted is that one occurrence or type of occurrence is a sign of another, these claims presuppose explanatory subjunctives, either physical or personal. (1) and (2) clearly assert that physical occurrences are nomically connected, while (3) asserts nomic connections that could be used in personal explanations. That the negotiators are making progress explains why the negotiations have continued over such a long period. But this explanation would be carried out in terms of psychological dispositions and perhaps intentionally willed human actions. (1)–(3) support subjunctive conditionals that may straightforwardly be made explicit.

1′. If smoke were to be coming from the chimney, the plant would be operating again.

(2′) and (3′) clearly follow this pattern. Again, we see that this type of interpretation can be explicated in terms of the explanatory subjunctive.

Interpretations Presupposing General Nomic Connections

Singular Causal Statements. We have distinguished causal generalizations, which assert nomic connections, from singular causal statements, which we saw presupposed them. Singular causal statements are nonetheless causal statements and interpretations. We may analyze these statements of the form *A* caused *B* or *B* occurred because *A* occurred according to the pattern:

a. *A* occurred.
b. *B* occurred.
c. If conditions relevantly similar to *A* were to occur, *B* would occur.
d. No other condition *C* sufficient for *B* to occur (i.e., $C \boxed{n} \mapsto B$) occurred.[6]

Clause (d) is required, as it is possible that *B* could be caused by several alternative antecedent circumstances, $A_1, A_2, \ldots, A_n$. A_1 could have occurred, but it was A_2 that caused *B*. The assertion that A_1 was the cause of *B* presupposes the denial that any of $A_2, \ldots, A_n$ occurred (at least before A_1 occurred). This pattern may be applied whether we are dealing with a case of physical, personal, or institutional causation.

1. The presence of oxygen in what was thought to be a vacuum made the match light when struck.
1a. Oxygen was present in what was thought to be a vacuum and the match was struck.
1b. The match lit.
1c. If oxygen were present and a match were struck, it would light.
1d. No other condition *C* (such as the match when dry being tossed into a fire) sufficient for the match to light occurred.

Hence, singular causal statements may be analyzed as conjunctions, one of which asserts a general causal connection, that a condition is either a sufficient or precipitating condition. Clauses (a) and (b) are clearly descriptions. Clause (d) is a description also, a nonprojective generalization. Presumably the set of alternative sufficient conditions is finite. Clause (d) asserts that none of them occurred. To be sure, identifying such conditions presupposes recognizing that they are sufficient causes of *B*, which in turn presupposes recognizing certain subjunctives. However, the singular causal statement itself does not enumerate these conditions but simply asserts that the set of them is empty.

Interpretive Classifications. How may we analyze the types of statements which in Chapter 5 introduced the category of interpretation, statements such as

> 1. Brutus's killing Caesar was an act of murder.
> 2. Brutus's killing Caesar was an act of self-defense.

The classic rhetorical understanding of interpretations as raising issues of definition does seem to fit well this class of interpretations. Surely to argue cogently that Brutus's killing Caesar was an act of murder one would need to know the legal definition of murder and to design one's argument to show that Brutus's action satisfied the definition. According to one widely used characterization, murder is the offense of unlawfully killing a human being with malice aforethought. In turn, malice aforethought characterizes any state of mind that intends committing an illegal act recognized illegal without recognizing any condition that in law will justify, excuse, or extenuate it.

Given these definitions, to justify the claim that Brutus's killing Caesar was an act of murder, once it is established that Brutus did in fact kill Caesar, one would have to show that

> 1a. Brutus believed that using his specific means would bring about Caesar's death.
> 1b. Brutus intended Caesar's death.
> 1c. Brutus recognized the *prima facie* illegality of his act.
> 1d. Brutus recognized no conditions rebutting the *prima facie* illegality of his act.

Given this analysis, the interpretation asserts the conjunction of four statements, the first two of which constitute a personal explanation, the remaining two being belief statements. It is the conjunction then of four interpretations. We can give a parallel analysis of the claim that Brutus's killing Caesar was an act of self-defense. Clauses (a) and (b) remain the same. To these we add:

> 2c. Brutus believed that Caesar posed a distinct threat to his life and limb.
> 2d. Brutus acted to avoid that threat.

(2) then also involves a personal explanation, together with further claims about Brutus' beliefs and intentions. Again, once the definition is spelled out, the individual clauses are interpretations in their own right.

Although (1) and (2) presuppose personal explanations, this is not the case for all interpretive classifications. Some presuppose just that an explanation of a certain type holds, be it physical or personal.

   3. The eruption of Mt. Vesuvius was a natural occurrence.

   4. That inscribed sequence of 0's and 1's representing the prime numbers between 0 and 99 is the result of human agency.

Here again, a cogent justification of these claims involves first analyzing the interpretive concept predicated. But such an analysis reveals that to predicate that concept is to claim or presuppose that an explanation of a certain type holds. What does it mean to say that some occurrence is natural as opposed to artificial (or supernatural)? Surely it involves saying that one need appeal to no nomic connections other than those in the physical world, that some antecedent event physically necessitates the occurrence. Where "$\boxed{n}\mapsto$" represents nomic necessity, we might let "$\boxed{p}\mapsto$" represent physically nomic necessity. So (3) asserts, at least in part, that there is an event E that physically necessitated the eruption of Mt. Vesuvius, that is, E occurred and if any event sufficiently like E were to occur, Mt. Vesuvius would erupt (or an event sufficiently like the eruption of Mt. Vesuvius would occur) as a matter of physical necessity. To say that an event or condition is the result of human agency is to say that some human being believed that by performing an action (here making an inscription), he or she was bringing that event or condition about and that the person had the goal to bring the event or condition about.

By contrast, interpretive classifications may presuppose particular causal explanations of various levels of generality.

   5. The tides are a gravitational phenomenon.

   6. The tides are a phenomenon of the moon's gravitational pull on earth.

   7. Werther's sorrows are literary induced.

   8. Werther's sorrows were induced by reading romantic novels.

Here we have straightforward appeals to physical or psychological explanations. Although we cannot pause to give analyses of these statements, clearly if any of them are true, some explanation presupposed by the statement will be correct. But the explanation will involve an explanatory subjunctive. We shall discuss the implications of this for determining whether interpretive classifications are ever properly basic beliefs in Section 8.9.

Some Rhetorical Classes of Interpretation Reducible to These Modes of Expressing Nomic Connection

Further types of interpretation might be included in a rhetorical catalogue. Although for understanding persuasively effective argumentation, it may be useful to give these interpretations their own separate classification, for seeing how these interpretations involve the explanatory subjunctive, they may be viewed as special cases of the types of interpretations we have already identified, if indeed we are to regard them as interpretations at all.

Comparisons. Sproule (1980, pp. 146–51) identifies comparisons as a type of interpretation. By contrast, Fahnestock and Secor (1982, pp. 99–112) classify comparisons under "fancier statements about what things are," suggesting that they are descriptions. Without doubt, some comparative statements are not interpretations in the logico-epistemological sense but descriptions. To say that

    1. The dress is like the car in being blue

is just to assert

    1′. The dress is blue and the car is blue.

(1) is an example of a simple comparison, a statement of the form

    2. A is like B (with respect to being $P_1, P_2, \ldots, P_n$)

where the various points of comparison may be unstated. Comparisons do assert interpretations where items are said to be like in sharing some interpretive property. For example,

    3. Demonstrations involving both sides of the abortion controversy are peaceful as armed confrontations between opposing parties are peaceful. If one side goes home, the other will not disturb the peace.

Here, a rather ironic sense of "peaceful" is defined dispositionally. From the logical point of view, then, we have a conjunction of (generalized) dispositional statements. This interpretive comparison, then, does not require distinguishing any new logical category of interpretation. It can be viewed as a conjunction of interpretive classifications, explicable in terms of dispositional statements.

Analogies, statements of the form

4. *A* is to *B* as *C* is to *D*

asserting that one relation or type of instance of a relation is like another relation or type of instance of that relation, mark a special type of comparison. As such, they can be a rhetorically effective way of making causal assertions. If *A* has some type of causal influence on *B* and the relation of *C* to *D* is the same, then *C* has this same type of causal influence on *D*.

5. The Munich appeasement of Hitler was to avoiding World War II as appeasing terrorists is to future prospects for peace.

Here we have two causal claims. We know that the allies' appeasing Hitler at Munich had certain causal effects (psychological causation at least). This makes the claim that appeasing terrorists would have a similar negative impact on future prospects for peace seem plausible.

Besides simple comparisons and analogies, we may have comparisons with degree.

6. Chess players are more *macho* than football players. (Fahnestock and Secor 1982, p. 108)

This statement can be straightforwardly analyzed as a conjunction:

6'. Chess players are *macho* (to some degree).
Football players are *macho* (to some degree).
The amount of *macho* displayed by chess players is greater than the amount displayed by football players.

The first two sentences clearly express dispositional statements. Should we have an operational definition of *macho* behavior, the third sentence clearly would express a description. Likewise, if one could give more examples of chess player *macho* than football player *macho* or more examples of types of such behavior on the chess players' part, one would be basing the third claim on the fact that the count for *macho* behavior for chess players exceeds that count for football players. But a statement reporting an empirical count or the results of a count is a description.

Minimization-Maximization. Because, according to Sproule, this type of interpretation involves highlighting details that would put one's case in a favorable light and downplaying contrary considerations, some would call this slanting. As such, we are dealing not with a type of statement but a rhetorical technique. However, one can highlight a detail by pointing out its causal or dispositional consequences or that it is a sign of something deemed important. Likewise, one can downplay a fact by denying that it has some significance or denying its causal efficacy. For example,

> 7. Since 95 percent of students who took the test passed on the first try, including many minority students, the instances of minority students who did not pass the test do not show it discriminatory.

That is

> 7′. It is not the case that the instances of minority students who did not pass the test constitute a sign that the test was discriminatory.

(7′) is clearly a denial of an attribution of significance.

Denials add a further dimension to our understanding of interpretations. Are negations of interpretations themselves interpretations? Interpretations are contingent intensional statements. Clearly, the denial of a contingent statement is a contingent statement. Because an intensional statement is not built up from simple atomic components solely by means of truth-functions neither is its negation, which thus is intensional also. Notice that because conjunctions of interpretations are clearly themselves interpretations, and – as is well known – all truth-functions can be defined in terms of negation and conjunction, we see that the class of interpretations includes not just simple interpretations but their truth-functional compounds. Minimization-maximization then introduces no new basic type of interpretation.[7]

Subjunctive Disjunctions. Another type of interpretive statement rhetoricians consider which can easily be reduced to the subjunctive we may call, for want of an established or better terminology, the subjunctive disjunction. The qualification "subjunctive" serves to distinguish these statements from truth-functional disjunctions. They do not simply claim that one or the other of their two disjuncts are true. Rather, they suggest that their two alternatives are possible and the only possibilities there are. Disjunctions in this sense may serve as premises in arguments endorsing some policy. If following that policy is one of only two possible alternatives and the other is grossly unacceptable or the greater rather than the lesser of two evils, then we have justification for following that policy.

> 8. Either we start developing alternative sources of energy now or we shall all freeze in the dark.

Likewise, subjunctive disjunctions can be used in arguments against some policy. Should adopting that policy bring about one or the other of two alternatives both of which are undesirable, we have justification for not adopting that policy.

9. If you go into politics, you will either be beholden to big corporate interests or big labor. But if you are beholden to any interest, you have lost your integrity.

One shows a dilemma false by showing that some additional alternative is possible. We can begin to develop alternative sources of energy ten years from now. Someone going into politics might have the personal financial means to reject contributions from corporate interests and from labor. These considerations focus how subjunctive distinctions can be easily reduced to subjunctive conditionals. Just as a truth-functional disjunction "$P \vee Q$" is logically equivalent to the material conditional "$\sim P \supset Q$" or "$\sim Q \supset P$," so a subjunctive disjunction is logically equivalent to "If it were not the case that Q, then it would be the case that P."

8'. If we were not to start developing alternative sources of energy now, we would all freeze in the dark.

9'. If you were not beholden to big corporate interests, you would be beholden to big labor interests.

We can easily imagine situations where the antecedents of these conditionals are true (and thus one of the possible alternatives does not hold), yet the consequent is false (the other alternative does not hold either), because some third alternative holds.

These considerations also highlight the difference between subjunctive and indicative disjunctions. If it is true that

10. Tom is a baseball player

then it is also true that

11. Tom is a football player or Tom is a baseball player

where (11) expresses an indicative inclusive disjunction. But it is *not* true that

12. If Tom were not a football player, he would be a baseball player.

Tom quite possibly could have been a soccer player.

The concept of possibility invoked by subjunctive disjunctions is not broadly logical possibility. For want of established terminology we might call it subjunctive possibility. We may think of it as a generalization of causal possibility, definable in terms of subjunctives in general as opposed to subjunctives expressing physical causal regularities. To complete our logical account of types of interpretations, we consider now how such statements may be defined in terms of the subjunctive conditional.

Ascriptions of Subjunctive Necessity and Possibility. In Section 8.3, we defined the notion of a nomically sufficient condition (see p. 154). This allows us straightforwardly to define the notions of subjunctive necessity and possibility, better nomic necessity and possibility. Clearly, we should not want to say that A was logically necessary if, given changes in the values of certain relevant variables, A should be false. But if whenever the causal laws true of the actual world held together with the other nomic regularities of the actual world, that is, given that a world is nomically inclusive of the actual world, A also holds in that world, we shall want to say that A is nomically necessary. Clearly, because any truth-functional tautology will hold in all worlds, it will be true in all worlds nomically inclusive of a given world. Hence where "τ" abbreviates some truth-functional tautology, "$\tau \boxed{n} \!\!\mapsto A$" is true in a world w just in case A is true in all worlds nomically inclusive of w. We may take this then as defining nomic or subjunctive necessity:

NN: "$\boxed{n} A$" $=_{df}$ "$\tau \boxed{n} \!\!\mapsto A$"

Nomic or subjunctive possibility then may be defined in terms of nomic necessity in the usual way:

NP: "$\langle\!\!\langle n \rangle\!\!\rangle A$" $=_{df}$ "$\sim\!\boxed{n}\!\sim\! A$".

A very significant use of the concept of nomic possibility occurs in the explication of statements attributing responsibility. Consider

1. Cedric through his marital infidelities is responsible for estranging his wife Beatrice.

Surely, we would not count (1) as true if Cedric could not avoid marital infidelities. This does not mean simply that it is logically possible for Cedric not to engage in these infidelities. It means that given the laws of this world, there is no condition determining that Cedric engages in marital infidelities, that is, it is consistent with the laws of this world that he refrain from such behavior, that is,

2. $\langle\!\!\langle n \rangle\!\!\rangle$ (Cedric does not engage in marital infidelities.)

Furthermore, it seems it also needs to be nomically possible that Beatrice not be estranged. If given the laws of this world, no matter what Cedric did Beatrice would be estranged, we would not say that he is *responsible* for estranging her or that his marital infidelities were responsible. Hence,

3. ◇ (Beatrice is not estranged.)

must be true also.

8.5 TYPES OF SUBJUNCTIVES, TYPES OF EXPLANATIONS, AND INTUITION

Our survey of interpretations shows that no matter how statements properly classifiable as interpretations may vary, they all somehow involve a subjunctive. The question then of whether interpretations can be acceptable basic premises becomes the question of whether and under what circumstances subjunctives (or in some cases their negations) are ever acceptable basic premises. The key is whether they may under certain circumstances be properly basic beliefs. In Section 8.2, we connected subjunctives with explanations. In Section 8.1, we distinguished between types of explanations on the basis of how their covering law generalizations came to be discovered and thus on the basis ultimately of the belief-generating mechanisms involved. This leads us to an epistemological classification of subjunctives. As we have distinguished physical, personal, and institutional explanations, so we may speak of physical, personal, and institutional subjunctives.

What then are the mechanisms generating basic beliefs expressed by these various subjunctives? Physical and personal subjunctives are ultimately supported "from below," by appeal to our experience of the events and persons in the world around us. Institutional subjunctives are ultimately supported "from above" through our understanding of the systems of constitutive rules which back those beliefs. More broadly, then, we may distinguish empirical from institutional subjunctives. In approaching the question of whether subjunctives are ever properly basic beliefs, we should treat these two classes of subjunctives separately. In each case, we believe we may identify a belief-generating mechanism that generates properly basic beliefs. We believe we should call these mechanisms empirical intuition and institutional intuition, and, further, that we should distinguish physical and personal modes of empirical intuition. The former is empirical in the sense that it begins with experience and is applied to experience. But it is an intuition of nomic, genuinely intensional, connections within experience.

That we denominate both mechanisms as forms of intuition gives us a key to understanding how they operate and how we may assess the reliability of their operation. As Cohen points out in (1986), as certain analytic philosophers use the term, intuition concerns "what counts as a reason for what" (1986, p. 73). Again, an intuition "is an inclination of mind that is taken to originate from the existence of a system of tacitly acknowledged rules for making judgements about relevant topics. That is how intuition can come to suggest what is a reason for what" (Cohen 1986, p. 76). To use Toulmin's terminology for the layout of arguments, intuitions concern warrants, the principles by virtue of which we get from data to claim. Intuition is one way in which warrants are grasped, and because warrants, properly understood as inference rules, are implicit in an argument rather than stated explicitly (compare Toulmin 1958, p. 100), intuition may be the principal way of grasping warrants. What does this have to do with subjunctive conditionals?

As Peirce has pointed out, our inferences are guided by habits of thought. When expressed propositionally, these habits of thought are the leading principles of our inferences (see 1955, p. 130). We may express this habit of thought not only propositionally but through an inference rule or schema, that is, a warrant. What is the relation between the warrant and the leading principle? Consider the following old saw:

1. Socrates is a man.
   Therefore Socrates is mortal.

The warrant of this inference is the material inference rule

2. From   x is a man
   We may take it that   x is mortal

But corresponding to the inference rule is the generalization

3. All men are mortal.

Peirce would refer to this as the leading principle. But this clearly is not an accidental generalization. It supports a subjunctive conditional, namely

4. $(\forall x)\,(x \text{ is a man} \;\square\!\!\rightarrow\; x \text{ is mortal})$

So, corresponding to the warrants of inferences are generalized subjunctive conditionals. Conversely, corresponding to subjunctive conditionals are inference rules. To

5. $(\forall x)([x$ is a piece of sugar & x is placed in water$] \;\Box\!\!\to\; x$ dissolves$)$

corresponds

6. From   x is a piece of sugar
                           & x is placed in water
   We may take it that   x dissolves

As our examples illustrate, to grasp the warrant is to come to believe at least implicitly the corresponding subjunctive conditional. Thus, if a type of intuition is a mechanism for grasping the warrants of arguments of a certain type, it is also the mechanism for generating beliefs that the corresponding subjunctive conditionals or universal generalizations of subjunctive conditionals hold. Furthermore, what bears upon the reliability of the inference warrant bears upon the acceptability of the subjunctive conditional. If one can reliably infer a conclusion from certain premises according to a given inference pattern and one recognizes this reliability, then one can take the corresponding subjunctive as a premise in some further argument. The reliability of intuition to grasp reliable warrants and the reliability of intuition as a mechanism generating beliefs expressed in subjunctive conditionals amounts to the same thing. Hence, we may investigate the presumptive reliability of intuition as a belief-generating mechanism by investigating its presumptive reliability in grasping warrants. This will be our procedure in the next section, when we first investigate the reliability of physical causal intuition in generating beliefs expressed through causal subjunctives by considering the reliability of inferences with causal warrants.

Making contact with one further structural distinction in Toulmin's layout of arguments indicates the fruitfulness of this approach. Toulmin distinguishes between warrants, which explain why data are relevant to claim, and backing for those warrants, which may be brought forward to establish why a warrant is acceptable. We may think of the backing as the input on which some form of intuition intuits that from certain premises we may infer some conclusion. Thus, the backing is the input for the mechanism generating subjunctive beliefs. So we may expect to get insight into the reliability of these belief-generating mechanisms as we get insight into the reliability of the corresponding inferences given how they are backed. Furthermore, as Toulmin points out, how warrants are backed differs widely from field to field. Various types of explanation correspond to various fields of argument. We should expect the inferences and their warrants to be backed in different ways and thus modes of intuition as subjunctive belief-generating mechanisms to operate differently in different fields. Thus, we should expect our task of assessing whether these modes of intuition are presumptively reliable to be much more straightforward if we can concentrate on just one field at a time and on how inferences in those fields are backed. We shall begin with the field of physical arguments whose backing concerns events or conditions in the physical world.

8.6 PHYSICAL SUBJUNCTIVES AND PHYSICAL INTUITION

By means of physical intuition as a belief-generating mechanism, we come to believe certain subjunctive conditionals or their universal generalizations that express nomic or lawlike relations in the physical world. I propose that the operation of physical intuition involves two factors: detection of covariation and imposition of an interpretive category. In the paradigm instance, that category will be causal dependency. In nature, some features regularly occur together, φ is generally accompanied by ψ, if not universally, then with some statistical uniformity. Such occurring together is covariation and the ability to recognize this is covariation detection. We may not only come to believe that there is a constant conjunction here, we may come to apprehend φ as an independent variable and ψ as the dependent variable. This is an intuition of agency involved with ψ. For example, one may notice that dropping a stick is always accompanied by a noise. But one may further apprehend dropping the stick as the independent variable and making a noise as the dependent variable. One is apprehending dropping the stick as the causal agent. But this means that we have brought the interpretive category of relevant variables or causal dependancy to our experience.

Although the paradigm case of physical intuition is physical causal intuition, at least one other category can be imposed subsequent to the detection of covariation, that of natural kind. As we see it, whether physical intuition is presumptively reliable as a basic belief-generating mechanism depends on what interpretive category is being imposed in a given employment of intuition. Intuitively grasping a causal connection, forming a causal hypothesis in a flash of insight, although generating a basic belief, would ordinarily not be thought to generate a properly basic belief. Clearly, to believe the hypothesis with justification, one ordinarily needs to test the hypothesis. But then the belief is no longer basic but based on propositions reporting the results of the test. However, when the interpretive category of natural kind is imposed, physical intuition is arguably presumptively reliable as a basic belief-generating mechanism, at least under certain conditions.

In (1993), Kornblith argues for the reliability of certain inductive inferences involving this category of natural kind. He seeks to establish the reliability of these inferences by arguing for the reliability of a mechanism which allows us to infer – Kornblith would say project – from an object's having certain features to its having certain properties. In light of our argumentation-theoretic considerations of the last section, we can easily appreciate why Kornblith's argument is relevant to our inquiry. If an inference is reliable, so is its warrant. Thus, the subjunctive conditional corresponding to that warrant will, if not literally true, still possess a high degree of verisimilitude. We may thus view the mechanism allowing us to make these inferences as a belief-generating mechanism.

Central to Kornblith's argument is the concept of a homeostatic property cluster. This notion is straightforwardly illustrated. At the level of observable properties, we may easily recognize that some tend almost invariably, even uniformly, to go together. For example, if something is an apple, it will have skin and flesh, each of a certain texture, small brown seeds, a shape within certain roughly anticipated parameters. Likewise, there are properties that rarely if ever occur together. Should this happen, their co-occurrence would not last very long. Should we perceive what we take to be an apple, yet the skin over half its surface was that of an orange, we would expect tampering – in fact a tampering which could be easily undone.

These stable collections of observable properties are subsets of wider stable collections that include unobservable properties also. Furthermore, having these unobservable properties explains why objects have their observable properties and why these properties standardly occur together. For example, knowing something of the physiology of an animal species may explain why the bodily temperature of such animals standardly falls within a certain range. Further yet, these unobservable properties may explain why certain configurations of properties can hold together and others are not possible (causally possible). Generalizing on the biological principle of homeostasis, we may describe these stable clusters of properties where the unobservables causally explain both the observables and the overall stability of the set as homeostatic property clusters.

Given this definition, we may now lay out Kornblith's argument for the reliability of causal inferences involving natural kind concepts quite straightforwardly:

1. Certain features of objects reside in homeostatic clusters. Therefore
2. The world is objectively divided into natural kinds.
3. Human beings apprehend the world as divided into natural kinds.
4. Human beings are sensitive to those features of objects tending to reside in homeostatic clusters, that is, human beings are sensitive to the indicators of objective natural kinds. Therefore
5. Natural kinds as apprehended by humans match up with real kinds in nature.
6. Humans are oriented to apprehending as essential to a real kind what *is* causally essential and thus universal to that kind.
7. Humans project, that is, make inferences, on the basis of what they apprehend as essential to natural kinds. Therefore,
8. These projections, inferences are reliable at least to a significant degree.

How does Kornblith develop his argument? By virtue of motivating our definition of a homeostatic property cluster, we have virtually presented the case for (1). We can easily recognize that our experience presents us with properties that cluster together. The one point which may need further arguing concerns explaining this clustering through unobservable properties. But this is straightforward. Why an organism displays many of its properties is causally due to its genetic makeup – something ordinarily unobservable. But members of a given species will have a significant common genetic inheritance, which causally determines that many of their observable properties will cluster together within a given range and renders this fact causally explicable. Likewise, water has the observable properties of freezing at $0°C$ and boiling at $100°C$ at sea level. But that water has these observable properties is causally explained by its molecular structure. Recognizing that instances can be easily multiplied completes the case for (1).

That (2) follows from (1) is straightforward, given two additional premises. One expresses Kornblith's understanding of a natural or real kind. The other cites certain scientific facts. For Kornblith, the concept of natural kind "involves a collection of unobservable properties, inseparably united in nature, which are jointly responsible for the salient observable properties by which we are initially inclined to classify objects into kinds" (1993, p. 35). The unobservable properties – or a core of such properties which causally explain the clustering of the remaining properties – constitutes the definition of the real kind. But now the scientific facts that there are in nature core clusters of unobservable properties, and that science has been successful in explaining homeostatic property clusters involving observable characteristics in terms of these cores become salient. Given this scientific explanatory success, "one can no longer reasonably doubt the real existence of such structures" (1993, p. 41).

Kornblith next turns to our cognitive mechanisms for apprehending the world. He argues first that humans conceive the world as divided into natural kinds, that is, (3). Kornblith argues that this is the expression of an innate mental structure. He first points out that the capacity to make discriminations according to similarity, to rank objects being more or less similar in some respect, is innate. Thus, we can recognize that a rectangle is more like a square in shape than it is like a circle, and that an ellipse is more like a circle than like a square. As Quine points out, "Without some such prior spacing of qualities, we could never acquire a habit. . . . Needed as they are for all learning, these distinctive spacings cannot themselves all be learned; some must be innate" (1969, p. 123, quoted in Kornblith 1993, p. 62).

These rankings concern observable properties. That this innate structure is the minimum all humans share and for some, that is, children, this is all the innate structure that is operative, Kornblith calls the minimalist assumption. He claims that this sets the minimum far too low. He argues by citing results of certain studies done on children. In one study, four-year-old children were shown triads of pictures. In the first two pictures, they were told what natural kind each object belonged to – the two objects were of different natural kinds in each case – and were told some other contrasting feature of the two objects that was not shown in the picture, for example, feeding behavior with different kinds of animals. Thus, we have two kinds, K_1 and K_2 and two features, F_1 and F_2. In the third picture, the children were shown an object that was also of kind K_1 but had a distinct observable similarity to the K_2 object as pictured. They were asked whether this object had feature F_1 or F_2. The right answer was F_1. An object's having F_1 was causally determined by its being of kind K_1. Sixty-eight percent of the children's answers were correct. "Perhaps more importantly, over a third of the children consistently answered the questions on the basis of natural kind groupings, whereas none at all followed a consistent strategy of answering on the basis of observable similarity"

(1993, p. 65). This shows that the children could recognize natural kinds, could see being of a natural kind as a more significant similarity than a mere observable similarity. Further studies of young children confirm and enhance the results of this study. Turning to adults, Kornblith finds evidence in psychological studies that humans have concepts of natural kinds parallel in structure to the natural kinds into which, we have seen, nature divides. He quotes Douglas Medin, who advances a view called *psychological essentialism*: "People act as if things (e.g., objects) have essences or underlying natures that make them the thing that they are" (1989, p. 1476, quoted in Kornblith 1993, p. 70).

Surely this evidence indicates that natural kinds are part of the conceptual structure of human beings from an early age. But are they part of an innate mental structure? Kornblith points out first that there is no evidence for the minimalist position that innate structure concerns just an ability to rank observable properties according to their similarity. But he goes beyond this. He argues for innateness directly on analogy with Chomsky's argument for innate constraints on language learning. Children at an early age learn to recognize and construct syntactically or grammatically correct sentences. The children have heard a finite number of sentences. They are able to construct new grammatically correct sentences. Thus, they have projected formation rules. However, there are infinitely many different grammars all compatible with the sentences a child has heard. As Kornblith puts it "There must . . . be something constraining the rules which the child considers, severely restricting the class of possible grammars" (1993, p. 74). According to Chomsky, innate linguistic universals effect this constraining.

Analogously, the system of concepts children develop has a common structure. What a child experiences greatly underdetermines the structure. Why then do children develop this common structure? The best explanation is that "there are innate restrictions on the kinds of concepts we form and that these restrictions sufficiently delimit the class of concepts which are possible for us so as to make learning of the common conceptual structure inevitable" (1993, p. 76). In light of the psychological evidence, then, the presumption is for innateness of psychological essentialism.

Having argued that the world is divided into natural kinds and that humans apprehend the world as divided into natural kinds, we come to the crucial question: Do the natural kinds humans apprehend match up with the natural kinds objectively in the world? Premise (4) claims that they do. A necessary condition for sensitivity to those features of objects tending to reside in homeostatic clusters is being able to detect covariation reasonably accurately (1993, p. 95). Kornblith admits that when it comes to detecting covariation in general, there is significant evidence that humans do not do a good job. But he does not need to establish that humans reliably detect covariation in general, but just those covariations indicative of homeostatic property clusters. For this, he feels he has some evidence.

Studies show that when there is only a weak correlation between properties, people may fail to detect it. But when there is strong correlation, when with one property another is always or almost always correlated, "we do quite well in detecting it" (1993, p. 100). But, in many instances with natural kinds, this is the degree of covariation. Substances will ordinarily have fixed boiling and freezing points – at least relative to a constant air pressure. Substances that do conduct electricity invariably conduct it. Combining substances may uniformly or near uniformly produce certain reactions.

In addition, as Kornblith points out, tests of covariation ability are artificial in that only one pair of properties is correlated to some degree. But natural kinds involve a whole cluster of covariant properties. Although the covariation of given pairs of properties may be imperfect, given instances of covariation may have a distinct resemblance. Furthermore, empirical evidence "suggests that we are, indeed, quite good detectors of multiple, clustered covariation, in spite of our limitations when it comes to detecting isolated cases" (1993, p. 101).[8] Hence, it appears that our covariation detection mechanism, when employed in an appropriate cognitive environment (and not one artificially oversimplified), such as an environment structured by natural kinds, does make us sensitive to the indicators of objective natural kinds.

Having argued that humans apprehend the world as divided into natural kinds (3) and that humans are sensitive to the indicators of objective natural kinds (4), it follows that (5) there is a matchup – admittedly imperfect – between real kinds as apprehended by humans and real kinds objectively in nature. However, one can object to this inferential move on two grounds, questioning whether the matchup is so imperfect that it becomes misleading to say that apprehended and real natural kinds match up. First, in some circumstances persons have a preconception of what properties should be found together. This leads them to read their theories into a situation, "seeing" covariation which is not there. In addition, even without any antecedent notion or theory about what properties should occur together, persons may upon an incomplete observation of certain data claim that certain properties do covary when in fact they do not.[9] A portion of the data suggests a covariation that the full data nonetheless disconfirms.

Kornblith believes that he can blunt the criticism of reading theory-driven anticipations of covariation into situations in which none is present. Such anticipations are expressions of the human "tendency toward belief perseverance: once we acquire a certain belief, there is a strong tendency to hold on to it, even in the face of undermining evidence" (1993, p. 104). Although in certain circumstances, belief perseverance will result in our acquiring mistaken beliefs, in the overall picture it may aid our efficiently acquiring true beliefs. If our background expectations are true or very good approximations to the truth, they should give us insight on how to interpret new data properly. Hence, looking at our belief-generating mechanism as a whole, belief perseverance may be a way of increasing its ability to generate true beliefs reliably. In light of this, it seems that the burden of proof is shifted back to the challenger to show that mistakenly reading in preconceptions is so prevalent as to render talk of any general matchup between natural kinds as apprehended by humans and real natural kinds misleading.

Remember there is empirical evidence that under certain conditions humans can reliably detect covariation. This fact gives us a reply to the issue of mistakenly detecting covariation in a portion of the data which the full data disconfirms.[10] Does this evidence of imperfect reliability show that human apprehension of real natural kinds is so faulty that we should not speak of a matchup between apprehended natural kinds and real natural kinds? One who claims this is accepting a significant burden of proof. Natural kinds involve clustered and not single covariation. Humans may read some covariation into a situation; but do they ever read in enough covariation to imagine they "see" a natural kind? Do humans read covariation *clusters* into a situation in a significant number of cases?

We have still to consider how statements (6) and (7), both basic premises in our layout of Kornblith's argument, are justified. That (6) humans are oriented to apprehending as essential or universal in a real kind what is essential or universal in that kind follows from Kornblith's discussion of the structure of natural kind concepts. Even small children apprehend natural kinds as having insides and outsides, underlying properties and superficial similarities. Furthermore, children "presuppose, from the very beginning, that the features which unite a kind are underlying rather than more superficial ones. But it is precisely those underlying properties which form the essence of natural kinds" (1993, p. 106).

Again, for adults, as the psychologists Medin and Ortony put it, "people act as if their [natural kind] concepts contain essence placeholders that are filled with 'theories' about what the corresponding entities are" (Medin and Ortony 1989, p. 186, quoted in Kornblith 1993, p. 106), that is, theories that identify what is essential and thus universal to that kind. This is not to say that what is apprehended as essential *is* always essential to that kind. Children may have a very faulty view of what those similarities are. Theories of the essence of a natural kind may need to be refined and revised. But, as Kornblith remarks, the structure of natural kind concepts points us in the right direction. We are oriented to apprehending, however imperfectly or incompletely, the underlying essences of natural kinds.

(7) asserts that humans make inferences on the basis of their apprehending what is essential, that is, universal to natural kinds. To justify this claim, we need to look at Kornblith's account of just how these inferences are carried out. How does one move from the backing to the intuition of the warrant? Observation of a small number of cases gives the backing. Kornblith cites the example that at one time the wives of both President Ford and Vice President Rockefeller underwent mastectomies. "Immediately thereafter, the number of visits to cancer detection clinics increased dramatically" (1993, p. 90). The backing is the observation that these two middle-aged women – both prominent in public life – had needed mastectomies. We may phrase the warrant this way:

From	x is a middle-aged woman
We may take it that	x has a non-negligible risk of developing breast cancer

In this context, "middle-aged woman" is functioning as a natural kind term. Part of the theory filling the essence placeholder includes a recognition, however preliminary, that there is a causal connection between a middle-aged woman's internal physiology and her susceptibility to certain diseases. We expect the instances of an organic natural kind to be constant in internal physiology. That is why causal beliefs involving this internal physiology may be entered into the essence placeholder for the kind. So, upon observing two middle-aged women who have a particular health problem, one makes inferences according to the above warrant, that is, on the basis of apprehending what is essential to a natural kind, that is, (7). By contrast, properties in which there is no intuition of causal connection are not projected. Should Mrs. Ford and Mrs. Rockefeller both have worn blue dresses on a given occasion, one would not project that middle-aged women have a tendency to wear blue dresses.

In light of (5), (6), and (7), the inference to (8) is straightforward. If real kinds as apprehended by humans and real kinds objectively in nature match up – at least to a certain extent, if what is apprehended as essential to a real kind may very well be an apprehension at least in part of what is causally essential to that kind, and if humans make inferences on the basis of what they apprehend to be essential to natural kinds, then those inferences have a significant degree of reliability, that is, (8). We must admit, as Kornblith points out, that the theories which replace the essence placeholders may be more or less accurate, and that this affects the reliability of an inference. But, "Insofar as that knowledge is accurate, our inductive inferences will be reliable. . . . Our conceptual and inferential tendencies jointly conspire, at least roughly, to carve nature at its joints and project the features of a kind which are essential to it. This preestablished harmony between the causal structure of the world and the conceptual and inferential structure of our minds produces reliable inductive inference" (1993, pp. 106, 94). But, as the inferences are reliable, the subjunctive conditionals corresponding to the warrants of these inferences are true or at least verisimilitudinous.

As these last remarks indicate, with this account of how we make inferences involving natural kinds and of the argument for their reliability, we have an account of one type of operation of physical intuition – that involving natural kinds – as a belief-generating mechanism and its reliability in generating beliefs expressed through subjunctive conditionals. Given our perception or acquaintance with one or more instances of a natural kind, and our apprehending them as being of that kind, we recognize that certain features of those instances – mode of nutrition or reproduction, conductivity or nonconductivity of electricity, boiling or freezing point – are connected to the essence of the kind. Should our information indicate what exactly these features are in this case – what *is* the mode of nutrition of these particular organisms before us, whether these instances of metal *do* conduct electricity, at exactly what point *do* these samples of liquid boil – then we project that property to other members of this kind. But we also come to believe, if only tacitly, that if something *were* of this kind, it *would* have this particular mode of nutrition, conductivity of electricity, boiling point. We come to believe a generalized subjunctive conditional.

Two critical questions immediately arise for natural kind guided physical intuition. Is it a mechanism that generates basic beliefs? Is it presumptively reliable? We may present two arguments that it generates basic beliefs. First, as we have seen, by virtue of this mechanism we make certain projections, that is, inferences. But, as Toulmin reminds us, these inferences have warrants. Our empirical observation of the particular instances of the natural kind constitutes the backing for this warrant. What is the relation between backing and warrant? Given that a warrant is an inference rule or inference license, again that it is appealed to implicitly rather than explicitly in argumentation (compare Toulmin 1958, p. 100), it would seem odd and indeed distorting to say that this license was *inferred* from propositions expressing the backing. Inference licenses do not enter into inferential relationships as conclusions inferred from premises. We grasp the warrant and thus the corresponding subjunctive conditional directly.

Second, Toulmin points out that backing is expressed in certain factual statements. The warrant, by constrast, draws a moral about what can be inferred from what. One can then challenge us: If this drawing a moral is not a form of inference, what is it? Following Audi, we distinguish conclusions of reflection and conclusions of inference. Audi asks us to imagine that we are listening to someone complaining about a co-workers's performance on a given task. The person cites many instances of ways in which the work was deficient. On this basis, we conclude that the work was shoddy. This is clearly a case of inferred belief. But now suppose the question arises of whether the reporter is biased toward the co-worker.

One might now recall his narration in one's mind's eye and ear, and from a global, intuitive sense of [his] intonations, word choices, selection of deficiencies, and omission of certain merits, judge that he is jealous of her. This is a response to an overall impression.... [I]t emerges from thinking about the overall pattern of [his] critique in the context of his relation to [the] coworker, but not from one or more evidential premises. (Audi 1997, p. 43)

In observing a small number of instances of a natural kind and identifying a property shared by those instances as essential to that kind, one is already bringing a pattern to what one observes. Is not seeing that something as an instance of a kind recognizing a gestalt in what one sees, a gestalt involving an essence? As we have seen, this essence may include certain determinable properties such as, for organisms, having a characteristic mode of interaction with their environment or a characteristic mode of reproduction. By means of this determinable, the perceived determinate falling under it is also identified as an essential property. We may then project from something's being an instance of this natural kind to its having that determinate property. But have we *reasoned* to this property's being essential from premises that it is a determinate of a certain determinable and that the determinable is an essential property of this natural kind of which the observed objects are instances? Have we not simply apprehended the determinate property as essential given our understanding of the essence of the natural kind? In projecting according to this determinate essential property, do we reason from the essence to the warrant? Do we not simply make projections based on our apprehension of the determinable property as essential? Thus, the warrant is intuitively grasped, as is the corresponding subjunctive conditional.

One might object that conclusions of reflection are really inferred. One has inferred that the person complaining is jealous from premises that he expressed his complaint using certain emotive means including being slanted in a certain way. Likewise, one could object that one infers that if something were an instance of a certain natural kind, it would instance some particular determinate essential property from premises that the corresponding determinable is part of the essence of the natural kind, that the natural kind concept indicates that a unique determinate for that natural kind falls under the determinable, and that observed instances of that natural kind are also instances of the particular determinate. Audi's reply to the first objection serves to reply to the second. The objection confuses "the grounds of one's judgment with beliefs expressing those grounds" (1997, p. 43). Just because one can frame premises for a judgment does not mean that one has inferred the judgment from those premises. Upon perceiving a book, one can give reasons from one's perceptual experience why the object perceived is a book. But the judgment was not inferred from those premises. One perceives the book immediately.

Even if one grants that natural kind guided intuition generates basic beliefs, the question still remains of whether any are properly basic beliefs. Granted, Kornblith has given us an argument that natural kind guided intuition has an overall reliability. But has he shown that this reliability is high enough to justify our taking a particular dispositional subjunctive which is the product of this intuition as a basic premise? One objection is readily apparent. As Kornblith admits, reliability of natural kind guided intuition is a function of what fills the essence placeholder. Our inferences will be reliable insofar as our apprehension of that essence is accurate (compare Kornblith 1993, p. 106). But in a given case of natural kind guided intuition, what guarantee is there that this apprehension will be accurate?

I believe we must distinguish two ways in which the theory which fills the placeholder may lead us to acquire mistaken beliefs. First, the theory may contain an inaccurate nomic or lawlike statement of the form "$(\forall x)(\phi x\boxed{n}\mapsto \psi x)$" or "$(\forall x)(\phi x \Box\mapsto \psi x)$," and through perception or testimony we believe for some particular a that ϕa. Hence, we come to believe – either by projecting according to the corresponding warrant or by inferring from the generalized subjunctive together with the instance of the antecedent – that ψa, where this proposition is erroneous. But this is an *inferred* rather than a *basic* belief. It is not a belief generated by natural kind guided intuition, and thus this problem, although legitimate, is not a problem for the belief-generating mechanisms we are discussing here.

Inaccurate knowledge of a kind's essence will affect intuition guided by natural kind N, if where "Nx" is the predicate that x is of that natural kind and "Δx" is a determinable property, the theory of the essence includes inaccurate statements of the form "$(\forall x)(Nx\boxed{n}\mapsto \Delta x)$" or "$(\forall x)(Nx \Box\mapsto \Delta x)$." Should δ be a determinate of Δ, natural kind guided intuition would be proceeding on inaccurate grounds in generating a belief of the form "$(\forall x)(Nx \Box\mapsto \delta x)$," for example. Likewise, should not all instances of N fall under just one determinate δ of Δ, but our understanding of the essence indicate that they do, statements of the form "$(\forall x)(Nx \Box\mapsto \delta x)$," will again not be true, and natural kind guided intuition be operating on inaccurate grounds in generating such a belief. It is hard to see how the second case could arise. Suppose we discovered two living organisms resembling each other closely, yet one bore its young live and the other laid eggs. Would both be classed as instances of the same species, that is, natural kind?

Again, that some determinables are broad concepts expected to be true not only of all instances of a certain species but of all instances of wider genera – Do not all animals have a characteristic mode of nutrition and a characteristic mode of reproduction? – one can question under what situations generalizations of the form "$(\forall x)(Nx \Box\mapsto \Delta x)$" will be false or inaccurate. More important, for the question of the presumptive reliability of natural kind guided intuition, if a theory filling the essence placeholder of some natural kind includes such generalizations, can one presume their truth? It would seem that in many cases their truth would be vouched for by common knowledge or by scientific practice and thus in effect by expert testimony. As we shall see in Chapter 10, there are presumptions for both of these sources of testimony. This is not to say that the presumption cannot be overturned. Advances in science might produce a restructuring of natural kind concepts. But, absent recognition of such advances or indications that such advances are genuine nomic possibilities, why should one not presume true these laws or lawlike statements indicating that natural kinds have certain determinable properties? But, if there is a presumption for these statements, there is a presumption of reliability for natural kind guided intuition in generating beliefs expressed by generalized subjunctives indicating that natural kinds have determinate properties falling under these determinables.

Contrast physical intuition guided by natural kinds with physical intuition of causal dependency, forming beliefs constituting causal hypotheses. Such beliefs are basic, but they would ordinarily not be regarded as properly basic but in need of evidence based on tests. It is nomically possible that other relevant variables are operating here. Those possibilities need to be ruled out before the belief is acceptable, but then the belief will no longer be basic but based on the results of these tests. Whether one carries out these tests is voluntary. Cohen sees here the criterion for distinguishing belief-generating mechanisms (or specific employments of such mechanisms) yielding presumptively acceptable beliefs from those that are not presumptively acceptable. I am appeared to treely and form the belief that there is a tree outside my office window. Unless I also have defeating evidence, my belief is also acceptable. My having the belief is a presumptive reason for my taking it as a premise (compare Cohen 1992, p. 130). But notice that also unless I am aware of defeating or rebutting factors, the issue of testing or gaining corroborating evidence does not arise. But, as Cohen points out, mistaken causal beliefs – at least about how Nature works – are quite common and therefore causal beliefs about nature's operations are not by themselves presumptively acceptable (Cohen 1992, p. 130).

What is the crucial difference between the kind of mechanism that generates presumptively acceptable beliefs and the kind that generates beliefs which are not presumptively acceptable? ... Wherever there is standardly some opportunity for the intrusion of a voluntary element into the mechanism, the kind of belief generated is not presumptively acceptable, because a mistake may be made in the discharge of this voluntary element. (1992, pp. 130–1)

So, where the question of testing genuinely arises, the belief-generating mechanism is not presumptively reliable. For there to be a presumption in favor of the belief, we must know that the tests have been carried out reliably, making the resultant belief nonbasic. But should the belief-generating mechanism be physical intuition applying the category of causal dependency, just forming a causal hypothesis, no tests will have been carried out. Thus, the mechanism is not presumptively reliable.

Notice that in natural kind guided intuition, the issue of test need not arise. Kornblith offers this illustration. Suppose I do not know the mode of platypus reproduction. I visit the zoo and see several female platypuses brooding eggs. I perceive these animals to be instances of the natural kind platypus. Part of the theory filling the essence placeholder of that natural kind term is the causal regularity that given the internal physiological structure of platypuses – whatever that might be – members of the species reproduce in a certain particular way – whatever that is. Furthermore, the theory includes the claim that it is not the case that some members of the species reproduce in one way, others in another way. But these principles would seem to be part of our very understanding of the concept of natural kind. Surely there is a presumption for them. Why should they be tested? Hence, once my experience discloses the specific mode of reproduction of the species, I may project that mode to the entire natural kind in accordance with these principles. Hence, there is also a presumption for the subjunctive claim corresponding to the warrant of that projection. So, unless I am aware of evidence bringing the operative principles in my theory of a natural kind into question, the issue of test does not arise for natural kind guided intuition.

We said at the beginning of this section that physical intuition operates by detecting covariation and imposing an interpretive category. Because in imposing the category of causal dependency, physical intuition is not presumptively reliable, it is not presumptively reliable in general. However, as we have seen, in the particular case of imposing the category of natural kinds, physical intuition is presumptively reliable.

8.7 PERSONAL SUBJUNCTIVES AND PERSONAL INTUITION

Recall from Section 8.1 that the hallmarks of a personal explanation are making reference to the beliefs and goals of some conscious agent. In Section 8.4 we saw further that beliefs and intentions could be understood as dispositions and thus ascriptions of belief and intention rendered as subjunctives (see pp. 158–62). The epistemological question now is whether one can form basic beliefs concerning the mental dispositions of others and their nomic connections, and whether or under what circumstances these beliefs are properly basic. This involves forming beliefs about other minds. As we saw in Section 7.2, Reid presents a theory of natural signs according to which on the basis of certain bodily appearances on the part of other persons, we form beliefs about the contents of their minds. Some of these beliefs concern occurrent mental states. But surely, just as "anger," "depression," "joy" may refer not only to occurrent mental states but to dispositional states, it seems that natural signs also may be signs of dispositions. Ascriptions of what they are signs of are thus explicable in terms of subjunctives.

It would be tempting to say that by means of these natural signs we perceive these dispositions through personal perception. However, since such predicates are unpacked in terms of subjunctives, ascriptions of dispositional predicates are interpretations rather than descriptions. We prefer to regard perception as generating descriptive beliefs and intuition as generating interpretive beliefs. So although this may be only a terminological cavil, we regard coming to believe that someone is dispositionally angry or dispositionally benevolent upon observing certain natural signs in his countenance or behavior as an employment of personal intuition rather than personal perception.

As with personal perception, personal intuition in this employment generates basic beliefs. Upon being appeared to by certain natural signs, we believe immediately that the person is in a certain dispositional state. As Reid puts it: "When I see the features of an expressive face, I see only figure and colour variously modified. But, by the constitution of my nature, the visible object brings along with it the conception and belief of a certain passion or sentiment in the mind of the person" (1983, p. 281).[11]

Is the evidence for an occurrent mental state also appropriately evidence for a dispositional mental state? The following remark of Perelman and Olbrechts-Tyteca is suggestive. In enumerating various presumptions, they note "the presumption that the quality of an act reveals the quality of the person responsible for it" (1969, p. 70). If an act is benevolent, we may presume that the person who performed it has a benevolent disposition. Clearly, what Perelman and Olbrechts-Tyteca say here can be generalized. For example, if someone appears angry, is there not a presumption that he *is* angry? Natural signs of someone's occurrent feelings of anger then are natural signs that if he were confronted with or reminded of the object of that anger, then *ceteris paribus* he would occurrently feel and perhaps display anger. In general, then, there is a presumption that the occurrent reveals the dispositional.

So far, our examples have mostly concerned affective mental states. But one should not conclude that the only mental states about which personal perception and personal intuition may form beliefs are affective states. Suppose we have perceived Jones igniting the fuse. Jones's act is intentional. It is thus a natural sign both that Jones believed igniting the fuse would cause the bomb's exploding and that Jones intended the bomb to explode. We propose calling this belief and goal the proximate intention of the act. We claim that intentional behavior reveals proximate intention. Notice that belief and goal are both dispositional. We do not expect that Jones only occurrently believes now that igniting the fuse would cause the bomb to explode or that he only intends now that the bomb explode.

The overt act would not ordinarily reveal less than proximate desires or goals motivating the act. Suppose we perceived Jones igniting the fuse but that we had no further information about Jones's intentions. Although we could intuit that Jones intended the bomb to explode, could we further intuit that he wanted to spread terror through the land? If we knew that Jones was a terrorist, we might come to believe that Jones intended the bomb to explode in order to spread terror. But would this belief be basic? Given our background knowledge of terrorists, of what bombs cause in the immediate vicinity of their detonation, of what Jones believed about the further consequences of his acts we would *infer* (using some material warrant) our conclusion concerning Jones's motivation. But this belief is the result of inference to an explanation. This particular inference may not be a reliable way to come to that belief, since other explanations which have not been ruled out may be equally or perhaps even more plausible. But such possibilities do not show personal intuition unreliable. The problem is with our *inferential* mechanism. We also may infer that others hold certain beliefs that are not part of the proximate intention of their acts. Suppose our background knowledge indicates both that polls show the prospects for Jones's winning are not good and that Smith supports Jones. We see that when the conversation turns to Jones, Smith betrays a lack of enthusiasm. We form the belief that *Smith* believes that Jones will not win. Our belief about Smith's believing is the result of inference to an explanation, not personal intuition.

We argue that as long as personal intuition is forming a belief concerning the proximate intention whose natural signs are manifest in some act, or a belief concerning the affective disposition of another on the basis of a manifest natural sign of the corresponding occurrent state, personal intuition is presumptively reliable. This is straightforward. In Section 7.2, we argued that personal perception is presumptively reliable. But, personal perception recognizes certain publicly observable features as natural signs of occurrent mental states, thus forming beliefs about those occurrent mental states. On the basis of the same natural signs, personal intuition generates beliefs concerning the corresponding dispositional states. But as we have indicated, there is a presumption that the occurrent reveals the dispositional. So if personal perception generating beliefs about occurrent mental states is presumptively reliable and there is a presumption that those mental states signify the corresponding dispositional states, there is a presumption of reliability for personal intuition in generating beliefs that those dispositional states hold.

There is, however, a further way in which personal intuition may generate beliefs expressed by personal subjunctives. Consider:

1. If one were to learn that one's spouse was engaging in marital infidelities and one cared about one's spouse's fidelity, then one would feel distinct hurt over that behavior.

Suppose I saw a friend, Beatrice, crying. Suppose she tells me that her husband Cedric has been unfaithful, where throughout their marriage she had trusted him. Would I not come to believe immediately that learning of Cedric's infidelity together with her valuing his supposed fidelity psychologically caused Beatrice's distress and would I not also come to believe that the corresponding generalization was true? But why would I form the belief that a particular instance of psychological causation held in Beatrice's case and would I be justified, given the evidence I was aware of, in moving to the general case?

Actually I need not personally observe the natural signs of Beatrice's emotional distress to come to have these beliefs. Suppose I learn from reliable testimony that Beatrice has just found out that Cedric has been unfaithful, where I could presume that his faithfulness was something she cared about. Would I not come to believe immediately that Beatrice was feeling hurt, that she was feeling hurt because of what she learned, and that this connection held generally? I propose that we come to believe this connection because we empathetically put ourselves in Beatrice's place so characterized and see that *we* would feel distinct hurt. When we encounter the case through testimony, we are encountering that case as characterized in a certain way, as a case of one spouse learning of the infidelity of her marriage partner, whose fidelity she prized. So in imaginatively putting ourselves in Beatrice's place, we imaginatively put ourselves in the place of anyone who has just learned that his or her spouse has been unfaithful. But this characterization is enough for us to feel empathetically the hurt of the betrayed spouse. We claim that it is sufficient also for our personal intuition to grasp a general connection between learning of one's spouse's unfaithfulness (where this was someone one cared about) and being hurt.

Some will object that although we come to hold these beliefs, they are inferred through analogy. I do not believe this is true to the phenomenology of how we come to hold these beliefs. Clearly, there is a presumption that people care about their spouse's fidelity, so we can set aside specific mention of this consideration. I hear that Beatrice has just learned of Cedric's infidelity. I immediately wince over the hurt I believe she is feeling over this betrayal. I empathetically feel not only that hurt but that it is a hurt intending Cedric's action. Notice that I do not entertain this argument from analogy:

2. a. In imagination I learn that my spouse has been unfaithful and I feel hurt over it.
   b. Beatrice has just learned that Cedric has been unfaithful. Therefore probably
   c. Beatrice feels hurt over it.

My belief is a matter of "feeling her pain" and what that pain is over. My empathy supplies the connection between learning that a spouse has been unfaithful and feeling pain. My personal intuition grasps the general connection manifested through empathy.

I do not believe we need to hold that we form the general beliefs immediately upon observing the instances. Even if we do not, we may still form these beliefs in a basic way. Should someone ask us whether in general if one were to learn of a spouse's unfaithfulness, one would feel hurt, mindful of our empathetic response, we might very well consciously form the belief that the general statement held. But are we inferring this from our self-knowledge? Do we not, rather, recognize the general connection because the hurt is hurt over the infidelity, that the hurt intends the infidelity? The belief again is basic.

Are these general beliefs properly basic? Here I believe a Reidian constitutional argument is apropos. Is not empathy, feeling the pains, sorrows, joys, pleasures of others part of our constitution? But when through entertaining a description that a person's situation satisfies certain conditions, either through personal observation or testimony, one enters empathetically into that situation, one's personal intuition grasps that it is because of these conditions characterizing the situation that one has the feelings one does, that if anyone were likewise in such a situation, one would feel as one does now. Surely, it is of our constitution and nature to form such beliefs, just as when being appeared to in a certain way we form a perceptual belief that there is an object satisfying certain properties before us in the external world. Surely in both cases, it seems that the beliefs formed express the basic evidence from which we reason. If perception is presumptively reliable, personal intuition in this employment should be presumptively reliable.

There are, however, personal subjunctives which go beyond the ascription of affective dispositions, proximate beliefs or intentions, or empathetically recognized connections. These are subjunctives of psychological causation that may be presupposed in explanations of events or conditions through intentional actions or in explanations of actions through motives. Consider:

> 3. Andy received an *A* in Symbolic Logic through his studying the subject assiduously.

According to our pattern of analysis in Section 8.4, this statement presupposes:

> 3′. If anyone with Andy's scholastic aptitude were to study symbolic logic as assiduously as Andy, he would get an *A* in Symbolic Logic.

(3) is an explanation with respect to intentional action. Consider also:

> 4. Cassius plotted the death of Caesar because he bore an inbred hatred of tyrants.

Here we are explaining Cassius's action with respect to a motive. It presupposes:

> 4′. If anyone with a relevantly similar psychological and cultural background as Cassius were to bear an inborn hatred of tyrants and were to believe that a certain individual were a tyrant, he would plot the death of that individual.

Both (3′) and (4′) are subjunctives of general psychological causation.

Although through my personal intuition I may come to believe that effort improves performance, this claim of psychological causation requires the corroboration of common knowledge if not the experience of testing. It will not be a properly basic belief on the basis of personal intuition alone. Again, although one's empathetically attempting to feel Cassius's hatred for a given type of individual might lead one to grasp a connection between harboring this hatred and having murderous thoughts toward that individual, to be justified in believing or accepting (4′), one would need evidence that this psychological causation held in general. But to be justified in accepting this statement, we would certainly need information about Cassius's psychological and cultural background, information that would furnish us with premises for our subjunctive belief. Personal subjunctives involving such psychological explanations then are causal hypotheses, as are physical subjunctives involving physical explanation. Although through a flash of intuitive insight one may come to hold them in a basic way, without confirmation or corroboration one's resulting belief is not justified. With such confirmation, they are no longer basic beliefs.

8.8 INSTITUTIONAL SUBJUNCTIVES AND INSTITUTIONAL INTUITION

We turn now to subjunctives corresponding to warrants backed by systems of constitutive rules, what Searle calls institutions (1969, p. 51), as opposed to the empirical subjunctives of the last two sections. Our questions in this section, then are first how do we learn these systems of constitutive rules and under what circumstances, if any, is there a presumption for the reliability of how we learn them? Second, does having learned these rules then "translate" into forming properly basic institutional subjunctive beliefs?

Let us recall from our discussion of presumption for institutional perception in Section 7.2 that we may learn rules either by "picking them up" informally or by consulting some authoritative formalization or formulation, or by a combination of the two methods. As we shall see, the second method ultimately reduces to the first. Learning a system of rules informally is clearly how we humans learn most of our first language, including its rules of syntax. Children hear a number of sentences spoken by others. They utter sentences of their own construction and in some cases are corrected. On the basis of these experiences they come to be able to abide by the rules of syntax for generating sentences of English – they know how to speak grammatically – even if they are not able to formulate any of the rules of grammar. We shall see the importance of this point shortly. For now, let us emphasize that knowing how to participate in a practice correctly does not entail being able to articulate general principles or constituting rules defining that practice. Hence, asking someone to state those rules is not a proper test for showing that he or she has learned them. Rather, the test would be overt behavior in accordance with those rules in a context calling for observance of the practice.

Clearly, observing such a display of knowing how would shift the burden of proof to anyone who says the person does not know the rules. It would establish a presumption for his having learned them. Notice that this observing involves institutional perception and presupposes that *our* institutional perception is presumptively reliable in this case.[12]

This means that constitutive rules learned informally or our knowledge of them are unique among the types of backing standing behind warrants and their corresponding subjunctive conditionals. In all other instances, backing could be expressed propositionally. One could meaningfully talk of forming beliefs that the backing held. One could thus talk of learning that the backing obtained independently of our acquiring the inference habit corresponding to the warrant. But in learning a system of constitutive rules in the manner of coming to know how, as Ryle points out, "we never speak of a person believing or opining *how*" (1949, p. 28).

I believe this indicates a far more intimate connection between backing and warrant in this case. Unlike the empirical, in particular physical, case where upon awareness of certain backing one comes to make projections conforming to a warrant, here to learn the rule – backing – is to acquire the warrant. The paradigm form of a constitutive institutional rule is "*X* counts as *Y* in context *C*" (Searle 1969, p. 52), for example, receiving a football counts as scoring a touchdown when standing in the endzone. Surely someone who had mastered this rule would project from Jones's catching the football while standing in the endzone to his scoring a touchdown. It is not that his mastering the rule would be input for his projecting according to the warrant – or his acquiring the inference habit corresponding to the warrant – as output. Here input and output would be one.

But just as in the empirical case, corresponding to the warrant is a subjunctive. To come to project according to the warrant is to come to believe the subjunctive. Surely, someone who from "Jones caught the football while standing in the endzone" took it that "Jones scored a touchdown" would believe that "If Jones were to catch the football while standing in the endzone, he would score a touchdown." The belief-generating mechanism is structured that upon learning the rule we acquire the subjunctive belief. But this means that the belief-generating mechanism is reliable to the extent that one has genuinely learned the rule (or system of constitutive rules of which that rule is a part). Thus, the belief-generating mechanism is presumptively reliable to the extent that there is a presumption one has learned the rules – a presumption that we saw is established by one's performance in undertaking the activity constituted by those rules or in correctly understanding or perceiving the activities of other in accordance with those rules.

Let us turn now to the other way in which one might learn constitutive rules, by encountering some formulation of those rules. As such, formulations back warrants in certain fields, so encountering these formulations constitutes the input of the belief-generating mechanism whose output is constituted by the beliefs expressed by subjunctives (or their universal generalizations) corresponding to these warrants. What may we say concerning the presumptive reliability of this mechanism? Let us approach this problem through Searle's speech act theory. What kind of speech act is this formulation? Clearly, whether this formulation is a record of the terms of some acts or other legal provisions passed by some legislative body together with the dates of enactment, a formulation of the rules of some game such as bridge, chess, or soccer, or a formulation of a system of taxonomy, we are dealing with two speech acts here, in tandem. The formulation itself is an assertive. It is asserting that certain constitutive rules containing certain provisions have been enacted in the case of legislation, or agreed to in the case of games, or promulgated in the case of a taxonomic system.

But in each case this is to report that another speech act has taken place – an act of legislation of one of these types: A formal legislative body has enacted a given piece of legislation. A body entrusted with the constitutive rules of a game has agreed to certain provisions or modifications of previously agreed-to provisions. Someone with authority – presumably a function not only of the person's expertise in a given area but also of the respect with which that person is held in the community of scholars in that area – has put forward a classification system. Searle points out that such speech acts have a twofold illocutionary force or part, "a declarational status (the propositional content becomes law) and a directive status (the law is directive in intent)" (1979, p. 28).

Searle defines a declaration as an illocutionary act whose successful performance "brings about the correspondence between the propositional content and reality, successful performance guarantees that the propositional content corresponds to the world" (1979, pp. 16–17). Thus, if Parliament successfully declares that those born in British colonies are British subjects, then those born in British colonies *are* British subjects. In general, successful performance of a declarative presupposes an institution. Parliament can make no successful declaration unless there is an institution of laws in which it occupies the position of law maker.

Directives by contrast "are attempts . . . by the speaker to get the hearer to do something" (1979, p. 13). Although the attempts may be expressed with varying degrees of force, the point is to get the world to conform to the word by having the hearer H do some future action A (compare 1979, p. 14). Of course, with a law enacted through some declarative, there may be no specific hearer H addressed or action A requested. But, surely, laws entail directive consequences for certain hearers under certain circumstances. British subjects have certain rights. Hence, the law declaring that those living in British colonies are British subjects entails that those persons have these rights and thus enjoins on certain persons in certain circumstances that they do what accords these persons certain of their rights.

When one comes to believe a subjunctive conditional when one is confronted with the formulation of some constitutive rule (when one is the hearer of an illocutionary act of assertion that this rule has been successfully declared), when is this belief reliably formed? It would seem that the following two conditions are prerequisite: First, one must understand the assertion that a successful declarative has been made. Second, that assertion must be true. But, notice that if these two conditions are satisfied, then the hearer in effect is in the illocutionary position of someone who has heard the declarative directly and not through the mediation of some further act of assertion. For someone in the latter position to form the subjunctive belief reliably, that person would need to understand the propositional content of the declarative act, that content would need to support the subjunctive conditional, and one would need to understand that the declarative act was successfully performed. Under what circumstances is there a presumption that these conditions are satisfied?

Consider first the truth requirement for the assertive that this declarative has been performed. There would be a presumption that the assertion is true just in case there is a presumption that the assertor's report is trustworthy. This brings us to the issue of when taking one's word is a reliable belief-generating mechanism, the subject of Chapter 10. To anticipate our discussion briefly, if a source vouches for a claim, taking that word will be presumptively reliable only if one is aware of signs that the source has the requisite competence or authority to state truly that the claim holds. For example, an authorized record of the Acts of Parliament will presumably have been authoritatively prepared and will contain some indication of its being an authorized publication.

When does one understand that a declarative with a given propositional content has been successfully made? Applying Searle's speech act
analysis, we have a situation where either a formal legislature or some
body or individual with legislative authority is the speaker *S*. The hearer
H is whoever encounters a formulation of what *S* is uttering or has uttered.
The utterance expresses the particular declarative. By this utterance, *S*
is trying to tell *H* something, that is, to produce a certain illocutionary
effect. This effect has two factors – *H*'s recognizing that *S* intends to tell
him something and *H*'s understanding exactly what it is that *S* is trying to
tell him. Notice that both of these factors require that *H* understand *S*'s
utterance. To recognize that *S* intends to tell him something by means
of his utterance, it is not enough that *H* perceive or otherwise come to
believe that *S* has made the utterance. *H* must understand it. But for
sentences in general, according to Searle,

1. Understanding a sentence is knowing its meaning.
2. The meaning of a sentence is determined by rules, and those rules
    specify both conditions of utterance of the sentence and also what
    the utterance counts as. (1969, p. 48)

A sentence expressing a declarative can be factored into two parts, a
declarative illocutionary force indicator and a sentence by whose utterance one may express the proposition being asserted. Understanding the
meaning of that sentence would involve knowledge of certain rules of reference and predication. Searle discusses such rules in Chapters 4 and 5
of (1969). Although Searle does not discuss declaratives in (1969), from
his characterization in (1979), I believe we can carry out an analysis of
declaration as an illocutionary act analogous to his analysis of promises
presented in Chapter 3 of (1969):

If *S* utters a sentence *P* in the potential presence of a hearer *H*, then
by uttering *P*, *S* declares that *p* (to *H*) if and only if

1. *S* and *H* share the same language, *S* can produce utterances and
    H receive them, and there are no further barriers to linguistic
    communication between *S* and *H*.[13]
2. *S* expresses the proposition that *p* in the utterance of *P*.[14]
3. That *p* does not obtain in the normal course of events.
4. *S* is in a position of legislative authority.
5. *S* intends that *S*'s uttering of *P* will bring it about that *p*.

This is the essential feature of a declarative, the bringing about of a state of affairs or proposition that *p* through an utterance of *P*.

6. *S* intends to produce in *H* the knowledge *K* that the utterance *P* counts as the bringing about of *p*. *S* intends to produce *K* by means of the recognition of *S*'s intention that his uttering of *P* will bring it about that *p*, and *S* intends *S*'s intention to be recognized by means of *H*'s knowledge of the meaning of *P*.

7. The semantical rules of the dialect spoken by *S* and *H* are such that *P* is correctly uttered if and only if conditions 1–6 obtain.[15]

We may now extract from these conditions for successfully making a declaration rules for using the illocutionary device indicating that a declaration is being made. Such a device is the phrase "I declare" – better "It is being declared that," which we may represent with "D" (following Searle 1979, p. 19). The procedure is straightforwardly analogous to Searle's for extracting rules for the promise indicating device.

Rule 1. D is to be uttered only in the context of a sentence *P* used to express that *p*.

Rule 2. D is to be uttered only if that *p* does not obtain in the normal course of events.

Rule 3. D is to be uttered only by a speaker in a position of legislative authority.

Rule 4. Uttering D in the context of *P* brings it about that *p*. (Compare Searle 1969, p. 63.)

Thus, the hearer *H* understand the sentence "It is being declared that *p*," that is, "D*P*" if and only if *H* knows Rules 1–4 together with the rules for understanding "*P*."

Thus, the Searlean analysis has reduced the case of acquiring warrants and coming to believe their corresponding subjunctive conditionals through encountering the formulation of some constituting legislation as backing for the warrant to the case of acquiring warrants and their corresponding subjunctives through learning constitutive rules. Here we are dealing with special rules governing meaning, but rules nonetheless. The mechanism then works this way. Through encountering a declarative utterance of some legislative body – this is the input – we come to believe certain subjunctive conditionals through understanding the utterance. We understand the utterance through having mastered (some of) the semantic rules of the language common to ourselves and the agent who produced the utterance. Our belief-generating mechanism, then, will be reliable to the extent that we have learned correctly these rules determining sentence meaning. The mechanism is presumptively reliable to the extent that there is a presumption that we have learned such rules.

8.9 INTERPRETATIONS IN GENERAL AND INTUITION

In the past three sections, we have argued that instances of three types of subjunctives can be intuited and thus constitute basic beliefs. We have shown both that subjunctives are interpretations and given that a statement is an interpretation, it can be analyzed as involving a subjunctive. Does intuition then vouch for interpretations in general? We need to consider the various types of interpretations we have identified. Because our discussion indicates that some types of interpretations can be defined in terms of others, we shall consider only the "primitive" types. Besides identifying the personal belief-generating mechanisms for these types of interpretations, be it intuition or something else, we need to consider the question of whether that mechanism is presumptively reliable. We have argued that under certain circumstances, physical, personal, and institutional intuition are presumptively reliable in generating subjunctive beliefs. How does this extend to interpretations in general?

Our survey of the types of interpretations shows that there are different levels at which a subjunctive can be embedded in an interpretation. At the first level, besides explicitly subjunctive conditionals (or explicitly generalized subjunctive conditionals, as we are using "subjunctive" to cover both) are those interpretations that can be straightforwardly paraphrased as subjunctives, such as dispositional statements. The question then of whether such statements could ever be basic beliefs becomes the question of whether their subjunctive paraphrases can be generated as basic beliefs by some mode of intuition. The question of whether such a belief is ever properly basic becomes the question of the circumstances under which that mode of intuition is presumptively reliable. Our survey in Section 8.4 of the modes of expressing general nomic connection shows that all the statements in these categories are interpretations at this first level.

Singular causal statements and interpretive classifications, by contrast, embed subjunctives one level down. We saw that both could be analyzed as conjunctions. With singular causal statements, one conjunct would be an explicit subjunctive. Interpretive classifications might involve several subjunctives. Let us grant that a belief expressed by a conjunctive statement will be a basic belief just in case each conjunct is a basic belief and furthermore that the belief is properly basic if and only if each conjunct is a properly basic belief. We saw that singular causal statements of the form event *A* caused event *B* could be analyzed according to the pattern:

   a. *A* occurred.
   b. *B* occurred.
   c. If conditions relevantly similar to *A* were to occur, *B* would occur.
   d. No other condition *C* sufficient for *B* occurred.

We also saw that instances of (a), (b), and (d) were descriptions, whereas (c) is an explicit subjunctive asserting some causal generalization. We saw further that (c) could assert either physical, personal (psychological), or institutional causation.

In Section 8.6, we saw that although certain physical dispositional statements might be properly basic beliefs, statements asserting general causal connections, if the result of causal intuition, are hypotheses. To hold an intuited hypothesis as a justified belief on the basis of one's personal belief-generating mechanisms, one must have subjected that hypothesis to test. But then the results of that test, if confirming, constitute evidence for premises supporting that hypothesis, which is thus no longer a basic belief. Hence, if such a physical causal generalization is a conjunct of a singular causal statement, that statement cannot be a properly basic belief. By contrast, an intuitive hypothesis may be corroborated by common knowledge or expert opinion and accepted on the basis of these sources. But then it is no longer a belief generated by physical causal intuition.

Personal explanations standardly appeal to motives – psychological causes – or intentions – reasons. The former involve subjunctives of psychological causation; the latter dispositional subjunctives of belief and intention. We saw in Section 8.7 that the class of psychological explanations involved not only explanations of an individual's particular actions, such as

   1. Cassius plotted the death of Caesar because he bore an inbred hatred of tyrants.

but also explanations of events or conditions brought about by some intentional action or series of actions.

   2. Andy received an *A* in Symbolic Logic through his studying the subject assiduously.

Both of these examples straightforwardly fit our four clause pattern. But in either case, the third clause is a subjunctive of general psychological causation which, as we saw in Section 8.7, would not be a properly basic belief of personal intuition. So, singular causal statements involving psychological causal explanation will not be properly basic statements of intuition.

By contrast,

3. The terrorist ignited the fuse in order to explode the bomb.

can be analyzed as

3a. The terrorist ignited the fuse.
3b. The terrorist believed that igniting the fuse would bring about the bomb's exploding.
3c. The terrorist intended for the bomb to explode.

Clause (a) is a description, whereas (b) and (c) are both interpretations, dispositional statements of belief and intention, according to our analysis in Section 8.4. In Section 8.7, we saw that personal intuition concerning proximate belief or intentional dispositions, dispositions that could be read off from certain overt actions that were their signs, could be properly basic, while beliefs concerning the nonproximate beliefs or intentions of others would not be basic beliefs. The question of intuitions involved in singular statements involving intentional explanation concerns whether their component clauses attributing beliefs or intentions to an agent are matters of proximate or nonproximate belief or intention.

Singular causal statements involving institutional causation can again be analyzed straightforwardly according to our four clause pattern. Consider our paradigm:

4. The case was decided against the defendant because two witnesses agreed.
4a. Two witnesses agreed.
4b. The case was decided against the defendant.
4c. If in a relevantly similar case two independent witnesses were to agree, *ceteris paribus* the case would be decided against the defendant.
4d. No other condition sufficient for deciding the case against the defendant occurred.

Again the issue of intuition arises just for clause (c), which is an institutional subjunctive. But we discussed the conditions under which institutional intuition generates properly basic beliefs expressed by institutional subjunctives in Section 8.8.

As we saw in Section 8.4, some interpretive classifications, such as our paradigms

5. Brutus's killing Caesar was an act of murder.
6. Brutus's killing Caesar was an act of self-defense.

may be analyzed as conjunctions, some of whose conjuncts are analyzable as subjunctives.[16] Hence, the issue of whether these interpretive classifications can be believed in the basic way and if so whether this belief can be properly basic reduces to the question of whether the conjuncts can be so believed. However, when we assert

7. The eruption of Mt. Vesuvius was a natural occurrence.
8. That inscribed sequence of 0's and 1's representing the prime numbers between 0 and 99 is the result of human agency.

as we pointed out in Section 8.4, we are asserting or presupposing that an explanation of a certain type holds. What we in effect are doing in asserting these statements is to embed the subjunctive one level further down. To assert (7) is to assert that some event E physically caused the eruption of Mt. Vesuvius. It is to assert an existentially generalized singular physical causal statement. Its logical form, then, is an existentially generalized conjunction, one of whose conjuncts is a subjunctive of physical necessity. Now one might come to believe such a statement through observing the causing event and coming to believe the instance of this existentially generalized conjunction that concerns this particular event. Such an instantiating statement is a singular causal statement and one might come to believe its subjunctive clause through physical intuition. Let us allow that one can believe an existential generalization in a basic way if one comes to believe an instance of it in a basic way. So, in this case, one would believe the existentially generalized statement in the basic way. But if one comes to accept the physical causal subjunctive clause as a matter of physical intuition, as we saw, the belief will not be properly basic. By contrast, upon coming to believe that Mt. Vesuvius had erupted one might come to believe that some event physically necessitated it as a matter of common knowledge. So one could come to believe the existentially generalized causal statement as a basic belief without coming to believe an instance of that statement. But here we are dealing with the testimony of common knowledge, not physical or some other type of intuition. We discuss the presumptive reliability of common knowledge in Chapter 10.

Likewise, an analysis of (8) indicates that the statement means there is a human agent and an activity of that agent caused the existence of the inscription of the sequence of o's and 1's. Here again we have an existentially generalized singular causal statement, although one which involves psychological causation. Again, one might come to believe (8) through observing the agent. Determining whether this belief is properly basic is parallel to the case for (7). By contrast, one might come to believe (8) by inference to the best explanation. The belief then is not basic but inferred. Hence, as long as we restrict ourselves to the issue of personal basic belief-generating mechanisms, the issue of whether an interpretive classification can be a basic belief and if so whether it can be properly basic reduces to the issue of this status for the components of an instance of that interpretive classification.

On the question of whether truth-functions of interpretations can be the object of intuition, let us set aside those interpretations that involve conjunctions of subjunctives with descriptions or existential generalizations of conjunctions, and consider just the question of whether beliefs expressed by truth-functions of subjunctives are generated by intuition. We need consider only two cases – conjunction and negation. Such subjunctives in general need not be the objects of intuition. A negation of a subjunctive may be an object of basic belief although it is not an object of causal, personal, or institutional intuition. Under what circumstances might I come to believe that a causal subjunctive is false? Clearly if I come to believe that the antecedent is true while the consequent false, then I should come to believe – and justifiably believe – the negation of that subjunctive. But my belief may be generated by perception.

Can we argue that basic beliefs expressed by truth-functions of subjunctives in general (as long as they are generated by a personal basic belief-generating mechanism) will be generated either by physical, personal, or institutional intuition or by perception (or by introspection or memory – we shall refer just to perception as the paradigm of a description-generating mechanism)? We offer this straightforward argument by mathematical induction. Because basic subjunctive beliefs are generated by intuition, they are generated either by intuition or perception. Let us assume then that beliefs expressed by truth-functions of subjunctives with less than n connectives are generated through intuition or perception. Consider the case of a truth-function φ of subjunctives with n connectives. φ is either of the form $(A \ \& \ B)$ or $\sim\!A$. But clearly if each of A, B is generated either by intuition or perception, so is the conjunction. Consider $\sim A$. Clearly, the issue of whether such an interpretation can come to be believed through intuition or perception reduces to the question of whether one can come to believe in this way that the negated interpretation is false. We have already seen that if A is a basic subjunctive belief, we can come to believe its negation through perception. Two cases remain. The negated interpretation could itself be a negation or it could be a conjunction. Thus, we are dealing with interpretations of the form $\sim(\sim A)$ or $\sim(A \,\&\, B)$. But the question of whether an interpretation of the form $\sim(\sim A)$ is generated through intuition or perception clearly amounts to the question of whether A is generated in this way, for they are logically equivalent. As long as A and B are logically compatible,[17] the question of whether $\sim(A \,\&\, B)$ is generated through intuition or perception reduces to whether one can come to believe in this way either that the component A is false or the component B is false. But this is to ask whether one can come to believe either $\sim A$ or $\sim B$ in this way. But this is immediate from our inductive hypothesis. Whether any of these beliefs can be properly basic depends upon whether the belief-generating mechanism may be presumed reliable in these circumstances of employment.

The final type of interpretation which we identified in Section 8.4 consisted of ascriptions of subjunctive or nomic necessity and possibility. Recall that we defined these interpretations in terms of a special subjunctive conditional of the form $A\,\boxed{n}\!\!\to B$, claiming that its antecedent A was a nomically sufficient condition for its consequent B.[18] Hence, where "τ" abbreviates some truth-functional tautology, "$\boxed{n}A$" is defined as "$\tau\,\boxed{n}\!\!\to A$" and "$\Diamond\!\!\!\!{\scriptstyle n}\,A$" as "$\sim\!\boxed{n}\!\sim A$." A statement of the form "$\boxed{n}A$" will be true in a given world w just in case A is true in all worlds nomically inclusive of w, that is, all those worlds where the causal and other nomic regularities holding in A also hold. How might one come to believe that a statement A was nomically necessary through one's personal belief-generating mechanisms? Notice that a statement of the form "$A\,\boxed{n}\!\!\to B$" will be true at a world w just in case "$\tau\,\boxed{n}\!\!\to (A\,\boxed{n}\!\!\to B)$" is true at w. Statements of nomically sufficient conditions then are included in the class of nomically necessary statements. Now, through physical, personal, or institutional intuition, one might come to believe a statement of the form "$A\,\boxed{n}\!\!\to B$" and also that such a statement was nomically necessary, as with *a priori* intuition, one might come to believe both that some logical truth was true and that it was necessarily true. A necessary condition then for one's belief that $\boxed{n}\,(A\,\boxed{n}\!\!\to B)$ being properly basic in this case would be that one's belief that $A\,\boxed{n}\!\!\to B$ was properly basic.

But something more seems to be involved here. If one believes that $\boxed{n}(A \boxed{n}{\mapsto} B)$, one believes that "$A \boxed{n}{\mapsto} B$" not only accords with the laws of nature but is a consequence of them, that given the laws of nature, things could not be otherwise than $A \boxed{n}{\mapsto} B$. But would one be justified in holding that belief without seeing that the laws of nature necessitated that $A \boxed{n}{\mapsto} B$? One ordinarily would be justified in believing that claim if one could see how to derive "$A \boxed{n}{\mapsto} B$" from an appropriate subset Γ of the laws of nature. But then one's belief that $\boxed{n}(A \boxed{n}{\mapsto} B)$ would not be basic, but based on the existence of the derivation. By contrast, one might see intuitively that "$A \boxed{n}{\mapsto} B$" followed from Γ, but this would be a matter of logical or *a priori* intuition.

If a statement S were not of the form "$A \boxed{n}{\mapsto} B$," how, if at all, could one come to believe $\boxed{n}S$ other than by seeing, either through some argument or by *a priori* intuition, that S followed from some set of laws of nature or other nomic regularities? There is perhaps one other way. One might believe both that $A \boxed{n}{\mapsto} B$ and that A were true. One might then conclude that $\boxed{n}B$. But besides the statement's being a conclusion of inference and thus not basic, the inference is also an invalid, confusing the necessitation of the conditional with the necessitation of the consequent. If a statement of the form "$\boxed{n}S$" is to be a properly basic intuitive belief, then, we must go beyond physical, personal, and institutional intuition, but the intuition involved is *a priori*.

How might one come to believe a statement of the form "$\lozenge_n A$"? Of course, if one believed that A were true, one would believe that the laws of nature did not necessitate $\sim A$'s holding. But if one did not believe that A held, one might imagine A's holding. If this did not violate any laws of nature or other nomic necessities, then one could believe that A was nomically possible, that is, $\lozenge_n A$. But this is to construct a counterexample to "$\tau \boxed{n}{\mapsto} \sim A$," and to the extent that intuition is involved, it is logical intuition. Hence, to the extent to which ascriptions of nomic necessity and possibility can be known in a basic way, they involve no other basic belief-generating mechanisms than the ones whose presumptive reliability we have already discussed, although logical intuition will need to be included among these mechanisms.

Our analysis in this section has shown that answering the question of what personal belief-generating mechanisms vouch for an interpretation involves ascertaining what type of interpretation is involved. For simple physical, personal, or institutional subjunctives, or interpretations that may be straightforwardly paraphrased as such subjunctives, the vouching mechanisms will be physical, personal, or institutional intuition. For interpretations involving descriptive conjuncts in addition to a subjunctive, some descriptive mechanism or mechanisms also will need to vouch for the interpretation. For certain truth-functions of interpretations, descriptive mechanisms may be sufficient, whereas ascriptions of nomic necessity and possibility involve *a priori* intuition.

It is now time to tie together the investigations of this long chapter. We saw in Chapter 5 that paradigm cases of interpretations in classical rhetoric presupposed explanations involving assertions of contingent but nonetheless nomic or lawlike connections. This gave us the key to understanding interpretations. We saw first that explanations could be divided into empirical and institutional. Empirical explanations in turn could be divided into physical and personal. In each case, however, at the core of the explanation is a lawlike statement that supports a subjunctive conditional. We took subjunctives then as the basic type of interpretation and explicated other types of interpretations in terms of the subjunctive. As there are three types of explanations, so there are three types of subjunctives and three corresponding modes of intuition for interpretations. We have argued that each mode of intuition is presumptively reliable in certain circumstances or given certain conditions. Thus, we can have properly basic beliefs of subjunctive form. Given our analysis of types of interpretation in terms of subjunctives, in some cases involving also descriptions or statements of logical entailment, we have now indicated how we may in general assess what personal belief-generating mechanisms vouch for an interpretation. That certain types of subjunctives may be properly basic beliefs only under certain circumstances has implications for the proper basicality of interpretations in general, which we can straightforwardly recognize, given our analysis. If our arguments are cogent, we have shown that although interpretations believed through personal belief-generating mechanisms in general will not be properly basic beliefs, some interpretations can be believed in a basic way and that these beliefs can be properly basic. Such interpretations should be acceptable basic premises.

8.10 OBJECTIONS AND REPLIES

Our account of interpretations and the conditions of their acceptability as basic premises makes at least two major philosophical assumptions that would not be readily granted by those of a skeptical temper. First, our explication of interpretations through subjunctives assumes that there is a difference between accidental and nomic universality. But Hume through his analysis of causation in effect rejects this distinction in favor of maintaining that there is only accidental universality. How might we reply to a Humean? Second, when we project according to natural kinds, we are assuming that the future will be like the past. Here again, Hume is the skeptic. Are we justified in making this assumption? Also in making these projections according to natural kinds, we are assuming that we can reliably identify the projectable property. But does not our experience radically underdetermine what we project? I see an egg-laying platypus in the zoo and project according to the concept of natural kinds from something's being a female platypus to its being an egg-layer. But does not my experience also support saying that this platypus has been observed before midnight on January 1, 2050, and is an egg-layer, or it has been observed on or after midnight on January 1, 2050, and is viviparous? Why can I not project *that* property? Goodman, obviously, is the skeptic here. By assuming that we can project according to natural kinds, our account encounters both the old and new riddles of induction. What may we say to these problems? Let us begin with Humean skepticism over distinguishing accidental from nomic universality.

According to Hume's well-known analysis, the relation of causation can be analyzed into contiguity between cause and effect, temporal priority of cause to effect, and necessary connection of cause and effect. Hume's analysis of necessary connection contains his rejection of nomic universality. That the relation of causation involves necessary connection is evident in our inferring effects from causes (or causes from effects). Hume quite rightly points out that this is not logical inference. Even if we believe that event *A* is the (sufficient) cause of *B*, *A*'s occurring without *B* involves no logical contradiction. Hume claims that we may perform this inference through experience of constant conjunction.

We remember to have had frequent instances of the existence of one species of objects; and also remember, that the individuals of another species of objects have always attended them, and have existed in a regular order of contiguity and succession with regard to them.... We likewise call to mind their constant conjunction in all past instances. Without any farther ceremony, we call the one *cause* and the other *effect*. (1888, p. 87, italics in original)

But Hume's explanation does not present a completed analysis of the necessity in causal connection. One experience of *A* being followed by *B* would not inform us of a necessary connection between *A* and *B*. Why should our experience of a hundred such successions disclose such a necessary connection?

But, Hume suggests, it may be that our analysis of the inference may indicate the nature of the necessary connection, rather than the nature of the connection putting a constraint on the analysis of the inference. We either make this inference by reason or through imagination. If by reason, then we presuppose in effect the principle that the future will be like the past. But this principle cannot be demonstrated. It is not a necessary truth. Further, it is presupposed in probabilistic reasoning and thus probabilistic reasoning cannot be used to justify it. Hence, reason cannot satisfy us that we are justified in projecting beyond our experience of constant conjunction. Because this inference is not determined by reason, it is determined by an association of ideas, of which cause and effect is one mode. The necessity in causation thus is not conceptual. Upon observing a sufficient number of instances of constant conjunction, our imagination sets up a connection between the idea of the cause and the effect so that the idea of one or observation of one conveys us to the idea of the other. There is nothing more to the necessary connection of cause and effect than this.

Has Hume here confused justification with meaning? Could one argue that there is a conception of necessary connection in causation even if one is never justified in asserting causal connections? To judge that A *causes B*, we need to see A as an independent variable and B as a dependent variable. Hume's analysis of causation does not accommodate this conceptual component. Going beyond our analysis in Section 8.6, can we give further argumentation that causation involves this conceptual component of variable dependency? I believe we can. Recall the experiment with four-year-olds[19] shown triads of pictures. The first two depicted instances of different natural kinds, K_1 and K_2, and the children were told that each instance has some further feature F_1 or F_2, the feature being causally dependent on the kind. The object in the third picture distinctly resembles the object in the second, but the children are told that it is an instance of K_1. Is F_1 or is F_2 true of this object? Answering F_1 constitutes evidence that the child has a concept of natural kinds and is projecting according to the natural kinds concept and not according to superficial resemblance.

I believe we can construct an analogous experiment with instances of covariation of the sort Hume considers. Suppose we show the four-year-olds a number of red candles. (Suppose we have also selected the children so that they have not seen candles before.) We light each one and let the children feel, each time, the heat produced by the candle in the region of the flame. We also show the children an equal number of low-wattage blue electric lights. We light each one and let the children feel that the lights remain cool. We then show the children a blue gas flame. Is it cool or hot? On Hume's analysis, we would expect the children to be totally confused. We might expect a divergence of answers. But if a significant number of children said the gas flame should be hot, this should show that they were projecting not according to a simple association of ideas but according to an intuition of causal dependency. These experimental results would count as evidence that Hume's account of causation was wanting as a conceptual analysis, whether or not one was ever justified in applying the concept of causation.

Can we accommodate the notion of causal variable dependency through accidental universality? There is a motivation for attempting this analysis. If one accepts that there is a necessary connection between *A* and *B*, the question of the nature of this necessity arises. Is it logical necessity or some other? Logical necessity is a clearly understood concept. The view that causal laws are logically necessary faces significant objections,[20] however, the most telling being that many sentences commonly regarded as laws are not logically necessary. A nomic or causal necessity that is nonlogical but nonetheless *necessary* seems obscure. As Nagel puts it,

> Those who maintain that the necessity of universals of law is *sui generis* and at bottom not further analyzable postulate a property whose nature is essentially obscure. . . . Moreover, since it is generally supposed that this allegedly special type of necessity can be recognized only by some "intuitive apprehension," predicating such necessity . . . is subject to all the vagaries of intuitive judgments. (1961 pp. 52–53)

Accidental universality will not do however to explicate nomic universality. It yields the wrong truth-conditions. Suppose that a disease is caused by a certain virus, which becomes virulent enough to precipitate the disease if and only if certain environmental conditions *EC* are present. Suppose that these environmental conditions can be manipulated, allowing people some control over the disease. But suppose the virus is never isolated as a relevant variable. However, it could be isolated. That is, there is a nomically possible world in which *EC* obtains at some point but the virus has been destroyed or neutralized at the same time. Thus, also at that time the disease does not occur. Now it is true in the actual world that any instance, past, present, or future of *EC*'s obtaining is also an instance of the disease occurring. But it is not true that this is a causal law or that we can truly assert nomic universality. The generalized subjunctive

"For any circumstances, if *EC* were to obtain, then the disease would occur" is not true. There is a nomically accessible world where the antecedent is true and the consequent false. The accidental generalization is true in the actual world but falsified in this nomically accessible world.[21]

If the above argument is cogent, it shows that attempting to understand nomic necessity through object language statements expressing accidental universals is not viable. But there remains an approach to the analysis of the subjunctive conditional, ordinarily carried out as an analysis of the counterfactual conditional, which promises to accommodate intuitions of necessity but to interpret causal laws – at least, those of the form Every F is a G – purely indicatively. This is the metalinguistic approach. As Nagel presents it, to assert a subjunctive of the form "If Fa were the case, Ga would be the case" is to assert that "Ga" follows logically from "Fa" together with both the conditional "$(\forall x)([Fx \ \& \ (IC_1x \ \& \ldots \& \ IC_nx)] \supset Gx)$" and "$(IC_1a \ \& \ldots \& \ IC_na)$," where "$IC_1x \ \& \ldots \& \ IC_nx$" state initial conditions of the law to the effect that F's are also G's.[22]

There is a distinct and obvious analogy between this approach and analyzing enthymematic arguments as involving suppressed or implicit premises. The metalinguistic approach in effect treats a subjunctive conditional as an enthymematic claim of entailment. We may then bring against this analysis Hitchcock's phenomenological criticism of the analysis of enthymematic arguments as involving unstated premises (1985). If we inspect enthymematic arguments that we have constructed, we shall find that we are not conscious of having omitted a premise, or of having some further premise or premises in mind. Likewise, we can ask whether when we assert a subjunctive conditional, we also are assuming some law together with a statement of initial conditions or even whether we are in general conscious that we are assuming something, although "we are not clear in our minds what tacit assumptions we are making" (Nagel 1961, p. 72). If we assert that "If Pres. Kennedy had been riding in a closed car rather than a convertible limousine in Dallas on November 22, 1963, the assassination would not have happened," what laws and initial conditions are we assuming? If we are not conscious of making these assumptions, then we should accept the metalinguistic analysis only if other analyses are more problematic. In particular, we should prefer the metalinguistic analysis over a modal analysis only if the latter involves invoking a modality in itself obscure.

But is our notion of nomic necessity, allowing nomic universals to be necessary, but not logically necessary, obscure? Given the semantics we sketched in Section 8.3, a nomic universal or nomic generalization, a statement of the form "(∀x)(Fx $\boxed{n}\mapsto$ Gx)" will be true (in the actual world) just in case the corresponding material universal "(∀x)(Fx ⊃ Gx)" is true in all nomically accessible worlds, that is, those worlds where all the causal laws holding in the actual world also hold. From a logical or formal semantical point of view, there is nothing obscure in this notion, for there is nothing obscure in the mathematical notion of a nonempty set (of worlds) on which there is a binary reflexive and transitive relation. To charge this notion with obscurity, one would have to charge the notion of possible worlds with obscurity. But, in view of the centrality of this concept in the tools of philosophical analysis, such a charge would encounter a heavy burden of proof.

A critic might still not be satisfied. Granted that the formal explication of nomic necessity is not obscure, but what about its philosophical motivation? Where w is the actual world, wRw' just in case all the causal laws true in the actual world are also true in w'. But what are the causal laws of the actual world w? Are they not the statements true in all w' such that wRw'? But do we not have a circularity here? To motivate R, we need to know what are the causal laws, but to identify the causal laws, we need to have defined R? But *is* circularity a problem here? Can we identify a causal law without specifying the truth-conditions for causal laws in the formal semantics we have sketched? It may be a necessary condition for a generalization to be a causal law that it support subjunctive conditionals. But one can certainly recognize intuitively that a generalization does or does not support a subjunctive conditional without having specified the truth-conditions for subjunctives. A number of issues, logical and epistemological, are involved with identifying laws of nature.[23] But these do not require settling the truth-conditions for these statements.

Our critic may still not be satisfied. Granted, given your explication, your notion of nomic necessity is neither logically obscure nor ill-motivated, but is it not epistemologically obscure? According to your account, a form of intuition is involved in generating basic beliefs expressed through subjunctive conditionals. Can you answer Nagel's complaint of "the vagaries of intuitive judgments"? Is in fact the notion of nomic necessity epistemologically obscure? When one asserts a nomic universal, one is asserting a nomic or causal dependency. Whatever F and G may be, being F is a causally or nomically sufficient condition for being G. Epistemologically, what is involved here? As we indicated in Section 8.6, we bring the notion of causal dependency to our experience. Given a covariation we have detected, we recognize an independent variable and a dependent variable within it. This is to apply an innate conceptual notion. But, again, as our discussion in Section 8.6 shows, saying that a concept is innate indicates neither that it is obscure nor illegitimate. If there is an epistemological obscurity here, it must be with the notion of causal dependency itself. But is this notion obscure? If one hypothesizes that one factor has caused another, what is obscure? Even if a's being G is surprising, if one sees that a's being F would render a's being G a matter of course, has one seen something obscure? Given our explication of nomic necessity, we find no substance to the charge of obscurity. Consequently, we believe that we have discharged the burden of proof for placing such a heavy emphasis on the subjunctive in our analysis of interpretations. We have given an analysis of the subjunctive conditional and of nomic necessity that distinguishes nomic from accidental universals and nomic necessity from logical necessity, but that is neither logically nor epistemologically obscure.

It still seems however that throughout our discussion, we are assuming that the future will be like the past, a belief Hume held could not be justified by reason because it could be shown neither demonstratively nor probabilistically. We may reply with Reid to Hume that the principle need not be defended through reason, either demonstratively or probabilistically, because it is a principle of our constitution and needs no justification. This principle is presupposed in all learning from experience. As a first principle of our constitution, there is a presumption of reliability for it.

The bald statement that the future will be like the past, that what we have not experienced will resemble what we have experienced, is very general. It does not imply that nature will be uniform in all respects and such a claim is not part of our constitution. We learn to distinguish accidental similarities from projectable features. As Reid points out, "We learn to be more cautious in the application of [the principle]. We observe more carefully the circumstances on which the past event depended, and learn to distinguish them from those which were accidentally conjoined with it" (Beanblossom and Lehrer 1983, p. 283). This leads us from Hume's old problem of induction to Goodman's new riddle of induction. Experience displays to us green emeralds and emeralds of no other color. So we believe the next emerald we encounter will be green. But when we define "grue" to mean examined before midnight tonight and green or not examined before midnight and blue, apparently experience just as well teaches us that emeralds are grue. But then what should we expect about any heretofore unseen emerald observed for the first time after midnight tonight? That it also will be grue, that is, blue? Notice that Goodman has framed this problem with reference to a natural kind term. Does the paradox then pose an objection to claiming the conditional presumptive reliability of empirical intuition as we have claimed?

The issue here is what makes a property projectable. Why is green projectable and not grue? Goodman's answer is that properties are projectable to the extent that they are actually projected in practice. This is what he calls entrenchment. This makes projectability an empirical matter. Projectability is dependent on actual human behavior. Being green is projectable because people actually do project it. Being grue is not projectable because people do not project it. "The more frequently a predicate . . . has been projected, the more projectable it is" (Plantinga 1993b, p. 130).

Against Goodman's solution, Plantinga suggests the following scenario. Suppose human behavior were to change as a result of some burst of radiation, so that a significant number of persons began to project "grue" instead of "green." Suppose an additional effect of the radiation was to increase greatly the birthrate of the revised projectors, whose progeny also projected "grue" rather than "green." Suppose the result of all this was that in a relatively short period, the majority of humans would be projecting "grue" rather than "green." Would "grue" then be projectable? Intuitively this seems wrong and this cuts against Goodman's explanation. It is not hard to explain this intuition, for we clearly expect that after midnight tonight, or January 1, 2015, or whatever time t is selected, those projecting that all emeralds are grue would accept that all heretofore unobserved emeralds are blue. Such an induction, we would expect, would not meet with much success.

The problem with entrenchment is precisely its empirical character. It is not actual behavior, but proper function which determines projectability for Plantinga. If a properly functioning human being prior to a certain date observed a number of emeralds all of which were green, she would not project that they were grue, with its consequence that the first emerald observed after that date would be blue. She would certainly not expect that. Such an expectation, her forming the belief that the first emerald observed after that date would be blue, would signify an improperly functioning belief-generating mechanism. The fact of her not making these projections is part of our design plan or constitution. This accords with an interesting comment Quine and Ullian make in this connection, which we may construe to be about our design plan. Even if we cannot define what projectability means, "We do have a natural knack for spotting such traits, with better than random success; they are the traits we notice" (1978, p. 87).

In light of our discussion of natural kind terms, I believe we can go further to say why we project properties like green rather than grue and why green but not grue is projectable. Notice that we always project a property with reference to some other property. We project "green" with respect to "emerald." But "emerald" is a natural kind term. As such, if the concept-forming segment of our physical intuition has been functioning properly, our concept of emerald will contain an essence placeholder filled with some theory, no matter how vague or preliminary, about the internal structure of emeralds. Part of this theory would be the claim that the "inside," "essence," internal structure of an emerald causally determines that the color of the emerald will fall within certain parameters. Our observing green emeralds makes more determinate that determinable. It is not part of this theory, however tentatively realized, that emeralds unobserved before some time t will after that time be found to have a color lying outside the parameters. There is nothing in the preliminary theory to indicate that given the internal structure of emeralds, we can expect those first observed after t to be blue. Hence, to project the property "grue" rather than "green" would be to go against the theory filling the essence placeholder. It would flagrantly, even pathologically, disregard how our concept of the essence leads us to identify certain properties of the emerald as projectable.

That we can distinguish between natural kind and other properties also shows that our view does not stumble over Hempel's famous raven paradox of confirmation but, rather, gives us a way to diagnose the paradox. Recall that we would count a raven which is black as a confirming instance of "All ravens are black" but not a gray stone. But a gray stone is an instance of a nonblack nonraven. So it would seem to be a confirmatory instance of "All nonblack things are nonravens," logically equivalent to "All ravens are black." Why is there this reluctance then to count the gray stone as evidence for "All ravens are black"? Obviously, "ravens" is a natural kind term, whereas "nonblack" is not. There is no essence placeholder associated with "nonblack" for us to fill with some theory about how the internal structure of nonblack things causally determines certain of their properties. Indeed, the idea makes no sense, because the extension of "nonblack" lacks the requisite unity for such a theory. The expectation that there is one is pathological. The situation is completely different with "raven" as a natural kind term. This suggests that we may deal with the paradox of confirmation by saying that for generalizations – at least those of the form "All A are B" – to receive confirmation by instances of A that are also B, A must refer to a natural kind term or express some property whose extension displays the unity of a natural kind. Without this unity, what is there to have confirmation about?

Finally, Quine's thesis in (1969) suggests the objection that, although the notion of natural kinds, together with similarity, is in certain contexts legitimate, in those contexts it is not ultimate but reducible to other notions. As Quine puts it,

> The notion of similarity or of kind changes as science progresses. . . . [I]t is a mark of maturity of a branch of science that the notion of similarity or kind finally dissolves, so far as it is relevant to that branch of science. That is, it ultimately submits to analysis in the special terms of that branch of science and logic. (1969, p. 121)

Quine's initial discussion suggests that he does not distinguish – as we expect he would not – between nominal and real kinds. He says "Green things, or at least green emeralds, are a kind" (1969, p. 116). We can take issue with Quine right at this point. "Emeralds" is a kind term, but neither "green" nor "green emerald" are. Remember that natural kind terms involve essence placeholders. But "green" involves no such essence placeholder, nor would we expect that "green emerald" would, over and above the placeholder for some theory about the internal structure of emeralds. All sorts of things are green. This is a superficial similarity, and our predication of this concept presupposes no essence. Although Quine admits that attempts to understand the concept of natural kinds in terms of the concept of similarity or *vice versa* are fraught with problems, it is clear that he considers kinds identifiable in terms of similarities, no matter how superficial.

Given this understanding of the human concept of natural kind, Quine continues that we revise our system of particular natural kinds as empirical science progresses. Inductive success is the standard here, leading to grouping objects together in terms of a developing "scientifically sophisticated" notion of similarity. "This development is a development away from the immediate, subjective, animal sense of similarity to the remoter objectivity of a similarity determined by scientific hypotheses and posits and constructs" (1969, p. 133). But, having arrived at this level, the notions of similarity and the notions of natural kind, together with the notions of dispositions and the subjunctive conditional, all of which Quine claims can be defined in terms of similarity, although scientifically legitimized, all become superfluous and ultimately dissolve in favor of the structural specifications of scientific theories. Our understanding of the mechanism as discovered by science suffices. "One can redefine water-solubility by simply describing the structural conditions of that mechanism" (1969, p. 135).

We reply that Quine has not discharged the burden of proof here, and indeed may give the appearance of establishing his claim only through legerdemain. Although in (1969) he suggests programmatically how dispositions might be defined using kinds rather than the subjunctive conditional, he nowhere indicates in this paper how the subjunctive conditional might be reduced using kinds or similarity. But, when Quine claims that we can describe the structural conditions of the mechanism of solubility, we must ask how these conditions are described. Quine gives no indication. Do they involve universal generalizations? We would expect so. Do these universal generalizations support subjunctive conditionals or are their truth-conditions adequately accounted for by accidental or *de facto* universals? Without showing the latter, Quine has not met the burden of proof and is open to the charge that he has hidden the problem simply by referring to the existence of these mechanisms and their scientific specifiability, without examining what that involves. The mere fact that these mechanisms might be specified for scientific purposes through a system of equations does not mean that proper understanding of the import of that specification could be had without the notion of the subjunctive conditional.

We may, then, agree with Quine that as science progresses, our notions of natural kinds will have greater projective reliability. But it does not follow that the notion of a natural kind will disappear or that we shall cease to make projections on the basis of natural kinds in favor of making such projections on the basis of the theories filling the essence placeholder. For one thing, because of our perception of certain covariant properties, our experience may indicate that an object is an instance of some natural kind. Although a theory may explain in terms of the internal micromechanisms of the object why one can reliably make certain projections on this basis, our experience may give us no information about what internal microconditions are satisfied and thus give us no information on which to make projections according to the theory. Instead of showing that the notion of natural kind is epistemologically eliminable, scientific progress shows that the notion can be put on a reliable ground. Scientific theories postulate unobservable structures. The success of science is a strong indication of the reality of these structures. But if these structures are real and their existence explains why certain properties reside together in homeostatic clusters, then defining natural kinds in terms of such homeostatic clusters would be a scientifically well grounded and reliable procedure. We conclude then that Quine has not shown that the notions of natural kind or subjunctive conditional are dispensable – at least not epistemologically.

9

Evaluations and the Moral Faculties

In this chapter, we follow the same overall procedure as in the last three. We first identify the types of evaluations or value judgments one may distinguish, presenting a standard philosophical account. We inquire for each of these types whether some mechanism generates such evaluations as basic beliefs and whether there is a presumption for its reliability in this employment. We see two mechanisms, moral sense and moral intuition, involved in generating basic beliefs expressing value judgments. Before asking about their presumptive reliability, we discuss how they are related and what types of evaluations may be basic.

9.1 THE STANDARD ACCOUNT OF TYPES OF EVALUATIONS

There is a standard threefold division of value judgments into judgments of nonmoral value, of moral obligation, and of moral value. Following Frankena, we call judgments of moral obligation deontic judgments and judgments of moral value aretaic judgments (1973, p. 10). Similarly, we may speak of deontic value and aretaic value. "Right" is the paradigm term for ascribing deontic value and "virtuous" for aretaic value. Deontic value is a property of acts, whereas aretaic value is a property of the motives and characters from which acts proceed.

"Good" in one sense is the paradigm ascription of nonmoral value. "Good" and "bad," however, have several senses. Some things are *morally* good or *morally* bad. As Ross points out, moral goodness belongs to actions "in virtue of the motives that they proceed from" (1930, p. 156).[1] Moral goodness and moral badness then are terms ascribing aretaic value. This means we must understand "good" and "bad" as having wider application than just nonmoral value. However, where "good" or "bad" occur by themselves, not modified by "morally," we understand that they express nonmoral value.

"Good," of course, has further senses. We distinguish instrumental from intrinsic value. As Ross points out, judgments of instrumental value have causal components. Such judgments involve both interpretations – the causal component – and evaluations – the state of affairs caused is intrinsically good or bad. Clearly, there will be a presumption for a judgment of instrumental value only to the extent that there is a presumption for its component judgments. We may thus set judgments of instrumental value aside and inquire here only into whether there is a presumption for judgments of intrinsic value.

Ross calls attention to another distinction between uses of "good" and other expressions of value – the adjunctive and the predicative. When we speak of good carpenters or good knives, our use of "good" is adjunctive. We are saying that something is good relative to its kind, that it satisfies well what that kind is designed to be or do. By contrast, when "good" is used predicatively, as in "Pleasure is good" or "Existence is good," "good" is an absolute term. Pleasure is not a good something; it is good outright. Although Ross's distinction is straightforward, surely to each adjunctive use of "good," there corresponds a predicative. Suppose Jones is a good carpenter. Can we not say that this fact is good, or that the states of affairs produced by Jones's carpentry are good, where "good" is now being used predicatively? That is, is not satisfying the criterion for being a good carpenter or being a good example of carpentry something that is intrinsically good? Are not these facts good absolutely precisely because the criteria for the adjunctive attribution of good are satisfied? One might object that someone could be a good thief in the sense of thieving efficiently. But would we want to say that his being a good thief is intrinsically good? We shall discuss this objection in Section 9.3, when we discuss what makes intrinsically good things intrinsically good. For now, it is sufficient that we acknowledge this point of procedure: In discussing whether there is a presumption in favor of our judgments of nonmoral value, whether the mechanisms generating them are presumptively reliable, we shall confine our attention to judgments where the evaluative expression is being used predicatively and where the sense of value is intrinsic.

Also following Frankena, we should point out that there are particular and general, singular and universal instances of each of these three types of evaluations. One can say

1. The performance of the orchestra last night was very good.
2. Pleasure is intrinsically good.
3. I ought to give the $100 I promised for disaster relief.
4. One ought to keep one's promises.
5. Mother Theresa was a virtuous woman.
6. Patience is a virtue.

It is important to notice this distinction, since in the case of each universal judgment, something is said to be intrinsically good, obligatory, virtuous in virtue of its having some other property, being an instance of pleasure, promise-keeping, or a patient disposition. This means that value, whether intrinsic, deontic, or aretaic, supervenes upon other properties. What mechanism generates beliefs in this supervenience? Can we ascribe it to a basic belief-generating mechanism of moral intuition? We turn to answering these questions directly in the next section.

9.2 SUPERVENIENCE, MORAL INTUITION, AND MORAL SENSE

Our noting that there are general judgments of value – intrinsic, deontic, or aretaic – points directly to how we may frequently argue for singular value judgments.

1. Eating ice cream is good because it is enjoyable.
2. You ought to pay the $100 because you promised to.
3. Mother Theresa was a good woman because she practiced benevolence.

We may see each of these arguments as instancing a warrant:

1'. From	x is a pleasurable experience
We may take it that	x is *prima facie* intrinsically good
2'. From	x is a promise
We may take it that	x *prima facie* ought to be kept
3'. From	x has practiced benevolence
We may take it that	x is *prima facie* a morally good person.

Notice that in each case, the warrant tells us that we may get from a premise expressing a nonevaluative description to a conclusion expressing an evaluation. One may come to believe the premise by one or more of the mechanisms for coming to believe descriptions discussed in

Chapter 7 – introspection, institutional perception, personal perception and memory in our examples respectively. But should the premise be acceptable, why is the conclusion also acceptable? Why are the warrants reliable and how may we recognize their reliability?

In the deontic case, Ross held that the principles of *prima facie* duty corresponding to these warrants were knowable *a priori*. They are self-evident, witness "To make a promise . . . is to create a moral claim on us in someone else" (1930, p. 21 footnote).[2] We must, however, come to recognize these general principles and their self-evidence. For Ross, just as we come to recognize by experience that instances of two and two make four and then by reflection apprehend the general computational principle, so we see the *prima facie* rightness of particular instances of promise keeping and by reflection come to recognize the general principle that keeping promises is *prima facie* right. This is how we come to recognize principles of *prima facie* duty in general (see 1930, pp. 32–33). Two points demand special emphasis. The elementary computational principles which Ross sees analogous to *prima facie* moral principles are substantive mathematical statements and not analytic propositions. Recognizing the self-evidence of *prima facie* moral principles then is not a matter of conceptual analysis. For Ross, we do not come to apprehend the principle that stealing is wrong by coming to recognize that "being wrong" is part of the meaning of "stealing." Ross is an ethical intuitionist as opposed to an ethical logicist.[3]

Second, if principles of *prima facie* duty are not analytic, then neither are the judgments of the rightness or wrongness of particular acts on which they are based. How, one may ask then, before we apprehend principles of *prima facie* duty do we see certain *prima facie* right acts as right? Ross apparently does not address this point, but his discussion suggests that these are examples of basic beliefs. I believe Ross's discussion indicates that there are two mechanisms involved in the generation of basic evaluative beliefs. First, there is a mechanism for generating beliefs that a particular act is *prima facie* right, a particular state of affairs *prima facie* intrinsically good, or a character trait *prima facie* morally good. Let us call this the *moral sense*. Its relation to the moral sense tradition in moral epistemology will be developed later. Second, as Cohen reminds us, we can have intuitions of what is a reason for what or what can be inferred from what both in general and particular cases.[4] Hence, there is both the recognition that in a particular case an act is a duty because it is an instance of some property and that this holds as a general principle of *prima facie* duty. The case is similar for the other types of evaluations. The mechanism here is *moral intuition.*

That we must recognize moral sense in addition to moral intuition as a mechanism generating basic evaluative beliefs merits further discussion. According to Ross's scheme, in coming to apprehend a general principle of *prima facie* duty, such as if one has made a promise, one is *prima facie* obligated to keep it, we apprehend several instances in which we recognize that someone has made a promise – a matter of perception, institutional perception at least – and perhaps introspection in our case – and recognize also that the person has an obligation to keep it. What belief-generating mechanism is involved in this singular apprehension of *prima facie* duty? Can I apprehend that *A* is a reason for *B* without apprehending *B*? Can I see in a particular case that having made a promise is a reason for being obligated to keep it if I do not recognize that I have an obligation to keep it? Moral intuition may recognize the former, but what does moral intuition depend on in making this recognition?

It is here that our inquiry makes contact with the moral sense tradition in moral epistemology. Suppose *S* made an utterance to the effect that "I, *S*, promise to do *A*," but that shortly thereafter, *S* renounced that obligation by performing an illocutionary act of renunciation. How would we *feel* about *S*'s behavior here? Clearly, we expect feelings of disapproval. Does this disclose something pertinent to the operation of the belief-generating mechanism we have called the moral sense? Suppose some observer *O* upon apprehending that *S* had promised *H* to do *A*, further apprehends that *S* did not perform *A*. (Let us assume there are no significant countervailing considerations to defeat *S*'s obligation to perform *A*.) But suppose also that *O* had no feeling of disapproval over *S*'s not performing *A*. Suppose *O* were incapable of feelings of approval or disapproval? Would one expect *O* to be able to make basic judgments of *prima facie* deontic value? It would seem that a capacity to have these feelings would be necessary for the proper functioning of a mechanism which generated judgments of the deontic value of particular acts as basic beliefs, what we have been calling the moral sense.

I believe that we can similarly argue for the indispensability of feeling in generating judgments of intrinsic value. Suppose someone took no pleasure in any activity or accomplishment and received no pleasure from any experience or even imagining a state of affairs. Suppose also this person took no dislike to any of his activities and felt no aversions to anything either experienced or contemplated. Could we expect this person to make judgments of intrinsic goodness or badness? I think not. This is not just a matter of expectation, but one for which there is empirical confirmation. Damasio in (1994) points out that patients with significant damage to the area of the brain controlling feelings have great difficulty making decisions. One patient, when asked to chose between two dates for his next appointment, went into an elaborate and tedious analysis of the pros and cons of each date, without coming to a decision after upwards of a half hour of deliberation. The process was terminated when Damasio himself picked the date. This the patient accepted with complete equanimity.

Damasio analyses the patient's problem as involving the absence of a somatic-marker mechanism. In contemplating various alternative actions, one may consider, if only fleetingly, the consequences of an alternative. The image of an alternative with a bad outcome will be accompanied by "an unpleasant gut feeling" (1994, p. 173). Because the feeling is about the body, Damasio terms it somatic. Because it marks an image, he terms it a marker (1994, p. 173). The somatic-marker system serves as a cut-down mechanism, eliminating alternatives from further consideration. It sounds an alarm that an alternative will lead to negative consequences and this may lead us to reject that alternative immediately. Damasio allows that we also may have positive somatic markers, which function as "a beacon of incentive" rather than "an alarm bell" (1994, p. 174). The indecisive patient then was unable to have these feelings when contemplating the alternative dates. Besides their role in decision making, these feelings allow us to make value judgments. "By dint of juxtaposition, body images give to other images a *quality* of goodness or badness, of pleasure or pain" (1994, p. 159). If these considerations are cogent, we have shown that basic beliefs concerning particular *prima facie* values are the products of a moral or more broadly evaluative sense. Moral intuition, like empirical intuition then, is not purely *a priori*. Both involve detection of covariation or cooccurrence. Whereas with empirical intuition, covariation detection is a matter ordinarily of perception and memory, moral intuition presupposes the moral sense.

Because Ross speaks of intuiting the general principle that promise keeping is a *prima facie* duty by inspecting several instances of promise keeping that are duties, one may ask whether the general judgment is nonetheless inferred. We regard this as mistaken. As Audi points out, intuition does not exclude reflection, and in many cases may be the outcome of reflection. "The conclusion of a reflection is a wrapping up of the question, similar to concluding a practical matter with a decision. One has not added up the evidences and formulated their implication; one has obtained a view of the whole and characterized it overall" (1997, p. 43). To those who would object that our judgment is inferred nonetheless from the propositions indicating a situation's various value-making features, we may reply with Audi that this "is to confuse the grounds of one's judgment with beliefs expressing those grounds" (1997, p. 43). If one comes to the judgment before articulating the grounds, the judgment is basic. The situation is analogous with perception. I am appeared to "treely" and form the belief that there is a tree outside my office window. If challenged, I might list a number of features in how I am appeared to which are tree-indicating. I might offer the propositions expressing those features as premises from which one may infer that there is a tree in front of me. But that is not what I do in perception. I do not form judgments that I am appeared to in such-and-such ways and from them infer that there is a tree in front of me. Rather, I am simply appeared to and on the basis of that sensory input form the belief that there is a tree in front of me.[5] Moral intuition, then, like perception, is a mechanism generating basic beliefs.

A state of affairs is actually intrinsically good just in case its *prima facie* good-making characteristics outweigh its *prima facie* bad-making characteristics. Likewise, an act is an actual duty just in case its *prima facie* right-making characteristics outweigh its *prima facie* wrong-making characteristics. For Ross, this weighing will frequently involve some form of intuition, because we do not in general have principles indicating that one characteristic is weightier than or takes precedence over another. However, if we form to ourselves beliefs to the effect that a situation has certain *prima facie* positive value-making characteristics and certain *prima facie* negative value-making characteristics, that one set outweighs the other, and that, because all this is the case, the situation has actual positive or negative value as the case may be, our judgment of actual value is inferred and thus not a basic belief.

Can one ever form a basic belief concerning actual as opposed to *prima facie* value? Certainly it is conceivable that one could be in a situation that manifested only one *prima facie* value-making characteristic or in which one took account of only one such characteristic. On that basis, one could infer immediately that the *prima facie* value was the actual value of the situation. But even here, the belief concerning actual value is inferred, not basic. Notice that to assess this inference, one would need to assess whether other *prima facie* value-making characteristics should have been taken into account. But this would seem to be the critical question for assessing whether a basic belief of actual value were properly basic. Hence, for the purpose of assessing the acceptability of basic premises, we need not treat statements of actual value as basic.

A fortiori we need not consider basic beliefs concerning general judgments of actual value. Ross would have little interest in such judgments, because he would regard them as mistaken. For Ross, conflicts of duties are always possible. Hence, one and the same act may, *qua* possessing certain attributes, be *prima facie* right and *qua* possessing certain other attributes, be *prima facie* wrong. Whether the act *is* right or wrong depends on which of these factors is more morally stringent. No matter how stringent the *prima facie* right-making attributes of an act, it is possible that the act possesses even more stringent *prima facie* wrong-making characteristics in light of which it *is* actually wrong. Hence, for Ross, a general principle that acts of a certain sort are always actually right or wrong is mistaken. Given Ross's argument, any claim that there are general principles of actual value, that certain *prima facie* values will *always* trump all other *prima facie* values with which they could come into conflict, incurs a significant burden of proof. The burden is to identify such values and to show that they will always override all other evaluative considerations. That is an issue beyond our scope here. Hence, we may set aside inquiry into how beliefs expressed by general principles of actual right or wrong are generated and whether there is a presumption of reliability for the generating mechanism.

Because we have distinguished three types of value, we shall consider each type separately in each of the next three sections. It is appropriate that we consider intrinsic value first. Surely, if there is intrinsic value, its wanton destruction is *prima facie* wrong. Hence, some cases of deontic value may supervene upon intrinsic value. Clearly also in some cases an act is *prima facie* right because it leads to good consequences. Hence, a comprehensive understanding of how deontic evaluations are generated presupposes an account of the generation of judgments of intrinsic value. It is also appropriate that we consider judgments of aretaic value last. In some circumstances, we may judge a person's character virtuous precisely because that person has consistently preferred right acts. Moral goodness then may supervene on deontic value.

Within each section, we shall address ourselves first to the question of what sorts of things have those evaluative properties. We shall then ask how the moral sense generates beliefs concerning when these values *prima facie* occur in a given case. Given this account of its operation, may we appraise the reliability of moral sense as a belief-generating mechanism? May we also explain why or under what circumstances moral intuition is reliable in generating particular or general beliefs that some condition is a reason for a *prima facie* evaluation? Our goal in this discussion will be to see whether there are conditions under which we may presume that moral sense and moral intuition are reliable belief-generating mechanisms.

Some readers may be left with a final question or misgiving. We have been speaking of moral intuition and moral sense in connection with the three types of value standardly distinguished. But intrinsic value, intrinsic goodness or badness, is frequently referred to as nonmoral value. Is it not anomalous to use the term "moral" in speaking of the mechanisms generating beliefs expressing nonmoral value? This objection is terminological and can be met terminologically. In speaking of the mechanisms involved with intrinsic value, we could speak of protomoral intuition and protomoral sense. The "proto" is appropriate here, for as we have pointed out, deontic value, in some cases, supervenes upon intrinsic value. But, because intrinsic value has a bearing on moral evaluation, requiring the prefixing of "proto" when discussing the mechanisms generating beliefs of intrinsic value is scrupulous. We shall then continue to speak of moral intuition and moral sense in connection with intrinsic value. Disquieted readers may use our prefix to allay their qualms.

9.3 JUDGMENTS OF INTRINSIC VALUE

What sorts of things are intrinsically good? Ross identifies four kinds of things which he regards as the primary intrinsic goods, "virtue, pleasure, the allocation of pleasure to the virtuous, and knowledge (and in a less degree right opinion)" (1930, p. 140).[6] Ross is confident that anything that is intrinsically good will either fall under one or a combination of these kinds (1930, p. 140). This immediately raises two questions: Do we agree that all these are intrinsically good? Are there further intrinsic goods that cannot be reduced to these? Let us begin with pleasure.

The case of pleasure brings home that we are discussing first *prima facie* intrinsic value or goodness. On the one hand, it may seem obvious that pleasure is good in itself. It would seem that this is neither something to be argued for, nor that judgments that particular pleasures are good would need to be argued for. On the other hand, someone might easily object: "Is pleasure always good?" Suppose a cruel, sadistic person experiences distinct pleasure in inflicting pain on others. Surely we do not want to say that the pleasure of this individual is a good thing, that *this* pleasure is good. But here, of course, something more is affecting the intrinsic value of the situation besides the pleasure involved. The state of affairs of experiencing pleasure is here part of a more complex state of affairs involving further considerations relevant to intrinsic value. Hence, we distinguish *prima facie* goodness or badness from overall or overriding goodness or badness. The fact that a sentient being is feeling pleasure creates a presumption that the total state of affairs is good, a presumption which can be undercut by other factors. (Compare Ross 1930, p. 137.) In the sadist's case, the presumption *is* undercut.

If argument that pleasure is *prima facie* intrinsically good be needed, Ross has three arguments for this point. First, he asks us "to suppose two states of the universe including equal amounts of virtue but the one including also widespread and intense pleasure and the other widespread and intense pain" (1930, p. 135).[7] Can one say that the former is not better than the latter? Second, even those who apparently value pleasure the least approve of kindness and disapprove of cruelty. But in kindness we give pleasure to others and in cruelty pain. "This seems to imply the conviction that pleasure is good and pain bad" (1930, p. 135).[8] Finally, "if virtue deserves to be rewarded by happiness . . . , this seems at first sight to imply that happiness and unhappiness are not in themselves things indifferent, but are good and bad respectively" (1930, p. 135).[9]

Judgments that a particular pleasurable state of affairs is *prima facie* good seem different from deontic judgments that a particular promise is a *prima facie* duty or even other judgments of intrinsic value, for example, that a particular instance of knowledge or virtue is *prima facie* good. Recall that judging that a particular instance of promise keeping is a *prima facie* duty involves both perceiving that a promise has been made and feeling disapproval towards the promisor's breaking the promise. Here, both perception and feeling are factors involved in judgment. Likewise, in a judgment that a particular virtuous action is *prima facie* good, I would seem to need to recognize both that the action was an instance of virtue and to feel positively in some way toward it. (This to be sure is a provisional statement, which will be refined in due course.) When judging that a particular instance of pleasure is *prima facie* good, it would seem that just feeling is involved. To feel the intrinsic goodness of the pleasure one must feel the pleasure and it would seem, conversely, to feel the pleasure is to feel its intrinsic goodness. Is pleasure unique among intrinsic values in this respect?

In part, this may depend on just what we are willing to count as pleasure. However, Audi has argued that there are instances of satisfaction that are clearly intrinsic goods but that are not obviously pleasurable. Conversations that we find intrinsically rewarding but that "are too much work or too fraught with tensions or problems to be enjoyable" (1997, p. 254) are instances of satisfaction but not of pleasure, if we understand pleasure as involving such feelings as making "one smile or glow inside" or having "visceral manifestations of the engagement with their objects" (1997, p. 254). Unless one wanted to widen one's concept of pleasure to include all such satisfactions, it would seem that we would need to count such satisfactions as intrinsic goods in addition to pleasure. But notice that such satisfactions, like pleasures, are experienced. Furthermore, in one feeling one feels both the satisfaction and the *prima facie* goodness. Audi reminds us that absence or reduction of pain is another type of experiential *prima facie* good. "On any plausible understanding of pleasure and the absence (or reduction) of pain, they are substantively different values: neither is simply the negation of the other" (1997, p. 254). Hence, satisfaction and reduction of pain – with absence of pain as the limiting case – are two basic types of *prima facie* intrinsic goodness.

The more general concept of satisfaction as opposed to pleasure may give us the key to understanding how we come to judge that instances of other types of *prima facie* goods on Ross's list are *prima facie* goods. Consider knowledge (and in a lesser degree right opinion). Surely, many aspects, features, events in the world arouse our wonder. This wonder in itself is a feeling or involves a major feeling component. One consequence of this wonder, at least on some occasions, is a desire to understand the world or at least to come to know more of it. But if so, the acquisition of knowledge is accompanied by a felt satisfaction. If one felt no satisfaction in learning anything, we question whether that person would apprehend any goodness in knowing.

Why should virtue be counted among the intrinsic goods? To say that a character or one of its traits is virtuous is to ascribe aretaic value. But surely it is also intrinsically valuable that such a character or trait exist. Price points out that beauty and deformity can be predicated of actions. (See Raphael 1947, pp. 104–5.) In speaking of beauty in particular, Price is speaking "of our feeling of pleasure and admiration at the performance of moral action" (Raphael 1947, p. 104). Should we need convincing that marks or signs of virtue arouse feelings of pleasure, consider this thought experiment. Suppose we hear of a man who, learning that a new neighbor had recently taken up residence on the property adjoining his, went and presented her with a beautiful oriental vase simply as a gesture of welcome and friendliness. Surely, we feel pleasure at this deed and for the generous disposition it betokens. Suppose we hear further testimony that this action is not an isolated incident in the man's life but quite in character with his dealings with people, that taken all together we have very strong signs of a very generous disposition. Surely, this increases our feelings of admiring pleasure. Suppose we further learn that this man has devoted his life as a college professor to helping others to think in an ordered and critical way and to appreciate the wisdom contained in the history of philosophy, giving himself unstintingly to doing his best in each classroom presentation. Surely, our feelings of pleasure grow stronger yet. We may have moral respect for the man but contemplating his generous disposition also gives us pleasure. Ability to take satisfaction also underlies our recognition of the fourth primary good Ross recognizes – the "apportionment of pleasure and pain to the virtuous and the vicious respectively" (1930, p. 138).[10] Pleasure or happiness befits the virtuous as unhappiness befits the vicious. We find this fit or apportionment according to merit satisfying and upon it we judge instances to be intrinsically good.

Because Ross regards virtue, pleasure, the allocation of pleasure to the virtuous, and knowledge as the four basic types of intrinsic goods, for him, what has intrinsic value are states of mind and certain relations between states of mind. Indeed, Ross specifically admits that he "can find no plausibility" in the claim "there are or may be intrinsic goods that are not states of mind or relations between states of mind" (1930, p. 140).[11] But is Ross's view plausible? Knowledge is intrinsically good but that what is known is true – that the state of affairs intended by the state of knowledge corresponds to the world – would seem to have no intrinsic but at best instrumental value. Without such agreement there could be no truth[12] and thus no knowledge. Truth itself would have no intrinsic value.

It would seem to follow from Ross's view that the contemplation of excellence – in particular, teleological excellence, something's fulfilling its *telos*, properly functioning or functioning as designed – that is, knowledge that such excellence obtains together with taking pleasure in this obtaining, has intrinsic value but the teleological excellence itself has no intrinsic value. But consider an electric gadget, computer program, or natural mechanism. If it works, it functions as designed. Surely this proper functioning is good, that is, *prima facie* good, and its goodness supervenes upon the congruence of its functioning with its *telos* or design plan. Surely, any kind of excellence possesses at least *prima facie* intrinsic value.

To help justify his view of the completeness of his list Ross offers the consideration that knowledge, pleasure, and virtue dovetail nicely with "a widely accepted classification of the elements in the life of the soul," namely "cognition, feeling, and conation" (1930, p. 140).[13] Knowledge, pleasure, and virtue are ideal states of these elements (1930, p. 140). But what about the mind itself as a whole? It would seem on Ross's view that states constituting the excellence of the life of the mind have intrinsic value but the mind itself does not. What of the intrinsic value of the whole person on Ross's view? Note that we are not asking about the value of a person as instancing some virtue or excellence, moral or intellectual. We are asking about the value of a person *qua* person possessing the dignity and due the respect incumbent upon someone as a human being. Personal value is not aretaic value. Surely, many believe that human persons are intrinsically valuable, indeed that they are of infinite intrinsic worth. Recognition of such value underlies the Christian concept of *agape*, and Ross apparently seems to have left no room for this value. He allows that mutual love has intrinsic value. He sees it as a compound or complex of virtue, knowledge, and pleasure. "Mutual love seems to be a blend of virtuous disposition of two minds towards each other, with the knowledge which each has of the character and disposition of the other, and with the pleasure which arises from such disposition and knowledge" (1930, p. 141).[14] So, for Ross, apparently love has intrinsic value but the person loved does not! This seems plainly counterintuitive.

Here the defender of Ross may reply that personal value can be reduced to deontic value. As we shall discuss in Section 9.4, we may recognize a number of duties that we are bound to observe in our relations with others. Persons have rights to the extent that we have duties to treat them in these particular ways. Hence, to talk of the value of persons is to talk of persons as bearers of these rights, as persons to whom certain duties are due. The value of a person consists in the duties other persons must observe toward him. Personal value is a construct out of deontic value.

But what is the ground of these obligations? Would it not be because contrary behavior would denigrate the person as person, as bearer of personal value? Contrary behavior would treat the person as a means and not an end, and so would not be fitting or appropriate to the person as a bearer of personal value. The objection, by attempting to reduce personal value to deontic value, seems to get the cart before the horse – better the objection seems to identify the cart with the horse. Our discussion of how we come to hold deontic judgments will corroborate our reply here. These considerations should be sufficient to show that attempting to reduce personal value to deontic value is distinctly problematic.

Could one object that personal value is not intrinsic value because it is *sui generis*? If so, then again Ross would not be at fault for not including persons among the things having intrinsic value. One might think this question more terminological than substantive, as long as personal value, if legitimate, were included in our survey of types of value. But there are good reasons for us to count personal value an intrinsic value. Again, as we shall see in Section 9.4, certain duties supervene upon the fact that certain objects have certain intrinsic values. Likewise, certain duties supervene upon the fact that certain persons have personal value. By analogy, then, personal value is a type of intrinsic value.

Our discussion, of course, presupposes that there is personal value. The most radical reply to our objection would deny just that. Is there then such a thing as personal value? Like Ross, Moore does not seem to recognize personal value. He does say that the object of personal affection has great intrinsic value, but this intrinsic value is consequent upon "some of the *mental* qualities of the person towards whom the affection is felt" (1903, p. 203, italics in original). Indeed, Moore speaks of affection as being more or less valuable and its positive value depending on appreciating a person's character and its bodily expression. What is the primary bearer of value is the whole containing the appreciation of a person's admirable mental qualities and their corporeal expression. Furthermore, these admirable mental qualities "consist very largely in an emotional contemplation of beautiful objects; and hence the appreciation of them will consist essentially in the contemplation of such contemplation" (1903, p. 204). The admirable mental qualities will also include an "appreciation of a person's attitude towards other persons" (1903, p. 204), and so our love of the person will include a love of love. Moore then apparently does not recognize persons as having value apart from their aretaic value and its bodily expression being able to form part of an intrinsically valuable whole.

I think we may say that the view of Ross and Moore, if pushed to its limits, entails a thoroughgoing elitism. If what has value are the states of mind of a person which involve virtue, intelligence, or pleasure, if a person is valuable for his appreciation of beauty and the admirable qualities of others and their physical expression, then the more virtuous, intelligent, or pleasurable are the person's mental states, the more valuable is that person – the more refined a person's appreciation of aesthetic enjoyments and the pleasures of human intercourse and affection (Moore 1903, p. 203), the higher that person's value. There seems nothing here to ground or justify regarding persons *qua* persons as having equal rights before the law. Why should not those manifesting capacity for greater virtue, intelligence, or pleasure have greater rights before the law? Should a person whose capacity for intelligence or pleasure is somehow lower or impaired have less rights before the law because of this "lesser" personal value?

For many, these results will seem preposterous – this being sufficient to show that Ross and Moore have overlooked a significant type of value. For those recognizing personal value, human beings have intrinsic value simply because they are persons, and apart from any mental or physical qualities the person may possess or the intrinsic value of any of his or her states of mind as involving virtue, intelligence, pleasure, or aesthetic and personal appreciation.

Unless one can show that the additional types of intrinsic goods we have identified can somehow be reduced to combinations of Ross's basic four, we are justified in claiming that Ross's account of intrinsic good is incomplete. Hence, we recognize besides pleasure or more generally satisfaction as an intrinsic good, both those states of affairs instantiating some excellence or constituting a part of such excellence, and human persons as having intrinsic value. Hence, our account of the presumptive reliability of the mechanisms generating beliefs that intrinsic value holds or beliefs concerning reasons for or principles of *prima facie* intrinsic value must take account of beliefs involving all these kinds of intrinsic value. Notice that ontologically, there is a distinct difference between persons and the other bearers of intrinsic value. Persons are not states of affairs. Hence we shall proceed to consider the moral sense and moral intuition in their employment to generate beliefs concerning the intrinsic value of states of affairs involving satisfaction and excellence first.

Beliefs Concerning the Intrinsic Value of States of Affairs

As Audi points out, there is an intimate connection between intrinsic value and reasons for action. "Surely anything intrinsically good would provide *one* kind of basic reason for action. To grant that pleasure, for example, is intrinsically good and then to deny that there is any reason to seek or promote pleasure would be at best inexplicable and would seem irrational" (1997, p. 248). Surely, also, to have a basic reason to seek or promote something for its own sake – or at least to desire it for its own sake – and not as a means to something else is to have a reason to recognize it as *prima facie* intrinsically good. But, when one feels pleasure, more generally when one experiences a state of affairs involving some satisfaction, does one not, thereby, have a reason to desire that state of affairs precisely because it involves this pleasure or satisfaction, and a reason to act to secure relevantly similar states of affairs? Likewise, should one anticipate that a state of affairs will involve pleasure or satisfaction, does not one thereby have a *prima facie* reason to desire it and take action to secure it? So here feeling the pleasure and having a (*prima facie*) reason for action are one and the same. But surely coming to believe that the object or goal of an action is (*prima facie*) intrinsically good upon having that reason for action is to come to have as basic a belief as coming to believe there is a tree outside one's office window upon having certain visual sensations. Our capacity to form these beliefs upon feeling or experiencing pleasure or satisfaction, at least in anticipation, is one expression of the moral sense in its employment to generate basic beliefs of *prima facie* intrinsic goodness. The case for pain is parallel, *mutatis mutandis.* To feel pain is to have a reason for avoidance. But this is the input from which the moral sense generates a belief of *prima facie* intrinsic badness.

Are these beliefs properly basic? Again, we must keep in mind that these are beliefs that states of affairs that are pleasurable or painful, more generally involve satisfaction or dissatisfaction, are *prima facie* intrinsically good or bad. Keeping this in mind, recognizing proper basicality is straightforward. If I experience a state of affairs as involving pleasure, my state of mind of feeling pleasure is part of that state of affairs. But what more evidence do I need to justify the belief that this state of affairs is *prima facie* intrinsically good? My feeling the pleasure is sufficient evidence, justification for the belief generated. As Audi points out, "The same individual experiences in virtue of which a kind of experience is intrinsically desirable, for instance pleasures in viewing a painting, can render believable the proposition that experience of that kind is intrinsically good" (1997, p. 267). These considerations obviously apply to satisfaction in general.

Likewise, we may ask about the proper basicality not of the belief that something pleasurable is *prima facie* intrinsically good but that pleasure is a reason for *prima facie* intrinsic goodness, a judgment of moral intuition. But surely, if one gives as a reason why a state of affairs was *prima facie* intrinsically good the fact that the state of affairs was pleasurable or involved one's being in a pleasurable mental state, one has given a legitimate reason for that judgment, at least to anyone who has experienced pleasure. This adequacy of the reason we recognize immediately, and with this recognition the proper basicality of such judgments of moral intuition.

Beliefs that states of affairs involving pleasure or pain are *prima facie* intrinsically good or bad, then, are based on completely internal evidence. The situation is analogous to avowals, generated by introspection, which as an internal belief-generating mechanism is reliable, *a fortiori* presumptively reliable. Likewise, the moral sense when employed to generate beliefs that states of affairs involving pleasure or pain are *prima facie* good or bad and moral intuition when employed to form judgments that the intrinsic value supervenes upon the pleasure or pain involved are reliable.

One might admit that the moral sense is reliable when forming a judgment about the subject's own pleasure or pain, but question whether it is reliable when forming a judgment about the pleasure or pain of others. I perceive the natural signs of someone in pain and form the belief that the person is in pain. I also form the belief that this state of affairs is *prima facie* intrinsically bad. But I certainly did not feel that person's pain. So it would appear that my argument for the reliability of the moral sense would not work in this case. We may grant this, but we may straightforwardly construct an argument for the conditional presumptive reliability of the moral sense in generating judgments that the satisfaction or dissatisfaction of others are *prima facie* intrinsically good or bad. In Section 8.7, we indicated that we may empathetically enter into the situation of others. This may very well not leave us unaffected. As Wilson points out, "We are affected by the distress or pleasure of another. . . . A man winces when the hero in a motion picture is wounded, exults when he is triumphant. A woman is saddened by the sight of an abandoned kitten or a lame dog, delighted by the spectacle of a stranger's new baby" (1993, p. 29). Even if we do not occurrently feel some pleasure or pain upon contemplating someone feeling pleasure or pain, we can certainly recognize (through personal intuition of psychological causation) that were we to be in that person's situation, we would feel pleasure or pain. We are feeling at least in anticipation pleasure or pain, more generally satisfaction or dissatisfaction, over the satisfaction or dissatisfaction of someone else. Notice in this case that the satisfaction or dissatisfaction we feel is internally available to us and it is open to the moral sense to recognize its *prima facie* intrinsic goodness or badness immediately. But our mental state intends the satisfaction or dissatisfaction of someone else. Our experienced satisfaction or dissatisfaction are signs of the *prima facie* intrinsic goodness or badness of the satisfaction or dissatisfaction our mental state intends. But, in such a case, the moral sense will be reliable to the extent that our perception or personal intuition of the situation is reliable, to the extent, we could say, that our empathy genuinely enters into the other's situation. Again, should we be aware of the signs of pleasure or pain in this situation not directly, but learn of them through the word of others, there will be a presumption for our moral sense's judgment of *prima facie* intrinsic value conditional upon there being a presumption for the reporter's account.

These considerations about the presumptive reliability of moral sense in generating beliefs of the *prima facie* intrinsic goodness or badness of the satisfaction or dissatisfaction of others can be generalized. Indeed, they lead us to the next type of intrinsic goods we need to consider. In perceiving the pleasure of others, we are experiencing something pertaining to human excellence. Recall Ross's pointing out the parallelism between knowledge, pleasure, and virtue, on the one hand, and cognition, feeling, and conation, on the other. So, coming to believe either that particular states of affairs of others that we perceive to be pleasurable for them are intrinsically good or coming to believe that states of affairs involving knowledge or virtue are intrinsically good are of a piece. They are coming to believe that states of affairs constituent of ideal states of the mind are intrinsically good. Notice that we are not saying that belief in the intrinsic goodness of these states of affairs is somehow consequent upon our recognizing their ideal status. Although they *are* ideal, one might come to believe that they are intrinsically good without entertaining a belief concerning their being ideal. However, one could. Certainly, in coming to believe that states of affairs one recognizes as involving teleological or criterial excellence are intrinsically good, one does. So, we may consider together all of these instances of coming to believe that certain states of affairs have intrinsic value. How does the moral sense's coming to form judgments concerning the satisfaction or dissatisfaction of others serve as a paradigm for how it forms beliefs concerning the *prima facie* intrinsic goodness of instances of excellence in general?

Notice that contemplating a state of affairs involving the constituent of some ideal or the realization of some end or excellence involves satisfaction, whether that constituent be pleasure or some other excellence. Again here besides the feeling of satisfaction itself, what that satisfaction is taken in or intends is also said to have intrinsic value. Consider virtuous dispositions and actions. We can take satisfaction in someone's having a disposition to act from benevolence, or that an action was performed from a desire to do one's duty. The input for moral sense is the belief that the disposition is benevolent or the action done from duty together with the experienced satisfaction. Now we may generalize on the case of how the moral sense comes to recognize the *prima facie* intrinsic value of the pleasures or pains of others. The experienced satisfaction is a sign that the intended state of affairs is (*prima facie*) intrinsically good. As certain sensations are presumptively sufficient evidence for the resultant perceptual belief that there is an object in the external world satisfying certain properties, so the experienced satisfaction is presumptively sufficient evidence that the intended state of affairs is *prima facie* intrinsically good. For consider: Is not my experienced satisfaction a reason to desire the intended state of affairs? Does not this constitute a reason to believe that the intended state of affairs is intrinsically good? Such a belief is the output of the moral sense.

Now for a belief that someone's benevolent disposition is intrinsically good to be true, the input belief that the person has a benevolent disposition must likewise be true. The same holds for the belief concerning action from duty. Hence, the reliability of the moral sense in this employment is dependent upon the reliability of the mechanism generating the input belief. But if that mechanism is presumptively reliable, then the moral sense in this employment is presumptively reliable. For, to offer a Reidian argument, if it is a first principle of our constitution to form certain perceptual beliefs upon being appeared to in a certain way, so it is likewise a first principle of our constitution to form certain beliefs of *prima facie* intrinsic value upon having certain experiences of pleasure or satisfaction. As Audi puts it:

Propositions about what is intrinsically desirable are believable on the basis of my experiences of the kinds of things in question, such as pleasures and pains. . . . An experience of green justifies (renders believable) the proposition that there is something green before one . . . ; an experience of pleasure in viewing a painting indicates the desirability of that viewing [and we would add that it indicates the desirability of the painting itself]. . . . The first kind of experience can render a belief justified; the second kind can render a desire rational. (1997, p. 267)

But the same experience which renders a desire rational can render believable the proposition that what is desired is (*prima facie*) intrinsically good. (Compare Audi 1997, p. 267.)

This same analysis can be applied both to apportionment of pleasure and pain to the virtuous and vicious, and to knowledge. One takes satisfaction in the fact that a particular virtuous disposition or a particular virtuous action is rewarded or that some instance of vice has met with punishment. One takes satisfaction in that one knows that *p*. Indeed, one may take satisfaction in that someone else knows that *p*. Likewise, in seeing that some artifact works as designed, or that some criterion is satisfied, one may take satisfaction in that there is this instance of teleological or criterial excellence. Hence, in all these cases, the operation of moral sense as a belief-generating mechanism is parallel to its operation in generating a belief that some instance of virtue is intrinsically good. The input can be characterized as an ordered pair consisting of a belief that φ and an experienced satisfaction, while the output is a belief that it is *prima facie* intrinsically good (or intrinsically bad) that φ.

In each of these cases, we have been talking of taking satisfaction in just one aspect of a state of affairs – its being pleasurable (for someone), or involving virtue or some other form of teleological or criterial excellence. Now it is quite possible for a state of affairs to involve several grounds of *prima facie* intrinsic goodness and, as we have already seen, states of affairs can involve a mixture of good-making and bad-making properties. If one weighs these features against each other to form an overall judgment of the actual value of a state of affairs, the resulting belief is not basic. But one can maintain that one can take several aspects of a state of affairs into account in forming a judgment of its value and this judgment still be basic. This involves what Audi calls moral reflection (see 1997, p. 43), which we see here as a special employment of the moral sense. Can one recognize a pattern in the state of affairs, similarly to the way one recognizes a pattern or *gestalt* in a painting, a pattern that overall tends to be intrinsically good or intrinsically bad? More specifically, can one take satisfaction (or experience dissatisfaction) in the overall pattern the state of affairs displays? If so, then that the state of affairs displays that pattern becomes the input belief for moral sense in generating a basic belief of *prima facie* intrinsic value. On the basis of that belief and the experienced satisfaction or dissatisfaction, the moral sense then generates a basic belief of the *prima facie* intrinsic goodness or badness of the state of affairs.

The factors determining the overall presumptive reliability of moral sense are the same in the cases of apportionment of happiness to virtue, of knowledge, and of teleological and criterial excellence as they were for virtue. Notice that the input belief in each of these cases is an interpretation. As such it need not be a basic belief. But the evaluative belief, generated from that interpretive belief as input together with the experienced satisfaction, is not inferred, but basic. Again, as the truth of the input belief is presupposed, the overall reliability of the mechanism is conditional upon the reliability of the mechanism whereby that belief was arrived at. By contrast, the experienced satisfaction constitutes the evidence for the intrinsic value of that state of affairs which is the object of the input belief. That the resultant evaluation ensues is as much an expression of our design plan as our coming to hold perceptual beliefs on the basis of sensory experience. If perception is presumptively reliable, why not the moral sense in this employment?

One might object that this account apparently assumes that people will take satisfaction in what has positive intrinsic value and experience dissatisfaction over what has negative intrinsic value. But is this true? What may we say of sadistic pleasure? A sadist correctly perceives some suffering, takes satisfaction, and forms a belief of the suffering's intrinsic goodness. Is the sadist's moral sense working reliably here? Notice that taking satisfaction in the pain of others is not the only "perverted" satisfaction imaginable. It is conceivable that someone would take satisfaction in someone else's being ignorant, knowably acting contrary to duty, or in some mechanism's being broken. This could be an expression of a satisfaction system warped by envy. Jones begrudges Smith the intrinsic goods she has, believing her having them is a (*prima facie*) bad thing. He is pleased over her misfortunes and believes them to be a (*prima facie*) good thing – *Schadenfreude*. By contrast, in what may be the most extreme case – epistemically – a masochist would take satisfaction in his own pain, judging it to be *prima facie* intrinsically good. In light of these considerations, may we maintain that the moral sense is presumptively reliable conditional just upon the presumptive reliability of the mechanism generating the belief that the state of affairs judged *prima facie* good or bad actually holds?

One could reply that the problem here is not with the reliability of the moral sense in these instances, but with the proper functioning of the satisfaction mechanism. We are dealing with pathology, psychological, moral, or perhaps of some other kind. The mechanism to feel satisfaction has been warped. The situation here is analogous to perception in a distorting environment. Although perception is presumptively reliable, operating in a medium for which it was not designed results in distorted perceptual beliefs. Likewise, our satisfaction mechanism is at least part of the medium in which the moral sense operates. In effect then the moral sense of these warped individuals is operating in an environment for which it was not designed. Just as mistaken perceptual judgments made by someone wearing distorting lenses would not count against the presumptive reliability of our visual perceptual mechanism, so mistaken evaluative judgments made by someone whose satisfaction system was warped by a vicious disposition should not count against the presumptive reliability of the moral sense. In both cases, awareness of the distortion undercuts the presumption for the reliability of the mechanism in a given case, but does not cancel the general presumption of reliability.

One may still object. If humans were standardly in a perceptually distorting environment, then there would not be "a high objective probability that a belief formed" (Plantinga 1993b, p. 19) through perception would be true. The nonreliability of perception would cancel any presumption for its reliability. But perception *is* presumptively reliable and the burden of proof is on someone to show that this reliability fails in a given case. Thus, there is a presumption that the environment is not distorting. May one likewise presume that one's satisfaction mechanism is reliable? Two considerations support a positive answer. First, to feel satisfaction over certain states of affairs and dissatisfaction over others is part of our constitution. Hence, we can apply a Reidian constitutional argument here. Such satisfactions form the data upon which we base judgments from which we reason, as sensations form the raw material for perceptual judgments from which we reason. We do not need to justify our constitution. Second, that evidence of defeaters for the presumptive reliability of one's satisfaction mechanism are commonly denominated as evidence of pathology, as evidence of deviation from the norm or ideal, indicates that absence of such evidence is reason not to question the reliability of our satisfaction mechanism. Hence, we can still maintain that the presumptive reliability of the moral sense in generating judgments of intrinsic value is conditional upon the presumptive reliability of the mechanism generating the interpretation constituting partial input for the moral sense. But we have to acknowledge that in particular cases, the presumptive reliability of the moral sense will be undercut by factors dealing with our feeling of satisfaction.

Understanding the operation of moral intuition and its presumptive reliability follows straightforwardly upon the considerations we have just entertained. In each individual case, one takes satisfaction *that* a certain state of affairs manifesting a certain condition or property holds because it manifests that property or condition – I take satisfaction in that Mother Theresa displayed a benevolent disposition. Intuition can recognize that *because* the state of affairs manifests virtue, one takes satisfaction in it. But the experienced satisfaction gives a reason to desire and promote, if possible, the state of affairs in which one has taken satisfaction. By the same token, it is the evidence for that state of affairs being intrinsically good. So, to recognize ultimately that because a state of affairs manifests a certain property, one takes satisfaction in it is to recognize that because it manifests that property, it is *prima facie* intrinsically good.

On this account, moral intuition is a completely internal belief-generating mechanism in these employments. My taking satisfaction in a certain state of affairs because it manifests a certain property is something open to my inspection. But if our discussion of the structure of moral sense is correct, my satisfaction is a reason for desire or action and thus a reason for the *prima facie* intrinsic goodness of that state of affairs. This also is open to my inspection. So in seeing that the value-making properties of the state of affairs are reasons for its *prima facie* intrinsic value, moral intuition is relying on internal evidence open to inspection.

Notice that if one takes satisfaction in a state of affairs because it manifests a certain property φ one would take satisfaction in other φ-bearing states of affairs because they manifest φ, unless those states of affairs manifested other properties canceling the satisfaction. Thus, one would accept appropriate counterfactuals of the form – If that state of affairs had manifested φ, I would have taken satisfaction in it. But this indicates that moral intuition does not presuppose the belief that the φ-bearing state of affairs obtains, as does the moral sense, and thus the reliability of moral intuition does not depend on the reliability of the mechanisms generating this belief.

Again, the reliability of moral intuition, like the reliability of moral sense, is subject to compromise from a distorted satisfaction mechanism. If a sadist takes satisfaction in other's pain, that sadist could recognize by intuition that because certain states of affairs involve pain, he takes satisfaction in them and thus further form the general belief that the pain (of others) is *prima facie* intrinsically good. But this no more counts against the presumptive reliability of moral intuition than it counts against the presumptive reliability of moral sense. Hence, moral intuition, at least in these employments in connection with *prima facie* intrinsic value, is presumptively reliable.

Beliefs Concerning the Intrinsic Value of Persons

Persons are not states of affairs, and so we should expect our discussion of how we come to have beliefs concerning their intrinsic value will differ from the other instances of intrinsic value that we have discussed. Indeed, to take pleasure in a person in the sense of finding satisfaction in holding concourse with him, or in contemplating various features he manifests, would seem to value the person only as a means to our satisfaction. But the intrinsic value of a person involves recognizing the person as an end. The concept of the intrinsic value or dignity of persons has been subjected to thorough analysis by MacLagan in (1960a), and his analysis gives us the key to understanding how we come to have beliefs that persons have value. To speak of persons as having intrinsic value and to say that persons are due respect as persons are equivalent ways of speaking. Hence, in what follows we shall speak of respect for persons in addition to their intrinsic value.

Respect for persons includes respecting them simply because they are persons. This attitude towards persons, MacLagan points out, is the type of love the New Testament calls "Agape." This attitude is manifested in a type of experience MacLagan calls the Agape-response. This has epistemic import. This response discloses the intrinsic value of persons as persons, as our experience of pleasure or satisfaction, in the first instance, discloses the intrinsic value of pleasure or satisfaction. On MacLagan's analysis, two factors are involved in making the Agape-experience possible or in generating it. The first is "our general consciousness of obligation, the awareness that there are or may be claims upon us that run counter to our wishes and that have an authority that cannot be expressed in terms of any mere psychological urgency" (1960a, p. 209). This capacity becomes occurrent in situations where we recognize a difference and indeed conflict between what we want and what we ought to do (1960a, pp. 209–10). The other factor MacLagan calls "our capacity for sympathy" (1960a, p. 210). He distinguishes passive sympathy or empathy, attempting imaginatively to feel what others feel, from active sympathy, "the sympathy of practical *concern for* others as distinguished from simply *feeling with* them" (1960a, p. 211, italics in original).

Passive sympathy is a necessary condition for Agape. Without it, there could be no consciousness of the other as a subject, that there is a moral universe (as opposed to a protomoral universe) to be experienced. But it is also "the natural matrix of active sympathy" in "that it is psychologically impossible genuinely to sympathize with anyone in the passive mode without at the same time having *some* measure of active sympathy also, *some* degree of practical concern for him" (1960a, p. 212, italics in original). Agape is "the fusion of active sympathy with the general moral interest that is involved in, or represented by, any really 'lived' sense of obligation" (1960a, p. 216). Agape, then, is a moral concern for the other. The other is a person for whom one is actively concerned, where this concern expresses principles of moral obligation. As such, the other has moral worth or importance, is due respect as a person.

It would seem that this experience discloses immediately the intrinsic value of persons as the experience of pleasure or pain discloses the intrinsic value of pleasurable or painful states of affairs. One experiences the other as subject, in particular as subject to or capable of experiences or states of mind that have intrinsic value, and as the object, that is, end, of one's practical concern. Furthermore, this practical concern is not just a matter of feeling but of moral obligation. If the experience discloses this and such beliefs arise from or are generated from this experience, what more is needed to come to believe both of individual persons and of persons collectively that they have intrinsic value or dignity?

Given our experience, what more is needed to convince us of the reliability of the mechanisms generating these beliefs? We may again see both the moral sense and moral intuition working here. The moral sense generates beliefs concerning the intrinsic value of individual persons; moral intuition the intrinsic value of persons *qua* persons, that their value supervenes simply on their being persons. MacLagan regards both factors contributing to the Agape-experience – sense of obligation and active sympathy – as part of our constitution as human beings. With Reid, we may argue that generating beliefs in the intrinsic worth of human beings is an aspect of our constitution. As such, the belief-generating mechanisms are presumptively reliable and the resulting beliefs are first principles from which we reason, acceptable as basic premises until we are presented with evidence to the contrary. One again might object that not all human beings have a sense of obligation, a capacity to empathize, or to be practically concerned for another on the basis of that empathy. A sadist might even have the capacity to feel another's pain but be concerned to foster that as a means to his own satisfaction, thus coming to believe that human beings are means, not ends. In all these cases, we may reply as we did to the sadist's case previously. That in individual cases, these systems might not function properly or function to create a distorted environment does not show that the moral sense or moral intuition are not presumptively reliable belief-generating mechanisms.

Agape involves not only a response or experience that discloses the dignity or intrinsic value of persons but has a directive import in a principle of respect for them. In (1960b), MacLagan develops how this principle of respect justifies certain *prima facie* duties. But these are matters of deontic value, to which we turn directly in Section 9.4.

9.4 JUDGMENTS OF DEONTIC VALUE

Recall that we can have basic beliefs that particular acts are *prima facie* duties, or are *prima facie* right or wrong, and basic beliefs expressing principles of *prima facie* duty, rightness, or wrongness. Being a *prima facie* duty is an objective feature of an act, supervening upon certain objective properties of the act. Our moral intuition recognizes this supervenience. Through the moral sense or moral sentiments we may form basic beliefs about the *prima facie* rightness of particular acts. How first of all does the moral sense generate such judgments?

As feeling pleasure or taking satisfaction constitutes the experience on which the moral sense generates beliefs concerning *prima facie* intrinsic goodness, so specific feelings or sentiments furnish the experience on which the moral sense generates judgments of deontic value. In (1993), Wilson distinguishes four types of sentiments – sympathy, fairness, self-control, and duty. All are relevant here, although, because we are speaking of all these as providing input from which beliefs concerning *duty* are generated, it is better to speak of a sentiment of fidelity rather than duty. Also, for the purpose of classifying duties, it is more precise to speak of a sentiment of personal integrity which is a component of, although it need not be the whole of, self-control. Ross catalogues six main types of *prima facie* duties, disclaiming any completeness or finality for it (1930, p. 20). For our purposes, I believe we can organize Ross's list around Wilson's four types of feeling or moral sentiments as amended. This organization will suggest an obvious and valuable expansion of Ross's list. Sympathy discloses to us individual acts that are *prima facie* duties of beneficence, nonmaleficence, or reparation. Duties of beneficence "rest on the mere fact that there are other beings in the world whose condition we can make better in respect of virtue, or of intelligence, or of pleasure" (1930, p. 21).[15] Duties of nonmaleficence are duties not to harm others, whereas duties of reparation rest on previous wrongful acts (1930, p. 21).

The moral sentiment of fairness is centrally concerned with three issues – equity, reciprocity, and impartiality (Wilson 1993, p. 60). Equity means that "things should be divided among people in proportion to their worth or merit" (1993, p. 60). People may differ on what counts for merit, but this does not gainsay the place of equity as a component of fairness. Duties of equity include, but need not be limited to, Ross's duties of justice, duties to prevent or upset a distribution of goods not according to merit. Reciprocity, as Wilson points out, "is a special case of equity: it is fairness *in exchanges*" (1993, p. 65, italics in original). Equal pay for equal work is a question of equity, but helping a co-worker who has given one help is a question of reciprocity. Duties of reciprocity include what Ross calls duties of gratitude. Impartiality means treating people without prejudice, favoritism, or disregard of the rules of procedure, giving them an opportunity to present their side of the story (compare 1993, p. 69).

Duties of personal integrity include first Ross's duties of self-improvement, to "improve our own condition in respect of virtue or of intelligence" (1930, p. 21).[16] These duties promote or realize our human flourishing. Their exercise enables the development of what Aristotle calls our human *aretē*. They are duties of integrity because realizing such *aretē* is part of our being true to ourselves. But there is another class of duties of personal integrity, one that Ross apparently does not recognize. These are duties incumbent upon us simply because of who or what we are as human beings, including our human condition and its limitations, and not in virtue of any ideal of human excellence. We may call them duties of self-respect. For example, at least in some cases, we can either use our bodily organs as they were designed or contrary to their design. In one case, we respect these organs and ourselves as "embodied persons and personalized bodies" (Meilaender 1991, p. 41); in the other we disrespect them and thus ourselves. Duties of self-respect enjoin that we refrain from disrespecting who or what we are.

Fidelity corresponds directly to a group of duties Ross recognizes. These are duties resting "on previous acts of my own" (1930, p. 21).[17] We may further subdivide this class into explicit and implicit duties of fidelity. An explicit duty of fidelity is the result of an explicit promise one has made. An implicit duty is the result of an implicit promise. By addressing myself to others in a manner or a context which entitles them to presume I am telling the truth, I am implicitly promising not to tell lies and thus am incurring the implicit *prima facie* duty of telling the truth (Compare 1930, p. 21).

We may summarize this classification of *prima facie* duties and the moral sentiments that may generate basic judgments or beliefs about these duties in Figure 9.1.

This classification associates duties not only with moral sentiments but with various types of human relations. I may be related to other human beings in a number of morally significant ways. I may simply be another human being whose actions can affect, for good or ill, the well-being of those around me. My neighbors then will be related to me as possible beneficiaries of my action (compare 1930, p. 19), and by virtue of this relation certain *prima facie* duties of beneficence and nonmaleficence are incumbent upon me. Should I harm my neighbor, either intentionally or unintentionally, I have brought an additional relation into being between myself and my neighbor, and by virtue of this relation I incur duties of

FIGURE 9.1 Table of moral sentiments and concomitant *prima facie* duties

reparation. As a human being, I may contribute with others to some joint effort – and thus enter the relation of co-worker or co-contributor with them. Being in this relation again founds duties concerning the equitable distribution of the outcome of the project. Similarly, my receiving good or favors from others or my being put in a position to adjudicate some matter brings me into additional relations to others, relations upon which *prima facie* duties supervene.

I may further intentionally enter into certain relations by my commitments of various sorts, relations "of promisee to promisor, of creditor to debtor, of wife to husband, . . . of friend to friend, of fellow countryman to fellow countryman" (1930, p. 19).[18] All these relations that I may bring into being by specific acts and commitments of my own require me to be faithful to these relations and thus the relations ground *prima facie* duties of fidelity. Duties of self-improvement and duties of self-respect do not in any obvious way supervene upon special relations to others. But to attempt to view *all prima facie* duties as depending on various interpersonal relations may be wrongheaded.

The question we must ask is what makes a relation morally significant. We are related in all sorts of ways to other people. But these relations, in general, do not found *prima facie* duties. If Jones and Smith are wearing ties of the same color, they are in the relation "x is wearing the same color tie as y" to each other, but it is hard to see that any *prima facie* duties of one to the other supervene upon that relation. The reason why, I believe, stems from this fact: That two persons are wearing the same color tie will not, except in very unusual circumstances, affect, increase or decrease, their affiliation for each other or their tending to engage in affiliative behavior. But "the desire of attachment or affiliation" is what Wilson identifies as the "mechanism underlying human moral conduct" (1993, p. 127). The earliest functioning of this mechanism in the life of a human being is "the instinctively prosocial behavior of the newborn infant," which is met by "the instinctively caring response that parents make to that behavior" (1993, p. 127).

Taking our clue from this, I believe we can begin to see how the moral sense generates basic judgments of the rightness of acts. The affiliative mechanism leads to behavior which forms morally significant relations to others. In the first instance is the parent-child and especially mother-child bond. On the basis of this bond or relation, the child senses that his or her needs are being responded to by others – that others have empathy for him. There is a positive correlation between the strength of the bond and the child's later sociable behavior (1993, p. 147). "Securely attached children show greater empathy than do avoidant children, probably because, having experienced empathy themselves, they have a greater capacity to display it toward others" (1993, p. 146). But one displays empathy or sympathy through concern for the welfare of others – minimally, at least, through concern for their occurrent happiness or unhappiness – their pleasure or pain – which would be overtly expressed through acts fulfilling duties of sympathy – acts of beneficence, nonmaleficence, reparation – however naively a child might understand how these are expressed. But, surely in the desire for affiliation or attachment to others we can see the root of felt obligation – that it is right to perform acts of beneficence, wrong to perform acts of maleficence, and that if you have hurt someone, acts of reparation are duties.

To see how our moral sentiments or deontic belief-generating mechanisms operate here to generate beliefs that particular acts are *prima facie* right, wrong, obligatory, I believe we should draw a distinction between attachment and affiliation. One is attached to another when one desires, seeks out, enjoys that other's esteem, warm regard, company. One is affiliated with another when one in addition has regard for that other as a person. That is, one is affiliated with another when one regards that person as the bearer of personal intrinsic value. A person P might desire to be attached to certain others *O*. By virtue of sympathy, *P* would apprehend that certain acts he could perform would foster or inhibit attachment. Given this connection between *P*'s acts and *P*'s desire for attachment to members of *O*, it is certainly prudentially right for *P* to perform certain acts of beneficence, prudentially wrong for *P* to perform certain acts of maleficence, and prudentially obligatory for *P* to perform certain acts of reparation. Given *P*'s desire for attachment to members of *O*, the prudential rightness, wrongness, obligatoriness of the acts supervene upon their effects on *P*'s attachment to *O*. But given this desire and given *P*'s apprehension of the connection, will *P* not come to believe that the contemplated acts are *prima facie* prudentially right, prudentially wrong, or prudentially obligatory? Surely, one module of *P*'s belief-generating mechanism should function to produce such beliefs.

These prudential obligations are matters of self-interest. However, if *P* desires not just attachment but affiliation with members of *O*, the judgments generated will be moral and not just prudential. This can be easily seen. Should I act to improve someone's virtue, intelligence, or pleasure, I have not only done something nice, something that we would expect would increase his or her affection and so attachment to me, but something that respects that individual as a person, something that is morally right. Likewise, should I injure someone, I have not only done something that could alienate the affections of that individual toward me, I have done something that disrespects that person. My act then is not just prudentially but morally wrong. Having committed this wrongful act, some act of reparation is morally necessary not only to repair the person's affections toward me but also to reestablish that the person is an object of my respect.

The *prima facie* moral rightness, wrongness, obligatoriness of my acts supervene upon such affiliative connections. Given my desire to be affiliated with members of *O*, my apprehension of these affiliative connections should constitute the input upon which judgments of *prima facie* deontic value of my acts regarding members of *O* are generated. Our desire for affiliation, then, not only impels the development of our capacity for empathy or sympathy, but includes our capacity to value other individuals as persons. We are thus constitutionally set to form certain judgments of the deontic value of certain individual acts, in particular, acts of benevolence, maleficence, and reparation. We can make similar remarks for the deontic judgments of fairness and fidelity. Indeed, we can regard the sentiment of fairness as primarily the sentiment of sympathy applied to situations calling for an equitable distribution of goods. We have already seen that such situations involve additional relations between people. Why are these relations morally significant? Consider first the relations upon which *prima facie* obligations of fairness rest.

Equity, as we have said, deals with the just distribution of goods. That there is some good to be divided already brings those who may share in this division into a particular relation with each other, that of potential sharer of this good. It is easy to appreciate how this relation is morally significant. For surely, if a potential sharer is not allowed to share in some good in a way that both is and is apprehended to be equitable, the attachment or affiliation of that person to the other potential sharers in this good – at least to those of them who *do* in fact share – will be impaired. As with duties connected with sympathy, we can again distinguish a recognition of prudential obligations from genuine judgments of deontic value. Wilson claims that the first motivation for fair behavior on the part of young children is self-interest. Fairness manifests itself first in sharing. It may very well be in a young child's self-interest to share, "to get attention, induce co-operation, or resolve disagreements" (Wilson 1993, p. 56). But if sharing were solely a means to advance self-interest, we would expect that as a child grows older and is thus capable of advancing his self-interest more forcefully, his basic sharing behavior would be abandoned or significantly modified. But this is not what happens. "The commitment to fairness grows stronger as the child grows older" (1993, p. 57). Not only do children share even when it is not in their self-interest, they recognize its deontic value. "Children begin to speak in ways that make it clear that sharing is something they *ought* to do" (1993, p. 57). This suggests that sharing is not just a way of cultivating attachment but of promoting affiliation. To share is to show respect. From this sense of the rightness, indeed obligatoriness, of sharing there develops "a fairly clear sense of rules and justifications" (1993, p. 59) concerning possessions and their distribution, a sense which becomes more sophisticated as the child grows. Parallel analyses obviously show the moral import of the relations involved in reciprocity and impartiality.

Again, with duties of fidelity, seeing the moral significance of the special relations that occasion these duties is completely straightforward. Broken promises recognized as broken, lies told recognized as intentional falsehoods obviously have a negative impact on the attachment or affiliation between the unfaithful promisor and the promisee, or the person who tells lies and the person to whom they are told. In all these cases of fairness and fidelity, our deontic belief-generating mechanism operates basically in the same way to generate beliefs that particular acts are *prima facie* right (or *prima facie* wrong or are *prima facie* duties). Given the desire for affiliation entailing respect for the other, taking as input the apprehended effect of an act upon one's affiliation with others, including the effect of this act upon respecting their personal value, the judgments of deontic value result. That the acts are *prima facie* right, wrong, or are *prima facie* duties supervenes upon these effects on affiliation. Our corresponding deontic beliefs are formed on the basis of our apprehension of this supervening effect.

The case will be obviously different for the duties of personal integrity – self-improvement and self-respect – because here our relations with others do not occasion these duties. How do beliefs that we have such duties arise? Duties of self-improvement, resting "on the fact that we can improve our own condition in respect of virtue or of intelligence" (Ross 1930, p. 21),[19] are obviously parallel to duties of beneficence. We might call them duties of self-beneficence. Although we may not recognize a duty to promote our own pleasure, surely to frustrate *all* one's desires for pleasure would be to do oneself an injury. Indeed, given our makeup as psychophysical beings, there are many ways we can harm ourselves. Duties of self-respect would be duties to avoid such injuries, and thus could be described as duties of non-self-maleficence.

Duties of beneficence and nonmaleficence are both duties of sympathy. Now it is by virtue of sympathy that we imaginatively enter into the minds of others to judge what effects our acts will have on them. But clearly then sympathy presupposes that we can feel for ourselves how certain acts or conditions will contribute to pleasure or pain and more generally our overall respect or disrespect for ourselves as persons. Duties of self-improvement and self-respect then supervene on the fact that certain acts of ours will definitely be in our interest or to our detriment. We may speak of a desire for self-regard. Our deontic belief-generating mechanism presupposes this desire in generating judgments concerning duties of personal integrity. Given that presupposition, taking our apprehension that certain acts will be to our interest or against our interest, including our interest as persons, as input, deontic judgments concerning *prima facie* duties of self-improvement or self-respect result.

In all these cases, we have been discussing the moral sense, which generates basic beliefs that particular acts are *prima facie* duties, or *prima facie* right or wrong. Can we argue that the moral sense is presumptively reliable in this employment? Recall that empathy leads us to recognize the effects on attachment or affiliation of contemplated acts connected with sympathy, fairness, fidelity, or personal integrity. Empathy in this employment is an aspect of empirical, indeed personal intuition, since these statements asserting these effects are claims of psychological causation. We view this operation of empathy as preliminary to the operation of the moral sense proper, as forming a theory of the essence of a natural kind is preliminary to the empirical intuition of subjunctives connected with that natural kind. Given this intuition, when inspecting an act, either imaginatively considering the act or perceiving its performance, one is able to project the affiliative consequences of this act. Given these projected consequences, both our ability to empathize with that person, to feel how that person would experience the consequences if the act were performed including the person's feelings of affiliation towards us (passive sympathy), our practical concern (active sympathy), and our sense of obligation – that what bears on affiliation bears on the respect due that person – in combination and concert produce the judgment or belief that the act is a *prima facie* duty, is *prima facie* right or wrong.

Now, given our discussion in Section 9.3, sympathy in both its passive and active forms and a sense of obligation are part of our constitution. Hence, we may again appeal to our Reidian argument. It is part of our constitution or design plan to form judgments that certain acts are *prima facie* duties when we apprehend their affiliative consequences. Such judgments of *prima facie* duty (or rightness or wrongness) are the beliefs from which we reason, basic principles or premises of our moral arguments, and are thus acceptable until we have reason to question the reliability of the moral sense in this employment.

Of course, these judgments are defeasible. We have reason to question the reliability of the moral sense just when we have reason to question the reliability of the personal intuition of the effects of affiliation preliminary to the operation of the moral sense (or, should the statement of these effects be inferred, we have reason to question the reliability of the inference). As we discussed in Chapter 8, personal intuition is presumptively reliable only given certain conditions. Discussing the reliability of inferential belief-generating mechanisms is beyond the scope of this essay. So, we shall have to say that the moral sense is only conditionally presumptively reliable, the condition being that the mechanisms generating the interpretation on which the belief is based are presumptively reliable.

Given this explication of the structure of the moral sense generating judgments of *prima facie* deontic value, our understanding of how moral intuition generates beliefs expressed by general principles of *prima facie* deontic value and its conditional presumptive reliability becomes straightforward. Not only does our personal intuition allow us to project that an inspected act will have certain affiliative consequences, given that it is of a certain type, it will allow us to form in general the belief that acts of that type will have these consequences. But then from sensing that particular acts of this kind are *prima facie* right or wrong in view of their projected affiliative consequences, it is easy to generalize that acts of this kind are in general *prima facie* right or wrong. Hence, we basically agree with Ross on how we come to recognize general *prima facie* moral principles. We recognize the *prima facie* rightness of a particular act of a certain kind. By reflection or abstraction upon these recognitions of *prima facie* rightness, we come to recognize general principles of *prima facie* rightness or duty (compare 1930, p. 33). This is not a matter of inductive enumeration. The recognized cases of *prima facie* rightness or wrongness do not so much constitute evidence for the general principles as illustrations. The presumptive reliability of moral intuition in intuiting these general deontic principles is conditional upon the reliability of the mechanism involved in recognizing the affiliative consequences. Should this mechanism be presumptively reliable in a given employment, so should moral intuition.

9.5 JUDGMENTS OF ARETAIC VALUE

We not only speak of acts as right or wrong, but as morally good or bad. Ross urges that it would be clearer if we spoke of actions rather than acts being morally good or bad, where an act is a thing done while an action is the doing of it from a certain motive (compare 1930, p. 7). Obviously, right acts can be done from bad motives, whereas wrong acts can be done from good motives. So "right" and "morally good," "wrong" and "morally bad," are not equivalent. What does it mean to speak of morally good or bad motives? More generally, what is involved in predicating moral goodness or badness?

We indicated when presenting our overall classification of value into intrinsic, deontic, and aretaic, that aretaic value concerns primarily the praiseworthiness or blameworthiness of persons and their characters. It is the character which in the first instance is morally good or bad, and other things will be morally good or bad by virtue of how they are related to character. In what does the moral goodness of a morally good character consist? Ross sees it as possessing certain desires. Actions will proceed from certain motives, but these motives will be determined by certain desires. Likewise feelings will proceed from desires. For Ross, the primary desire making a character good is the desire to do one's duty or devotion to duty. Indeed, the stronger one's devotion to duty, the greater one's goodness.

Ross sees two other desires as contributing to the goodness of character, "the desire to bring into being something good [thought of as good and] . . . the desire to produce some pleasure, or prevent some pain, for another being" (1930, p. 160).[20] Parallel to this there are three desires that corrupt one's character: "(1) the desire to do what is wrong [for the sake of its wrongness], (2) the desire to bring into being some particular evil, (3) the desire to inflict some pain on another" (1930, p. 163).[21] There are also indifferent desires, that is, for indifferent pleasures, such as a pleasure of the senses. Selfish action springs from an indifferent desire. Such actions are bad because they consist "in acting on an indifferent desire to the exclusion of an action to which a good desire prompts us, or would prompt us if we stopped to think" (1930, p. 168).[22] Good actions then proceed from good desires, bad actions from bad desires or the lack of self-control.

This account of desire as in effect being the primary bearer of moral goodness meets with an obvious objection. As Cohen points out and as we have already remarked in Section 8.4 (see p. 159), desires are involuntary. Does character then just consist of the desires one has? Is aretaic value determined just by desire or is something more involved? As Kant points out in *The Groundwork of the Metaphysic of Morals*, "character" applies to the will in so far as it makes use of the talents and temperaments which nature has entrusted to the person of whom it is the will. (Compare Paton 1948, p. 61.) But, as Kant claims in the very first sentence of Chapter 1 of the *Groundwork*, "It is impossible to conceive anything at all in the world, or even out of it, which can be taken as good without qualification, except a *good will*" (1948, p. 61). Can desires then be given the place of primary bearers of aretaic value? Indeed, if desires are involuntary, can we ascribe to them any aretaic value at all?

Viewing desire as involuntary does not prevent Cohen from seeing desires as proper subjects of aretaic evaluation. It also does not prevent him from saying that we have some moral responsibility for the desires we have. For, although we may not have direct voluntary control over our desires, we may try to cultivate some and weed out others. We may also decide on a given occasion whether to satisfy a desire or to resist it (Cohen 1992, p. 44). But this leads to a crucial point. Whether or not we attempt to foster or check a desire is voluntary; it is a matter of adopting certain goals. As Cohen points out, *goal adoption* is the counterpart to desire as acceptance is the counterpart to belief. It is voluntary and something for which we standardly are held accountable. Hence, we see the moral goodness of a morally good character as consisting in having adopted certain goals or having made certain commitments. These commitments are the counterparts to the desires Ross sees as constituting the goodness of a good character. Likewise, the moral badness of a morally bad character consists in having made commitments counterpart to the desires Ross identifies as constituting a bad character.[23]

How are commitments related to desires? Clearly, desires may be in accord with commitments or contrary to them. The moral value of a desire then is determined by the moral value of the commitment with which it accords or conflicts. If a commitment is morally good, so are the desires which accord with it. If a commitment is morally bad, so are the accordant desires. If a desire conflicts with a morally good commitment, for example, is a desire not to do one's duty, it is morally bad. If a desire conflicts with a morally bad commitment, then it is morally good.

What may we say then about the aretaic value of actions, feelings, or characters overall? Consider actions. Some actions may arise from certain commitments, without the aid of or even in opposition to certain desires. But if the commitment is morally good, so is the action. Other actions may arise both from a commitment and from desires in accord with that commitment. But if the commitment is morally good, so are the accordant desires and so is the action. In some cases, an action might arise from a desire together with a failure of commitment or a failure to maintain a commitment in a given case – an instance of *akrasia*. But if the commitment, had it been made or maintained, would have been morally good, then the desire would conflict with it and thus both the desire and the concomitant action would be morally bad. Could *akrasia* go the other way? The resultant action would be morally good. This is an interesting question that we cannot explore further here. Feelings proceed from desires and perhaps also commitments. So the aretaic value of the feeling is consequent upon the moral goodness or badness of the desire. Finally, the moral goodness or badness of a character overall is consequent upon the moral goodness or badness of its commitments or lack of them. So, moral goodness and badness go back to or are consequent upon the aretaic value of commitments or to the value of desires consequent upon their accord or lack of it with appropriate commitments.

How then are our judgments of moral value generated? Wilson has addressed this issue in (1993), where on philosophical matters he is distinctly indebted to Adam Smith's treatise, *The Theory of Moral Sentiments* (1976). Our discussion will draw significantly on these sources and we believe extend them. The question of how judgments of aretaic value are generated raises a challenge straight off. Acts are publicly observable. Actions, doing acts from certain motives, have an aspect which is not directly observable, for we cannot experience someone's desires or commitments directly. Likewise, we cannot experience another person's feelings. However, as we discussed in Section 7.2 in connection with personal perception, we may perceive signs of a person's feelings and immediately form the belief that the person has those feelings. This is personal perception, and thus we may be said to perceive those feelings. Likewise, we may speak of natural signs of desires both occurrent and dispositional. Acts, especially when taken in context, may be signs of desires, commitments, or both. Feelings might be most straightforwardly read off from these overt signs. Hence, we shall begin by discussing judgments concerning the aretaic value of feelings, and then consider judgments of desires, commitments, actions, and, finally, judgments of character.

Again in the first instance, we are considering the moral sense as our belief-generating mechanism. Feelings have aretaic value as signs of desires, commitments, or the lack of self-control to maintain proper commitments or curb unruly desires. Feelings proceeding from or in accord with morally good commitments will be appropriate to the situation, while those in conflict will be inappropriate. We judge feelings then as to their appropriateness or propriety. We may distinguish three levels of judgments of deepening moral import. At the first level, what we might call the level of self-referential judgments of propriety, we form the judgment that a feeling of someone other than ourselves is appropriate just in case it is congruent with the feeling or feelings we would have if we were in that person's situation, basically if we would feel the same way. For example, we perceive someone reacting angrily to a certain situation. We vicariously feel the anger the person is displaying. We may enter into that situation and imagine what anger we might feel. We judge the anger appropriate should we judge that we would be comparably angry.

Sympathy, thus, is at the core of these judgments. By sympathy we have the data which constitutes the input for the moral sense as a belief-generating mechanism. The moral sense generates an evaluation on the basis of the congruence we have felt. Adam Smith sees this recognition of congruence as a general criterion for evaluative judgments at this self-referential level:

When the original passions of the person principally concerned are in perfect concord with the sympathetic emotions of the spectator, they necessarily appear to this last just and proper, and suitable to their objects; and, on the contrary, when, upon bringing the case home to himself, he finds that they do not coincide with what he feels, they necessarily appear to him unjust and improper, and unsuitable to the causes which excite them. (1976, p. 16)

We may express the criterion for judgments at this self-referential level this way:

the other's feeling is appropriate from the point of view of *myself*	iff	*my* feeling would be congruent with the *other's* should *I* be in the *other's* situation

Our desire for attachment impels us beyond the level of self-referential judgments of propriety. At the second level, we judge our *own* feelings as we anticipate *others* will judge them. We may call this the level of other-referential judgments of propriety. By contrast, we may express its criterion this way:

my feeling is appropriate from the point of view of *the other*	iff	*the other's* feeling would be congruent with *my* feeling should the *other* be in *my* situation

The desire for attachment is operating here because we want to be liked, indeed praised, by others. We thus judge our feelings on how we believe they will be seen by others. Here again, passive sympathy is producing the data upon which the moral sense is generating its evaluation. This involves a reflexive empathy, if you will.

Taking the point of view of others in judging our own feelings already impels us a significant way toward the moral point of view. It introduces some amount of objectivity to our judgment. But there are still self-regarding elements at this level. We are concerned with taking the point of view of others because we are concerned with maintaining their attachment – something *we* desire. Our judgment is based on what we empirically project others will praise or blame. At the third level, by contrast, according to both Smith and Wilson, we judge our feelings and motives from the perspective of an impartial spectator. We want to *deserve* the praise we receive, and not just receive it. Smith memorably develops this contrast: "Man naturally desires, not only to be loved, but to be lovely; or to be that thing which is the natural and proper object of love. He naturally dreads, not only to be hated, but to be hateful; or to be that thing which is the natural and proper object of hatred" (1976, pp. 113–14). To judge whether he is in fact a natural and proper object of love or hatred, a person must view himself not from his own perspective nor that of some other particular person who may be anticipated to love or hate him but from the perspective of a third-party spectator. This perspective is the level of impartial-spectator-referential judgments of propriety:

my feeling is appropriate from the point of view of *the impartial spectator*	iff	*the impartial spectator's* feeling would be congruent with *my* feeling should *the impartial spectator* be in *my* situation

Smith feels it is entirely natural for us to assume this perspective and that without assuming it we could little take into account our neighbor's interests. We may correct for our moral perspective in weighing the size of our interests against those of our neighbor just as easily as we correct for our visual perspective in judging of the sizes of objects at various distances from us.

The impartial spectator may judge not just my but anyone's feelings. Hence, we may speak of the feelings of other persons as being appropriate or inappropriate from the impartial spectator's perspective. Someone else's feeling is appropriate just in case the impartial spectator would have a congruent feeling were he in that person's situation. The input for our moral sense then is an empathetic assessment of how the impartial spectator would feel were the spectator in x's situation and whether that feeling would be congruent with x's feeling as we empathetically experience it.

The impartial spectator is clearly a personification of conscience. But as such, we can question whether "impartial" is an adequate characterization of this figure. Impartiality means not favoring one party over another, giving to each party equal consideration. As MacLagan points out, although this suggests that each party is due some consideration, it does not entail that proposition. It is consistent to say that each person should receive equal consideration and that each person should receive none at all. "Impartiality, considered strictly, is consistent with our having no respect for persons at all" (1960a, pp. 197–8). Qua impartial, the spectator may have no practical concern for others or be committed to their welfare. Hence, referring questions of the appropriateness of feelings to "the" impartial spectator need no longer result in a univocal verdict. Consider the following thought experiment: Suppose I feel anger after hearing that a judge doubled the bail of a poor defendant when a person came forward willing to post the originally set bail. Is my feeling of anger appropriate? How would the impartial spectator feel in this case? If the judge raised the bail for the poor person but not for an accused who was rich and could pay the bail out of his own resources, then we would expect the impartial spectator to share our anger. But suppose the judge treated rich and poor alike. After setting bail, should the accused be able to make it, the judge would increase it to a level where the accused, at least at that point, could not. Suppose the judge was not alone in this. All the other judges proceeded in the same way. So the poor person was not being treated differently from any other accused. Would the impartial spectator then share my anger? If this figure disapproved of this aspect of the judicial process, he could be expected to be angry. But this would not be anger of the impartial spectator *qua* impartial. An impartial spectator not sharing such disapproval might have no anger at all. Referred to this spectator, it seems my anger is inappropriate.

But we want to say that the anger *is* appropriate. If anything, the judge inflicted pain and seemingly unnecessary pain on the accused by raising the bail. If this were the general practice of judges, anger toward the whole system would seem appropriate. This shows that to be a proper referee, the spectator must be more than impartial. Ability to feel imaginatively the pain of others is part of empathy. A practical concern that others avoid unnecessary pain is part of active sympathy. A sense that preventing such pain is an obligation is an expression of the sense of duty. Surely someone with these sentiments would feel anger over the judge's behavior. This shows that we want not just an impartial spectator but an agapic spectator as the personification of conscience.

I believe we need to clarify the concept even further. It is not enough that this spectator, besides having empathy, simply have certain feelings of concern for the well-being of others or a desire for their advancement. It is also not enough to add that the spectator also have a desire to do his duty or that duty be done. The spectator needs to be committed to these ends, to have voluntarily adopted them as goals, to be fully praiseworthy or morally good. The spectator needs to have made the commitments which constitute the moral goodness of a character, those commitments which are counterparts to the desires that Ross identifies as central.

Notice that by characterizing our spectator as agapic, we have already indicated that he has the commitments counterpart to Ross's morally good desires and ordinarily will share those desires. Active sympathy, a practical concern for others, should involve desires to bring about actual good *qua* good and to bring about others' pleasure or avoidance of pain, so long as it is not part of a desire to bring about some larger whole with intrinsic disvalue. A commitment to actual duty will ordinarily be accompanied by a desire to do one's duty. We speak of actual duty or actual good or pleasure which is not part of some intrinsically bad whole to highlight that in having these desires, an agapic spectator does not also have the desire to see performed some *prima facie* duty whose moral stringency is outweighed by other *prima facie* duties. Again, although the agapic spectator will in general share the desire to produce pleasure and foster avoidance of pain for others, he may not share or sympathize with desires to bring about specific pleasures or avoidances of pain when they are part of larger wholes with intrinsic disvalue. For example, surely the impartial spectator would not sympathize with a desire to have someone avoid pain if that would foster irresponsible behavior.

Insofar as impartiality is an aspect of fairness and fairness is one type of duty, our agapic spectator will be an impartial spectator. Notice that by virtue of sympathy and duty, the agapic spectator has the sentiments of sympathy, fairness, and duty that Wilson identifies as components of the moral sense. One sentiment has not been mentioned – self-control. We need not consider this sentiment because the agapic spectator is not a flesh and blood person with desires that may conflict with commitments. Rather this figure has just the desires arising from a morally good character.

Given this characterization, we can straightforwardly see that referring one's feelings to the projected feelings of the agapic spectator provides an appropriate reference point from which to judge whether the feelings are morally appropriate. In the case of anger over the judge's actions, the impartial spectator is committed to the avoidance of unnecessary pain and presumably desires none be inflicted. The judge's raising bail for the poor person accused of some crime would then go against that commitment and frustrate the desire. Thus, the agapic spectator would feel anger. Our feeling anger is then congruent with the agapic spectator's. By contrast, suppose we feel anger over some frustration to our self-seeking. Would the agapic spectator share this anger? Because it is a frustration to our self-seeking, let us assume we are trying to gain an unfair advantage over others. Clearly, given what we know of his commitments, we can project that should he be in our position, the agapic spectator would not share our commitment to this self-seeking goal. Hence, he would not experience our frustration and thus would not feel the anger we feel. Our feeling of anger here is not appropriate.

How may we generalize this discussion from feeling to judgments concerning the moral value of desires, commitments, actions, characters? Clearly appropriateness for desires as for feelings is a ternary relation. Another's desire is appropriate from my point of view if my desire would be congruent with his were I in his situation. By contrast, suppose someone's desire is selfish. By putting myself in his position, I need not and ordinarily would not share the desire that *he* be the beneficiary of certain gratifications. So we may judge of the appropriateness of another's desire from our point of view by comparing our sympathetic awareness of that desire with what we expect of our own desire in that situation. But if we can make such a comparison with our own desire, surely we can make such a comparison with the desire of the agapic spectator as we already understand his desire to be formed. And surely a desire – whether our own or someone else's – is morally good, if the agapic spectator would have the desire were he in that situation. Likewise, a desire would be morally bad should it be for something that would frustrate the desire of the agapic spectator in that situation. Should a desire neither be shared by the agapic spectator nor frustrate any of his desires, the desire would be morally neutral, neither morally good nor morally bad. This might be a desire for a simple pleasure of the senses, which is not in itself or in context selfish. Hence, one forms a judgment of the moral goodness or badness of a desire as one recognizes that desire to be congruent with the desire of the agapic spectator.

One point in the above paragraph bears further elaboration. Following Ross, we allow that some desires are morally indifferent. For Ross, "It seems clear that the desire of an indifferent pleasure is in itself indifferent" (1930, p. 166).[24] But surely could we not imagine that if the agapic spectator were in the same position as some particular person, he might very well share the person's desire for some innocent pleasure? But then it would seem that such pleasures are not indifferent but morally good. But this is to mistake the agapic spectator for a concretely particular person. Rather, as we discussed in connection with whether the agapic spectator needed to exercise self-control, we should take this figure as having just the desires in accord with a morally good character. We need not worry then about an impartial spectator sharing the indifferent desires of a particular individual with the apparent consequence that these desires become morally good.

We may formalize this discussion through the following definitions:

x's desire is morally good	iff	the agapic spectator would share x's desire were the spectator in x's situation
x's desire is morally bad	iff	the agapic spectator would find x's desire contrary to or in conflict with his commitments were he in x's situation
x's desire is morally indifferent	iff	the agapic spectator would neither share x's desire nor find the desire in conflict with his commitments, were he in x's situation

Having clarified what it is for desires to be morally good or bad, we may now go on to understand what it is to predicate moral goodness or badness of commitments, actions, and ultimately characters. The analysis of commitment follows a similar pattern:

x's commitment is morally good	iff	the agapic spectator would share x's commitment were the spectator in x's situation
x's commitment is morally bad	iff	the goal of x's commitment would conflict with the goals to which the agapic spectator would be committed were he in x's situation
x's commitment is morally indifferent	iff	the agapic spectator would neither share x's commitment nor find the goal of that commitment to conflict with his goals, were he in x's situation

Actions, as we have said, are acts done from a certain motivation. But motivation concerns the desires and commitments from which the act was performed. An action then will be morally good just in case the desires and commitments from which it proceeds are morally good, and similarly for its moral badness or moral indifference. Finally, judgments of character involve overall judgments of the person. We judge a person to be of good character overall just in case his actions, including his manifestations of feeling, seem consistently to show or are consistent with the core commitments constituting moral goodness. To the extent that a person's actions and overtly expressed feelings are signs of those commitments and desires that are in accord with the core commitments, we judge the person morally good.

With actions and character overall, what is epistemologically primary are the desires and commitments expressed through the person's overt behavior. Hence, in discussing whether the moral sense is presumptively reliable in generating beliefs expressing particular judgments of aretaic value, we can concentrate just on beliefs concerning feelings, desires, or commitments. If we consider such beliefs or judgments as we have analyzed them, we may resolve them into two conjuncts:

1. x has a feeling, desire, commitment
2. if the agapic spectator were in x's position, he would share x's feeling, desire, commitment

We thus have a schema for particular judgments of aretaic value. Notice that this schema presupposes that x has in fact the feeling, desire, commitment attributed to him. Notice also that we may make aretaic judgments both about ourselves and about others. But whether we replace the variable "x" by expressions referring to ourselves or to others raises distinct epistemological issues. Hence, it will be profitable to distinguish the question of whether the moral sense is presumptively reliable when rendering judgments about *our* moral goodness or badness from whether in judging others it is presumptively reliable. Let us consider the second issue first.

Is the Moral Sense Presumptively Reliable in Judging the Aretaic Value of Others?

Because judging the aretaic value of others presupposes forming beliefs about their feelings, desires, or commitments, such judgments presuppose beliefs about other minds. This raises an interesting question concerning what beliefs about the aretaic value of others may be basic. Consider:

1. Jones's anger over the slow-moving line at the toll plaza was clearly an overreaction.
2. Smith's wanting to provide scholarships for economically disadvantaged inner-city children is commendable.
3. The Rev. Martin Luther King's commitment to racial justice, maintained through many personal attacks, well deserves our admiration.

In each case, we may ask how the proponent came to have a belief concerning the contents of the mind of the subject of this judgment. The proponent's belief in each of these cases could be basic. He may have witnessed Jones's overt expression of anger and his belief be generated by personal perception. A proponent making a claim about Smith's mind may have heard Smith declare his desire to provide these scholarships, and immediately formed the belief that Smith in fact *did* have this desire. This involves personal testimony. We discuss why there is a presumption for it in the next chapter. That Martin Luther King had a commitment to racial justice is a matter of common knowledge. Receiving common knowledge is another form of receiving testimony, which we also discuss in the next chapter.

By contrast, a prosecutor might present a good deal of evidence to show that a defendant had a certain motive, most likely a combination of desire with voluntarily adopted goals. Should members of the jury come to believe that the defendant *did* have this motive on the basis of this argument, their belief would not be basic although it still might be justified. In such a case, members of the jury could also come to believe that

4. The defendant's motive in this case is morally reprehensible.

Can we speak of their belief that (4) as a basic belief? Their presupposed belief about the defendant's motive, that is, a belief about an other's mind, is not basic, but what of the aretaic judgment? Once they formed the belief that the defendant had this motive, could they not immediately form the belief that the motive was morally reprehensible? To use our image of the agapic spectator, could they not form the belief that were the spectator in the defendant's situation before committing the crime, he would never have had this motive and indeed would have commitments with which it was completely incompatible? The presupposed belief that the defendant had this motive is not basic, and so we could say that the judgment overall is not basic. But the purely evaluative part of the judgment is immediate and thus basic.

To take a positive example, I may hear of a benevolent act. But I may question whether the *action* was benevolent, that is, proceeding from a desire or commitment to do something good for someone else. Suppose I am presented with a good argument that the motive was in no way self-serving. May I not immediately form the judgment then that the motive was morally good and praiseworthy? I see no reason why this could not happen, at least in some cases.

Some may object that such aretaic judgments are inferred, according to the quasi-syllogistic pattern:

5. The motive behind action *A* was benevolence.
   <u>All benevolent motives are morally good.</u>
   Therefore, the motive behind action *A* was morally good.

Against this reconstruction I believe we can bring Hitchcock's phenomenological argument to which we have already referred. (See p. 210.) When I form my judgment of the moral reprehensibility of the defendant's motive or the moral praiseworthiness of a benefactor's motive on the basis of being convinced by argument that they had these motives, am I aware of reasoning quasi-syllogistically? If not, why should I accept this reconstruction of how I came to hold these beliefs?

The challenger, however, has a rejoinder. The aretaic judgment is inferred but not quasi-syllogistically. Rather, it is inferred directly or immediately from the belief concerning the motivation. The quasi-syllogistic reconstruction confuses the warrant of this immediate inference with a universal premise. So from the single premise that the person had a certain motivation, we infer immediately that the motive was morally good or morally bad, the warrant being

From *M* is a motive of type τ
We may take it that *M* is morally good (morally bad).

We cannot deny that this may describe how we come to believe aretaic judgments on some occasions. But as an account of how we always form them, we find it too rationalistic. Once we become convinced that the criminal acted from a self-serving nature, do we *infer* from the nature's having this property that it was morally bad or do we *feel* the repugnance of the motive, that it would be in opposition to the commitments and desires of the agapic spectator, should he be in that situation? To my mind, the latter certainly describes how we come to hold these beliefs, at least on a number of occasions.

Hence, forming a judgment concerning the aretaic value that pertains to some other person presupposes having formed a belief pertaining to the mind of that other person, a belief concerning the person's feelings, desires, or commitments. This belief may be basic or inferred, but this does not affect whether the value judgment itself is basic or inferred. Of course, for the value judgment to be justified, for it to be properly basic, the presupposed belief must be justified. Hence, a judgment as to whether the overall belief-generating mechanism here is presumptively reliable entails that the mechanism whereby we come to hold a belief concerning the other person's mind is presumptively reliable. But this now focuses the question we must answer here. Given that the mechanism generating the presupposed belief is presumptively reliable, is the moral sense presumptively reliable in generating the aretaic value judgment concerning this feeling, desire, commitment of this other person? What may we say to this question?

In effect, we are judging whether the agapic spectator would share a particular feeling, desire, or commitment, or would have a conflicting desire or a commitment with a conflicting goal, were the spectator in the same position as the person whose feeling, desire, or commitment is subject to our judgment. Can we presume that the moral sense is reliable in generating such beliefs? Given our understanding of the commitments of the agapic spectator, this might seem obvious. The agapic spectator is committed to fulfilling the requirements of duty, to bring intrinsic good *qua* good into being, and to increase the pleasure of others or to let them avoid pain. His desires and feelings accord with these commitments. Surely then judging that a feeling, desire, or commitment as we apprehend it would either match or clash with those of the agapic spectator seems a judgment we could make immediately.

However, a presumption for this judgment presupposes a presumption for several further judgments. Consider a judgment that a feeling of anger on someone else's part was an overreaction. To say that someone feels anger is ordinarily not simply to say that the person is experiencing a certain mental state. The person is also angry *over* something. The feeling is intensional, as would be a desire or commitment. We expect that one's being angry over a situation would typically not be just a matter of what one has simply perceived in that situation but, rather, with how one has interpreted it, and thus how one understands what that anger intends. Are certain features of the situation seen as signs of something further? Is a given overt gesture a sign of some individual's respect or disrespect, for example?

In judging whether someone else's feeling is appropriate, we are bringing *our* interpretation to that situation. We are judging whether the agapic spectator would share this feeling were he in the situation *as we understand it*. But does the other person, whose feeling of anger I am judging to be inappropriate, share my interpretation? Perhaps, if the agapic spectator were not only faced with the same externals of the situation but also shared the same interpretation as this other person, he might share this person's feelings. We must distinguish between seeing the other person's anger as understandable and seeing it as appropriate. Should one have insight into how the other person interprets the situation, one might see that the agapic spectator would share the anger *should the spectator share the interpretation.* But he need not share the interpretation and surely in some cases would not. Has the other person arrogated to himself certain privileges and prerogatives that have not been met or respected? Surely the agapic spectator will not share the other's arrogation of these privileges and prerogatives.

These considerations raise the question of whether in empathetically entering the situation of someone else, there is a presumption for *my* interpretation of the situation. Should a person be livid over having to wait two minutes to pass through a toll both, it is a matter of common sense that whatever interpretation the person may be making of the situation which might render the anger legitimate in his eyes would be inadequate or unjustified. In many cases, there will be a presumption for our interpretation of the situation, that we may view the situation from our perspective. There may be no evidence to call the presumption for our interpretation into question. By contrast, there may be such evidence. Suppose the person about whom we are rendering this judgment were a member of another culture, fostering a different interpretation of the situation, ultimately better grounded than ours. If one were aware that this was a real possibility, the presumption for one's interpretation would be undercut.

Notice that since the agapic spectator is committed to fulfilling duty, bringing intrinsic good into existence, and increasing the pleasure of others or decreasing their pain, our interpretation of the situation will also include a judgment about what may actually be a duty, not just a *prima facie* duty, or bring about actually as opposed to *prima facie* intrinsically good or bad results. Again the question of whose understanding comes to the fore. Perhaps we see X contrary to duty, while o sees X as a duty and is committed to bringing X about precisely because it fulfills his duty. When we empathetically enter into o's situation, asking whether the agapic spectator would share o's desire or commitment to doing X, is the agapic spectator bringing our understanding of duty to the situation or is he assuming o's? On the one hand, the agapic spectator apparently must assume o's deontic judgment that X is his duty. If o sincerely desires to do his duty and has conscientiously come to believe that X is his duty, we would not judge his desire or commitment to do X morally bad if we judged X to be contrary to duty. In asking whether the agapic spectator would share o's desire or commitment in this instance, we assume that the agapic spectator shares o's view that X is a duty.

On the other hand, o need not have come to believe that X was a duty by his best lights. Indeed, there are cases where even if o said he believed X to be his duty, we would ask whether the agapic spectator would share his desire to do X not if he viewed the deontic properties of X as o does but as we do. Why? Although we believe o's deontic judgment in both this and the previous case is mistaken, as Plantinga suggests, in the first case we regard the error as nonculpable – since o conscientiously came to believe that X was his duty – whereas in the second the error is culpable. Suppose X is the act of participating in a racist lynching. Suppose o believes that it is right to participate in this lynching and desires to do it. Because o believes that X is right, if the agapic spectator should share that belief, he would not find the desire to conflict with his desires or commitments. Does this mean that o's desire is not morally bad? It does not, because the agapic spectator will not share o's belief that X is right. Plantinga comments: "There are many moral beliefs we don't think a properly functioning human being can (in ordinary circumstances) nonculpably acquire" (1993a, p. 17).

These considerations that where an aretaic judgment presupposes a judgment of actual deontic or intrinsic value, if there is evidence that the person whose feeling, desire, or commitment is being judged does not share our judgment of deontic or intrinsic value in this case, but that the person has come to his or her deontic or intrinsic judgment conscientiously, nonculpably, then there will be a presumption for our aretaic judgment only if sharing the other's deontic or intrinsic value judgment is part of the agapic spectator's being in the other person's situation. If otherwise, that is, if there is no evidence that the other has a different understanding of the deontic or intrinsic values in the situation or if the other has not conscientiously come to his different understanding, then there will be a presumption for our aretaic judgment only if sharing *our* understanding of the deontic and intrinsic values is part of the agapic spectator's being in that situation and there is a presumption for our beliefs of deontic or intrinsic value in this case.

Should there be a presumption for our belief about the mental state of the other person and for our interpretation of the situation including from whose point of view the questions of deontic or intrinsic value need to be assessed, our judgment that the other's feeling, desire, or commitment accords or conflicts with those of the agapic spectator, were he to be in that situation, is now immediate. The moral sense in its are-taic employment is again an internal mechanism. Once we have formed the presupposed belief concerning the other's feeling, desire, or commitment, and as long as there is a presumption that our understanding of the situation is reliable, we can see whether the feeling, desire, or commitment accords or conflicts with that of the agapic spectator, were he to be in this situation. This derives directly from our understanding of the spectator and his commitments. The evidence for the *aretaic* part of our judgment or belief is internal and as with the other internal belief-generating mechanisms, we can see directly that the mechanism is reliable.

Because the aretaic value of actions depends on their underlying motives, ordinarily composed of commitments and desires, as we have pointed out, judging the aretaic value of an action involves first identifying those underlying desires and commitments and then judging whether the agapic spectator would share them, were he in that situation. This adds nothing new to our discussion, but it raises an interesting question. Suppose one judges that an action has mixed motives, say that it proceeds both from a genuine desire to do good to someone else but also from a desire to manipulate that person, to put her under a debt of gratitude. Given our analysis of the motive, what becomes of the judgment of the action's aretaic value? Two responses are possible here. One is that given the conflicting motives, one does not judge the action but judges the motives separately. The other is to judge whether one of the motives is dominant. Was the action done basically from benevolent intentions or did the desire to manipulate predominate? If one is able to make this determination, one can judge the aretaic value of the action overall.

What may we say of judgments of the character of others? Judging that a character is morally good or bad presupposes sizing up that person's character. Sizing up involves reflection, if the presupposed belief concerning the character overall is basic. (See p. 237.) Upon observing certain overt acts and expressions of feeling, which we take to be salient in revealing the person's character, we come to an overall view of that character. Forming the belief in this way conforms to a common presumption already noted in Section 8.7, identified by Perelman and Olbrechts-Tyteca, "that the quality of an act reveals the quality of the person responsible for it" (1969, p. 70). By contrast, we might infer a belief concerning a person's character from premises concerning what we take as particular expressions of that character. Our overall judgment might say that the person is prideful or humble, miserly or generous, envious or magnanimous. But these all connote dispositions to have desires or commitments of a certain sort, which we can judge to accord or conflict with the desires and commitments of the agapic spectator.

In discussing aretaic value, we have not spoken of feelings, desires, or commitments as being *prima facie* morally good or *prima facie* morally bad, but as being *de facto* or actually one or the other, if not morally indifferent. We believe that this is proper in discussing moral value. Any of the core desires Ross identifies as morally good and from which morally good actions proceed are morally good without qualification. A desire to do one's duty is actually morally good. Should it become alloyed with a desire to make oneself look good, a desire for self-promotion, the desires may be judged separately, as we noted above. We may judge the motive overall to be actually mixed in aretaic value, because it incorporates these two desires, one actually morally good and the other actually morally bad.

Is Moral Intuition Presumptively Reliable in Making General Judgments of Aretaic Value?

So far, we have considered just the moral sense as a mechanism generating basic beliefs concerning aretaic value. Does the moral intuition also make general judgments of aretaic value, judging that certain features or properties of feelings, desires, commitments are reasons for saying that something is morally good or morally bad? This should be obvious. As Ross points out, goodness – including moral goodness – is a consequential property. (See 1930, p. 155.) Something is good by virtue of having some other property. Having these other properties then is a reason for being morally good. There is something for intuition to grasp here. The moral goodness of desires and commitments is consequent upon their having the properties Ross has identified as being at the core of moral goodness. The properties upon which the moral goodness of characters, actions, and feelings are consequent comprise being properly related to such desires or commitments.

We have seen that one can recognize the moral goodness of a particular desire or commitment in a particular case by seeing whether the agapic spectator would share that desire or commitment were he in that situation. But the agapic spectator is a personification of our sense of sympathy – both passive and active – and our sense of duty. We judge a commitment or desire to be morally good in so far as it accords with our active sympathy, as informed by our empathy, or as it accords with our sense of duty (or both). But why do these desires and commitments accord with sympathy or the sense of duty? It is because they are desires or commitments to do one's duty, to bring instances of intrinsic good into existence, or to increase the pleasure or decrease the pain of others! The moral goodness of the desire or commitment supervenes on these properties. This is what moral intuition recognizes. Similarly to the case of deontic judgments, the moral sense recognizes particular desires or commitments to be morally good (or bad) by virtue of their according with sympathy or duty. Moral intuition then forms this general judgment. The evidence for our intuitive judgments is internally available to us and thus also the reliability of moral intuition in its aretaic employment.

Is the Moral Sense Presumptively Reliable in Judging One's Own Aretaic Value?

Generating beliefs concerning the moral goodness or badness of one's own feelings, desires, or commitments presupposes judgments concerning the contents of one's own mind as opposed to other minds. Now my desires are open to my direct inspection. This seems true whether I am considering occurrent or dispositional desires. Introspection is the mechanism generating my beliefs about my desires and, as we saw in Section 7.3, introspection is presumptively reliable when generating beliefs specifically about my mental contents. Hence, in coming to form a belief about the moral goodness or badness of a desire of one's own, the desire itself is open to one's inspection and our introspective beliefs that our desires have these qualities are presumptively reliable.

To judge the aretaic value of my feeling, desire, commitment, I need to ask whether the agapic spectator would share that disposition or find it conflicting, should he be in my position. As with judging the aretaic value of others, whether there is a presumption for my judgment presupposes there is a presumption for my understanding of the situation. It is still possible that my understanding may be mistaken, even though we are not dealing with the perspective of some other person. First, one might correctly introspect that one has a desire or commitment, but be mistaken about the nature of that desire or commitment. For example, I desire to perform a certain act X. I perceive X as a duty. I believe that in this case I desire to do X *qua* requirement of duty. But suppose that my performing X will result in others' praising me, praise that I crave. Do I desire to do X *qua* duty or *qua* precipitating praise? Am I deceiving myself if I say that I desire to do X out of duty? Without answering that question, we can surely say that any awareness I may have of my desire for the praise of others in this situation is awareness of a defeater to my belief that I desire to do *X* out of duty. Now clearly I may suppress this awareness. This does not mean that my desire to be praised for doing *X* does not exist. Under certain circumstances, I may be confronted with it full force. But it does show that my understanding that I desire to do *X* out of duty may be mistaken.

Again, suppose I feel anger over a person's behavior toward me. Does the person's behavior frustrate some presumptively legitimate right or some claim which I have arrogated to myself? Evidence for the latter is evidence against my understanding of the situation and evidence that the agapic spectator would not share this anger, were he in my position. Notice that in cases where I think I desire to do *X* out of duty but really desire to do *X* out of praise or where my anger is not legitimate, we might very well be reluctant to recognize this as a case of honest error. My not taking account of my desire for praise or the arrogant nature of my claim in coming to my belief is something for which I am ordinarily culpable. This is why the agapic spectator will not see this desire or this feeling as we see them and thus will not share them.

My judgments of actual duty, right, wrong, actual intrinsic good or intrinsic bad in a situation are also subject to error, sometimes culpable. If I have conscientiously attended to the relevant factors in a situation, an act may be a subjective duty for me, even if objectively it differs from what duty requires. If there is a presumption for my judgment that I desire to do this act *from* duty, *ceteris paribus* there is a presumption for my judgment that the desire is morally good, for should the agapic spectator be in my position, he would share that desire. But as another person may come to believe or accept evaluations in a culpable way, so may I. If the rightness of one's participating in a lynching is a belief one can only acquire culpably, can we not expect some awareness of one's culpability in acquiring this belief? Awareness of evidence of culpable error then defeats any presumption for the view that the agapic spectator would not have a conflicting desire were he in my position.

Now should there be a presumption for my understanding of the situation, that my desire is a desire to perform my duty *qua* duty, or to bring some intrinsic good into being *qua* intrinsic good, and should there be a presumption for my judgment that an act is a duty or that a state of affairs is intrinsically good, then judging that my desire is either in accord or conflict with the desires of the agapic spectator is no less internal and immediate than judging the congruence of the putative desires of others with those of the agapic spectator. Given there is a presumption for the presuppositions of the judgment, given my grasp of the concept of the agapic spectator, I can immediately and thus reliably judge whether my desire would be congruent or conflict with his, were he in my situation.

A significant objection can be brought against our whole project in this section on aretaic value. We are claiming that if we have rightly discerned someone's feelings, desires, commitments, our own or others, we form an objective judgment of their moral goodness or badness by taking the point of view of the agapic spectator. But does the agapic spectator represent a point of view which is ethically objective or can this figure be simply a projection of values prevalent in a particular culture? This, of course, is the objection of ethical relativism, an objection which applies also to our discussion in the previous two sections. There is an additional significant objection we should address. Our view sees the moral sense as the prime evaluative belief-generating mechanism. But there have been a number of objections brought against moral sense theory. Do these objections affect our view and if so, how may we address them? Considering these objections, however, deserves treatment in a separate section.

9.6 OBJECTIONS AND REPLIES

How may we reply to the objection that the agapic spectator is simply a cultural projection? On this account, by taking the point of view of the agapic spectator, our judgment that some feeling is appropriate or some desire or commitment is morally good indicates no more than that such a feeling would be regarded as appropriate or such motivation as morally commendable in our culture. The perspective of the agapic spectator, then, does not reflect a judgment of objective moral goodness. We reply by asking our challenger to look again at how singular judgments of aretaic value are generated. Such judgments presuppose that someone, ourselves or others, has a certain feeling, desire, or commitment. In the case of ourselves, this is a matter to which we have internal access. Barring self-deception, there is a presumption for such judgments. Indeed, it would seem that in many cases such judgments would be indefeasible.

In the case of others, our judgment, if basic and not a matter of testimony, involves either personal perception or personal intuition. Now, as we developed in Chapter 7, some overtly physically perceivable signs are natural signs of the internal or mental states of others. We need not be taught the meaning of a frown to understand its meaning and form a belief concerning the attitude of the person who is frowning, a matter of personal perception. Through our experience, we acquire knowledge of further signs, increasing our capacity to form judgments of personal perception.

Clearly, this growth in personal perception is affected by our experience and may very well be culturally conditioned. People in one culture may learn that certain overt expressions are signs of feelings or desires, occurrent or dispositional. People in other cultures may not learn to attach any such significance to these outward expressions. This can obviously make for cross-cultural misunderstanding. Now we have already admitted that beliefs generated by personal perception or personal intuition are defeasible. In the case of cross-cultural personal perception or interpretation, where a person of one culture forms a belief about some mental state of someone from some other culture, any presumption for such judgments may be extremely vulnerable. But to form a belief that some other person has a certain feeling, motive, or some other mental state, occurrent or dispositional, is to render no value judgment about that mental state, aretaic, intrinsic, or otherwise. The value judgment is a further judgment.

In evaluating the relativist objection, the question we must ask concerns the belief-generating mechanism of this further judgment. Given our judgment that someone else has a certain feeling, desire, or commitment, a judgment that may be culturally conditioned, especially when we take into account how that state or disposition is characterized, understood, or interpreted, is our judgment that the agapic spectator would share that feeling, desire, commitment, were he in that person's situation, also culturally conditioned? The agapic spectator is a personification of the senses of sympathy and duty. Are the commitment or desire to do our duty and the commitment or desire to bring about intrinsic good for others valued only in certain cultures, reflecting only the values or preferences of those cultures?

We have already seen that MacLagan is confident that the senses of duty and sympathy – both active and passive – are universal. Human beings have a capacity to be aware that they are under obligation. But if one is conscious that one has a duty, and in addition that one has a commitment or desire to do one's duty in this case even when tempted not to, how could one fail also to believe that this commitment or desire was a good or praiseworthy thing – morally good? How does this simply constitute a cultural preference? If such a commitment or desire would be universally regarded as morally positive by those aware of them, then ascribing such a desire or commitment to the agapic spectator is not to culturally condition his image.

How would we regard someone who is devoid of passive sympathy? For MacLagan, this, rather than the presence of empathy in a human being, requires explanation. "The breakdown of empathy . . . is not simple non-existence but the non-existence of that the absence of which, rather than its presence, should be accounted strange and deserving of explanation" (1960a, p. 211). What may we say of active sympathy? We have already noted that for MacLagan active sympathy is a psychological consequence of genuine passive sympathy (compare 1960a, p. 212). A preoccupation with self can conflict with and even deaden a natural sense of empathy, but such a preoccupation will clearly conflict with a sense of duty. So we may recognize that we have a practical duty to have at least some concern for others. But if we can recognize this as a duty, cannot we then regard a commitment or desire to do that duty, which would amount to a commitment or desire to bring about some intrinsic good or the increase of pleasure for others or a decrease of their pain, as a morally good or praiseworthy thing? Can we not ascribe such motivations to the agapic spectator? If the recognition of the duty is potentially universal, so is the recognition of the positive moral value of a commitment or desire to accomplish what that duty requires. But then this judgment does not express a mere cultural preference, and ascribing such desires or commitments to the agapic spectator does nothing to make the image culturally conditioned.

Our argument presupposes the universality of sympathy and duty. But, the objector might press, this is an empirical, psychological claim. "What is the hard evidence that these sentiments are universal?" Wilson, as a social scientist, advances this discussion by arguing "that people have a natural moral sense" (1993, p. 2), the sentiments of sympathy and duty being major components. He points first to two universal facts about human societies – that they are "organized around kinship patterns and that children, no matter how burdensome, are not abandoned in large numbers" (1993, p. 15). But, as he points out, one cannot account for the motivation maintaining kinship ties or the motivation behind childrearing practices solely through self-interest. Kinship relations constitute channels of reciprocity. Members of families help each other. But even when family members live at a distance, so that help might easily be gotten from or given to one's more proximate friends and neighbors, "kinship ties continue to exert a powerful pull on us" (1993, p. 16). Grown children feel a sense of obligation to their parents which in most cases cannot be explained by what the children expect still to receive from their parents. By contrast, the care and nurturing parents give children cannot be explained simply out of self-interest on *their* part.

We can thus speak of a universal sense of kinship. One salient expression of this sense is "the affection a parent, especially a mother, bears for its child" (1993, p. 226). This is met by "the desire to please that the child brings to this encounter" (1993, p. 226). This desire to please is at the core of what Wilson regards as a child's innate sociability, which "is the vital embryo in which a capacity for sympathy and an inclination to generosity can be found, and from which parents may help produce a sympathetic adult" (1993, p. 45). "The innate sociability of children makes them sensitive to the moods and actions of others.... For most children the ability to be affected by the emotional state of others leads to a concern for the well-being of others" (1993, p. 46). Passive sympathy leads to active sympathy. Wilson feels there is a good deal of empirical evidence to support this picture of how a sense of sympathy develops.[25] Although examining his empirical sources and detailing his argument further is beyond our scope here, we have said enough to show the critic that there is distinct evidence to believe that the sense of sympathy, a core sentiment of the agapic spectator, is not culturally provincial.

What may we say of the sense of duty? For the purposes of our discussion here, we may speak of conscience or the sense of duty interchangeably. To argue that this sentiment is universal, we may give an account of how conscience is formed that does not make reference to the practices of a particular culture. Part of universal childrearing involves attempts by parents to direct the child's behavior in certain ways. These involve punishments for some behavior and rewards for others. Another universal human characteristic – universal in the sense that its absence in an individual denotes pathology – is the disposition to develop emotional reactions to objects, events, situations of a certain type, given the circumstances in which we have met with things of that type. "We can be frightened by a fire or a spider and ever after get nervous in the presence of a flame or a bug" (1993, p. 105). Notice that we have these reactions even if the flame or the bug cannot possibly hurt us. We can likewise be conditioned to have certain pleasurable reactions. If when growing up, every time the home team wins there is a celebration, a child may very well acquire a sense of elation whenever hearing of a home team victory. This sense persists, even when there is no one around to join in a celebration.

Wilson sees this as significant. If rewards and punishments are apportioned consistently, the emotional reaction associated with the reward or punishment is experienced, even if there is no one there to reward or punish, even if, for all we know, an act will remain unobserved. Keeping this in mind, we can argue that our sense of duty, like our sense of sympathy, is an outgrowth of our drive for attachment or affiliation. A child's desire for the affection of others, in particular of his or her parents and other members of the family into which he or she is born, leads the child to become sensitive to what the parents approve or disapprove in his behavior. But expressions of such approval or disapproval leave their mark in emotional reactions to contemplated behavior, even if that behavior will not meet with parental reward or punishment. Although this account does not give us a complete picture of the development of conscience, it is enough to show that we have reason to believe a sense of duty is universal. Attributing it to the agapic spectator then is again not provincial.

In addressing why scholars are skeptical of moral universals, Wilson suggests that they may be looking for the wrong thing – seeking "universal rules rather than universal dispositions" (1993, p. 225). Rules seek to adjust the moral sentiments to local conditions – economic, social, cultural. As those conditions vary widely, so may the rules. What we can agree as universal are the dispositions that animate systems of rules. Hence, we can reply to the charge that our agapic spectator is a cultural projection. Given certain empirically ascertainable facts about human nature, we can argue that the dispositions, the desires and commitments, that are at the core of this figure are universal.

How may we reply to the other principal objection that may be brought against our approach, that the very notion of a moral sense is incoherent? One objection presses that speaking of a sense presupposes a sense organ. Where is the organ for the moral sense? Indeed, some have sought to satirize the moral sense view by saying that those who hold it have claimed to have found "a moral nose" or "a moral ear," a sense organ not noticed before! (See Sprague 1967, p. 386.) More seriously, some objections may be understood as amplifying the following point: Our senses generate perceptual judgments. Hence, one would expect a moral *sense* to generate judgments that have the features of perceptual judgments. But moral judgments and the circumstances of our forming them are so unlike perceptual judgments that to talk of a moral sense makes no sense.

We cannot have a perceptual judgment without the object perceived being physically present. But suppose the faculty for forming basic particular beliefs concerning deontic or aretaic value is the moral sense. One cannot then judge of the rightness or wrongness of acts – at least in a basic way – without actually observing the performance of those acts and sensing them morally. To come to the conclusion inductively that acts of a certain type are right I must have morally sensed a sample of such acts and found them all to be right. This seems plainly contrary to fact. Yet some have understood this as an implication of the moral sense position, one that discredits the view. I can judge in a basic way that an act is *prima facie* right or wrong or a motive morally good or bad, just on the basis of a report concerning the act or motive, or considering such an act or motive in imagination. This criticism again takes the "sense" in "moral sense" too literally or on too close an analogy with perception. When we speak of a moral sense, we are speaking of a mechanism which generates basic *particular* beliefs – *this* particular act is right; *that* particular motive is morally good. In this way it is analogous to perception that generates basic beliefs about particular objects. But that does not presuppose that the sense needs to perceive the act or motive to generate a basic judgment. Deontic and aretaic properties are consequent on other properties. By contemplating acts or motives with certain properties, even if this contemplation be done in imagination, we can see that they have certain deontic or aretaic properties.

Taking the moral sense on analogy with a perceptual belief-generating mechanism has led to a much deeper critical probing of the moral sense approach developed by Broad. Consider judgments of the form

1. That act is *prima facie* right.

If this is analogous to a perceptual judgment, then it would seem that we would need to understand this statement according to some theory of perception. On a naively realistic view, such a statement is analogous to "That thing is yellow," where a sensed quality of yellow is actually present and pervades the object, when one is appeared to yellowly. So the quality of rightness is in the act and one's having a moral feeling upon contemplating the act is analogous to being appeared to yellowly.

This account however seems to involve significant problems. Broad asks us to consider first the case where we predicate rightness of the act of someone else.

2. Jones's repaying the debt was right.

Broad argues that we cannot come to know this in any manner analogous to sense perception. We can see that Jones is signing a check, but can we *see* that this is an act of repaying a debt? Jones could be forging the check or bribing the person to whom the check was drawn. To know what Jones was doing, we would need to know his intentions and not just his overt behavior. "Now one person can contemplate another's intentions only in the sense of making them objects of *thought* and never in that of *perceiving* them" (1952, p. 371). It is by virtue of the act's being an act of debt-paying or forgery or bribery that it is right or wrong. But this is not perceived and our being appeared to by some moral feeling – pro or con – is not a perception of the act's having this right- or wrong-making property as being appeared to yellowly is a perception of yellow. Broad thinks "that this suffices to wreck the Moral Sense Theory in its naively realistic form as applied to singular deontic judgments made by one person about the acts of another" (1952, p. 371).

But does it? Are there not two judgments here? (2) presupposes

2'. Jones's act is one of debt repayment.

For one to come to believe the singular judgment (2) in a basic way analogous to the basicality of sense perception, must (2') also come to be known in that way? Could not (2') be an input judgment for moral sense? On the basis of this belief and being appeared to by a moral feeling one forms the belief that the act was right or wrong. As we have indicated, we can have basic evaluative beliefs that presuppose others, which may not be basic. But this does not rule out the basicality of the overall evaluative judgment, although it may make whether there is a presumption for it conditional on whether there is a presumption for the presupposed judgment.

We can also question whether Broad has too narrow a view of perception here. Recall our discussion of personal perception in Chapter 7. If one claimed that one perceived that Jones was repaying the debt, would one base that judgment just on seeing Jones sign a check or on one's knowing Jones had a debt to repay to the person to whose order he was drawing the check and perhaps knowing other pertinent facts? In short, could we not have a case of combined personal and institutional perception here? If not, could not our belief that Jones was repaying the debt involve a basic belief of personal intuition? But, apart from these speculations about perception or intuition, we need see the moral sense as generating only the evaluative belief and not the belief presupposed by the evaluative judgment. Hence, Broad's point about the difference between how we come to hold overall deontic judgments about the acts of others and judgments of sense perception does not affect our view of the moral sense as generating basic beliefs of deontic value. Broad does not discuss aretaic value in (1952) but expects that his conclusions will apply, *mutatis mutandis.* We trust that our account in Section 9.5 of coming to hold beliefs about the aretaic value of others is sufficient to construct a reply to Broad here.

Broad allows that in judging our own acts, we are or may be directly aware of our intentions. So it seems that the problem of conception versus perception does not arise for these judgments. So a moral sense theory might allow that judgments of our own acts are primary. Through them, we acquire the notions of rightness and wrongness, which we later apply to the acts of others. Broad counters that we do have moral feelings both when contemplating our acts and those of others. "Now I cannot detect any relevant difference between my moral feelings in the two cases" (1952, p. 372). Hence, since judgments of the latter cannot be construed analogously to sense perception on a naively realistic interpretation, "it seems unreasonable to suppose that the precisely similar moral feelings which one has when introspectively perceiving or remembering one's own acts is susceptible of a naïvely realistic interpretation" (1952, p. 373). But if Broad's analysis of deontic judgments of others is mistaken as we have argued, his objection here is unsupported. In both cases, beliefs about intentions may be presupposed in the evaluative judgment. But the question concerns generating that judgment proper.

Believing that he can set aside naive realist accounts of deontic properties and our coming to hold beliefs that they are instantiated in particular instances, Broad turns to a dispositional account. For perceptual properties, to say "This object is yellow," for example, is to say "If a normal human being were to view this object in white light, then it would present a yellow appearance" (1952, p. 368). Broad analyzes singular deontic statements of the sort "That act is right (or wrong)" as "That act would evoke a moral pro-emotion (or anti-emotion) in any human being who might at any time contemplate it" (1952, p. 375). Broad admits that "any" may have to be restricted to "any which is normal" or "any which is in a normal state." The aretaic analogue would render "That feeling, desire, commitment is morally good (or morally bad)" as "That feeling, desire, commitment would evoke a moral pro-emotion (or anti-emotion) in any human being who might at any time contemplate it."

Prima facie this analysis is distinctly different from ours, first and foremost appealing to all human beings rather than the agapic spectator. This is very significant for dealing with a problem Broad sees as central for the moral sense theory, given this understanding of deontic (and by implication aretaic) judgments. He points out that the connection between a right-making property and rightness (and similarly between a morally good-making property and moral goodness) seems to be necessary. (Philosophers may also regard such connections as self-evident and synthetic, as Broad indicates in his discussion.) This leads Broad to give the following analysis of the general statement or principle "All acts of promise-keeping are *prima facie* right":

> It is necessary, self-evident and synthetic that any human being who should contemplate an act which he believed to be one of promise-keeping would tend to feel a moral pro-emotion towards it. (1952, p. 377)

But, as he points out, this claim seems clearly false empirically. Some human beings lack moral sentiments, and hence will not feel these emotions. But even if the generalization were true, it would seem to be a contingent and not a necessary truth. Broad summarizes the problem this way: "If the present form of the Moral Sense Theory were true, certain propositions which are in fact necessary and knowable *a priori* would have been contingent and knowable only empirically. Therefore the theory is false" (1952, p. 377).

Broad feels that there are only two ways out for the moral sense theorist at this point. He needs to argue either that "All acts of promise-keeping are *prima facie* right" is not necessary or that "All human beings who should contemplate an act of promise-keeping will feel a moral pro-emotion towards it" is not a contingent statement. We believe there is a third way out, at least if we carry out our analysis with respect to the agapic spectator rather than with respect to all human beings (with possible restriction to normalcy). Consider:

> If the agapic spectator were to contemplate an act which he believed to be one of promise-keeping, he would tend to feel a moral pro-emotion towards it.

The "tend to" provides for cases where the agapic spectator is aware of overriding wrong-making characteristics of the act.

What may we make of this statement? I believe we can argue that it is both necessary *and* contingent, although the necessity is not alethic or broadly logical. What the statement in effect says is that if one contemplates an act of promise-keeping from the point of view of the agapic spectator, in particular sharing the agapic spectator's commitment to doing one's duty and its concomitant desire, one would tend to have a moral pro-emotion toward it. The subjunctive here may not express a causal law, but it does express a "personal law." We have a personal subjunctive, which is nomically necessary in the sense of nomic necessity defined in Chapter 8. By contrast, worlds where the agapic spectator has the core commitments but feels no moral emotion are conceivable. Hence, the statement is not logically necessary but contingent. By contrast with Broad's proposed explication in terms of all human beings, which seems false, our explication in terms of the agapic spectator states a true "law" of human nature, both nomically necessary and contingent. We submit that this rises to meet Broad's challenge.

We have thus replied to the two major objections we anticipate could be brought against our approach, that it seeks to absolutize or universalize moral perspectives that are culturally relative and that the notion of a moral sense is not coherent. We have argued that given our analyses in this chapter, these objections do not apply to the position we have developed. Dialectically speaking, then, until further telling objections are brought forward, the presumption rests with our side.

10

Taking One's Word

The Interpersonal Belief-Generating Mechanism

In Chapters 6 through 9, we surveyed the personal basic belief-generating mechanisms. These mechanisms form beliefs upon the basis either of how we are appeared to in various ways or of connections we intuit. The mechanism in this chapter, by contrast, takes beliefs ready formed by someone else and makes them our own. This is a central belief-generating mechanism for argumentation. In accepting the basic premises of an argument, in many cases, one may be taking someone's word for it, either the proponent's or someone else's. Let us begin by reflecting on just how central is taking one's word.

10.1 IMPORTANCE OF TAKING ONE'S WORD

Certain recent work in epistemology has called attention to two facts: the significant extent to which in forming our beliefs we rely on the word of others and the meager extent to which philosophers have considered this mode of forming beliefs. Simple reflection should reveal the extent to which our beliefs are formed by taking someone else's word. Coady makes this point with great persuasiveness (1992, pp. 6–7). He invites you to suppose you are visiting Amsterdam for the first time. You rely on the word of the airplane's crew that this really is *Amsterdam* where your plane had landed. You enter your date and place of birth on the hotel registration form. The belief that a certain date is one's birthday or that a certain place is one's place of birth is always received from others. Likewise, the hotel clerk is relying on your word when he receives from you all the information requested on the form, and anyone to whom he transmits this information would likewise be relying on the clerk's word.

Suppose you ask the clerk for the time. You again rely on testimony. When you begin to explore Amsterdam on foot, you consult a map and proceed to buy a newspaper. In consulting the map, you are again relying on a form of testimony, as you are when you form beliefs about current events on the basis of reading your copy of the paper.

As Coady points out, trusting the word of others is extensive in science as well as everyday contexts. Not only may social scientists take testimony from the subjects of their studies but also both social and natural scientists will consult the data of other scientists. Furthermore, the very process of having one's scientific work refereed indicates reliance on the word of others within the scientific community, for confidence in one's work increases with the corroboration of a positive referee's report (compare 1992, pp. 11–12). Not only in scientific contexts but also in common sense, we seek corroboration: "The judgments of others constitute an important, indeed perhaps *the* most important, test of whether my own judgments reflect a reality independent of my subjectivity" (1992, p. 12, italics in original).[1]

Plantinga points out that this cumulative nature of human knowledge is central and necessary to "intellectual achievement and culture, testimony is the very foundation of civilization" (1993b, p. 77). Indeed, testimony may be a presupposition for the richness of the very language we use to formulate our beliefs. Reid was one of the few figures in the history of philosophy to acknowledge the importance of testimony, witness this high appraisal:

> If I had not believed what [my parents and tutors] told me, before I could give a reason of my belief, I had to this day been little better than a changeling. And although this natural credulity hath sometimes occasioned my being imposed upon by deceivers, yet it hath been of infinite advantage to me upon the whole; therefore, I consider it as another good gift of Nature. (Beanblossom and Lehrer 1983, p. 87)

But testimony has received scant attention in the history of Western philosophy. This is explainable given certain main emphases within that tradition. Plato was concerned with knowledge for which necessity is a necessary condition. Even perception then would be a questionable source of knowledge for Plato, much less taking someone's word, where from the mere fact of receiving someone's word we cannot know whether that word is true. Again, Aristotle's view of a science as a body of self-evident first principles together with what may be deduced from them holds up necessity as a condition of knowledge. This view of knowledge as necessary was seminal. "Amongst the ancients and medievals, the view of knowledge as a kind of thoroughgoing rational understanding militated against treating beliefs based on testimony as part of knowledge" (Coady 1992, p. 6).[2] Coady points out that in the modern period, "the dominance of an individualist ideology has had a lot to do with the feeling that testimony has little or no epistemic importance" (1992, p. 13).[3] If the goal is to improve one's understanding to achieve certain knowledge on one's own, what would be the importance or motivation for consulting the word of others? From the point of view of this study, the need to redress this situation is paramount. If acceptability is to be understood in terms of presumption, and presumption for a belief or claim on our belief is a function at least in part of the source of that belief, and if the word of others is a major source of our own beliefs, then it behooves us to determine, as precisely as we can, whether and just when there is a presumption for beliefs generated by this source.

Even naming this belief-generating mechanism is problematic. Reid called it credulity. But this seems an unfortunate choice of word. "Credulity," as *Webster's* points out, strongly suggests a disposition to believe on slight or uncertain evidence, an over-readiness to believe. But assenting to a belief thus uncritically is certainly not a reliable way of forming true beliefs. How could we show that there was a presumption for the reliability of such a mechanism if we have already implicitly indicated its unreliability?

Is "testimony" a better choice of word? Here, also, there are problems. First, testimony is both given and received, and the word refers to what is transferred in this process. So, to refer to the belief-generating mechanism, we might speak of taking testimony rather than of testimony *simpliciter*. But "taking testimony" does not have the right connotations. Police investigators might take testimony from eyewitnesses to a crime or accident to develop a body of data to pass on to other authorities without assenting to that data themselves. For these investigators, taking testimony need not be a belief-forming process. "Relying on testimony" would be a better appellation here, for one who relies on testimony comes to believe that testimony with assent.

But this characterization is still problematic. Is everything a proponent says in a given situation an instance of testimony? A proponent may say that he saw the accused standing over the body of the victim. He also may say that the accused is guilty. Is he testifying in both instances? In the first, his statement is a description. But the claim that someone is guilty is an interpretation. That claim relates certain overt performances to personal intention and systems of law. Can one testify to an interpretation just as well as to a description? Can one testify to evaluations? Can one testify that abortion is murder? Testimony seems to presuppose some sort of authority which a proponent might not have in all cases. If all we know is that a proponent has put forward some claim, then the conditions need not be satisfied for according his statement the status of testimony.

But should the challenger accept the proponent's statement, she would certainly be taking his word. "Taking one's word" then is the most accurate or least prejudicial way of describing the cognitive faculty of forming beliefs based on what others say. Is there a presumption for this cognitive faculty in general or may there be a presumption for it only in certain of its employments? In those cases, is the word relied on genuine testimony? To answer that question, we must clarify what we mean by "testimony."

10.2 TESTIMONY DEFINED

Coady offers the following account of what he regards as the conventions governing the speech act of testifying:

A speaker S testifies by making some statement p if and only if:

(1) His stating that p is evidence that p and is offered as evidence that p.

(2) S has the relevant competence, authority, or credentials to state truly that p.

(3) S's statement that p is relevant to some disputed or unresolved question . . . and is directed to those who are in need of evidence on the matter. (1992, p. 42)[4]

We may define "testimony" as the product of a speech act of testifying. Clearly, on this account, testifying is not simply asserting and accepting testimony is not simply accepting someone's word. Clause (2) makes the most obvious difference. A proponent can assert just about anything, but his mere assertion does not in itself give him any "competence, authority, or credentials" in the matter. Indeed, should we recognize that a proponent's belief that p is without warrant, we should refuse to accord his stating that p the status of testimony.

The notion of testifying that Coady has defined and the notion of testimony that we have derived from it are externalist notions. Testifying that p requires that the proponent have the relevant competence, authority, or credentials to state truly that p, and that his stating that p *be* evidence that p. Now suppose a challenger receives an assertion from some proponent. Certainly that the proponent satisfies clause (2) is a fact about the proponent that is not revealed to the challenger by how she may see herself appeared to or by how she may see certain ideas combined or related. Suppose a challenger forms a belief that p on the basis of the proponent's asserting that p, and that the proponent's asserting that p is an instance of testimony. This may be sufficient to make the challenger's belief that p warranted. Should p be true, we may say that she knows that p. But does this have implications for doxastic practice, for saying that p is presumptively acceptable from the challenger's point of view?

We need to define an internalist notion of testimony from the challenger's point of view. Here Coady's definition proves quite fruitful, in particular his clause (2) even though that makes *his* definition externalist. Our being *testified* to by a proponent on some matter presupposes that we are appeared to in at least two distinct ways. First, the proponent must have stated or told us something. He has stated that p and we have heard that statement with understanding.[5] But, second, there must be some factor in how we are appeared to which is a sign of competence, authority, or credentials to state that p, a sign of authority for short.

Here we are using "sign" as Reid used "sign" in his accounts of perception and testimony. As we pointed out in Section 7.2, features of a sensation are signs of the existence and features of external objects or conditions. Recall that Reid distinguishes between two types of perceptions – natural or original and acquired. I become aware of a certain smell. My design plan generates a belief that there is a body existing externally to me that is in some sense causing this sensation. My perception here is natural or original. My sensation or features of my sensation then are a natural sign of the body having this corresponding feature. By contrast, suppose that when appeared to by this sensation I recognize it as the smell of a rose. I perceive a rose through this sense of smell. The sign is acquired, for I had to learn that a sensation having these particular features was a sign of a rose.

Reid feels there is a remarkable analogy between perception and testimony. In both, "Things are signified to us by signs; and in one as well as the other, the mind, either by original principles or by custom, passes from the sign to the conception and belief of the things signified" (Beanblossom and Lehrer 1983, p. 90). As we may distinguish original and acquired perceptions, so we may distinguish natural and artificial languages. As we discussed in Section 7.2, natural language involving various bodily gestures and appearances discloses to us features of other persons or other minds. Artificial languages are the spoken and written languages which we learn as a part of growing up. "In artificial language, the signs are articulate sounds, whose connection with the things signified by them, is established by the will of men. . . . And, after this connection is discovered, the sign, as in natural language, always suggests the thing signified, and creates the belief of it" (1983, p. 91). As with natural language and perception in general, the beliefs generated are basic. Upon hearing a certain articulated complete sentence, whose meaning we recognize, we may form a belief and form it directly. We have not argued that the person *S* who uttered this sentence has asserted that *p*, usually what *S* asserts is true, so (probably) *p*. (Compare Plantinga 1993b, p. 79.) We move to the belief that *p* directly from the asserted sentence as sign. This is what is involved in forming a belief by taking someone's word.

One might object, however, that although we may form basic beliefs on the word of others, those beliefs are never properly basic. That is, such beliefs need to be reasoned or argued for on the basis of other premises before they can be regarded as acceptable. Even if we can identify conditions under which someone's word is testimony, we must always *argue* that the word *is* testimony from premises that those conditions are holding. Our assenting to this supported belief is not forming a basic belief. But, we may reply, to revise our epistemic or doxastic practice to conform to the objector's view of rational acceptance or assent would not make that practice more rational. "On the contrary, it would surely be irrational to the point of insanity to withhold assent pending investigation of the respective premises" (Coady 1992, p. 144).[6] I dial a certain number and the person answering tells me that the person I wish to contact is no longer at that exchange. She gives me another number. I proceed to dial that number. Here, I have accepted the information she gave me as a premise for further action. I did not make any attempt to investigate her reliability. I simply accepted the information. My belief that the telephone number was correct was basic. Was it properly basic? Was this acceptance irrational? How could I have gotten access to information which would support her reliability? Would attempting to make such an investigation not be the height of neurotic suspiciousness?

We want to say that my belief that the telephone number was correct was properly basic and acceptable because it relied on testimony. But this returns us to the question of how we distinguish a person's testimony from his or her word in general. Here the notion of sign plays a crucial role. It seems patently obvious that when one is appeared to, one need not be appeared to by one sign only. The features of one experience might include several signs. A proponent may utter a statement in anger. Our reception of that statement – that particular experience – then has at least two signs among its features. The uttered sentence, part of an artificial language, is one sign. But the facial features, tone of voice signifying anger constitute another sign, a natural language sign.

It seems just as patently obvious that there are signs of competence, authority, and credentials. These may consist of or repose in some overtly recognizable feature of the person giving testimony or of the overall situation. I recognize my own personal physician. This means that I not only can identify him at sight when I see him, but can recognize him *as* a physician by virtue of being in a doctor's office, which is also his office. In an emergency room, I may perceive a person to be a physician by virtue of the distinctive clothing he or she is wearing or by virtue of how the person addresses or examines others. My recognition is acquired perception. I also have learned that the natural trust that as a child I reposed indiscriminately in the word of others may still be reposed in physicians when they are speaking on medical subjects. So the signs that one is a physician are also insignia of authority, in medical matters at least.

A sign of authority is simply that – a sign that there is a congruence between what a proponent has said and his authority, competence, capacity to state truly that he has said. This may not even be a matter of recognizing overt insignia of authority (such as a doctor's gown) but simply what type of statement is made. If someone jubilantly tells me that Holland has just won the World Cup in soccer, he is making a report, but a report ordinarily quite congruent with his capacities to state truly that something has happened. He may have witnessed the game himself, read of the win in the newspaper, or seen the game on television. It does not strain credulity to think that the proponent was in one or more of these situations. Hence that what he has said is a report with a certain content is a sign of his competence to make such a report. We shall discuss signs of authority more fully when we discuss each particular type of testimony.

This speaking of signs of authority gives us the internalist counterpart of Coady's externalist clause (2) for testimony. Whether or not S has the relevant competence, authority, or credentials to state truly that p is a fact about S independent of the challenger or the person to whom S addresses his remark. But that the challenger has been appeared to in a certain way and that a feature of that appearance is a sign of authority is a fact about the *challenger*. It is internal to the challenger. It is something of which she may come to full awareness through inspecting her experience.

Being appeared to authoritatively, that is, one's experience including a sign of authority, then, is a necessary condition of testimony from the challenger's point of view.

Does Coady's definition of testifying reveal further necessary conditions for testimony from the challenger's point of view? Let us examine the remaining two clauses. In defining testimony from a challenger's point of view, one might think that clause (3) was satisfied automatically. For, in a dialectical exchange, the proponent makes contributions in response to the challenger's questions, these responses being put forward as evidence or as premises. So, one might think that any statement a challenger would receive from the proponent as a premise would be in answer to one of her questions, and thus be relevant (or at least intended to be relevant) to this question and addressed to the challenger. But this overlooks one possibility for dialectical exchanges. The proponent may put forward some claim at the initial state of the "exchange," and the challenger regard it as so obvious as to need no questioning. She simply concedes it. There is a presumption for it from her point of view. Let us further assume that she recognizes this presumption because she recognizes a sign of the proponent's competence or authority to state truly what he has asserted. The "exchange" ends right there. Furthermore, the proponent makes his remark independently of any previous contemplation of some issue with the challenger. Must we deny that this statement is testimony from the challenger's point of view because the proponent did not put this statement forward in response to a question from her?

Is clause (3) really necessary for the definition of testifying? It underscores the jurisprudential inheritance of the concept. Coady distinguishes formal testimony, what is given in the courtroom, from natural testimony. A formal witness contributes only what answers the questions asked, where there are clearly identified persons who need the witness's testimony and to whom it is directed. In nonjudicial proceedings, testimony may also generally be given in answer to specific questions to benefit some specific persons, ordinarily those asking the questions. Natural testimony includes "giving someone directions to the post office, reporting what happened in an accident, saying that, yes, you have seen a child answering to that description, telling someone the result of the last race or the latest cricket score" (Coady 1992, p. 38).[7]

I believe there are a number of instances in natural contexts when testimony has been given, yet no question has been asked. When I turn on the radio or television for the news, am I explicitly aware of asking any question, if I inspect my consciousness? Perhaps someone will reply that there is an implicit question: What new and startling things have happened in the past few hours? But how are we to understand implicit questioning? Without some account, the answer seems *ad hoc*. But even with an account, I do not believe the answer would cover all cases. Suppose I am listening to some non-news program that is interrupted for a bulletin that severe tornado-spawning weather is heading toward the vicinity. Was there no testimony from the weather forecaster because I had not asked any question about the weather? Clause (3) is an unnecessary restriction on the concept of testifying and on the derivative concept of testimony. It points to the formal and dialectical ancestry of testimony without presenting a necessary condition for it.

Does clause (1) present a further condition to be incorporated into a definition of testimony from a challenger's point of view? For S to be testifying that p, S's stating that p must be evidence and offered as evidence that p. This clause again reflects the jurisprudential inheritance of the concept of testimony. The testimony of witnesses is one type of evidence, offered as evidence. Consider the second conjunct of the clause. If to offer a statement that p as evidence that p means that one is asking our audience to accept p because we claim that p, then we are vouching for it. Vouching for a statement means putting the weight of one's authority behind asserting that statement. It would be not merely to make a statement but to represent to one's audience that the statement is acceptable on one's own authority. By contrast, one may assert a statement that p not on one's authority but on the weight of evidence one has produced. Here one is not vouching for p but arguing that p. One might assert a statement simply to remind one's audience of what they already accept. This would certainly not be putting forward the statement on one's own authority, vouching for it.

With Reid we may distinguish testimony from judgment, which we express this way: In judgment one renders one's opinion which may but need not be supported by evidence to some degree. But, in asserting a judgment one does not vouch for that claim as a matter of fact; one makes no claim that he is staking his veracity and reputation on that judgment. By contrast, in giving testimony, one puts forward his claim as fact and puts the weight of his authority behind that assertion. So we see that there are a number of speech acts – reminding one's audience that p, arguing from evidence that p, voicing one's judgment or opinion that p – which do not involve vouching for p. All of these speech acts contrast with testifying and thus we may claim that vouching for p is a necessary condition of testifying that p.

Should we then add a further condition to our definition of testimony from a challenger's point of view – that there be some sign that the proponent is vouching for his statement? I believe we should. A proponent with the requisite authority to vouch for a statement, an authority recognized by the challenger, might put that statement forward not on his own authority but anticipating that the challenger already accepts it, or intending to defend the statement with argument if asked. From the challenger's point of view, do we have testimony here? Because, by our admission, the proponent was not testifying, it is hard to see why we should call what the challenger has received testimony – even though the proponent was in a position to give testimony. For an assertion to be testimony, then, from the challenger's point of view, there must be some mark or sign that the proponent is vouching for his statement. We need not develop at this point what is the nature of this sign, which will vary from case to case. Presumably aspects of body language, tone of voice, solemnity of the context in which the statement is made may constitute such signs.

We still must retain there being a sign of authority as a condition for testimony from the challenger's point of view. A proponent may vouch for a statement for which he has no authority, at least in the challenger's eyes. Is he testifying? What is it to put the weight of one's authority behind an assertion when that weight is nil? At best, this is testifying in a degenerate sense. And it is a sense we need not consider further. For why should there be a presumption for the reliability of degenerate testimony, where by definition there is no sign of authority or competence of the proponent putting forward that "testimony"?

What of the first conjunct of clause (1), requiring that S's stating that p be evidence that p? Does this clause require our modifying further the definition of testimony from a challenger's point of view? Whether or not a statement put forward as evidence that p *is* evidence that p depends on whether the proponent has any authority or credibility in this matter. Proper authority would make that vouching evidence. Lack of such authority would make the vouching worthless as a piece of evidence. Hence, for the assertion of a statement that p to *be* evidence, nothing further is needed than that the proponent vouch for it and have "the relevant competence, authority, or credentials to state that p." Thus, the first conjunct of clause (1) does not add anything further to the concept of testifying and thus does not necessitate any additions to our concept of testimony from the challenger's point of view.

We may then offer the following definition: A statement that p as put forward by a proponent in a dialectical exchange and received by the challenger of that exchange, heard and understood by her, constitutes *testimony from the challenger's point of view* just in case she is aware of signs both that the proponent is vouching for his statement that *p* and that the proponent has the requisite competence, authority, or credentials to state truly that *p*. We may say that our belief-generating mechanism of taking one's word is relying on testimony, then, if it generates a belief that *p* on the basis of being appeared to by someone asserting that *p* together with signs that the assertor was vouching for *p* and was an authority concerning *p*. Is there a presumption for testimony, that is, a presumption for the reliability of relying on testimony? We shall devote the rest of this chapter to answering that question.

10.3 PRESUMPTION FOR RELYING ON TESTIMONY: PRELIMINARY CONSIDERATIONS

As with the belief-generating mechanisms we have discussed previously, our question here is whether there is a presumption for the reliability of relying on testimony. In view of our definition of testimony from the challenger's point of view, this amounts to asking whether there is a presumption of reliability for taking the word of someone else when in addition it appears that the person is vouching for his claim and that he has the requisite authority to state the claim truly.

As with perception, Reid's views will prove central here in clarifying what a presumption for the reliability of relying on testimony means. Where it will not cause confusion, we shall speak more simply of a presumption for testimony or for the reliability of testimony. Reid acknowledges that humans have a distinct disposition to rely on the word of others. This is a basic principle of our constitution which he calls the *principle of credulity*. Reid sees the faculty of taking someone else's word as going through at least two developmental stages. In childhood, there is complete, generalized trust in the word of others – a necessary trust since one's abilities to find out the truth on one's own have not yet developed. In maturity, there need not be and will not be complete trust in the word of others. When children develop, grow up, they become capable both of finding out for themselves at least some matters for which they previously had to rely exclusively on the word of others, and they "find reason to check that propensity to yield to testimony and to authority" (Beanblossom and Lehrer 1983, p. 282). Reason "learns to suspect testimony in some cases, and to disbelieve it in others; and sets bounds to that authority to which she was at first entirely subject" (1983, p. 96). Yet, "the natural propensity [to rely on testimony] still retains some force"

(1983, p. 282). Reason will continue such reliance in cases where her own lights will not suffice.

I believe we can merge some of our conceptual apparatus into Reid's developmental account quite readily. As children, our constitutions or design plans are set always or almost always to take the word of others. The adult acquires through maturation the ability to recognize rebutting or defeating considerations for taking the word of others. Some justify merely suspicion of what is claimed, others justify outright withdrawal of belief. Coming to recognize such defeating conditions, that when such conditions are present, trust in the word of others should be curtailed or suspended, is not the same thing as coming to recognize positive signs of authority or competence or signs that someone is vouching for a proposition as opposed to performing some other kind of speech act. But neither are these two things incompatible. There is nothing incoherent or inconsistent in extending Reid's view of the maturational process to say that through this process the defeater recognition features or modules of our design plan become activated *and* we come to recognize signs of authority and marks of the speech act of testifying. These are all part and parcel of the mature faculty of relying on testimony. But there is still a propensity to rely on testimony. This is as much a part of our constitution as is assenting to perceptual belief claims.

Just as we could give a pragmatic justification for trusting the "testimony" of sense – it is indispensable for getting on in the world – so we may give a pragmatic justification for trusting the testimony of others. We can justify this for both children and adults. Trust in the word of others is necessary for children to learn what they need to get by in the world. Likewise for adults, without this trust "no proposition that is uttered in discourse would be believed, until it was examined and tried by reason; and most men would be unable to find reasons for believing the thousandth part of what is told them. Such distrust and incredulity would deprive us of the greatest benefits of society, and place us in a worse condition than that of savages" (1983, p. 95). Our considerations in Section 10.1 on the importance of taking one's word can enrich such a pragmatic argument.

We may present a further argument. Given Reid's account of relying on the word of others as also a first principle of our constitution, the case for the presumption of reliability of testimony is analogous to the case for perception. It is part of our constitution to form beliefs through relying on testimony. Just as in perception, when we are appeared to in a certain way through the senses, we automatically form certain beliefs as a consequence of our constitution or design plan, so when we are appeared to "testimonially" we are constitutionally set to assent to the belief formed through this experience. Not to assent to testimony would go against our constitution, indeed violate it, just as not assenting to a perceptual belief in the absence of evidence calling the perceptual mechanism that generated it into question would go against our constitution. Just as it is simply common sense that we accept the perceptual belief, so it is common sense that we accept the testimonial belief. As a presumption for the reliability of perception is a first principle of common sense, so a presumption for the reliability of relying on testimony is also a first principle of common sense. As such, there is no need to argue for these principles and indeed such an argument would be wrongheaded.

One might object to this analogy by pointing out that when we come to "years of discretion," we become aware that people sometimes lie and that they are sometimes mistaken. Does this awareness not defeat the presumption for testimony? How can one concede the general reliability of testimony in the light of these facts? One might counter this rebuttal by replying that when we come to years of discretion, we also become aware that our senses at times are deceived or deceive us. Yet this does not defeat the presumption for the reliability of perception. We still trust our perceptual mechanisms unless we have *evidence* of their malfunction, or of environmental anomaly, or of our holding doxastic goals other than getting at the truth. Why should the fact that some witnesses lie and some witnesses are mistaken be so significant as to undercut the general presumption of reliability for testimony?

Whatever the merits of this rejoinder, it leads us to overlook two important factors in the issue of the presumption for testimony. First, some philosophers, including Reid, have specifically addressed the issue of lying, arguing that lying can never be prevalent enough to undercut the general presumption for testimony. Second, when we come to maturity, we do learn to withdraw our trust from some sources and to rely on others because of signs of competence or authority. A presumption for the reliability of testimony includes a presumption for the reliability of the belief-generating mechanisms of the witnesses. This has important implications for clarifying just what the presumption for testimony involves. Let us examine each of these issues in turn.

Coordinate with the principle of credulity, Reid claims that the human constitution also contains a *principle of veracity*. Human beings have a natural propensity to tell the truth, even persons who are notorious liars. Even they will tell the truth more often than they lie. We must be tempted to lie and the act does "violence to our nature" (1983, p. 94). Telling the truth "requires no art or training, no inducement or temptation, but only that we yield to a natural impulse" (1983, p. 94). By virtue of this principle of veracity, there is a real connection between our words and our thoughts. Our words become reliable signs of our thoughts, and individual instances of lying are not able to deprive our words of this sign function. It is by virtue of this principle of veracity, together with the competence of witnesses, that the principle of credulity gains its reliability.

That in testimony our experience must include a sign of authority or competence highlights a unique feature of testimony and its presumption. Assume that challenger C receives the testimony of proponent R that p. There being a presumption for p from C's point of view depends not only on there being a presumption that C's belief-generating mechanism of relying on testimony is functioning properly but also on there being a presumption that R's belief-generating mechanism is functioning properly. Otherwise, C's experience would not include a sign of R's competence or the presumption of R's competence from C's point of view would be undercut by further evidence of which C is aware or how C is appeared to. That was why it was necessary for us to discuss the presumption in favor of personal mechanisms first before we could discuss a presumption for testimony. We shall develop this point further shortly.

Such considerations lead Plantinga to say that "testimony is ordinarily parasitic on other sources of belief so far as warrant goes" (1993b, p. 87). If the proponent does not have warrant for his claim, neither will the challenger have warrant for her belief formed by taking his word. Although clearly in testimony or taking one's word, warrant for the challenger's belief is dependent on warrant for the proponent's belief, I do not think we need evoke the negative connotations of the word "parasitic" in describing this dependency. I should like to say that the warrant is composed, in a sense analogous to functional composition. The conditions for warrant must have been satisfied by the cognitive faculty that generated the proponent's belief. The challenger receives the proponent's report through perception. This includes her understanding the proponent's statement, a matter of learning language and thus of acquired institutional perception. The challenger's perceptual mechanism must also be functioning properly for her belief that p to have warrant on the proponent's word that p. Her belief is the result of two (or more) belief-generating mechanisms working in tandem or composition on the original data of the proponent's experience. As the belief is a product of these composed mechanisms, so the warrant is dependent on the proper function of each and is thus composed.

As warrant for testimonial beliefs is composed, so is presumption of warrant. As we have noted, the challenger received the proponent's testimony through perception. Now the challenger does not – or at least need not – form the perceptual belief that the proponent has asserted or witnessed that p and on this basis infer or arrive at the belief that p. She forms the belief that p as a basic belief. However, the challenger's perceptual mechanism by which she received the proponent's testimony and that could have generated the belief that the proponent testified that p must be functioning properly for her belief to have warrant, as we have noted. Hence, for her belief to be acceptable, for there to be a presumption for her belief, there must be a presumption of warrant for the belief that the proponent has asserted that p, even if the belief is not formed. Again, we have noted, the proponent's belief that p must be warranted for the challenger's belief that p to be warranted also. The challenger does not – or again at least need not – form the belief that the proponent's belief that p has warrant. But for the proponent's report to be *testimony* there must be some sign of authority or competence in how the challenger is appeared to. It goes without saying that for there to be a presumption of warrant for the challenger's belief that p, there must be an absence of signs indicating that the proponent's authority has been compromised. That is, there must be a presumption that the proponent's belief that p is warranted, even if the challenger does not form that belief. The presumption of warrant and thus the presumption for her belief that p generated through relying on testimony is then dependent upon and in effect the composition of these two presumptions concerning her cognitive faculty and that of the proponent.

I believe this has distinct implications for formulating principles of presumption for testimony. Can we classify sources of testimony according to the areas for which the claims they put forward have warrant? Clearly, different sources of testimony will have authority or competence in different areas. For each source of testimony, we can talk about the area of reliability for that source. This means that we can become more specific in saying when a particular proponent is giving testimony and this means that we can present more specific presumptions of reliability for particular types of testimony, more specific principles of presumption. To do this, we must first survey the various types of sources which may give testimony, and then identify the area of competence for each type of source. In the next section we shall survey the sources. Then in the remaining sections of this chapter we shall identify the area of competence for each.

10.4 SOURCES OF TESTIMONY

Aristotle presents a classification of sources of testimony in connection with discussing dialectical reasoning in Book I of the *Topics*. Dialectical reasoning takes as its premises what is generally accepted, that is "accepted by every one or by the majority or by the philosophers – i.e. by all, or by the majority, or by the most notable and illustrious of them" (McKeon 1941, p. 188). Opinions that are accepted by all or by the majority are examples of common knowledge, whereas philosophers for Aristotle are analogous to experts for us. Experts are certainly sources that may vouch for a claim, and common knowledge, although not an individual like a proponent in a dialectical exchange, is nonetheless a source of beliefs to which we ascribe some authority and, in a somewhat metaphorical sense, say vouches for these beliefs.

There clearly are further sources of testimony. We would not say that someone is an expert concerning what he or she has perceived. But we certainly would ordinarily grant that persons are competent to report on their experiences of perception, introspection, and memory. Indeed, what more credentials could we ask for when a proponent reports on what he has experienced directly than that he is speaking of *his* experience? Such a report is a firsthand report. But a proponent may report what someone else has reported. Here we have a secondhand report and what we shall call a chain of testimony. Obviously, we may describe this as a chain of length 2. And, of course, we can have chains of length *3*, *4*, and indeed some of very significant length. It is by virtue of such chains that most of us gain most of our knowledge of current news events and of history. So, chains of testimony are another source.

Such chains frequently operate in the media. The reporter who has presented a story frequently does not report what he or she has perceived directly but relates what has been learned through various sources – indeed, through various chains of sources. But the media does much more than simply report the news. It not only reports but also interprets and even evaluates the news, that is, what the news concerns. Because of this and because of its significant and pervasive influence in our lives, the media deserves consideration as a source in its own right.

Finally, we have what Coady calls institutional testimony. This may be testimony in an extended sense, but it is a source of a significant number of our beliefs. When I consult a clock to determine the time, I am appeared to in a certain way by the face of the clock. But on the basis of this I form a belief not just or even that there is a clock in front of me, but that it is three o'clock, for example. In forming this belief, I am assenting to what the clock is "saying," its "testimony." And presumably by being a clock it has the "authority" to "vouch for" the time of day. "Road signs, maps, the measurement markings on rulers, destination-markers on buses and trams, the author attribution on the title page of a book" (1992, p. 51)[8] are further examples of institutional testimony.

All these sources give us their word on various matters. But do they give us genuine testimony in certain particular areas? That is, is there a presumption of reliability for what they vouch for, based on their authority or competence, which would lead us to say that their word in these areas was genuine testimony? We shall examine each of these sources in turn, beginning with personal testimony.

10.5 PERSONAL TESTIMONY AND ITS PRESUMPTION

It is important that we begin by clarifying just what we mean by personal testimony and its scope. Our remarks in Section 10.4 suggest that reports or avowals of what one has experienced directly through perception or introspection, or remembers having experienced directly are instances of personal testimony. Here let us be explicit that this is precisely what we mean. A statement put forward by a proponent is an instance of personal testimony just in case it is a description of some event or condition which that proponent has witnessed directly or some summary report or summary generalization of what he has witnessed directly. One gives personal testimony of what one perceives oneself, introspects, or remembers perceiving or introspecting. By contrast, descriptions of what others have witnessed are not *personal* testimony but, rather, a stage in a testimonial chain.

Seeing why there should be a presumption for personal testimony, that is, a presumption for the reliability of relying on personal testimony, is straightforward. When a proponent personally testifies that p and a challenger forms the belief that p on the basis of this testimony, the mechanisms involved in this belief formation are all mechanisms for which there is a presumption of reliability. As we have already indicated, the challenger receives the proponent's testimony that p through perception. She perceives that the proponent has asserted that p together with signs that he is vouching for p and has the competence to assert that p. But we have already argued that there is a presumption for the reliability of perception. What are the marks of competence in this case? They are marks that the proponent is speaking of what he has perceived directly or introspected within himself or remembered – or some combination of these. But these are all cognitive faculties which are presumptively reliable. As we indicated in Section 10.3, the presumption for personal testimony then is a composition of the presumptions for the reliability of the cognitive mechanisms of both the challenger and proponent which are involved in generating the challenger's belief that p.

Perhaps it would be best to think of this presumption for the reliability of testimony as involving three levels or stages of presumption. First, the challenger has perceived that the proponent has asserted that p and this is a matter of perception. Should she form the belief that the proponent has asserted that p, there would be a presumption of reliability for her belief-generating mechanism here. But she also perceives that the proponent is vouching for p. Let us assume there is a presumption of trust that this voucher is sincere. Should she form the belief that the proponent is sincerely vouching for p, as opposed to merely asserting that p, there would be a presumption for this belief. This is the second level of presumption. But, because the proponent's belief was generated through perception, introspection, or memory, there is a presumption for the reliability of those mechanisms. The challenger's belief that p then is a result of these presumptively reliable belief-generating mechanisms working in composition.

One might concede that both the proponent's and challenger's belief-generating mechanisms are presumptively reliable here but still question why the composition of these mechanisms is also reliable. But why under these circumstances should there not a be presumption for the reliability of forming the belief that p on the basis of the proponent's presumed sincere voucher that p and the presumed reliability of the mechanisms which generated the proponent's belief that p? Is this not simply a matter of common sense? If there is a presumption that a person is sincerely vouching for a belief, and thus a presumption for the reliability of generating *this* belief of sincere vouching, and a presumption that he came to the belief through reliable means, why should there not be a presumption for the belief vouched for and for the reliability of the mechanism producing this belief?

What may we say about the assumed presumption of trust? Why when a proponent is speaking should we presume that he is speaking sincerely, even if not accurately? We have already answered that question in Section 10.3 where we addressed Reid's principle of veracity and related arguments. We do presume that others are trustworthy and this presumption is well founded. We thus have our case for the presumptive reliability of

relying on personal testimony. We may presume that this mode of generating beliefs is reliable.

10.6 WHEN IS THERE A PRESUMPTION FOR TESTIMONY RECEIVED THROUGH A CHAIN?

Personal testimony is firsthand testimony. What may we say of secondhand reports? If a witness's statement expresses not what he has observed
in person, but what someone else has, who has reported that to him, is
there still a presumption for this claim? What shall we say then of third-
hand, fourthhand, fifthhand, in general n-hand reports? If the challenger
receives the report from the nth witness, is there a presumption for it?
The commonsense view holds that ordinarily strength of presumption
decreases as length of chain increases. This, at least, is the default situation. One expects that in the transmission process, each witness acts as a
filter, modifying the content of the testimony at each stage. Where "$T_x p$"
abbreviates "x testifies that p," the intuitive picture of the transmission
schema might be represented as a linear chain:[9]

1. $$ p \implies T_a p^1 \longrightarrow T_b p^2 \longrightarrow T_c p^3 \longrightarrow \cdots \longrightarrow T_n p^n $$

The expectation is that in the default case, the proposition expressed
by what is substituted for "p^1" is distinctly different from the proposition
substituted for "p^n." Even assuming that all the witnesses intended to tell
the truth and not to deceive, and assuming that a's initial statement that
p^1 accurately represents the state of affairs that p, one would ordinarily
be skeptical that p^n is a true or sufficiently verisimilitudinous statement.
Why? We expect that a person giving testimony will report those aspects
or details that have impressed him with a certain salience, where this
salience is conditioned by his grasp of what is important enough or relevant enough to be reported. An eyewitness to a crime will not report *every*
detail of the scene, such as the color of the rug or the style of the furni-
ture, deemed insignificant background details. That the perpetrator had
a gun and also wore a mask, that the victim pleaded for mercy – these
would be deemed relevant details.

Our witness acts as a filter. A secondhand report will have passed
through two or more filters, depending upon how many people have
passed the story from one to the next. As Coady points out, each person
may make an appraisal of the trustworthiness of the previous source or
sources and a decision on how much of the previous testimony to endorse

(1992, p. 212). It would be surprising if some relevant facts did not get excluded in this process, and the significance of other facts distorted. Besides judging data relevant, observers also may interpret what they have observed and infer certain descriptions on that basis. Hence, at some point in a chain of communication, a reporter may take a message as indicating some further fact, as meaning that some further statement is true, and report *that* as fact rather than the "original" message. The more filters our reports have passed through, the more chances such interpretations will have been made at some point in the chain. These interpretations may be mistaken, even assuming goodwill on the part of all our reporters. There is a distinct possibility that these descriptions, these secondhand reports, will involve distortion. Recognizing then that a person giving his word stands at the end of a chain of testimony weakens the presumption for that testimony. We would expect that if the chain were sufficiently long, n sufficiently high, the presumption might be weakened to the vanishing point.

This commonsense view accords with the legal practice of banning hearsay evidence, at least in criminal proceedings. As Coady points out, it seems in distinct agreement with the views of John Locke:

Any testimony, the further off it is from the original truth, the less force and proof it has. . . . A credible man vouching his knowledge of it is a good proof; but if another equally credible do witness it from his report, the testimony is weaker: and a third that attests the hearsay of an hearsay is yet less considerable. So that in traditional truths, each remove weakens the force of the proof: and the more hands the tradition has successively passed through, the less strength and evidence does it receive from them. (Locke 1961, Bk. IV, Ch. xvi, Sec. 10. Quoted in 1992, p. 199, italics in 1992)

These consideration show there is no blanket or overall presumption for testimony received through a simple or linear chain. Thus, if a challenger recognizes that the proponent testifying to some state of affairs is the last member of some chain through which someone's firsthand testimony has been transmitted, the challenger needs evidence – which may be contextually present – of the reliability of the transmission chain before she can regard reliable the word of this last member of the chain. If there is evidence or reason to believe that each person in the chain after the firsthand witness has been careful to transmit what he has received from the immediately preceding person in the chain, so that

$$2. \qquad p \implies T_a p' \longrightarrow T_b p' \longrightarrow T_c p' \longrightarrow \cdots \longrightarrow T_n p'$$

quite accurately represents the transmission chain, where a's testimony is presumptively reliable, then so is n's and *in this case* there is a presumption for p'. This could happen if the challenger had evidence or could presume that each of a, b, c, . . . , n had a responsibility to report accurately in this case, say if each were a member of a reputable news organization. We shall comment on this again in connection with whether there is a presumption for the news media in Section 10.9.

However, as Coady points out, the linear picture of the transmission of testimony is in many instances oversimplified. One may receive the word of the last members of several testimonial chains and these words may converge. Suppose three persons report to an individual **f** that there had been an explosion in a city some one thousand miles distant earlier that day, where **f** subsequently reports that to us. Because none of these reporters could have been physically present to witness the explosion and then travel the one thousand miles, the testimony of each is at least secondhand. Let us suppose that each has spoken by telephone to someone living in the city, each speaking to a different person. These persons were not eyewitnesses to the explosion themselves but, rather, spoke to eyewitnesses. To simplify, let us suppose that each of those contacted by phone spoke to the same eyewitness. Thus the transmission structure involves three chains and can be represented this way, where "E" stands both for the state of affairs that there was an explosion in the city that morning and the statement to that effect. Numerical superscripts indicate some modification of the testimony.

$$3. \quad E \implies T_p E \quad \begin{array}{c} \nearrow T_a E^1 \longrightarrow T_b E^4 \searrow \\ \longrightarrow T_m E^2 \longrightarrow T_n E^5 \longrightarrow T_f E \\ \searrow T_r E^3 \longrightarrow T_s E^6 \nearrow \end{array}$$

Surely, if the words of **b, n, s** agree that there was an explosion this morning, however statements "E^4," "E^5," "E^6," may differ from each other in detail, they all have statement "E" as their core, which is what **f** is reporting according to this schema. Hence, we can take our prime witness **p** and our final witness **f** as asserting the same statement. Given the convergence of **b, n,** and **s**'s testimony on "E," can they be presumed reliable in so far as they testify that E and is **f** a presumptively reliable source in reporting that E? The convergent testimonies of **b, n,** and **s** corroborate each other. So **f** receives corroborated testimony. Hence, we may say that the source for **f**'s word that E is the conjoint, mutually corroborative testimony of **b, n**, and **s**, a source whose reliability is higher than the reliability of either of **b, n**, or **s** alone. Hence, in virtue of receiving this convergent testimony and reporting its core, there seems good reason to regard **f**'s testimony as reliable as the testimony of this convergent source. But is this reliability high enough so that we can presume **f** reliable outright in this case? That is, would we be justified in accepting E, taking E as a premise, on the basis of **f**'s testimony under these circumstances?

Coady has an argument that in some circumstances, **f** may be in an even better epistemic position than is someone giving personal testimony. Let us modify our transmission diagram so that instead of **p** as the one prime witness **a, m**, and **r** are each prime witnesses. Let us assume that the statement "E" constitutes a common core of each of their messages and of the testimony of **b, n**, and **s**, so that we can represent the transmission of information through the following diagram:[10]

4. $\quad E \Longrightarrow \begin{array}{l} T_aE \longrightarrow T_bE \\ T_mE \longrightarrow T_nE \\ T_rE \longrightarrow T_sE \end{array} \Longrightarrow T_fE$

Suppose that the state of affairs E is unusual, but that **a, m, r** are experienced in things of this sort, as are **b, n, s**, and **f**. As Coady puts it, **a, m, r** "have a certain diffidence in their judgments. They are confident enough to pass the message on and to do so without qualification" (1992, p. 213). What about **f**? "He is somewhat doubtful when he hears from [**b**], impressed when he hears from [**n**], and quite convinced when he hears from [**s**]" (1992, p. 213). He is receiving testimony from three independent chains that he believes are independent, where "We may even suppose that he has good reason to believe so" (1992, p. 213). Coady concludes, "My point here is only that where such transmission patterns exist the later hearsay testifier may be in as good if not better position than even an original witness" (1992, p. 213).[11]

E's being unusual mitigates against the trust **a, m**, and **r** have in their perceptual mechanisms in this case, and thus also mitigates against the presumption for the reliability of their word as personal testimony. It seems **b, n**, and **s** should share their diffidence. But their testimony corroborates each other and this is the testimony **f** receives and transmits.

Hence, if one were willing to regard **a**, **n**, and **r**'s personal testimony as presumptively reliable, even with some diffidence, it seems that one should regard **f**'s testimony as presumptively reliable, dispensing with the diffidence. Hence, should our context indicate **f**'s epistemic position, we quite possibly may regard **f** as a presumptively reliable source in this case and his assertion that E acceptable.

There are even further possibilities for corroboration. Consider just the topmost chain in (4), viz

$$4'. \quad E \implies T_aE \longrightarrow T_bE \longrightarrow T_fE$$

Surely, it is possible that **a**'s testimony could be received by several persons, each of whom could testify to others. But each of these latter could receive testimony from at least two of the persons who received **a**'s testimony.

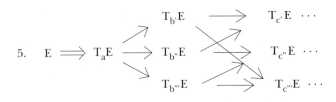

Thus, each of **c'**, **c''**, **c'''** is receiving corroborated testimony. Furthermore, both **c'** and **c'''** share a source, that is, **b'**, which has testified that E. Likewise, **c'** and **c''** share a source, **b''**, and **c''** and **c'''** share a source, that is, **b'''**. Hence, **c'** and **c'''** can "compare notes" over what **b'** has testified to. If **b'**'s testimony has been transmitted twice, is it consistent between these transmissions? Such possibilities of corroboration and cross checking can occur again as the chain proceeds. (Compare Coady 1992, pp. 214–15.) But if we could see how **f**'s testimony at the last stage of a convergent transmission chain could be accorded the presumptive reliability of personal testimony, certainly the testimony of one at the final stage of a ramified convergent chain may be accorded this presumptive reliability also.

10.7 EXPERT TESTIMONY AND ITS PRESUMPTION

As Rescher points out, in debate and in disputation more generally there is a presumption for expert testimony. "The attest of suitable 'authorities'" or "suitably qualified experts . . . is . . . generally conceded as entitled to a presumption of truth" (1977a, pp. 36, 37). The issue with expert testimony, then, is not whether there is a presumption in its favor but how it can be rightly identified. Under what circumstances is an authority suitable or an expert suitably qualified? What circumstances nevertheless require this presumption to be set aside? Clearly, not every word of a recognized expert counts as expert testimony. Indeed, as would be widely conceded, according a presumption to the word of an authority speaking outside his or her field of expertise constitutes a fallacious appeal to authority.

To count as expert testimony, someone's statement must be within an authority-conferring field and the person must be certified as an expert in that field. Once these two conditions are satisfied, there is a presumption for the person's statement, unless there is additional evidence that under the current circumstances, the statement is not credible. Each of these conditions requires development.

What is an authority-conferring field and how can such a field be recognized? As Coady points out, there seem to be two distinct types of such fields (1992, pp. 278–79). One comprises the informal fields of expertise. Included first are the practical fields. Artisans and practitioners of skilled trades are all experts in informal fields, as are those trained in making special evaluations, appraisers of real property or of objects of value. More informal yet, those with a special acquaintance with some area or individual, such as a wife with intimate knowledge of her husband, count as experts in an informal field. By contrast, a formal field of expertise consists of some organized branch of knowledge, typically a field of science. We say typically, because representatives of formal fields not ordinarily counted as sciences may nonetheless have expert status because of their standing in their respective fields. Is a book or movie obscene, lacking any redeeming social value? Could not a literary critic be called as an expert witness in this case? (Compare Coady 1992, p. 292.)

How does one properly recognize an authority-conferring field? It is commonly conceded that the informal fields are areas of expertise. Hence, it is common knowledge that these are authority-conferring fields. Now common knowledge is another source of testimony, whose presumption we discuss in the next section. Hence, *if* there is a presumption for common knowledge, then there is a presumption that commonly identified informal fields of expertise are indeed authority-conferring fields. Why should a formal field be regarded as a branch of science? Again, this can be a matter of the testimony of common knowledge. Is it not common knowledge that certain fields – physics, chemistry, biology – are fields of science? Are they not commonly identified as such and taught as sciences by university bodies? In addition, is there not also a commonly recognized informal field of "academics," including within its purview the divisions of knowledge, and would not it also be a matter of common knowledge that the faculty of university bodies are experts in this informal field? So if a university regards a field as a science, its faculty *ipso facto* assert as experts in the informal field of academics that it is a science. Surely recognizing this attestation is sufficient to recognize a field as a science should recognized academics be presumptively reliable in speaking on the divisions of academics. By contrast, that universities and other such bodies refuse to recognize some field as a branch of science but, rather, regard it as bogus shifts the burden of proof to those who would claim otherwise. These considerations also show why fields such as literary criticism might nonetheless count as formal authority-conferring fields, at least under some circumstances. Such fields are commonly regarded as fields of specialized knowledge. If they are taught in colleges and universities as such, then we have faculty, that is, academically expert, testimony that these are specialized and to some degree authority-conferring fields.

Whether we are dealing with a formal or informal authority-conferring field, certification would seem to be a matter of whether representatives of that field have admitted the person into the company of experts in that field or certified that he or she has acquired a level of competence within it. That is, the person has been properly certified through some institutional process. How does one recognize that a person has been properly certified? That is, when is there a presumption for one's belief that a person has been certified in some authority-conferring field? Clearly, there are several possibilities here. One could have examined a certificate. This is a case of understanding some document – a diploma or license – an instance of institutional perception. By contrast, one may receive testimony that such a certificate exists. To establish his credentials, the expert may attest that he has been certified by some institution or board which by common knowledge is recognized competent to certify in this area. Here we have the proponent's personal testimony concerning his institutional perception. Hence, there is a presumption of trust that the expert is speaking truly of what he believes through institutional perception, for which there is a presumption.

Instead of receiving testimony from the proponent himself, that he is certified, the challenger may receive this testimony from someone else. But here the situation is the same. We have personal testimony to institutional perception. The witness has either examined some document, observed some ceremony, or received through some chain the testimony of a witness who had. If this testimony has come through a chain where there is no reason to question its reliability, there again will be a presumption for it. By contrast, one may have seen the expert engaging in activity presupposing his certification or may have evidence allowing one to presume that the expert engages in such activity or holds a position for which certification is prerequisite. If one recognizes that the expert is employed in some academic or scientific institution, or engages in an occupation requiring licensing on the basis of certification, one can presume certification. Testimony also that can be presumed reliable, from the expert or a third party, that the expert holds such a position creates a presumption that the expert has been properly certified.

How would one recognize that what an expert has said on a given occasion pertains to a given field? This ordinarily would be a matter of understanding language, including the context of utterance, again a matter of institutional perception. Hence, as long as there is a presumption for common knowledge, it is straightforward to characterize the circumstances under which an expert's word constitutes expert testimony and how one can have a presumptively reliable belief that the word is testimony, and thus that there is a presumption for that testimony.

Under what circumstances will this presumption be undercut? Clearly, this might happen should there be a clash of testimony. If two experts give conflicting testimony, we obviously cannot accept both. Unless we have some reason to prefer one over the other, we should accept neither. This does not mean that the clash cannot be explained on grounds relevant to restoring presumption for one of the sides. Suppose two experts were called to testify whether using a certain procedure was correct and acceptable. The issue is central to determining whether the defendant in a civil lawsuit is liable for damages. One expert testifies that the procedure is acceptable; the other, that it is not. Now suppose the procedure is part of an overall practice. The practice is effective and efficient for achieving the end for which it was designed. The expert who testified that the procedure was acceptable is proficient in this practice. But this practice is not the only way to achieve that end. An alternative practice is equally effective and efficient, and the second expert is skilled in that practice. However, the procedure integral to the first practice has no place in the second and would be quite dangerous if carried out in that context. It would appear risky to anyone accustomed to the second practice. We can certainly understand why the experts would disagree. Their evidential situations are different. Was the defendant's use of the procedure part of the first or second type of practice? If that point could be established, the presumption for the testimony of one of the experts would be restored.

In this example, experts have come to an honest disagreement of opinion. There are less than honest factors which could lead experts to render conflicting opinions. Two experts may give conflicting testimony because each has a vested interest in the outcome of a case, vested interests in opposition. One expert is a witness for the defense, the other for the prosecution. Both are being paid and paid well for their testimony. Both could be called again to testify with promise of similar monetary reward. Both have a vested interest in giving testimony which bolsters their side of the case. Of course, conflict in testimony is not the only way in which suspicion of vested interest may arise. If we have distinct evidence that the expert giving testimony is employed by some person or firm which has a stake in people's accepting some claim, we have evidence that the expert has a vested interest, even if no other expert attempts to contradict him. In such situations, the presumption for expert testimony is compromised, if not completely undercut. Any evidence in fact that the person might be speaking disingenuously in this situation should also be distinctly compromising. As Coady puts it, "Inconsistency, overconfidence, vagueness, vested interest, prejudice, previous history of deceit or incompetence, clashing testimony, all have to be taken into account" (1992, p. 297).[12]

Notice that all of these factors are evidential. They can be recognized or come to be recognized in a given situation. It seems that such factors might frequently influence the word of experts. Can one maintain that in the absence of recognizing such factors in a given situation, we should still accord presumption to expert testimony? Let us again review our understanding of testimony from the challenger's point of view. If a proponent puts forward a statement that p and the challenger recognizes both that the proponent is vouching for p and that the proponent has the requisite competence, authority, or credentials to state truly that p, then the statement that p constitutes testimony from the challenger's perspective. But to talk of expert testimony is to say that the statement that p pertains to an area of recognized scientific or other expertise in which the proponent has recognized credentials. Our argument that a presumption for expert testimony should be the default position parallels our argument for why there should be a presumption for personal testimony. The challenger perceives that the proponent has not only asserted that p but is vouching for p. As this involves understanding a communicative utterance, we have institutional perception here, which is presumptively reliable. How does the challenger come to recognize that the proponent has the competence to assert that p? As we have seen, this is a matter of recognizing that there is a field, that the expert is certified in that field, and that he is speaking in that field, all matters ordinarily of common knowledge, institutional perception, or personal testimony, for which there is a presumption of reliability. Because the expert is vouching for p and there is a presumption of trust that he is speaking sincerely, this amounts to a presumption that he has come to accept that p through reliable means. Hence, as with personal testimony, given this presumed reliability and the presumed reliability of the challenger's perception that the proponent has vouched that p and that the proponent is a suitable expert, there is a presumption for her belief that p arrived at through expert testimony.

Cederblom and Paulsen raise a critical question about expert testimony which could constitute an objection to our argument. They ask, "If a supposed expert states a number of views on an issue, how can we tell which of these are based on expertise and which are based on personal political or moral preferences?" (1988, p. 140). This raises the issue of whether there is a presumption of trust when an expert speaks in his or her field. When asked to testify concerning a certain issue, can we presume that the expert is sincerely rendering his or her opinion based on or arrived at through the standard or accredited procedures of inquiry within that field? Is the possibility that the expert could be substituting personal opinion for expert opinion or that the expert's moral or political views could have colored his or her inquiry, carried out within the procedures of the field, such a significantly realistic possibility that we should in general withdraw a presumption of trust from experts when they render opinions in their fields? Such a claim clearly incurs a very significant burden of proof, one which Cederblom and Paulsen have not addressed. Clearly, certain issues calling for expert testimony lie within controversial areas where experts themselves may have ideologically influenced positions. But clearly also which areas these are will be a matter of common knowledge. Thus, it will be part of our challenger's evidential situation in receiving an expert's testimony that the testimony is within some controversial area. That in itself could be a reason to challenge the testimonial claim, to regard the presumption of trust as compromised if not undercut in this case. But notice that this is based on specific evidence about this situation, not on a recognition of the general bias or lack of trustworthiness of experts. Barring establishing that claim, the presumption of trust still stands.

As we have admitted, our argument presupposes that the testimony of common knowledge is presumptively reliable. We turn to the issue of common knowledge directly in the next section.

10.8 THE ISSUE OF COMMON KNOWLEDGE

In what sense is common knowledge a source of belief, like an individual person who gives us his word? Our examples in Section 10.7,

1. Physics, chemistry, biology are natural sciences.
2. Colleges and universities by awarding degrees certify that persons have some level of competence or expertise in a given area.

seem straightforward instances of common knowledge, at least for many persons in contemporary Western culture. Here are some further examples:

3. George W. Bush was inaugurated President of the United States in January 2001.
4. George Washington was the first president of the United States.
5. Cigarette smoking causes lung cancer.
6. Stealing is *prima facie* wrong.
7. There are many trees in Canada.[13]

How might one come to believe these statements? Many will claim to have witnessed President Bush's inauguration, whether they were physically present or saw it on television. Many others may come to believe (3) through news reports or ultimately through reading some historical account. So a variety of sources – perception, personal testimony, last member of a testimonial chain – may be responsible for people's holding this belief. But no matter what the source, it is a commonly held belief, at least of this writing. That George Washington was the first president is something all Americans learn in school, if not before. What does this mean but that someone whom we then trusted told us this was the case – last member of a testimonial chain – and we have remembered what we were told although we have forgotten the particular telling. But this is true not just of us individually but of people generally who have been brought up in American schools.

Some may remember news reports of the U.S. Surgeon General's findings on cigarette smoking and lung cancer – a report of expert testimony. Others may have heard reports of these reports or similar findings. Others may simply have been told this by someone in whom they reposed some trust. In individual cases, the particular source may very well be forgotten. But virtually everyone – at least in the United States and Canada – has heard statement (5). If our considerations in the last chapter are cogent, our moral intuition generates the belief that stealing is *prima facie* wrong at some point – we expect rather early – in our moral development. But coming to this realization concerning stealing is part of our common moral development, even if we have no philosophical view on how we came to have this belief.

Why should the claim that there are many trees in Canada be a matter of common knowledge? I expect that most of us believe through perception that there are many trees in our "immediate" vicinity. But we have also seen maps of Canada and have learned how to interpret them – this being a matter of acquiring institutional perception. Putting these two pieces of information together, we readily form the belief that there are many trees in Canada, or will form that belief if the question ever arises. We probably first came to believe that physics, chemistry, biology were natural sciences through being taught such subject matter as science or seeing these subjects regarded as natural sciences by those familiar with academic distinctions, thus receiving the word of some trusted authority figure. That college degrees signify that a person has passed a certain course of study and thus should have some level of competence is part of the meaning of "college degree." We come to believe such statements as we come to learn the language from authorities we trust. We may very well have forgotten what authorities transmitted this knowledge to us. But just about everybody else – at least those with a high school education – is in the same position and shares these beliefs with us.

This survey indicates that common knowledge is not some additional interpersonal source besides personal testimony, testimony through some chain, expert opinion, or the word of trusted authorities. Common knowledge has come to us through these various sources – different sources for different people. Standardly, we have forgotten the particular source, so that we cannot discuss the presumptive reliability of the particular source in this particular instance. However, the belief has been transmitted not just to us but to persons in our culture generally. As Govier characterizes it, "If, in a particular culture, P is accepted by virtually everybody, is presupposed in practical life even by those who purport to disbelieve it and who construct theories of science and philosophy, then P is a common sense belief in that culture" (1981, p. 40). We have, in general, then acquired common knowledge or commonsense beliefs through taking someone else's word. That the other members of our culture share these beliefs suggests that we can speak of common knowledge as a source. Questions of the presumptive reliability of common knowledge then rest on the commonality of the belief rather than the features of a particular source or a chain of sources.

Why should there be a presumption for common knowledge? That there is a presumption in favor of common knowledge, indeed of any statement in accord with the normal, usual, customary state of affairs, is a basic principle of presumption in debate. If our analysis is correct, we acquire common knowledge through some presumptively acceptable source, even if we can no longer identify the source. But if I already believe some statement in this way that is generally shared by others – at least those sharing my cultural and historical context – so that I am not aware of evidence against that belief or a challenge to it, why should I not accept the belief until or unless evidence against it comes to light? If a proponent puts forward a statement expressing that belief as a basic premise in an argument, why should I require argumentation for that premise before accepting it? As Govier points out, this would be "a violation of the social conditions of argument" (1985, p. 82). It also would seem to betray either a neurotic or a Cartesian doubt. The former needs therapy. The latter drives the classical foundationalism which we already argued in Chapter 1 cannot provide a proper account of premise acceptability.

We may offer another argument for why there should be a presumption for common knowledge or commonsense beliefs.[14] According to a common maxim for argumentation, we seek to defend the less certain on the basis of the more certain. In a good argument, the premises should have greater prior probability or plausibility than the conclusion. At least, the premises should not be less certain than the conclusion. But, in an intuitive sense of certainty, what could be more certain than the commonsense statements such as (1)–(7) above? To be sure, certain broadly logically true statements could be regarded as more certain. But from such premises alone, we could not argue to a substantive conclusion. If for there to be a presumption for a statement from the challenger's point of view, she should either concede it or argue against it, what premises of greater certainty or plausibility could a challenger use to argue against some commonsense proposition? If any argument against a common-sense assertion of a sort to properly transfer certainty from premises to conclusion invariably included premises which were less certain than the commonsense assertion being argued against, then all such arguments would involve the fallacy of problematic premise, failing to rebut the presumption for the commonsense assertion.

One could question this sense of certainty. Do we just *feel* more certain of commonsense beliefs than of propositions which deny them? Is there something more objective to the certainty? I believe there is. Because these beliefs are commonly held, they will in general not be subject to dialectical challenge. There will be a consensus on these beliefs, which will not be afforded to others. As Govier puts it, the fact that other philosophers and ordinary people may disagree with me over such a belief, that some may have no opinion, and that I have made mistakes over beliefs not as complex as these, "gives me some inductive reason to think that I may be wrong about this particular proposition. No such basis for doubt will apply to the common sense propositions which I believe" (1981, p. 43). As lack of consensus is an objective reason to feel less confident of a belief, presence of consensus is an objective reason to feel more.

10.9 PRESUMPTION FOR THE WORD OF THE NEWS MEDIA?

The issue of whether there is a presumption for the word of the news media seems settled by our discussion of the circumstances under which there is a presumption for testimony that has reached us through a chain of reporters. Although the reporter for the news service may not have personally witnessed the event he or she is describing, that reporter will be the last link in a chain going back to those who gave personal testimony. Moreover, the news service has a reputation to protect. Hence, we may presume that the reporter has not simply passively received and passed along the word of the next to the last reporter in the chain, but has checked the story, unless this has already been done by a recognized reliable reporter earlier in the chain. Hence, the news service report either goes back to the report of some presumptively reliable witness or to a report that has come through several convergent, mutually corroborating chains of testimony. Thus, if the news service is presumptively respectable, there is a presumption for this report from the news service.

However, the word of the news media does not consist simply of reports which have come through presumptively reliable reporters or presumptively corroborative chains of testimony. Many statements of the news media will not be reports, that is, descriptions, at all but interpretations or evaluations. These statements may express the point of view of the news service but may not be the word of any authoritative source or a reflection of common sentiment. Indeed, the news organization may be seeking to mold popular opinion rather than to express statements commonly agreed to. Even if statements disseminated are the word of an expert, they may reflect that person's ideological commitments or be outside the expert's field. Thus, the word of the media is a mixture of description, interpretation, and evaluation. There may very well be a presumption in favor of the descriptions, but not for the interpretations or evaluations.

Furthermore, news media convey many statements through suggestion as opposed to explicit assertion. This is a tool of slanting. A news service may make a number of factually accurate reports, but they may be selected so as to put the subject being described in a certain light, either bad or good, to communicate a certain attitude toward that subject and to foster that attitude in others. Thus, the cumulative effect of these reports is to suggest an evaluation, one for which there need not be a presumption. In addition, interpretations such as statements of causal connections, intentions, attitudes may be suggested by the juxtaposition of factual statements, and evaluations may be consequent upon these suggestions. Again, there may be no presumption for these suggested assertions as there are presumptions for the factual descriptions themselves. Finally, slanting may involve the use of emotive words, the resulting statements conveying distinct evaluations.[15] The moral is that in approaching the word of the news media, one must be careful to recognize what that word is. Insofar as that word is a simple descriptive report, there is a presumption for it as long as there is a presumption for the reliability of the news organization. But insofar as that word expresses an interpretation or evaluation, or intimates some suggested message, there need not be a presumption for it.

10.10 PRESUMPTION FOR INSTITUTIONAL TESTIMONY

Recall that institutional testimony concerns such information as we receive from maps, signs, timetables, measuring devices, scientific instruments. A map "tells" me that the train station is located at a point that I may reach by walking three blocks along one street and then two blocks to the left. The posted timetable at the station indicates that there is a train at 3:15. My watch tells me that it is 2:55. A sign with an arrow indicates the direction to the platform. Obviously, we accept such information and regard it as acceptable. No one would think me behaving in any way irrationally, should I want to get a train to a certain destination, if I followed the directions of the map, consulted the timetable, checked my watch, and then proceeded – but did not rush, after all I have twenty minutes – to the proper platform. Here I have used these pieces of information as guides for my action, even if I have not consciously used them as basic premises in reasoning about what I ought to do.

Do we have testimony here? Is institutional testimony genuine testimony? For a statement p to constitute testimony from the point of view of a challenger, she must be aware of evidence that the proponent of the statement vouches for p, and that the proponent has the requisite credentials to state truly that p. Although maps, timetables, signs, scientific instruments of various sorts obviously do not actually assert statements, by learning how to read them, I learn how I may read off statements from them. But clearly, once I formulate that statement to myself, I recognize that the source in an extended sense vouches for it. Those who have issued the map or timetable are vouching for the statements read off from them by those who know how to read them. Furthermore, although the particular artifact does not literally have competence or credentials, those who issued it have the requisite authority or competence to construct such an artifact and they have certified its proper construction. This in effect gives the artifact the proper credentials and makes what is read off from it genuine testimony. By the fact that I have bought the map in a reputable store, that it may be marked "Official Street Map of Amsterdam," that the timetable has been posted in a very public location, I have a sign that the competence or authority of the designers of these artifacts have been transferred to the artifacts themselves.

Is the trust commonly placed in institutional testimony well placed? The answer should be obvious. We come to believe that p by reading off the statement that p from some artifact. This is a matter first of institutional perception for which there is a presumption. By virtue of institutional perception, we also recognize both the instrument's vouching for p and marks of the instrument's certification. But these are marks that the instrument was constructed or issued by those with the authority and competence to make or issue such instruments, and there is a presumption that these marks are reliable. This is just a particular application of the general presumption for the *status quo*. Instruments bearing a certain company's trademark together possibly with other marks of certification ordinarily have been made by that company (as long as one buys the artifact in a reputable store). Signs posted publicly have ordinarily been placed there by those authorized to do so. But companies ordinarily have competence to produce the instruments they produce and public officials with the authority to place signs ordinarily have the competence and the responsibility to see that the signs are accurate. Hence, the construction of the artifact involves competence which has been transferred to the artifact to give competent readings. As we may presume the construction reliable, so we may presume the readings reliable. The presumption for institutional testimony, then, is a matter of the presumption for the reliability of institutional perception and the *status quo* presumption of competence for the sources that have produced the instruments of institutional testimony.

PART III

PRACTICE AND PERSPECTIVE

11

An Outline of the Practice of Epistemic Casuistry

Some premises are straightforwardly acceptable as basic premises without argument either presenting evidence for the premises or a case for their being justified in this instance. For example, given how a challenger is appeared to perceptually, she may be perfectly justified in her immediate acceptance of a premise expressing a perceptually generated descriptive belief. However, suppose one is faced with a "hard" case. One may feel constrained to justify to oneself that a statement is acceptable as a basic premise. Alternatively, one may need to show to someone else why a statement is acceptable – or not acceptable – as a basic premise under prevailing conditions. Here the request is to justify the *judgment* that a particular statement is or is not acceptable as a basic premise. Apart from the dialectical requirement of showing *someone* that a statement is acceptable, the epistemological issue remains of why one is justified in accepting a particular premise in a certain situation.

At the risk of raising hackles in some, we call making such a determination an exercise in epistemic casuistry. There is no need for hackles to be raised, given the way we use the word. For "casuistry" as we understand it means no more than what we have indicated – making determinations in particular cases. In its ordinary, moral context, casuistry deals with such questions as whether a particular act is right or wrong, or a particular state of affairs good or bad. The issue here is not some philosophical theory of what makes right acts right or what is the nature of intrinsic goodness. The question is whether one may truly or justifiably predicate "right" or "good" in a particular case. There would seem to be something distinctly unsatisfactory about someone's being able to discourse on theories of what makes right acts right or on theories of goodness and yet be unable to indicate whether a particular act was right or state of affairs good.

Questions about particular cases likewise arise when we turn from ethics to epistemology. Is a person S justified in believing that p? For example, is a particular description acceptable as a basic premise for a challenger at her point in a dialectical situation? There would again seem to be something extremely unsatisfactory in someone's being conversant about various theories of epistemic justification or general principles of premise acceptability and yet unable to answer such questions. It should be just as unsatisfactory as someone's being knowledgeable about theories of logical truth yet being at a total loss to determine whether a particular statement is a truth-functional tautology. No matter what theory of premise acceptability one may put forward, the situation will be unsatisfactory if one cannot also say when and why a particular premise is acceptable. Our aim in this chapter is to address this practical question.

As we indicated in Chapter 2, determining presumption involves three questions:

1. What type of statement is it?
2. What source vouches for it?
3. Does this voucher create a presumption for the statement?

In Chapter 5, we gave an account of the various types of statements and sources which may vouch for them. In Chapters 6 through 10, we explored whether certain sources were presumptively reliable. As we have pointed out, being presumptively reliable is a global or overall feature or property of a source. In a given situation, the presumption may be undercut. As we have seen in Chapter 3, two factors affect whether a presumption is undercut in a given situation. One concerns the epistemic stance of the source vouching for the premise. Given what I know of the proponent, his report constitutes personal testimony. But is there evidence that the proponent may be subject to an illusion in this case? The second factor concerns the cost of mistakenly accepting the statement versus the cost of gaining further evidence, the pragmatic dimension of premise acceptability. Question (3) then divides into three subquestions:

3a. Is the source presumptively reliable?
3b. Is the source epistemically compromised in this situation?
3c. Is the expected cost of mistakenly accepting the statement in this situation greater than the expected cost of procuring further evidence?

Recall that when we are discussing acceptability, we are assessing whether or not a statement is acceptable from the challenger's perspective. We view the challenger definitely not as a brain in a vat, but as a person not only physically embodied but embodied in a dialectical situation. Accepting premises ordinarily is not done in detachment from one's immediate surroundings but, rather, with awareness of those surroundings and taking direction from that awareness, even if such direction is not altogether consciously acknowledged. "Background knowledge" constitutes a significant factor in accepting premises. So if I hear a radio news report that a plane has crashed in Siberia and I form the belief that such a crash has indeed occurred, I am also aware – perhaps not altogether consciously – that the source of my belief about the plane crash is the radio news source. I frequently know, in the sense of being personally acquainted, the sources of my beliefs. We would expect this to be standardly the case for personal belief-generating mechanisms. How did we come to believe that there is a tree in full leaf outside our office window? We see it! That is, we recognize the source of our belief in our sense-perception.

We might expect frequently to know the source of our belief when we take the word of others. We "know" who that other is, even if we have not consciously formulated that knowledge to ourselves. Where these beliefs constitute the basic premises of an argument, we may very well know in many cases who the proponent of that argument is. Furthermore, we may very well "know" something of the proponent's evidential stance *vis-a-vis* the basic premises of that argument.

PROPONENT:	The keys are not lost.
CHALLENGER:	Why do you say that?
PROPONENT:	They are on the kitchen table.

If the challenger has every reason to believe that the proponent has just or very recently come from the kitchen, she "knows" that the proponent's premise is a matter of personal testimony, even if she has not consciously reflected on that question. In other cases, however, it may be very unclear, from the challenger's perspective, whether the proponent is in any position to vouch competently for a given premise.

A challenger also may be aware of signs of unreliability on the proponent's part, if the proponent displays such signs. Does he appear intoxicated? Does he seem to be hallucinating? Does he have a history of dissembling? Again, the proponent may display no such signs, and this may be evident to the challenger, even if she has not consciously formulated any such belief to herself. Finally, the challenger may very well "know" the expected cost of mistakenly accepting a certain premise, at least that the cost may be significant in a given case.

Just because an argument has been put forward by a proponent does not mean that the only way the challenger can accept the proponent's basic premises is through taking the proponent's word. The challenger may already accept the proponent's basic claims because she has already come to believe these premises through her own personal belief-generating mechanisms or by taking the word of some third party. Presenting the premise, then, does not function to increase the proponent's stock of beliefs or statements that she accepts. Rather, it may function to increase the salience of a belief the challenger already has. In determining whether the premise is acceptable from the challenger's point of view, it is quite appropriate then to ask which of her belief-generating mechanisms is the source of this belief for her. Hence, in practicing epistemic casuistry, much information about the challenger's beliefs about the proponent as a source and about possible other third-party witnesses as sources, about the challenger's own belief-generating mechanisms as sources, about the overall evidential stance of these sources, and about the situation is relevant. It is proper for the epistemic casuist to take all this information into account. To simplify our discussion, let us assume that when a challenger is asked to accept a basic premise on someone else's word, that person is the proponent.

As we indicated earlier, our casuistical procedure is determined by three principal questions. These should be addressed in order. Thus, our first question in determining premise acceptability is to ask what type of statement it is. The answer determines the rest of the course of inquiry into acceptability, for, as we have seen, different personal belief-generating mechanisms are associated with different types of statements. Even if we are being asked to accept the statement on the word of the proponent, asking what type of statement is involved is the appropriate first question. As our discussion in Chapter 10 shows, recognizing when the word of another is a form of testimony involves judgment that the proponent has the requisite competence, authority, or credentials to state truly the claim he is putting forward. But that surely in part is a matter of the proponent's belief-generating mechanisms which have been involved in his coming to hold this statement and what those are may be determined by what type of statement is involved. Hence, our inquiry in the rest of this chapter falls into four parts, one for each basic type of statement.

11.1 WHEN IS THERE A PRESUMPTION FOR A BASIC PREMISE WHICH IS LOGICALLY DETERMINATE?

Clearly, recognizing that a logically determinate statement is false closes the question of whether there is a presumption for it. As we saw in Chapter 6, the one personal mechanism that generates beliefs expressed by necessarily true statements is *a priori* intuition. But if *a priori* intuition vouches for a statement, as we have seen, one comes to believe both that the statement is true and necessarily true upon understanding the statement. In this way one "sees" ordinarily with distinct conviction that the statement is true. But under these circumstances, there is a presumption for the statement. Indeed, when one sees that the statement *is* necessarily true, the presumption for it cannot be defeated.

Cast dialectically, should a basic premise in an argument the proponent is putting forward be a necessarily true statement and the challenger recognize it as such, her *a priori* intuition is vouching for the statement, a source which is presumptively reliable. Unless the challenger is also aware of some condition that would defeat the presumption for *a priori* intuition, the premise is acceptable from her point of view. What defeating conditions might come to light? As we have seen, there are two types – epistemic and pragmatic. Now, it is imaginable that one's *a priori* intuition could be overly generous in attributing necessity – one has illusions that certain non-necessary propositions are necessarily true.[1] Suppose that for a set of propositions, all substitution instances of some particular form, some of which were necessarily true and others not, my *a priori* intuition vouched indiscriminately for their necessity. Should I be aware of this malady in the functioning of my *a priori* intuition, its voucher would no longer create a presumption for its judgments of necessary truth – at least for propositions within this set. But the point is that, setting aside pragmatic considerations for the moment, unless the challenger is aware of such improper functioning, the presumption for the reliability of her faculty of *a priori* intuition remains as does the presumption for the statements for which it vouches.

Could *a priori* intuition's vouching for a claim fail on pragmatic grounds, assuming that the presumption for it is not undercut on epistemic grounds? Here the expected cost of accepting the claim if mistaken is higher than the expected cost of gaining further evidence. We do not believe that this can happen for this belief-generating mechanism because through *a priori* intuition I "see" not only that a statement is true but necessarily true. Should I see the necessary truth of a proposition, what need is there of further corroboration or evidence? Hence, the pragmatic issue does not arise. So what may an epistemic casuist say? If a logically determinate statement is vouched for by a challenger's *a priori* intuition, and the challenger is not aware of any condition undercutting the presumption of the reliability of the mechanism in this case, there is a presumption for the statement for the challenger at this point and it is acceptable from her point of view.

A challenger, however, may come to believe a necessary statement not because she apprehends its necessary truth but because she takes the word of someone else. If this is the source that vouches for her belief, will there be a presumption for it? This raises the issue of expert testimony (which may possibly have come through a testimonial chain). If there is to be a presumption for this statement on the basis of this voucher, the testimony must go back to someone whose powers of reason – both *a priori* intuition and deduction – have enabled him to see the necessity of the statement for which he is vouching.

I believe it is highly unlikely that a challenger would ever accept a semantic or conceptual truth simply on the word of some "expert." Suppose the proponent put forward such a statement, where the challenger did not see its necessity. No matter who the proponent was, I believe the challenger would ask for an explanation of the necessity. Typically, this would be an explanation that a word had a certain meaning. Once this was recognized, the necessity of the statement would be apparent immediately. The challenger would accept it as vouched for by *her a priori* intuition. Hence, we may set aside the issue of expert testimony for semantic or conceptual statements. This leaves formal, mathematical, and metaphysical necessarily true statements to consider.

Let us suppose the challenger receives such a statement from the alleged expert directly. Presumption requires first that she must apprehend that the statement falls within the subject matter of an authority-conferring field. Could the statement then be a metaphysical statement? We can say that certain professors of philosophy are authorities in metaphysics. But this does not mean that such authorities are able to indicate authoritatively that certain metaphysical claims are true and others false. Rather, they are able competently to present arguments for or against metaphysical claims – their own arguments or arguments of historical importance – and to indicate the strengths and weaknesses of such arguments. But then should we accept some metaphysical claim after consulting an expert, we accept it not on the basis of that person's *voucher* for that claim but of his *argument* for it. The claim is no longer a basic claim and the issue of basic premise acceptability is transferred to the basic premises of that argument.

Hence, the issue of accepting a necessary statement on the basis of an expert's vouching for it arises just for the statements of formal logic or mathematics, both formal authority-conferring fields. So if the challenger recognizes the expert's status, there is a presumption for his claim, absent defeating or undercutting circumstances, such as dissenting opinion from another expert. Where the challenger does not see the necessity of the expert's claim, the pragmatic issue of the cost of mistakenly accepting that claim and mistakenly accepting what that claim is being used to support, whether some intermediate conclusion or the final conclusion of the argument, may arise. Should the expert's opinion support a conclusion whose mistaken acceptance involves a high expected cost versus the expected cost of securing further evidence, a converging voucher from another expert may be required for proper acceptance.

Suppose the challenger receives expert testimony not directly but through a chain? This chain might involve a media report of what the expert has said, for example that a famous open mathematical problem had been finally solved. Would there be a presumption for that mathematical claim under those circumstances from one's perspective? As we pointed out in Section 10.6, a presumption for the statement from the challenger's point of view depends on her being aware of various facts concerning the transmission chain. Does she have evidence or may she presume that each member of the transmission chain reported the result reliably and that the chain was initiated by an expert? If the intermediate transmitters were the science writers for a reputable news organization, we might expect this presumption to hold. If there were convergent testimony that an expert had testified to a certain claim or if convergent chains went back to the convergent testimony of several experts, then we would expect a presumption here also.

11.2 UNDER WHAT CONDITIONS IS THERE A PRESUMPTION FOR A BASIC PREMISE WHICH IS A DESCRIPTION?

As we saw in Section 7.1, in the case of descriptions the question "What type of statement is it?" can be followed by a subquestion "What type of description is it?" We may distinguish reports from generalizations and within reports, we may distinguish reports of individual events or conditions – individual reports – from summary reports. Within generalizations, we may distinguish those which are projective – making an extensional statement about an entire class on the basis of a sample – from those which are nonprojective – making a statement just about some observed set of objects. As we shall see, determining whether there is a presumption for a summary report involves the same issues as determining whether there is a presumption for a nonprojective generalization. We shall consider these two types of descriptions together. First, however, we shall consider individual reports.

Individual Reports

Let us assume that the proponent has put forward an argument with an individual report as a basic premise. As with logically determinate statements, the challenger may not need to base her acceptance of this premise on the proponent's voucher. One of her personal belief-generating mechanisms may vouch for it or perhaps she recognizes – this is part of her evidential situation – that someone besides the proponent of the argument vouches for that individual report, someone whose word in this case merits acceptance. There are thus four sources that may vouch for an individual report – perception, introspection, memory, and the word of others. Let us consider each of these sources in turn and see what must be ascertained to determine in a given case whether the source's vouching for an individual report creates a presumption for it.

Perception. Suppose that the challenger's own perception vouches for a basic premise presenting an individual report. As we saw in Section 7.2, physical perception and personal perception are presumptively reliable, as is institutional perception provided that there is a presumption that the challenger has learned the constitutive rules in terms of which she has acquired the ability to make such perceptions. Let us assume that we are dealing either with physical or personal perception, or with a case of institutional perception where the challenger is aware of no evidence that she has not learned the constitutive rules properly. Then the question of whether there is a presumption for this premise from the challenger's point of view concerns first whether the challenger is aware of any evidence undercutting the presumptive reliability of her perception in this case. Is the challenger aware of evidence that her perceptual belief-generating mechanism is not functioning properly or that the environment in which this perception is occurring is anomalous? If either question receives a positive answer, then unless the evidence is slight the challenger's perceptual mechanism has been compromised in this situation and its vouching for the individual report does not create a presumption for it.

The question of environmental problems arises in a special way for instances of institutional perception involving institutional testimony. In Section 10.10 we concluded that whether institutional testimony could be presumed reliable in a given case was contingent upon whether one's institutional perception by which one read the testimony was presumptively reliable and whether there was a presumption that the instrument from which this testimony was read off had been constructed competently. Evidence undercutting the presumption of competence is evidence that the perceptual environment is anomalous. The instrument is part of my perceptual environment. Indeed, it is part of the medium through which I am making certain institutional perceptions. Evidence then that the instrument is not functioning properly is evidence that my perceptual environment is distorted. Notice then that the issue of institutional testimony as a source vouching for a basic premise can be subsumed under the issue of institutional perception.

It is hard to see how the perceptual mechanism could be oriented to some goal other than seeking the truth. So if there is no evidence of perceptual malfunction or environmental anomaly, the perceptual mechanism in this case is not epistemically compromised.

Finally, we come to the pragmatic question of estimated cost. The question is whether the estimated cost of accepting the individual report, should it be false, is greater than the estimated cost of securing a voucher from some further source. That the individual report to be accepted has been presented in the context of an argument is significant. There will be some final conclusion of that argument. Should the argument otherwise properly support that conclusion, and indeed any intermediate conclusions along the way, the estimated cost of accepting the premise if mistaken includes the estimated cost of accepting these argumentative consequences, should they be mistaken. In many cases, we expect that the estimated cost of such mistaken acceptances versus the estimated cost of acquiring further evidence may be intuitively evident. If so, and the estimated cost of mistaken acceptance is less than the estimated cost of gathering further evidence, and it is evident that the challenger's perceptual mechanism has not been epistemically compromised, the individual report is acceptable from the challenger's perspective.

Introspection. As we indicated in Section 3.3, introspection generates beliefs first about our mental contents and mental operations. These beliefs

concern matters of internal access. Hence, we argued that introspection in generating these beliefs is not only presumptively reliable but
apparently immune to conditions under which that presumption could
be undercut. The evidence I am aware of completely certifies the truth
of my belief. In light of these considerations, can there be any question of introspection not functioning properly? Because I am aware of
the evidence directly, there is no question of a distorting environmental
medium. Again, as the belief is true in light of this evidence, what would
it mean for introspection not to be truth-oriented? Finally, again, as the
evidence, my being aware of a certain mental content or operation, completely "covers" the truth of the belief that I am currently appeared to in
a certain way or engaged in a certain mental operation, the question of
the expected cost of gaining additional evidence does not arise. So when
my introspection generates and thus vouches for such a belief, that belief
is an acceptable premise for me.

Recall that in Chapter 7 we allowed that not only beliefs such as "I am
currently having an in-the-left-leg-pain," but also "I am currently having
a pain in my left leg," where "pain in the left leg" refers to the cause
of the in-the-left-leg-pain, to count as introspective beliefs. This means
that certain introspective beliefs are defeasible, although introspection
in this employment is presumptively reliable. How could this presumption
for introspection be undercut? First, how could introspection in such a
circumstance be epistemically compromised? It is hard to imagine how
there could be a distorting medium. But one could possess evidence that
one's introspection in this employment was not functioning properly.
One may experience an in-the-left-leg-pain even if one has lost one's
left leg through amputation. One could be aware that one had a history
of psychosomatic disorders. Furthermore, one might have evidence that
one's belief-generating mechanism might be oriented to a goal other than
the truth here. One might be aware that it would be to one's advantage
to be in pain – to become an object of the attention and sympathy of
others, to be entitled to certain compensation. Given the possibility of
receiving compensatory damages, the question arises of the expected
cost of one's mistakenly accepting that the cause of one's feeling an in-
the-left-leg-pain is a condition in the left leg over the expected cost of
acquiring confirming evidence of that condition. But in the absence of
evidence that one's introspection in this employment is not functioning
properly, or that one may be imagining one is in pain for some ulterior
motive, or that the cost of one's mistakenly accepting that some condition
is causing one's pain would be greater than my obtaining corroborating

evidence, there is a presumption for one's belief and it is acceptable as a premise.

Memory. Memory, as long as what is remembered is distinct and not vague, again is a presumptively reliable belief-generating mechanism, as we discussed in Section 7.4. Should the challenger then be presented with a basic premise which reports an individual event or condition that she remembers happening or obtaining, the question of whether that premise is acceptable becomes the question of whether she is aware of any evidence that her memory has been epistemically compromised or that the expected cost of accepting what she remembers, should her memory be faulty, is less than the expected cost of gaining corroborating evidence. Recall that we remember only what we have witnessed. The question of a distorting medium may arise for the challenger's memory then if there is a question of whether the medium through which she witnessed the event or condition were distorting. Otherwise the question of environmental anomaly does not arise. If sensuous imagery triggers a memory belief, that imagery does not come to me through a medium. If I remember an event upon being asked about it, my remembering does not happen through a medium.

Epistemic evidence undercutting the presumptive reliability of the challenger's memory at a given point then consists of evidence either that her memory is not functioning properly or that her memory may on this occasion not be oriented toward the truth. Remember that the presumptive reliability of memory concerns just what is remembered distinctly and not hazily. Should the challenger be aware that her memory is vague on a given occasion, she would have evidence not that her memory was not functioning properly, but that the presumption for memory did not apply in this case. Awareness of malfunction could be awareness of defeating information – for example, personal testimony from a witness deemed reliable that the remembered event did not happen at all or otherwise than as remembered. If the challenger is aware of evidence that she wants desperately for things to be as she remembers them, she has evidence that her memory may be the product of wishful thinking and thus not oriented to the truth. But if she is aware of no such evidence, and if there is no reason to suspend presumption for pragmatic considerations, then the premise, vouched for by her memory, is acceptable.

Taking the Proponent's Word. Should the proponent put forward an individual report as a basic premise, three possibilities arise: The proponent could be giving personal testimony; he could be reporting what has come to him from some other reporter; or he could be simply asserting the report without evidential grounds. Hence, having identified the proponent as the source vouching for the statement, before we can apply any of our conclusions from Chapter 10 as to whether his word is presumptively reliable, we must determine first whether his word constitutes testimony of some sort. Should the challenger's dialectical situation then contain no marks of the proponent's word being testimony, his voucher would create no presumption for the statement from her point of view. Let us then consider in turn how the challenger would identify testimony – first personal and then received – and what factors would bear on whether the proponent's voucher would create a presumption for the statement.

PERSONAL TESTIMONY. As we indicated in Section 10.4, personal testimony concerns what one believes through one's faculties of perception, introspection, and memory. Should the proponent put forward an individual report, the challenger's first question is whether the proponent witnessed the event or condition reported. Can this be presumed? In some cases, the statement itself may bear the marks of personal testimony.

1. A bus is passing my office window.
2. I have a pain in my right leg.
3. The last time my friends were over for dinner I served chicken.[2]

In all these cases, there is a personal reference to the speaker. In other cases, the challenger's background information concerning her dialectical situation may indicate that the report is personal testimony, at least presumptively. Should a reporter at the airport say

4. The president arrived this afternoon and made a statement upon disembarking from the plane.

we may presume that the reporter is giving firsthand testimony of what she witnessed.

In other cases, information in the challenger's dialectical situation will definitely indicate that the proponent is *not* giving personal testimony.

5. Hannibal crossed the Alps.

No proponent today may assert (5) as a firsthand report. Again, in other cases, it may be unclear whether a report is personal testimony or not. Suppose proponent and challenger meet uptown, the proponent reporting that

6. There has just been an explosion at City Hall.

where City Hall is located downtown. Did the proponent actually witness the explosion or is he reporting what someone else witnessed firsthand? The challenger's background information may not settle this issue. She may simply have to ask the proponent (or find out in some other way) whether he personally witnessed the explosion before she can recognize or presume whether or not this statement is an instance of personal testimony.

Now, suppose that the challenger has identified the proponent's individual report as personal testimony. As we saw in Chapter 10, personal testimony is presumptively reliable. So the question of whether this premise is acceptable from the challenger's point of view concerns whether she is aware either of evidence epistemically compromising the source or of pragmatic considerations calling for acquiring further evidence. The pragmatic considerations would seem not to be different here from the cases of perception or memory. The expected cost of the consequences of mistakenly accepting a premise are not something affected by the fact that the premise was vouched for by some external witness rather than by perception or memory.

Evidence of two sorts pertains to whether the source is epistemically compromised. First, because personal testimony concerns what one has witnessed (or may be witnessing now), the proponent's memory, together with his perception or introspection, combine to generate the belief he puts forward. Hence, if the challenger is aware of evidence either that the proponent's perception or memory are not functioning properly or that the environment through which he perceived the event or condition he is now reporting was distorting, the challenger has evidence that the witness is epistemically compromised. Again, if the challenger has evidence that the proponent, although sincere, believing what he reports, may be subject to wishful thinking or that for some other reason his memory or perception are not oriented toward the truth, she will also have evidence that the proponent is epistemically compromised.

There are a number of particular ways in which these warranting factors can be compromised in the case of personal testimony which should be noted for purposes of epistemic casuistry. Most of the epistemically compromising factors concern perception. But memory ordinarily plays a significant role in testimony. One testifies to what one remembers having perceived rather than to what one is perceiving at the present moment. Hence, evidence that the memory may be vague or hazy rather than distinct is evidence that the witness is epistemically compromised. If the challenger's background awareness of the dialectical situation gives no indication of whether the proponent made his observations recently or some time in the past, the proponent's testimony may be epistemically compromised from her point of view.

There are several signs that the perception of a witness could be compromised. First, the challenger may be aware of an environmental circumstance which may render it highly unlikely that the witness made the observations which allegedly ground his report. For example, suppose two cars collide upon entering an intersection. Suppose the accident happens at 7:00 A.M. in mid-September. Suppose one car is traveling east and suppose an observer is standing at the intersection looking west. The question arises of whether there was anyone in the passenger seat. The observer testifies affirmatively. But at this hour of the morning at this time of year, the sun would be shining directly on the windshield of an eastward-bound car, causing significant glare for the westward-looking observer. Could the witness make this observation in these environmental circumstances? Surely, this information undercuts the presumption of reliability for the observer's personal testimony in this case.

There are two particular signs that the witness's belief-generating mechanisms were not oriented to the truth on a particular occasion. First, evidence may indicate that the witness was psychologically set to "observe" what he reported observing. His belief-generating mechanism then was oriented to confirming his preconceptions or stereotypes rather than to arriving at the truth. Second, the observer's perceivable emotional state may call into question whether his belief-generating mechanisms are oriented to the truth. Someone with an evident desire to find his watch, which has been stolen, may claim to have seen it in a pawnbroker's window. But can we be confident that in perceiving what he takes to be *his* watch in the pawnshop window, the observer's perceptual mechanism is oriented to forming true beliefs? Is wishful thinking here a distinct possibility?

Because the challenger's belief-generating mechanism of receiving testimony and forming beliefs on that basis is involved besides the proponent's giving testimony, we need to note ways in which that mechanism also can be epistemically compromised. Ignoring certain defeaters constitutes evidence of compromise. This can happen for three reasons. The challenger may be aware of conflicting testimony, of indications undercutting the presumption of trust that the proponent is speaking sincerely, and the implausibility, indeed astonishing nature of the proponent's report.

The challenger's being aware of testimony from another witness which conflicts with the testimony of the proponent would *prima facie* undercut the presumption for the proponent's individual report. This need not mean that there is a presumption for the word of the opposing witness. It could be that without further evidence, there would be a presumption for neither claim. We say that opposing testimony would *prima facie* undercut the presumption in favor of the proponent's personal testimony, because the challenger may be aware of evidence that the opposing witness is epistemically compromised or that the witness's testimony exhibits either of the two further defeaters we are about to discuss. Should the opposing witness's word not be a matter of personal but of received testimony, yet the challenger have no evidence for the reliability of the chain of reporters, the presumption for the proponent's word need not be undercut.

Evidence that the proponent is not sincere constitutes another way in which the proponent as a source can be compromised. Such evidence defeats the presumption of trust for the proponent. For example, is the challenger aware that the proponent has a reputation for inaccuracy or irresponsibility, that he has lied in making similar reports in the past, is prejudiced on one side of an issue, or even has a vested interest in his audience's accepting some view? (Compare Govier 1985, p. 83.) Such facts indicate unreliability and thus undercut the presumption in favor of the proponent's personal testimony. Should the challenger believe what the witness has reported without this defeating issue of insincerity being countered, she would have evidence that *her* testimonial belief-generating mechanism was not functioning properly.

One further problem relating to the presumptive reliability of a witness's personal testimony may arise: If the witness makes a report that the challenger finds implausible given her dialectical situation, is there still a presumption from her point of view for the reliability of the witness's testimony? The implausibility of such reports as

7. Yesterday some ghosts visited us for a tea party.
8. Boy lifts twenty-five-hundred-pound car through his own (unaided) muscle power.

seems clearly to undercut any presumption for the personal testimony of the proponent in this case. Reports exceeding normal sensory capability also are implausible, where recognizing the implausibility should constitute a defeater. For example,

9. We saw a whale at the aquarium yesterday

falls completely within the limits of visual sensory capability. But

10. We saw that the wire is one cm thick.

that is, we are alleging that our belief that the wire was of this thickness was generated through visual sense perception, falls outside the limits for which visual perception is presumptively reliable. The report presupposes a sensory capability far more acute than what is normal for human beings, and thus is implausible.

The issue of sensory capability involves contextual factors. Should our visual perception be aided by a vernier caliper, there would be a presumption for its reliability, as long as there is a presumption that we understood how to read the caliper and that the caliper were competently constructed. This is acquired institutional perception. The presence or absence of devices aiding our sensory capabilities is only one contextual factor affecting the presumptive reliability of perception in a given case.

11. My watch is on the kitchen table.

said by someone just coming from the kitchen is ordinarily completely within the bounds of reliability for sense perception. But

12. My watch is in the pawnbroker's window in the shop across the street at the end of the block.

raises clear questions of sensory capability. Given the context of the observer, that is, his distance from the object, we cannot presume his perception presumptively reliable.

A particular contextual factor affecting sensory capability concerns the care with which the witness has made the observation he is reporting. Suppose a witness is standing right in front of the pawnshop window, rather than a block away, and puts forward (12) on the basis of what he perceives in the window. Suppose however the witness has just glanced in the window. Has he exerted sufficient care to vouch for (12)? Is his visual sense perception presumptively reliable in this context? By contrast, our witness's looking carefully at the watch in the window constitutes no defeater for his visual sense perception's being presumptively reliable.

Will there always fail to be a presumption for any astonishing report and does this indicate that there will fail to be a presumption for reports of the unexpected in general? This issue has elicited distinct philosophical discussion, perhaps most famously in Hume's appraisal of reports of miracles. Hume would have us reject such reports out of hand, and not only reports of the miraculous but reports in general which do not conform to "our own knowledge, observation, and experience" (Coady 1992, p. 181). Hume's position is that whenever "the testimony of others vouching for their observation and experience" (1992, p. 181) conflicts with the uniformities or regularities that our own knowledge and experience have disclosed, the latter should "either be decisive or at least heavily preponderant" (1992, p. 182).[3] Hume will not even grant credibility to accumulated testimony to the unexpected or astonishing: "But as finite added to finite never approaches a hair's breadth nearer to infinite; so a fact incredible in itself, acquires not the smallest accession of probability by the accumulation of testimony" (1875, p. 424, quoted in 1992: 182).[4]

As Coady points out, the consequences of this position are absurd. If embraced in this extreme form, one would reject all reports of behavior in other cultures or at other historical periods that do not conform to the regularities of human behavior that our own experience in our own culture and historical epoch discloses. "There is no human sacrifice in my world so there can have been none in the past, reports notwithstanding" (1992, p. 188).[5] More forcefully yet, on this view scientific discovery, as portrayed by Kuhn, would be completely irrational and unwarranted. For, as Kuhn points out, "Discovery commences with the awareness of anomaly, i.e., with the recognition that nature has somehow violated the paradigm-induced *expectations* that govern normal science" (1970, pp. 52–53, italics added). On Hume's position, any report of anomaly is to be rejected precisely because it contradicts our paradigm-induced expectations, no matter how many will testify to the anomaly. This is to adopt a total conservatism in science, refusing to consider evidence which might lead to paradigm adjustment or paradigm shift. In light of this, we can set an extreme Humean skepticism aside.

The extreme skeptical position claims that not only will there fail to be a presumption for any astonishing or even unexpected report, but that the proponent can never discharge the burden of proof incumbent on him in advancing the report. A more moderate position would hold that being astonishing or unexpected undercuts the presumption for a report vouched for by personal testimony, but holds no brief that the burden of proof incumbent upon someone who makes such a report cannot be discharged. This position accords with a principle of presumption already recognized in debate, "the familiar standing presumption in favor of the normal, usual, customary state of things" (Rescher 1977a, p. 37).

In a conflict, the presumption for the normal, although defeasible, takes precedence over the presumption for personal testimony.

One question remains. If a report's being astonishing undercuts the presumption for the personal testimony of a single witness, will it under-cut the presumption for the personal testimony of several witnesses? Can several witnesses' testifying to the same incredible event in combination constitute a source for which there *is* a presumption? This seems intuitively plausible. But one can charge that our intuitions are guided more by our knowledge of how we *form* beliefs given multiple testimony than of intuitions concerning whether those beliefs are acceptable. Surely, if I hear an astonishing report from one witness, I may be little disposed to feel that report true. But now suppose that nine more witnesses come forward and vouch for that astonishing report. Unless *my* resistance is incredible, I should now be disposed to feel that report true. Is there a presumption for it? Could one rather charge that my testimonial belief-generating mechanism is not functioning properly in this case?

We may argue that as long as there is no evidence to undercut the presumption for each witness individually, apart from the astonishing nature of the report, there is a presumption for the belief from the point of view of the challenger. She is aware that ten individuals have testified to this report. Upon reflection, she could form beliefs for each of these witnesses that he or she has given this testimony. There will be a presumption for *these* perceptual beliefs for the challenger. Given the presumption of trust, she may presume that the witnesses are sincerely speaking their minds. But given that each of these ten witnesses has testified to the same astonishing report, the question arises of how to explain this convergence of testimony. That what they reported really happened and caused their perceptions of what they reported constitutes an explanation of the convergence. Given an appropriate number of witnesses, the explanation that they are speaking truly will be a best explanation. Recall that we are assuming that the only reason to withhold acceptance in these cases is the astonishing nature of the report. Hence, there is no evidence that the testimony of these witnesses is compromised by their emotional state, as would be the case in mass hysteria. But if the explanation is a best explanation, then – assuming that arguments to best explanation transfer presumption from their premises to their conclusions – the challenger would be justified in accepting the conclusion of the explanation on the basis of an argument to best explanation. The premises of that argument are the claims that each of these witnesses has given the same testimony, premises for which there is a presumption in each case. But the conclusion of this argument is the astonishing report. Hence, if accepting that report on the basis of an argument to best explanation is proper, so should be accepting the report as a basic belief on the basis of the combined testimony of the ten witnesses.

This general argument is nicely illustrated by an example from Laplace.[6] Suppose someone reported that he had tossed one hundred dice and they all landed on the same face. We would not believe him. Laplace claims that even if we witnessed this ourselves, we would not believe it unless we "brought in the testimony of other eyes in order to be quite sure that there had been neither hallucination nor deception" (1951, p. 118, quoted in Coady 1992, pp. 180–1). The astonishing nature of the event undercuts even the presumption for one's own perception of it. But should the testimony of others corroborate my perception, the statement that the event happened becomes acceptable. Because the corroboration rules out alternative explanations (hallucination and deception), the best explanation of the convergent testimony is the truth of what is attested to. But if the claim is acceptable as the conclusion of an argument to best explanation whose premises are that certain reports were made and perceptions had, surely it is acceptable as a basic belief on account of there being an unrebutted presumption for the reliability of those sources combined.

TESTIMONY RECEIVED THROUGH A CHAIN. Suppose the proponent put forward a report of an individual event or condition as a basic premise where the challenger has no reason to believe the proponent himself has witnessed that event or condition. The proponent's report then, for all the challenger knows, is at least secondhand and has come through a testimonial chain. As we saw in Section 10.6, there is not a presumption for testimony received through a chain unless there is evidence of the presumptive reliability of the chain. The question for determining whether the premise is acceptable now is not simply whether the proponent is aware of factors undercutting presumption. The question is whether she is aware of factors establishing a presumption in this case to begin with.

Recall that there are two types of chains which transmit the word of others, linear and convergent.[7] When considering the question of whether the challenger is aware of factors establishing the presumptive reliability of a chain, there are basically four structural possibilities to consider. Two involve linear chains; two convergent. If the challenger is aware that each reporter in a linear chain through which a report has passed to a proponent is reliable, say because each reporter had a reputation for reliability or a responsibility to be reliable, for example, because the proponent has received his report from a reliable news agency, then there would be a presumption of reliability for the chain as a source of testimony from her point of view. Structurally, the situation looks like this:

$$E \Rightarrow T_{\text{FIRST-HAND WITNESS}}E \rightarrow \ldots \rightarrow T_{\text{NEWS AGENCY}}E$$
$$\rightarrow T_{\text{PROPONENT}}E \rightarrow \text{CHALLENGER}$$

But, in general, we could not expect the challenger to have access to such information. Suppose the challenger were aware that the proponent received the report directly from a firsthand witness. Here we have a two-member chain, as our diagram shows:

$$E \Rightarrow T_{\text{FIRSTHAND WITNESS}}E \rightarrow T_{\text{PROPONENT}}E \rightarrow \text{CHALLENGER}$$

Because there is a presumption for personal testimony, from the proponent's point of view the firsthand witness is presumptively reliable. Since the challenger knows that the proponent has received this report from the firsthand witness, why is there not a presumption, from her point of view for the reliability of the chain

FIRSTHAND WITNESS → PROPONENT?

The problem, of course, is that the presumption of reliability for the firsthand witness can be undercut. In some cases, from the contents of the report, the challenger will know whether or not this is the case. The challenger can certainly recognize whether the report lies outside human sensory capabilities or whether the report is otherwise implausible or astonishing.

But, whereas the proponent, having direct contact with the firsthand witness, may be aware of contextual problems we have seen would undercut the presumption of reliability for the witness, the challenger will not in general be in this position. For example, the proponent through his contact with the witness might be aware that factors in the environmental circumstances under which the witness made his observations undercut the presumption that he is making a reliable report or the proponent might be aware that the witness was emotionally upset over what was observed. The challenger, by contrast, is just receiving the proponent's report of what the witness said. Since she does not have direct contact with the firsthand witness, she will in general have to trust that the proponent is not aware of any such problems in transmitting and thereby vouching for the witness's report. But can the challenger presume this? She can presume that the proponent understands what the witness has said, that he has come to believe this report on the word of the witness, and that he is sincerely transmitting what he believes. But can the challenger presume that the proponent exercises critical faculties in accepting reports and thus transmits only reports for which he is aware of no condition undercutting the presumption?

Recall that to recognize the proponent's statement that p as testimony, a challenger must be aware of signs that the proponent is vouching for his statement and that he has the requisite competence, authority, or credentials to state truly that p. Surely being able to assess whether the presumption for a firsthand witness is undercut and to refrain from accepting and vouching for a statement under these circumstances are necessary conditions for the proponent's competence in transmitting reports. So, for this chain to be a *testimonial* chain, the challenger must be aware of such marks of competence. But this is not a matter of general presumption but of special acquaintance with the proponent. Should the challenger then be aware of such marks of competence then, *ceteris paribus*, she may regard the chain of firsthand witness to proponent as presumptively reliable. But, without being aware of such assurances, there would not be a presumption.

Even if a chain is presumptively reliable, the presumption for the proponent's testimony may be undercut. Before discussing convergent chains of testimony, let us consider these rebutting factors, because they are germane to discussing whether certain convergent testimonial chains are presumptively reliable. What factors could undercut the reliability of a proponent as a transmitter of the word or testimony of others? First, and most obviously, there is the issue of whether the proponent understands what the reporter has said. The presumption is for linguistic competence. This is just a special case of the presumption for the *status quo*. But this presumption would be undercut if there was evidence that the proponent lacked facility in the language one could presume the reporter was speaking.

As observer preconceptions or emotions could affect the reliability of one's perception, so they could affect the reliability of whether one reports the word of others reliably. Surely should one have a negative stereotype of some group, one could "hear" in a report concerning a member of that group not what the reporter actually said but what one expected the reporter to say. If one were emotionally upset, one might very well "hear" in a report something that would solace the upset rather than what the reporter actually asserted. Furthermore, in transmitting the report, does the proponent remember correctly and accurately what the reporter said? Has he just now heard this report or did he hear it some time ago?

The implausibility of the proponent's report could be a sign of any of these epistemic problems. It could just as much undercut the presumption of his reliability in making a report as it could his reliability in giving personal testimony. Likewise, if the challenger were aware of signs that the proponent was not speaking sincerely or if she were aware of conflicting testimony from other witnesses, the presumption for the proponent's reliability as a transmitter of received testimony in this case would be undercut. So as with personal testimony, the rebutting factors of conflicting testimony, lack of sincerity, and the overall astonishing nature of the report may undercut whatever presumption there may be for a report of received testimony, as may evidence that the proponent was epistemically compromised.

Turning now to testimonial chains involving convergence and thus corroboration, there are again two patterns to consider. First, the challenger could receive a given report from several independent chains. The proponent and several others could all vouch for the report, yet none of these persons would have witnessed the reported event or condition firsthand. The structure of the transmission chain might be represented through the following diagram:

$$
\begin{aligned}
&\ldots T_a E \;\to\; T_{r'} E && \searrow \\
&\ldots T_b E \;\to\; T_{\text{proponent}} E && \to \quad \text{CHALLENGER} \\
&\ldots T_c E \;\to\; T_{r''} E && \nearrow
\end{aligned}
$$

Obviously, the challenger could receive reports from only two or from many more than three reporters. Confining ourselves to the above diagram for simplicity and concreteness, the point is that even if the challenger has no reason to believe either that the proponent or r' or r'' observed event E directly and thus the testimony of each of them is coming through some chain, and the challenger has no knowledge of these chains, still the fact that the proponent together with r' and r'' all report that E serves to establish some presumption for the reliability of these persons, provided that the best explanation of this corroboration is that event E really happened and was observed.

Alternatively, the challenger might know that the proponent has received corroborated testimony, although for all she knows, none of the reporters from which the proponent has received his information is a firsthand witness. The transmission structure might have this diagram:

$$
\begin{aligned}
\ldots T_a E &\rightarrow T_{r'} E \searrow \\
\ldots T_b E &\rightarrow T_{r''} E \rightarrow T_{proponent} E \rightarrow \text{CHALLENGER} \\
\ldots T_c E &\rightarrow T_{r'''} E \nearrow
\end{aligned}
$$

Even if the challenger knew that the number of penultimate reporters was sufficiently high so that the best explanation for the convergence, should their reports really corroborate each other, is the truth of the report, would there necessarily be a presumption from the challenger's point of view that the entire testimonial chain including the proponent is a reliable source under these circumstances?

The situation is distinctly analogous to that where the challenger knows that the proponent has received his report from one firsthand witness. The presumptive reliability of that witness can be undercut in various ways. The chain of firsthand witness to proponent then will be presumptively reliable from the challenger's point of view only if she is also aware both that the proponent is able to assess whether the presumption for the reliability of the witness is affected by any of these compromising factors and that the proponent will not vouch for compromised testimony. Now the proponent in the current situation has received the same report from each of three reporters. From his perspective, each of r', r'', r''' is a proponent claiming that E, where none of r', r'', r''' has observed E firsthand. But as we have just seen, there are factors that would undercut the reliability of these proponents as transmitters of reports. Unless the challenger is aware that the proponent has the competence to recognize these factors and will not vouch for a report if he recognizes that these factors undercut the presumption of reliability of a significant number of reporters from whom he received the report, there will not be a presumption for the proponent's report, indeed for reliability of the chain of which the proponent is the final member, from her point of view. Could one accept, take as a premise, what a proponent says knowing that the proponent has received that report from several reporters yet not knowing whether the proponent can recognize the factors undercutting the presumptive reliability of these reporters and would discount their reports upon evidence of sufficient unreliability? By contrast, should the challenger be aware that the proponent is competent to recognize that a source is compromised and to refrain from vouching for a report upon recognizing sufficient evidence of compromise, then her awareness of the fact that the proponent has received testimony through a convergent testimonial chain fosters a presumption of reliability for that chain, in particular if the truth of the report is the best explanation of the convergence.

Summary Reports and Nonprojective Generalizations

As we indicated in Section 7.1, in some cases it is quite possible that one could come to believe a summary report just through one's own personal belief-generating mechanisms.

> 1. Over the past two weeks, the cellar has been flooded six times.

One could remember having perceived the cellar flooded six times. The question of whether there is a presumption for this statement, should the proponent of an argument put it forward as a basic premise, concerns whether there is any reason to doubt the reliability primarily of his own memory in this case together with whatever pragmatic issues may arise. We also indicated that introspection could be involved in the question of summary reports.

> 2. During the course of the experiment, I felt a warm sensation flowing from both legs up my body ten times.

Here again, the primary belief-generating mechanism is my memory, although what is remembered is what I have introspected. One also would appraise this statement for presumption as one would appraise any memory statement.

Coming to believe a summary report just through one's own personal belief-generating mechanisms however seems atypical.

> 3. During the second week of January, thirty homeless persons were found dead on the streets of New York City.

It is possible that one could have found all thirty of these persons oneself. By contrast, if one worked for the medical examiner's office, it is possible one could have observed five of these unfortunates oneself and received reports from one's colleagues about the other twenty-five. Here one's belief-generating mechanism would be a combination of memory and taking one's colleagues' word concerning what they remember. The question of whether there was a presumption for (3) from one's point of view as a challenger would depend on whether the presumption for one's own memory were not compromised in this situation together with whether the word of whatever sources reported the remaining cases constituted testimony of some sort, and whether in this case there was a presumption for that testimony. Again, pragmatic considerations may arise here.

Unless one has been involved in such data gathering, it would be rather unusual for one's belief in a statement like (3) to be grounded even in part on what one remembers. Rather, one would be relying on the word of some other person. Let us assume the person is the proponent of an argument. Unless the proponent has simply made up this summary report, two possibilities arise. Either the proponent is vouching for the statement on the basis of his own personal belief-generating mechanisms or he is reporting the word of someone else. If we as challengers are aware simply that the proponent has put forward a summary report and are not aware of his grounds, there cannot be a presumption of reliability for the proponent from our point of view as challengers, just as there could not be in the case of individual reports. *We* need more information. If the proponent simply made up this report, his word is not testimony and not presumptively reliable. If he received the report from some further source, the question then becomes the question of whether there is a presumption for the chain of which the proponent is the last reporter. We cannot answer that if the chain is otherwise anonymous to us. Let us assume then in what follows that the proponent does have grounds for his summary report and that we as challengers are aware of the type of grounds on which the proponent came to vouch for his statement.

If the proponent is vouching for the statement on his own, two further possibilities arise. Either the proponent is reporting what he remembers – as homeowner he saw the cellar flood six times – or the proponent has some credentials to vouch for the statement. The proponent might be the spokesperson for the medical examiner's office and thus speak with the authority of that office, or the proponent might have special credentials or recognized competence in data gathering. In the one case, we are dealing with personal testimony, in the other with a form of expert testimony. The question then of whether there is a presumption for the proponent's claim from the challenger's point of view rests on whether she recognizes that his statement is a form of personal or expert testimony, and is aware of no factors undercutting the presumption for such testimony in this case. Is there reason to question the reliability of the proponent's memory? Does another equally authoritative person give conflicting testimony? Is the proponent's sincerity in question? We have already reviewed these factors. Again, should the proponent's summary report be astonishing, presumption could be restored if it were sufficiently corroborated.

Suppose then that the proponent is reporting the word of someone else. Here we are dealing with a chain. As we suggested in Chapter 7, perhaps most typically one would come to believe a report like (3) through encountering it in some news medium. Here the news medium is the proponent and the question of whether there is a presumption for the summary report becomes the question of whether the medium is presumptively reliable in this case. But a newspaper might frequently publish summary reports without using them as premises in some argument. More typically, where we are dealing with summary reports from news organizations in the context of an argument, the proponent of the argument would be using a summary report he came to believe on the word of some news organization. Here, should the challenger be aware that the proponent has learned this summary report through a reliable news agency, there is a presumption of reliability for the source, news organization to proponent, from her point of view. There will be a presumption for what the proponent has reported, provided that the presumption of trust that the proponent was reporting what he sincerely believed the news organization to have said is not compromised and there is also a presumption that the proponent understood the news organization's report.

By contrast, the challenger could become aware that a summary report like (3) was vouched for by someone certified to make statements about vital statistics in New York City or otherwise certified to issue this summary report authoritatively. Here the presumption-establishing issue is whether the proponent has not uncritically accepted the authority's statement in light of factors that would rebut the presumption of reliability for the authority. Unless the challenger can presume this, the source

ESTABLISHED AUTHORITY → PROPONENT

is not presumptively reliable from her perspective. Of course, whether there is a presumption for this report from the challenger's point of view again concerns whether there is a presumption that the proponent is reporting sincerely what he understood to be reported to him and whether he properly understood the source.

The situation is parallel should the challenger be aware that the reported testimony originates with a person who is making the summary report on the basis of his own experience. This is personal testimony to a summary report that the proponent is relaying. Presumption for it from the challenger's point of view is assessed just as one would assess presumption for a proponent's report of personal testimony to an individual report. Finally, the challenger may be aware that the chain through which the summary report has come to her is convergent rather than purely linear. Again, we may distinguish the case of where separate linear chains converge on the challenger from where they converge on the proponent who transmits the report to the challenger. In both these cases, determining whether there is a presumption for the report from the challenger's perspective proceeds parallel to the cases for individual reports.

The situation is parallel for nonprojective generalizations. We could look at these as summary reports concerning some finite class.

4. All of the plants injected with that compound survived.
5. None of the animals injected with the vaccine and then with anthrax developed the disease.
6. Seventy percent of the animals observed developed tumors when exposed to radiation.

Exactly the same cases arise here as for summary reports, and the question of presumption is the same in each case. It is quite possible that any of (4)–(6) could report what the challenger has observed. Alternatively, the challenger may have observed some cases and be relying on the word of others for the rest. By contrast, the challenger may need to depend on the word of others, especially the proponent, to come to believe and accept any of (4)–(6). Now, the proponent could have made the observations to ground these statements or have some authoritative credentials to put them forward. For example, he could be certified to speak for a research organization that made and collated the appropriate observations. By contrast, the proponent could be reporting the word of some further source. Here we have a chain of reporters, hopefully a testimonial chain. The various structural possibilities to consider are the same as for summary reports. The proponent could have received testimony from someone who made and collated the grounding observations or from an authorized source. By contrast, the challenger could receive convergent reports from several independent chains or be aware that the proponent has received such convergent reports. Clearly, this is structurally parallel to the cases for summary reports and the questions for establishing or undercutting presumption are the same.

Projective Generalizations

As we pointed out in Chapter 7, projective generalizations such as

1. All swans are white.
2. Sixty percent of the voting population approves of the president's job performance.

extrapolating to entire populations rather than reporting on a sample actually observed, involve inference. Consequently, the only way one could come to hold such a belief in the basic way is through taking the word of someone else. The first casuistical question then is whether this source is simply giving his word, perhaps because he believes he has reliably inferred this conclusion from acceptable premises, or is giving genuine testimony of some sort. Because inference is involved, testimony presupposes the word is either an instance of expert or authorized opinion or an instance of common knowledge.

As we have pointed out, recognizing expert testimony is a matter of recognizing that the statement made is within an authority-conferring field by someone who has in some way been certified in that field. We discussed how one recognizes this in Section 10.7. If the word has come through some chain of reporters, then as with summary reports and non-projective generalizations the background knowledge in one's dialectical situation as challenger must indicate one of various structural possibilities. The proponent has received the report either from some expert or authorized person directly or through a chain going back to such a person. If the challenger can presume that the report has been transmitted reliably, then there is a presumption of reliability for the source. Whether there is a presumption for the statement from the challenger's point of view then will be determined by whether there is any evidence that the proponent is epistemically compromised, in particular that the proponent would not recognize factors undercutting the presumption for that expert testimony, or by pragmatic considerations. Obviously, the two paradigm cases of convergent testimonial chains that have been considered in connection with received testimony could arise here also. The question of whether there is a presumption of reliability for these sources and a presumption for their word in this case would be answered as with the cases for expert or authorized opinion for summary reports and non-projective generalizations.

It might seem that a statement like "All swans are white" is a matter of common knowledge. Now the mark of common knowledge is that everyone, or virtually everyone, in an historical or cultural situation believes that statement. As we argued in Section 10.8, common knowledge is presumptively reliable. Hence, once we recognize this of a projective generalization, unless we are aware of some defeater – such as direct evidence of a counterexample – there is a presumption for it and it is an acceptable basic premise. The case of projective generalizations provides perhaps the best transition to the next section. Ordinarily, someone asserting that all swans are white means to assert something more than the accidental or purely extensional universal equivalent to "There is nothing which is a swan and fails to be white." Rather, the person is asserting a nomic universal supporting "If something were a swan, it would be white," a generalized subjunctive conditional and thus an interpretation. We turn to determining when there is a presumption for interpretations in the next section.

11.3 UNDER WHAT CONDITIONS IS THERE A PRESUMPTION FOR A BASIC PREMISE WHICH IS AN INTERPRETATION?

In Chapter 8, we saw that three types of subjunctives – physical, personal, and institutional – were at the core of interpretations. Corresponding to each type of subjunctive was a mode of intuition. In Section 8.9, we saw that the interpretations analyzable in terms of these subjunctives did not require us to introduce any further personal basic belief-generating mechanisms, although some interpretations involve descriptive conjuncts. Hence, in terms of personal belief-generating mechanisms in connection with interpretations, we need to consider just physical, personal, and institutional intuition.[8] We also saw in Chapter 8 that only under certain circumstances are these mechanisms presumptively reliable. Whether a belief generated by the mechanism under those conditions is a properly basic belief depends on whether any presumption rebutting factors are present. Now, one could come to hold or believe an interpretation not through one's personal belief-generating mechanisms, but through taking the word of others. Hence, there are four cases to consider to answer the question posed by the heading of this section: physical subjunctives generated by physical intuition, personal subjunctives generated by personal intuition, institutional subjunctives generated by institutional intuition, and interpretations in general generated by taking the word of others. We take each case in turn.

When Is There a Presumption for a Physical Subjunctive Generated by Physical Intuition?

As we saw in Section 8.6, physical intuition operates when in a moment of insight we "see" that certain events, phenomena, conditions are nomically related. This may issue in our framing a general causal hypothesis or a singular causal statement, presupposing a general causal connection. If in framing the hypothesis, we also come to believe it, the belief will be basic.

But, unless our background information indicates that we may presume that no other relevant variable operates here, the belief would not be properly basic. One is not justified in accepting the hypothesis unless one is aware that these other factors have been ruled out. Should one obtain this evidence through some systematic investigation, one's belief would be justified but not basic.

Although physical intuition is not in general reliable, a certain mode of physical intuition – natural kind guided intuition – is presumptively reliable. Such intuition generates beliefs expressed by (generalized) subjunctives of the form "$(\forall x)(Nx \,\square\!\!\rightarrow \delta x)$" where "$N$" is some natural kind predicate and "δ" is a determinate of some determinable "Δ." The question for epistemic casuistry then is how may one recognize in a given case of natural kind guided intuition that the presumptive reliability of this mechanism has been undercut from the challenger's perspective. The first question concerns whether the presumption has been undercut for the guiding generalization that all members of the kind instance some determinable Δ and that there is a unique determinate δ which all also instance. Perhaps some living organisms instancing distinct modes of reproduction will come to be counted as members of one species. Although it will still be true that every member of the species will have some mode of reproduction or other, observing members of the species displaying a particular mode will no longer justify projecting that mode to the entire species, accepting the corresponding subjunctive conditional.

But there are further factors, both epistemic and pragmatic, of which one could be aware which would undercut the presumptive reliability of one's natural kind guided intuition. First, as natural kind guided intuition is a species of empirical intuition, one's belief concerning objects observed that they are N's that are also δ's will typically involve a perceptual belief. Hence, it is at least possible that environmental distortion undercuts the presumption for the perceptual beliefs that back our intuition. Indeed, any factor undercutting the presumptive reliability of perception in generating the backing beliefs would constitute a factor undercutting the presumption for natural kind guided intuition in this case. If one has come to believe that certain members of a natural kind instance some determinate of a determinable through the word of others rather than through personal observation, problems with the word as testimony similarly undercut the presumptive reliability of natural kind guided intuition in such cases.

How might natural kind guided intuition not be oriented toward generating true beliefs about natural kinds but beliefs satisfying some other need? Suppose some natural kind elicited a strong emotional response, either positive or negative. The wolf, for example, has frequently been an object of fear and some may stereotype the animal as evil. Such circumstances might lead to distorting natural kind guided intuition in two ways. First, the distortion may arise at the level of backing. Instead of seeing that some instances of that natural kind display the determinate of some determinable property, one might only *think* one saw such instances. Likewise, instead of genuinely receiving testimony that certain instances of the natural kind displayed certain determinate essential properties, one might merely *think* one had received such testimony, misperceiving or misunderstanding what was said to satisfy a desire to confirm one's stereotypes. But should one recognize that the backing for natural kind guided intuition has been reached in an unreliable manner, the presumption for that intuition to grasp a genuine connection in this case is undercut.

Second, stereotypes can distort natural kind guided intuition by leading one to confuse "accident" with "essence." Suppose one reliably observes that these members of the natural kind display some property which confirms the stereotype. But it is an accidental property, rather than one following from the causal essence of the natural kind. Nonetheless, through natural kind guided intuition one projects according to this property and accepts the corresponding subjunctive. Clearly, natural kind guided intuition has not been operating in a reliable manner here. Awareness that one holds a stereotyped view of a natural kind then is awareness of a factor undercutting the presumption of reliability for intuition guided by a concept of that natural kind.

Besides the presumption of reliability for natural kind guided intuition being undercut by these specific factors pertaining to warrant (in Plantinga's sense), it is also subject to what we might call external defeaters. If one not only has perceived members of a natural kind displaying some property regarded as an essential determinate but also perceived some counterexamples, then one would be confronted with a defeater to one's natural kind guided intuition that if something were to be a member of this natural kind, it would possess that property. In this case, we have not only direct evidence against the belief which natural kind guided intuition has generated, but also indirectly against the beliefs filling the essence placeholder for this natural kind concept. Clearly, also, awareness of evidence in general that the theory filling the placeholder in light of which intuition operates, even if that evidence does not falsify what is intuited in a given case, nonetheless constitutes awareness of a defeater for the presumptive reliability of one's intuition in dealing with this natural kind. Finally, the presumption for physical intuition can be undercut by pragmatic considerations. The question of whether the expected cost of mistakenly accepting an intuited subjunctive versus the expected cost of obtaining additional information legitimately arises. Indeed, as natural kind guided intuition operates in the light of a causal theory for which there is a presumption liable to defeat, pragmatic questions in some cases may be distinctly acute.

When Is There a Presumption for a Personal Subjunctive Generated by Personal Intuition?

We have argued in Section 8.6 that when personal intuition apart from empathy generates beliefs of psychological causation, such beliefs are not justified simply on personal intuition's voucher. These include statements to the effect that certain mental states have caused certain overt results or overt behavior. However, we have seen that personal intuition *is* presumptively reliable to generate beliefs concerning dispositions manifested through certain overt signs such as facial expressions, bodily gestures, or tone of voice. Likewise, intentional acts are signs of the proximate intention of the person who performed them. We have furthermore seen that personal intuition is presumptively reliable in generating certain subjunctives of psychological causation where one can empathetically feel the effect produced by the cause. So we basically have two cases to consider in asking when there is a presumption for a personal subjunctive generated by personal intuition – the case in which intuition involves an overt sign and the case in which it involves empathy. Let us consider each in turn.

Consider a dispositional statement allegedly believed through personal intuition upon observation of an overt sign. The first question to ask in judging whether this statement is acceptable is whether it is actually based on an overt sign of that disposition. Does the overt appearance or behavior of the person manifest signs of the disposition or is some further motivation being asserted? Someone's mailing a package is a sign of the disposition that the person believes he is mailing the package and has mailing the package as a goal. Ascribing some further motivation goes beyond this sign. If we knew of some want that might explain why the person was mailing the package, and came to believe that this motivation explained the action, the belief expressed by the explanatory statement would not be basic but arrived at by inference to (best) explanation. If some nonmanifest motive is being attributed, we are not dealing with personal intuition.

Suppose, however, that we are dealing with personal intuition. What factors might undercut its presumptive reliability in a given case? First and foremost, is the person intuiting the disposition aware of any defeater? Is she aware either through her own personal experience or through the presumptively reliable testimony of others that the signs of the mental states that the person is manifesting are at best signs of occurrent states only – states that are out of character and thus not dispositional? True, there was a momentary flash of anger on the person's face. True, occurrently the person felt anger. But that was quickly dissipated, especially when he gained a different perspective on the situation. Now, if one were aware of this, one would have a "sufficient overriding reason" against one's judgment that the person is dispositionally angry – sufficient to undercut or rebut the presumption for one's personal intuition in this case. To form the belief that the person had the disposition in light of this counterevidence would indicate that one's personal intuition was not functioning properly.

Because personal intuition is empirical, one must perceive overt signs of dispositional mental states or receive testimony about those signs before one can intuit those dispositions. Hence, awareness that one's perceptual mechanism was not functioning properly, or that it was operating in a distorting cognitive environment, or operating in a way not oriented to the truth would be evidence undercutting the presumptive reliability of one's personal intuition in a given case. Likewise, evidence countering the presumptive reliability of the testimony from a witness concerning the overt signs of a disposition would undercut the presumption of reliability for personal intuition based on that testimony.

Could personal intuition itself not be oriented toward the truth? Suppose one wanted to take the moral high ground vis-à-vis someone else. It would certainly be very convenient if the person was inappropriately angry, believed something stupid, or intended some obviously unworthy goal. To regard some aspect of the person's countenance or overt behavior as a sign of such dispositions could certainly be part of coming to hold beliefs accommodating our psychological needs. Pragmatic considerations also may undercut the presumption for personal intuition. Should accepting certain beliefs concerning someone's mental disposition justify taking the moral high ground against that person, such acceptance has distinct consequences for interpersonal relations. Perhaps this acceptance should not be undertaken lightly and deferred until there is even more evidence that the person truly has those affective dispositions, beliefs, or intentions before we regard our stance as justified.

Turning to personal intuition involving empathy, one circumstance in particular will serve to defeat the presumption for such beliefs. When we empathetically enter into a situation, we ordinarily presume that the person in that situation would interpret it as we would. Should we judge that if someone were to learn that her spouse was unfaithful, she would feel hurt, based on our empathetically feeling that hurt in that imagined circumstance, we are presuming of course that people care about the fidelity of their spouse. This would seem to be a safe presumption. But it could turn out false in a given case. Perhaps one's spouse has been unfaithful so many times that one's feelings toward that individual have grown completely cold. Learning of one further instance of unfaithfulness will provoke no emotional response.

Examples could be easily multiplied. We have desires and aversions and we may presume that other persons share our desires and aversions when we empathetically enter into their situation. The presumption may be perfectly legitimate. But it may be defeated in given cases. If so, we may not be feeling the situation as they feel it, and the presumption of reliability for our personal intuition would be defeated in such cases. Notice that the presumption that others share our desires and emotions may be undercut not only by evidence about others but by evidence that our desires and aversions are disordered. Evidence that I am subject to irrational fears, disproportional anger, exaggerated emotional attachments would be evidence defeating the presumptive reliability of personal intuition guided by empathy involving such emotions. As for presumption of reliability being undercut by factors dealing with warrant or pragmatic issues, our comments on personal intuition based on signs suffice.

When Is There a Presumption for an Institutional Subjunctive Generated by Institutional Intuition?

As we developed in Section 8.8, institutional intuition is presumptively reliable on condition that we have properly learned the constitutive rules that back the warrant corresponding to the intuited institutional subjunctive.[9] Whether or not there is such a presumption is part of the background knowledge one brings to a given dialectical situation. Is one able to engage successfully in or at least follow successfully that practice? Have one's attempts to engage in the practice or express one's understanding of it been accepted by others? Is one able to understand successfully the language in which some constitutive rule has been put forward? Have one's attempts to communicate with others via that language been successful? Recognizing that the presumption of reliability for institutional intuition has been undercut in a given circumstance seems equally straightforward. Have others disagreed with, taken exception to what I thought was a correct application of the rule or permitted according to the rule? Have others questioned my understanding of the language or of the given expressions in which a given constitutive rule is formulated? I might even question my own understanding, if the rule according to that understanding seemed implausible. Again, if I am encountering the constitutive rule through some formulation asserting that the rule had been declared by some authority, evidence that the text of the assertion had been corrupted or that it did not constitute the testimony of a reliable source would undercut the presumption of reliability for my institutional intuition in this case. Similarly, if I had been present at the promulgation of the rule but had reason to believe I had not heard the promulgating authority correctly, that there was distortion in the medium conveying the message to me, the presumption of reliability would be compromised.

Furthermore, if there were evidence that I had a strong self-interest in the outcomes of the practice constituted by given rules – that I stood to gain significant monetary advantage if the team I was backing won the game – this could constitute evidence that my understanding of the rules was distorted. Institutional intuition might be operating in the context of a module oriented toward something other than the truth. Finally, pragmatic considerations could affect whether there is a presumption for institutional intuition in a given case. Suppose X has occurred in context C. By institutional intuition, I believe that if X were to occur in context C, then Y would occur or have occurred. But suppose the expected cost of Y is significant. I might then want to recheck my understanding of the constitutive rule backing this subjunctive before regarding it and its consequent as acceptable.

When Is There a Presumption for an Interpretation Believed on the Word of Others?

Notice that we are speaking of interpretations in general here and not just subjunctives. For an interpretation believed on the word of the proponent to be properly basic for the challenger, the interpretation need not be properly basic for the proponent. Hence, the question of the acceptability of interpretations on the word of others is not confined to the specific types of interpretations we argued could be seen acceptable on the basis of our physical, personal, or institutional intuition, together in some cases with other personal belief-generating mechanisms. It is quite possible that a proponent could vouch for a physical causal hypothesis as a basic premise, and for the challenger to find the premise acceptable, should she recognize the proponent's word as a matter of his expert testimony.

Clearly, in light of the types of subjunctives we have identified in Section 8.5, these signs of competence, if any, will not be signs that the proponent is giving personal testimony, since that pertains to events or conditions which one has witnessed. Even in the case of an empirical subjunctive that is a properly basic belief, a proponent's vouching for such a subjunctive is not an instance of giving personal testimony. One might give personal testimony to the backing, expressed in an individual report or a conjunction of individual reports, of a dispositional statement generated by natural kind guided intuition. However, the interpretation itself, for example,

1. Substance x has a boiling point of $y°$C under atmospheric pressure z.

goes beyond the backing. Where the boiling point of substance x is not a matter of common knowledge, if a proponent without recognized special competence simply puts forward that subjunctive, the challenger does not know whether the proponent has proper backing for the belief and indeed whether he has backing for it at all. Hence, the challenger would not be aware of any signs of the proponent's warrant to assert this statement. It would not be testimony from her perspective. For the judgment to be acceptable from her point of view, she would need for him to declare his evidence. But then *her* belief, should she believe (1), would no longer be basic.

Our discussion of types of interpretations and intuition in Section 8.9 indicates that with two possible exceptions, physical, personal, or institutional intuition is involved in coming to believe interpretations through one's own personal basic belief-generating mechanisms. The exceptions are ascriptions of nomic necessity and possibility, which involve *a priori* intuition and so again are not matters of personal testimony, and certain negations of interpretations that could come to be believed through one's descriptive mechanisms. But even the latter are not matters of personal testimony. Suppose the proponent asserted

2. It is not the case that substance x has a boiling point of $y°$c under atmospheric pressure z.

Assume the proponent has come to believe this negation of a generalized subjunctive through observing several counterinstances. Simply by asserting (2), the proponent gives no indication that he has made such observations. Why should the challenger accept the proponent's word, unless the proponent has also given personal testimony to his observations? Should he give such testimony and the proponent come to believe (2) on this basis, the belief again would not be basic on her part.

If the challenger's accepting the proponent's interpretation as a basic premise is to be acceptable for her, she must be aware of signs either that the proponent has the expertise to make this statement, that he is reliably transmitting the expert opinion of someone else, or that he is reliably transmitting common knowledge. (One might question whether this last alternative is a possibility. If an interpretation were a matter of common knowledge, would not the challenger have already come to believe it, independently of the proponent's word? This need not always be the case. For example, by virtue of the constitutive rules of some institution, it might be common knowledge among those familiar with the institution that if certain conditions were to hold, then some other condition would hold also. Familiarity with the institution might be widespread but not universal, and the challenger one of those not yet "initiated." Here the proponent could be rightfully described as transmitting common knowledge to the challenger, where should she take his word, she would form a belief new for her.)

As we saw in Chapter 10, there is a presumption of reliability for expert opinion and for common knowledge. The question for epistemic casuistry now concerns whether recognizing expert testimony or common knowledge and the conditions under which the presumption for that testimony is rebutted involve special considerations in the case of interpretations. Turning to expert opinion, suppose first the proponent himself is the expert. To recognize that the proponent's vouching for an interpretation expresses expert opinion, the challenger must recognize that the interpretation belongs to an authority conferring field and that the proponent has credentials in that field. If anything, dealing with interpretations should make this straightforward, at least in a number of cases. At the core of an interpretation is a subjunctive, physical, personal, or institutional. Recognizing what type of subjunctive is involved is a matter of understanding the interpretation. But a physical subjunctive may very well enunciate some causal law or nomic regularity of some physical science. A personal subjunctive may express some nomic psychological regularity. An institutional subjunctive will be a consequence of the constituting rules of some institution, which in some cases, for example, law, could itself be an authority-conferring field. In these cases, as least, recognizing the authority-conferring field should be straightforward.

By contrast, it also would seem straightforward that some interpretations would not belong to authority conferring fields. What are we to say concerning subjunctives ascribing dispositions to particular individuals?

3. John is pugnacious.
4. Jane believes that *p*.
5. Jones intends that *p*.

One must be careful here, since some of these statements might be included within informal authority conferring fields for which certain persons might have informally certified competence. Suppose John's wife of over thirty years asserts (3). Is she not in a position to speak authoritatively on which dispositions are in character for her husband? By contrast, someone's holding a belief or intending a goal may not be nearly as settled as a dispositional character trait. These statements may then not fall within an authority conferring field. This means that they will not be matters of expert opinion. A proponent's accepting such statements may be quite proper, but a challenger's accepting them may be proper only if the proponent also gives her reasons for them. But then the challenger is not accepting them as a matter of expert opinion.

Should one recognize that an interpretation falls within an authority conferring field, that we are dealing with an interpretation does not affect how we would recognize the proponent as an authority in that field. We have outlined these considerations in Section 10.7. Also, the fact that we are dealing with interpretations seems not to affect the circumstances under which the presumption for expert testimony needs to be set aside. No matter what experts may be testifying to, whether it be an interpretation or some other statement, conflicting testimony on the part of experts, awareness that the expert has a vested interest in what he is testifying to, indeed any evidence of disingenuousness or unreliability undercuts the presumption for expert opinion.

What may we say then if a proponent is not an expert but is transmitting the opinion of some expert? Here our considerations parallel those for what is ultimately personal testimony received through a chain, which we discussed in Section 11.2. Indeed, what we said there basically applies here, *mutatis mutandis*. This includes consideration of the four central structural possibilities. In particular, for the simple linear chain

EXPERT WITNESS → PROPONENT

there will not be a presumption for the proponent's word, unless there is a presumption for the proponent's judgment that the witness is an expert in the field to which the interpretation belongs and that the proponent can detect those factors rebutting the presumption for expert testimony. Should the expert be testifying to some technical interpretation, the challenger might need to be aware of signs that the proponent was competent to understand the expert's testimony for the proponent's word to *be* testimony in turn.

Finally, should one recognize that a proponent's premise expressing an interpretation is a matter of common knowledge, there will be a presumption for it. Not only oneself, but people in one's cultural and historical context have come to believe that claim. That the premise is an interpretation does not change the fact that these factors make it a matter of common knowledge, or change the fact that a presumption stands for it until evidence against that interpretation, such as evidence bringing a causal generalization into question, comes to light.

11.4 WHERE IS THERE A PRESUMPTION FOR A BASIC PREMISE WHICH IS AN EVALUATION?

In Chapter 9, we saw that two personal mechanisms generated basic beliefs expressed by evaluations – moral sense and moral intuition. Now someone could come to believe some judgment of intrinsic, deontic, or aretaic value by taking the word of someone else. Hence, in outlining the procedure for judging that an evaluation is acceptable as a basic premise, we need to include besides evaluations generated by moral sense or moral intuition the case of evaluations believed on someone else's word. For the latter, the issue of acceptability does not depend on the type of evaluation. We may treat all three cases together and consider this issue first. We shall then discuss for each type of evaluation separately how we may recognize whether there is a presumption for it, given that it is generated by the challenger's moral sense or moral intuition.

May There Be a Presumption for an Evaluation Taken
on the Word of Others?

A proponent may put forward claims not only of *prima facie* but actual goodness or badness, rightness or wrongness. When the challenger takes him at his word, she forms a basic belief concerning actual intrinsic or deontic value. In discussing then whether evaluations taken on the word of others could ever be properly basic, we are including more than just beliefs of *prima facie* intrinsic or deontic value, besides beliefs of aretaic value. As we have seen, for there to be a presumption for the proponent's word, that word must be testimony of some sort. Clearly, for evaluations this could not be personal testimony, since ultimately moral sense or moral intuition will be involved in generating such beliefs. Hence, the proponent must either be a moral expert, transmit the word of some expert, or convey common moral belief or common moral knowledge.

Can there be a moral expert whose word constitutes presumptively reliable testimony for an evaluation? As Coady points out, we do turn to others for their moral insights (1992, p. 73). What signs would indicate to a challenger that these others have the requisite competence, authority, or credibility? Following Coady, they include signs that these were good or virtuous people, or signs that they were persons of moral wisdom (1992, p. 74). "As Aristotle has it, 'we ought to attend to the undemonstrated sayings and opinions of experienced and older people or of people of practical wisdom not less than to demonstrations; for because experience has given them an eye they see aright'" (*Nicomachean Ethics*, 1143^b 10–14, quoted in 1992, p. 73). Surely we may know such individuals or know persons who believe they have encountered them, "intuitively" recognizing their moral authority. Thus, one would have some reason to regard their word on evaluative issues as testimony, sufficient for showing testimony outright should there be a presumption that these are persons of integrity.

Of the various factors which undercut a presumption for expert testimony, evidence of disingenuousness seems the most damaging. If recognizing someone as a moral authority involves recognizing signs of virtue or integrity, contrary signs jeopardize our continuing to accept our original appraisal of the person's character. Whether it would jeopardize that acceptance outright or just undercut the presumption for his word over this particular question would need to be decided on a case-by-case basis. By contrast, awareness that two recognized moral authorities disagreed over some question would undercut the presumption for their word in this case but not in general. Particular disagreement does not show that we cannot accept their word in those cases where they agree.

Suppose someone who claimed to have encountered such a moral authority reported the word of that person to us – some evaluative judgment the person vouched for. Would that statement be testimony for us from our point of view as challengers? Can we receive moral testimony through a chain? Such reception presupposes our recognizing signs that the reporter had the competence to recognize signs that the person from whom he received the statement was a moral authority. Here we are not encountering the alleged moral authority directly. Now although one might justifiably come to believe that the reporter sincerely believed he had encountered a unique individual who had vouched for a certain moral judgment, it is hard to see what signs would reliably indicate that the reporter had such a depth of insight into the person's character that one could presume the individual was a reliable evaluative authority and properly come to believe the evaluation simply by taking the reporter's word. The situation might be different, given convergent testimony.

There is one circumstance where we may recognize that taking the word of others seems justified, that is, where that word is a matter of common knowledge or commonly conceded moral opinion. This would seem to be a matter of general evaluative principles rather than particular judgments. Even if we do not remember from whom we learned a particular precept, that it is generally agreed to establishes a presumption for it. Our discussion in Chapter 10 of why there is a presumption for common knowledge covers the case of evaluations. Is the presumption for common evaluative knowledge undercut by disagreement between cultures? The question is ambiguous. Does the fact that there can be points of disagreement between cultures over what evaluations are commonly conceded in those cultures undercut any presumption for common knowledge in evaluative matters? But why should disagreement over certain points constitute a blanket rebuttal of the general presumption for common knowledge of evaluative issues? At most, disagreement seems to undercut the presumption for common knowledge over particular points. But we can question whether it shows even that in general.

Suppose a challenger has accepted an evaluation commonly conceded in her cultural context. Suppose she learns that in some other culture this evaluation is not commonly conceded and a conflicting evaluation conceded in its stead. Is this sufficient reason for the challenger to withdraw her acceptance of the evaluation until she gains proper evidence for it on other grounds? I do not believe this conclusion follows. Recall that evaluative judgments are supervenient. But evaluative properties may supervene over interpretive classifications. Take, for example, the wrongness of lying. Suppose our challenger had accepted the culturally common view that all lying is *prima facie* wrong. She learns of a culture that apparently disagrees. But lying is something more than uttering a statement knowing it is not true. One lies *to* some person. One may further understand that one can only lie to a member of one's moral community, which need not be the same as the community of all human beings. Suppose the challenger's culture regards the moral community as embracing all humans. The dissenting culture regards only persons within that culture as members of the moral community. An act that the challenger would regard as a lie would have a different meaning for someone in the other culture. Is the moral disagreement over lying or over the boundaries of the moral community? Because there is this alternative explanation for the disagreement, the challenger need not withdraw her acceptance of the general principle that lying is *prima facie* wrong. Indeed, apparently the only instances where withdrawing acceptance might be called for are cases in which the best explanation for the disagreement is outright basic disagreement between cultures over some issue:

Act *A* insofar as it is *P* is right.
Act *A* insofar as it is *P* is wrong.

If the only grounds for the challenger's acceptance of the former is her recognizing it part of common moral opinion, then her learning of the dissent may be reason to withdraw her acceptance.

Having discussed the conditions under which there may be a presumption for an evaluation taken at the word of others, we may in the rest of this section concern ourselves with identifying when there is a presumption for an evaluation generated by the personal mechanisms of moral sense or moral intuition. Following the order of our discussion in Chapter 9, we turn to intrinsic value first.

When Is There a Presumption for a Basic Belief of Intrinsic Value?

We saw in Section 9.3 that the sign of the *prima facie* intrinsic goodness of a state of affairs is the pleasure, more generally the satisfaction we take in it or judge we would take were we in that situation. Likewise, pain or dissatisfaction are signs of *prima facie* intrinsic badness. Should a challenger's moral sense vouch for the intrinsic goodness or badness of a state of affairs, we also saw in Section 9.3 that there were two sorts of evidence of which she could be aware that would defeat the presumption for her evaluation. First, she could be aware that there was something wrong with her satisfaction mechanism. Her awareness that she is envious of someone else rebuts the presumption that the satisfaction or dissatisfaction she feels over states of affairs the other person is experiencing discloses their *prima facie* intrinsic value. Awareness of any disordered attachments or desires, not just envy, is awareness of evidence that one's satisfaction or dissatisfaction consequent upon the fulfillment or frustration of those desires fails to disclose properly what is genuinely *prima facie* intrinsically good or bad. Finally, our awareness that our judgments of *prima facie* intrinsic value would not meet with either general consensus or agreement of those whose evaluations we respect is awareness of defeaters for the presumption for our satisfaction mechanism.

Section 9.3 indicated another type of evidence defeating the presumption for a judgment of *prima facie* intrinsic value. Except in cases of a belief that our own pleasure or pain is *prima facie* good or bad, where we are immediately, internally aware of what is judged good or bad, an introspective judgment reliable outright, the judgment of moral sense presupposes a belief formed by some other belief-generating mechanism whose presumptive reliability may be defeated in given cases. If there is not a presumption for that belief, there will not be a presumption for the evaluation generated by moral sense. For example, for there to be a presumption for the belief that someone else's pain is a *prima facie* bad thing, there must be a presumption for the belief that the person feels pain. Likewise, in forming judgments of the intrinsic value of particular instances of virtue, apportionment of happiness to virtue, knowledge, and criterial or teleological excellence in general, the moral sense presupposes that someone has performed a virtuous action, received their just deserts, possessed a certain piece of knowledge, or that something has satisfied certain criteria. All these beliefs are interpretations of various sorts. Awareness of epistemic or pragmatic factors that would undercut the presumption of reliability for the mechanism generating the interpretive belief would also undercut the presumption for the judgment of moral sense.

How may a challenger assess whether there is a presumption for her general belief that states of affairs of a certain sort are *prima facie* good or bad, a judgment generated by moral intuition? The feeling of pleasure or satisfaction in a given case is all the evidence one needs for the general judgment that the pleasure or satisfaction is a reason for the *prima facie* intrinsic goodness of a state of affairs, that is, that satisfaction is a *prima facie*

intrinsic good. Otherwise, our argument for the presumptive reliability
of moral intuition in Section 9.3 shows that in a given case the evidence
defeating this presumption is evidence defeating the presumption that
our satisfaction mechanism accurately reflects intrinsic value. Moral intuition in generating general beliefs concerning *prima facie* intrinsic value
grasps that because a state of affairs manifests a certain property ϕ, we
take satisfaction in it or would take satisfaction in it were that state to
be realized, and thus the state of affairs is *prima facie* intrinsically good.
We are internally aware of this connection and thus moral intuition is
reliable in grasping it. Hence, the question of whether a given general
judgment of *prima facie* intrinsic value vouched for by moral intuition is
acceptable becomes the question of whether one is aware of evidence
that one's satisfaction mechanism is disordered, at least in the subject
matter of this judgment.

May the presumptive reliability of moral sense and moral intuition
also be defeated on pragmatic grounds? Suppose one is aware of no
defeating evidence against one's satisfaction mechanism. May one need
in certain circumstances to grow in self-knowledge of factors that may
be disordering one's loves, desires, satisfactions? Surely in some contexts
taking mistaken judgments of *prima facie* value as premises could have
serious consequences. In such cases, self-examination before accepting
these premises may be in order.

Judgments of Personal Value

In Section 9.3, we argued that the moral sense was not just presumptively reliable but reliable in generating beliefs that persons had dignity
or personal intrinsic value, and moral intuition was reliable in generating the belief that this moral value supervenes simply on being persons.
To identify an object of our experience as having dignity, we must be
able to identify that object as a person. But if personal perception is
presumptively reliable in reading off signs of someone else's occurrent
mental states and personal intuition is presumptively reliable in forming
beliefs that persons have certain dispositions, surely they are presumptively reliable in allowing us to form beliefs that there are minds or persons who experience these states and have these dispositions. (Surely
also other persons' imputation of personhood to objects of their experience about which they are giving their word is presumptively reliable.) Indeed, to have reason to doubt such a belief we would need
evidence that the object before us is some cleverly constructed robot.

Although not logically impossible, this scenario is still technologically fantastic.

When Is a Basic Belief of Deontic Value Properly Basic?

In Section 9.4, we argued that moral sense and moral intuition were presumptively reliable in a given case on condition that our belief that an act has certain affiliative consequences is justified. There is little to add to indicate our procedure for recognizing in a given case that a challenger's belief that a given act is *prima facie* right, wrong, or a duty or that in general acts of a certain sort (e.g., promise-keeping) bear *prima facie* deontic properties is properly basic. Is there evidence undercutting the presumptive reliability of the mechanism by which the challenger came to hold the dispositional of affiliation that the deontic belief presupposes? If that belief were formed by the challenger's personal intuition, is there evidence that the intuition was not functioning properly in this case? Should the challenger have formed that belief by taking the word of someone else, is there reason to regard that word as testimony and if so, is there evidence that the presumptive reliability of testimony is undercut in this case? Should the challenger have formed the belief by basing it on other beliefs of hers (here the belief expressed by the dispositional of affiliation would not be a basic belief), do the challenger's premises justify her conclusion? If there is no evidence calling the justification of the dispositional belief into question, the belief that moral sense or moral intuition forms in light of this interpretation is properly basic. There is a presumption for it from the point of view of the challenger and she may take it as an acceptable premise.

When Is There a Presumption for a Basic Belief of Aretaic Value?

In Section 9.5, we saw that judging the moral goodness or badness of feelings, desires, commitments was epistemically primary and that such judgments, whether they concern the mental states of others or our own mental states, involve significant presuppositions. If there is a presumption for these presuppositions, there will be a presumption for the aretaic evaluation generated by moral sense. Given one's recognition that a feeling, desire, commitment satisfies certain conditions, seeing that it would either be shared by the agapic spectator, conflict with his commitments, or neither be shared or in conflict – the aretaic judgments of moral sense *per se* – would be immediate, given our understanding of the agapic spectator. The issue is whether there is a presumption that the feeling, desire, or commitment satisfies these conditions.

Suppose then that the proponent of our argument puts forward a basic premise concerning the moral goodness or badness of someone's feeling, desire, or commitment, a premise for which the challenger's moral sense vouches. Let us assume first that the proponent's premise concerns someone other than the challenger. Obviously, the first issue is whether there is a presumption for the existential belief that the person has this feeling, desire, or commitment. Is it a basic belief for the challenger generated through personal perception or personal intuition? If so, are the conditions for the relevant belief-generating mechanism's being presumptively reliable satisfied in this case and is there any evidence undercutting the presumption of its reliability here? Is it a belief the challenger takes on the word of someone else? If so, is that word testimony and is there any reason to regard the presumption for testimony undercut in this case? Is it a belief the challenger holds on the basis of other beliefs which constitute propositional evidence for it? If so, do these propositions constitute good reason for the belief? If the answer to the relevant question is negative, there will not be a presumption for the presupposition and thus not for the challenger's aretaic judgment.

As we saw in Section 9.5, in coming to believe that the agapic spectator would share some other person's feeling, desire, or commitment, should he be in that other person's situation, the challenger brings her interpretation of that situation to bear. Playing the role of the agapic spectator, although she empathetically enters the other person's situation, she enters it with *her* understandings. The casuistical question then is whether there is a presumption for these presupposed understandings. Although in many cases, this presumption may be a matter of common sense, of our seeing things as we ordinarily would take them to be, in others it may be undercut. Is the challenger then aware of any evidence which would defeat the presumption for her understanding of the situation?

If the person were a member of another culture, he might see the significance of certain features in a situation differently, but not in a way evincing culpable misunderstanding. This might lead him to feel differently about those features than someone not making that interpretation. In empathetically entering into the situation, we should attempt to view it from this perspective and ask whether the agapic spectator would share those feelings were he in this situation viewing it from this perspective. Again, is there evidence that this other person's view of actual duty or actual intrinsic value differs from ours and that this different view is not the result of culpable ignorance but a conscientiously held view? If so, is the challenger asking whether the agapic spectator would share the other person's feelings, desires, or commitments, given that he also shared these evaluations? By contrast, the challenger may be aware of no evidence that the other's understanding of the situation differs from hers, or if there is such evidence, there is also evidence that his understanding evinces culpable ignorance. The challenger then does not have to adjust for the other's possibly differing interpretation.

Should casuistical reflection confirm that there is a presumption for the challenger's interpretation of the other's situation, should such reflection not uncover any defeaters, then there will be a presumption for her judging that the agapic spectator would share the other's feelings, desires, commitments (or find them in conflict with his feelings, desires, commitments, or perhaps be neutral toward them). If there is a presumption that the other has a certain feeling, desire, or commitment, that his interpretation of the situation is legitimate, and there is a presumption that from his perspective the feeling, desire, commitment either accords with a commitment to do one's duty, bring intrinsic good into being qua intrinsic good, or to increase the pleasure or decrease the pain of others, conflicts with such a commitment, or is neutral to it, then seeing whether or not the agapic spectator would share that feeling, desire, or commitment or find it conflicting is immediate. There will be a presumption for the aretaic judgment from the challenger's perspective.

Suppose a basic premise in an argument expresses an aretaic judgment concerning one of the challenger's own feelings, desires, commitments. This may seem unusual, but it is not impossible. As we saw in Section 9.5, these judgments also involve presuppositions and a presumption for the judgment requires a presumption for the presupposition. Again, these presuppositions concern my understanding of the situation and I may be aware of evidence defeating a presumption for them. I desire to do X that is a duty, but doing X will bring me distinct praise. Is my desire a desire to do my duty or to be praised? If I am aware of a desire to be praised, is there an undefeated presumption for the view that my desire is to do my duty? Again, am I aware of evidence that I may have culpably come to hold a view about the deontic or aretaic value in the situation, for example that some act I desire to perform is right? In general, then, am I aware of evidence that I am misinterpreting the situation so that should the agapic spectator be in my situation, he would not share my understanding? Awareness of such defeaters involving such culpable ignorance is awareness of factors undercutting the presumption for the challenger's aretaic belief concerning her own feelings, desires, or commitments. By contrast, should the challenger be aware of no defeaters to her understanding of the situation, should she be aware that her judgments of deontic or intrinsic value are conscientious – that there are presumptions for them from her point of view – then there is a presumption for her aretaic evaluation of the situation and the premise expressing it is acceptable.

Finally, as we have seen in Section 9.5, moral intuition is reliable, and not just presumptively reliable, in reaching general judgments of aretaic value. Such judgments then are obviously acceptable as basic premises.

Theoretical Considerations

A Commonsense Foundationalism

We have accomplished the project of this book. We have given an account of acceptability for basic premises, explicating the concept and giving a rationale for why various conditions render certain basic premises acceptable. We also have outlined a procedure for determining in a given case whether a particular basic premise is acceptable. We conclude by putting this whole project in some theoretical or philosophical perspective. In contrast to the classical foundationalism that we criticized in Chapter 1, we call our position commonsense foundationalism. It is essentially the epistemological position Plantinga calls Reidian foundationalism (1993b, pp. 183–5) after Thomas Reid, the founder of the Scottish commonsense school of philosophy. We prefer "commonsense" to "Reidian," because we believe first that our explication of acceptability in terms of presumption is eminently in accord with common sense. Second, other philosophers, notably Peirce and Moore, are identified with common sense, and their views may enhance the philosophical rationale for our approach. Commonsense foundationalism raises some obvious "big" questions. Why should an epistemic approach to basic premise acceptability be a form of foundationalism? Why should one seek a commonsense approach? Are there objections that should be addressed? What questions remain open? We proceed to these questions in the following sections.

12.1 WHY FOUNDATIONALISM?

Although epistemologists may debate the nature of the noetic structure for our beliefs, it is clear that argument structure[1] is foundationalist. An argument will have basic premises, that is, premises that are not argued for at least in the context of that argument. These premises will be put forward to support further statements, which may be given as premises for yet further statements, which may support even further statements, until one comes to the final conclusions of the argument. Given any supported statement within the argument, we can trace its support back to some basic premise or premises. The basic premises thus are the foundations of a particular argument.

This is exactly parallel to our noetic structure on a foundationalist account. Certain beliefs are basic. We do not come to hold them by basing them on other beliefs or inferring them, either deductively or inductively, from other beliefs. Although some of these beliefs may in a sense be self-evident, others may be based on evidence, as perceptual beliefs are based on the evidence of the senses. But they are not based on further propositions. However, we do infer other beliefs from these basic beliefs or base other beliefs on them.

Some may object that our description of argument structure overlooks circular arguments. Is it not possible to have an argument where a statement S_0 is put forward to support a statement S_1, which in turn is put forward to support a statement $S_2, \ldots$, which in turn is put forward to support S_n, which in turn is put forward to support S_0? Where then is the foundation in that argument? Although such a structure is abstractly possible, such an argument is fallacious. In a good argument, justification for the premises will be transferred to the conclusion, *provided that* there is justification for the premises to begin with. The conclusion presumably needs justification. The premises may in turn receive justification from further premises, but if the conclusion is introduced as a premise, we have an unjustified and thus questionable premise and the argument fails to transfer justification to the conclusion.

Likewise, foundationalists reject circular reasoning for parallel reasons. According to Plantinga,

> If there is a *circle* in the basis relation – that is, a case where a belief A_0 is accepted solely on the evidential basis of a belief A_1, which is accepted solely on the evidential basis of $A_2, \ldots$, which is accepted solely on the evidential basis of A_n, which is accepted on the evidential basis of A_0 – then, says the foundationalist, the noetic structure in question is improper. The reason, in brief, is that warrant cannot be generated just by warrant transfer. A belief B can get warrant from another belief A by way of being believed on the basis of it, but only if A already *has* warrant. No warrant *originates* in this process whereby warrant gets transferred from one belief to another. (1993b, p. 178, italics in original)

Given this parallelism between argument structure and noetic structure, we hypothesize that should the basic premises of an argument express basic or foundational beliefs that are either self-evident or that are properly supported by nonpropositional evidence available to the challenger, the person evaluating the argument, those premises should be properly basic or acceptable for that challenger. It has been the burden of this book to clarify this hypothesis and present a confirming argument for it. That argument is the justification for the commonsense foundationalist position we have developed over the course of this book. But this leads to the second question: Why should a commonsense approach give us a proper account of proper basicality and thus of premise acceptability?

12.2 WHY COMMON SENSE?

Our answer to this second question is simple, if a bit contentious sounding. Any plausible account of proper basicality and premise acceptability will instance a commonsense approach. We hope that the commonsensicality of our position and its plausibility as an approach to basic premise acceptability is evident. If a basic premise expresses a belief generated by a presumptively reliable mechanism and one is aware of no defeaters, epistemic or pragmatic, why should one not find the belief properly basic and the premise acceptable until or unless one becomes aware of evidence of defeaters? To reject a commonsense approach is to embrace a form of skepticism. Can the skeptical alternative give us a plausible account of proper basicality and premise acceptability?

Could a thoroughgoing Pyrrhonian skepticism, for example, ever admit that any basic premises were acceptable? According to what may be our best reconstruction of Pyrrho's thought, he held that

All we know are phenomena, not the inner constitution of things – phenomena that cannot be classified as either true or false, since we do not know the things in themselves beyond them. . . . We must suspend judgment [concerning our relation to the things around us], must neither accept nor reject these things, since all we know of them are our own sensations. (Hallie 1967, pp. 36–37)[2]

Apparently, then, the only basic premises Pyrrho would allow are premises about our sensations and, further, he would not allow that we can argue from these to justify assertions about the things in the world around us. So, all arguments beginning from premises putatively describing objects in the external world, or stating the laws generally recognized to relate these objects, or asserting claims that certain states of affairs were *prima facie* good or acts *prima facie* right – in short, our deliberative arguments about what we ought to believe or do – would all have unacceptable premises, and thus be unacceptable arguments. For us, such an implication renders the Pyrrhonian skeptical approach totally implausible. Just consider: If, when appeared to in the manner of a tree outside my office window, the premises

> There is a tree outside my office window.
> There is not a tree outside my office window.

are equally unjustified, then how may we discriminate, judge better or worse, an argument that incorporates the former premise from one that incorporates the latter? Indeed, how can there be any evaluation of arguments as better or worse concerning our deliberating over what to believe or do in the external world, if all the premises of such arguments are unacceptable? If the skeptic allows that he may hold his skepticism only in his study and not when he ventures forth, we must ask whether he ever deliberates concerning what he should believe or do, once he ventures forth. If he does, we may ask what canons govern this deliberation, in particular what canons evaluate from what basic premises this reasoning may rightly proceed. Pyrrhonian skepticism stultifies any attempt to give an account of proper basicality of beliefs concerning the external world or acceptability for basic premises expressing statements about the external world.

Are other forms of skepticism less implausible? A full answer to that question is beyond our scope here. However, as some commentators have noted, the classical foundationalism of Descartes and Locke leads to the skepticism of Hume, as, as Popkin points out, Hume's is a Pyrrhonian skepticism. "His analysis revealed a skepticism about man's ability to gain knowledge about anything beyond the immediately obvious or demonstrable relationships of his ideas.... The quest for a justifiable basis for belief always reveals how unjustified are our beliefs about matters not immediately experienced" (1967, p. 455).

Reid developed his philosophy consciously in opposition to Hume's skepticism. We discussed in effect Reid's reply to Hume's skepticism and his defense of common sense in Section 3.4. (See pp. 49–52.) To our implausibility argument, Reid can add that skepticism confuses certainty with trustworthiness. To say that a belief-generating mechanism is trustworthy is to admit a presumption of reliability for it. It is not to say that the mechanism generates only beliefs which are certain. As we have seen, the demand for certainty is an unjustified and unwarranted demand of the skeptic.

We can see that Hume and Reid may be looking at the same facts concerning human nature but giving them a strikingly different philosophical interpretation. For Hume, nature constrains us to hold certain beliefs. For Reid, our constitution determines that under certain circumstances, when appeared to in certain ways, we form certain beliefs. Both recognize that these beliefs, in many cases, will not be certain. For Hume, demanding certainty, this means that we are in the grasp of forces which determine us to hold beliefs lacking justification. For Reid, not demanding certainty, the principles of our constitution whereby we form beliefs become the first principles of evidence. If we are constrained to form a belief in a certain way, why should we not accept it until or unless we become aware of some defeater? The belief is justified until rebutted because our constitution generates presumptively justified beliefs. It is an epistemically good thing to accept these beliefs, barring defeat or rebuttal. These considerations show how we can answer a Humean skepticism from within a Reidian framework.

By calling our foundationalism common sense, we identify it not only with the commonsense tradition founded by Reid. Peirce's critical common sensism can provide us with considerations corroborating our antiskeptical stance. We have noted that the skeptic may hold his skepticism while in his study, but not when he leaves it. Peirce urges, "Let us not pretend to doubt in our philosophy what we do not doubt in our hearts" (quoted in Skagestad 1981, p. 28). As Skagestad puts it, "We come to philosophy with a network of preconceived opinions which it never occurs to us to doubt, because we are not aware that they can be doubted, or even that they are there" (1981, p. 28). Our notion of a challenger's perspective is obviously aligned with this view. Should the challenger assess whether she should accept a given basic premise, she is not asking this question in a vacuum but from her perspective in a dialectical situation involving many beliefs. Ordinarily, most of these beliefs will not be certain or incorrigible. But it does not follow that the challenger should doubt them. Peirce holds that doubting all beliefs is psychologically impossible (Skagestad 1981, p. 28). From the perspective of commonsense foundationalism, it is epistemically unnecessary. If the source of these beliefs is presumptively reliable and the challenger is aware of no defeaters of this presumption or of pragmatic issues calling for suspension of acceptance until further evidence is available, there is a presumption for these beliefs. Awareness of a defeater would lead a rational challenger to doubt a particular belief. But surely awareness of such defeaters would produce genuine doubt as opposed to the Cartesian doubt of everything less than certain, which Peirce rejected as artificial. As with Peirce, our common sensism is a critical common sensism. Properly basic premises may be doubted under certain circumstances but not because they are less than certain but because we are aware of defeaters to their presumption. The skeptic goes wrong in confusing Cartesian doubt with genuine doubt.

<h2 style="text-align:center">12.3 OBJECTIONS AND REPLIES</h2>

Our commonsense foundationalism is open to objections that can be brought against a foundationalist approach in general, in particular to the claim that there are justified basic beliefs. BonJour argues that there cannot be such beliefs in the case of empirical knowledge. For BonJour, epistemic justification is essentially related to arriving at the truth (1978, p. 5). He argues:

> If basic beliefs[3] are to provide a secure foundation for empirical knowledge, . . . then that feature . . . in virtue of which a belief qualifies as basic must also constitute a good reason for thinking that the belief is true. If we let "φ" represent this feature, then for a belief B to qualify as basic in an acceptable foundationalist account, the premises of the following justificatory argument must themselves be at least justified:
>
> (i) Belief B has feature φ.
> (ii) Beliefs having feature φ are highly likely to be true.
> _____
> Therefore, B is highly likely to be true. (1978, pp. 5–6)

BonJour adds that, as B is empirical, it would not be the case that both (i) and (ii) can be given *a priori* justification, else an empirical statement would be justified *a priori*. He then proceeds to clinch his argument:

> If we now assume, reasonably enough, that for B to be justified for a particular person (at a particular time) it is necessary, not merely that a justification for B exist in the abstract, but that the person in question be in cognitive possession of that justification, we get the result that B is not basic after all since its justification depends on that of at least one other empirical belief. (1978, p. 6)

We believe that Alston's concept of epistemic justification which we presented in Chapter 4 straightforwardly allows us to reply to BonJour, and that Alston in (1983) in effect makes this point. What does it mean to be in cognitive possession of a justification? In the case of a perceptual belief, is it sufficient that we be appeared to in a way sufficiently indicating that the belief is true absent defeaters and we be aware of no defeaters? Must we in addition be aware that being appeared to in this way without awareness of defeaters is sufficient for justification – the meta-awareness requirement? In Chapter 4, we argued for the former against the latter. We saw that BonJour's meta-awareness requirement led to paradoxical, even absurd consequences (See pp. 76–78.), when taken in conjunction with his overall coherentist position. In (1985), BonJour in effect argues that unless one knows premise (ii) above, one will not see that the belief's possessing φ gives one a reason for thinking the belief true. But why should one think that? Suppose one is appeared to treely in the absence of any awareness of defeaters, but without any reflective thought of whether being thus appeared to makes it highly likely that one is truly confronted with a tree. Why does one not have a reason for thinking it true that one has a tree before him?

Alston comments that BonJour's article suggests "a confusion between *justifying a belief* and *being justified in a belief*" (1983, p. 87, italics in original). If one possesses certain evidence, one is justified in holding a belief even if one is not prepared to give a justification of that belief. The latter does involve giving an argument. But being justified in holding a particular belief does not presuppose that one can make that argument. By keeping these two notions distinct, one may avoid BonJour's objection. If one is aware of adequate grounds for one's belief and is not aware of sufficient or overriding reasons, one is epistemically justified in holding that belief. Such conditions strongly indicate the truth of that belief and thus believing it accords with the epistemic goal of maximizing true and minimizing false beliefs. One's being aware that the grounds epistemically justify the belief, that it is good from the epistemic point of view, do not make the belief an epistemically better thing.

BonJour may still have a reply here. Our illustration of adequate grounds for perceptual beliefs apparently appeals to the given. BonJour points out that to make such an appeal, one is not claiming that these grounds are certain or incorrigible or that they concern only the states to which a cognizer has private or internal access (1978, p. 9). One need not make such additional claims to hold a "givenist" position. But BonJour feels that even a moderate "givenism" is untenable (1978, p. 9). He argues that according to givenism, in an allegedly basic belief that p, we have a belief, a state of affairs that p, and an intuition or immediate apprehension of the state of affairs. But, BonJour asks, what is the nature of this intuition? "It *seems* to be a cognitive state, perhaps somehow of a more rudimentary sort than a belief, which involves the thesis or assertion that p" (1978, p. 10, italics in original). But is this true? Suppose I form the true belief that there is a tree outside my office window, being appeared to treely. It seems that the intuition or immediate apprehension is being appeared to treely. But how does that being appeared to involve the assertion that there is a tree outside my office window? For BonJour, the intuition's involving the cognitive thesis raises the problem of why the intuition does not itself require justification, a problem he does not see how to solve. But if what is immediately apprehended does not involve the cognitive thesis, the problem does not arise.

BonJour next considers the possibility that the intuition is not a cognitive state and does not need justification. But this makes "it difficult to see how the intuition is supposed to justify the belief. If the person in question has no cognitive grasp of that state of affairs (or of any other) by virtue of having such an intuition, then how does the intuition give him a *reason* for thinking that his belief is true or likely to be true?" (1978, p. 10, italics in original). But the antecedent of BonJour's question is not entailed by what is immediately apprehended not involving a cognitive thesis. I am appeared to treely. It is hard to see how being thus appeared to involves the thesis that there is a tree outside my office window. But, on the basis of this experience, taking it as "input," my perceptual belief-generating mechanism generates the belief that there is a tree outside my office window. The cognitive thesis is generated by the mechanism and is not part of the intuitive or given apprehension. BonJour thus believes that "The givenist is caught in a fundamental dilemma: if his intuitions or immediate apprehensions are construed as cognitive, then they will be both capable of giving justification and in need of it themselves; if they are noncognitive, then they do not need justification but are also apparently incapable of providing it" (1978, p. 11). We have shown that the second conjunct of this dilemma does not hold. We have grasped the dilemma by the horns. BonJour indicates that givenists will try to take a position like ours: "by claiming that an intuition is a semi-cognitive or quasi-cognitive state, which resembles a belief in its capacity to confer justification, while differing from a belief in not requiring justification itself" (1978, p. 11). BonJour feels that "This 'solution' to the problem seems hopelessly contrived and *ad hoc*" (1978, p. 11). But how is our answer in light of our illustration contrived and *ad hoc*? With this, we rest our reply to BonJour's objections to foundationalism.

Quine's web of belief is a current alternative nonfoundationalist paradigm for picturing our neotic structure. Fisher claims that work in the analysis and evaluation of "real arguments," arguments intended to convince others (2000, p. 109) strongly supports the paradigm. Examining the arguments one might bring forward pro and con these two accounts is beyond our scope to investigate properly at this time. We must be satisfied with two small points here.

First, Fisher admits that Quine's arguments for the web of belief, for seeing beliefs as mutually supporting and thus for implication as a symmetrical relation in some cases, do not suffice to show that "the traditional view that implication is an asymmetrical relation" (2000, p. 110) is false. They have thus not refuted that where a belief *A* justifies a belief *B* by implying or otherwise constituting evidence for *B*, where to justify *A* in turn we must appeal to some further belief *C*, that the regress of justification never properly circles back on itself but ends in some properly basic beliefs. The foundationalist may remain unconvinced of the web of belief view. Hence, foundationalism and its account of basic beliefs is still a viable paradigm, provided that objections to the philosophical coherence of the notion of basic or immediate belief can be answered. This we have already endeavored to do. Second, the existence of the web of belief account of neotic structure does not change the fact that according to the prevailing understanding of argument macrostructure, arguments have basic premises. What account can those who accept the web of belief picture give of premise acceptability and in particular of basic premise acceptability? What on that account does it mean for a basic premise to be acceptable and what are the criteria or conditions of acceptability? The burden is on the defenders of the web of belief approach to provide such an account.

12.4 PROSPECTS

Let us close this long project by noting several things which remain to be done. First, we have considered only intrinsic, deontic, and aretaic value, saying nothing of aesthetic value. But surely such statements as "This is beautiful," "That is ugly" are evaluations and such statements may appear as basic premises in arguments. Are such premises ever acceptable as basic? Surely it is too facile to say that all such statements concern matters of taste which we do not argue about, for surely art, literary, and music critics make cases for their aesthetic valuations and may argue from them. We should keep in mind that beauty is connected with certain pleasures at least. We may experience these aesthetic pleasures when confronted with certain objects that we may then judge to be beautiful. Ross characterizes aesthetic enjoyment as "a blend of pleasure with insight into the nature of the object which inspires it" (1930, p. 141).[4] Hence, if upon experiencing aesthetic enjoyment we form the belief that what is enjoyed is beautiful, we expect that belief would be properly basic just in case our insight, which we expect would involve some form of interpretation, were also properly basic. To ascribe beauty is to ascribe a special sort of intrinsic goodness. Hence, we anticipate that an account of proper basicality for aesthetic judgments might be developed along these lines. We leave this as an open problem for those interested readers familiar with the field of aesthetics or with better aesthetic insights than ours.

Our account of the sources that may vouch for basic premises may be criticized as incomplete, especially in light of our regard for the reformed epistemology of Plantinga and Alston. Sproule includes revelation as one source of our beliefs. Characteristically, revelation "involves a direct inspiration from the deity" (Sproule 1980, p. 60). Plantinga speaks of such belief-generating mechanisms as the *sensus divinitatis* and the internal testimony of the Holy Spirit. By not including these among the belief-generating mechanisms we consider, we incur the charge of stacking our whole enterprise with a naturalistic bias. To this, we reply with the theological principle that grace builds on nature. If so, then it behooves us to explore the natural belief-generating mechanisms first, before considering any putative supernatural mechanisms. At least, the principle gives us *prima facie* good reason for so proceeding. This indeed is Plantinga's procedure in (1993b), considering various natural belief-generating mechanisms there, reserving discussing the others for a sequel. The natural mechanisms have given us ample material for discussion here.

Finally, what some may find the most serious omission in this study is our not investigating the acceptability of basic premises which do not express basic beliefs – at least beliefs that are not basic for the challenger to whom the proponent is directing his argument. The proponent may put forward a premise without arguing for it and the challenger may believe and be prepared to accept that premise not because it is vouched for by one of her personal basic belief-generating mechanisms, nor because she properly takes the proponent's (or someone else's) word for it, but because she sees that it is based on other beliefs which she already accepts. But under what circumstances does this propositional evidence render the premise acceptable? We have endeavored to avoid answering this question by pointing out that the propositional evidence on which the challenger is basing her belief ultimately goes back to basic beliefs or propositions accepted in the basic way (barring a loop in the challenger's noetic structure). We can think of the proponent's argument being extended to reflect the propositional support the challenger accepts for the premise he leaves as basic and then ask whether the basic premises of that extension are acceptable. But we must also ask whether the connections between the premises and the conclusions in the extension argument are adequate. So the question of the acceptability of basic premises vouched for by propositional evidence raises the whole question of connection adequacy – the other principal question in argument evaluation. Should we have addressed that issue first before addressing basic premise acceptability?

There is good reason to think that the question of connection adequacy will raise the issue of basic premise acceptability. Let us assume that Toulmin's account of the layout of arguments is at least approximately correct for at least a certain class of arguments.

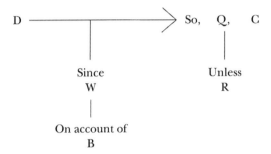

Toulmin's picture of how data and claim are connected raises the issue of basic beliefs in two ways. In Section 8.6, we discussed how the relation between backing and warrant should not be thought of as a premise-conclusion relation. (See pp. 183–4.) Now, because the warrant is properly thought of as an inference rule rather than a statement, the issue of its acceptability as a premise does not arise. But surely the question of whether the warrant is an acceptable inference rule *does* arise and, if the warrant is not defended, this would seem to raise the issue of basic acceptance. Again, as we saw in Section 8.5, corresponding to the warrant is a subjunctive or generalized subjunctive, whose acceptability stands or falls with the warrant. (See pp. 172–4.) Assessing the acceptability of the warrant involves assessing the acceptability of the corresponding subjunctive as a basic premise.

Furthermore, notice that a warrant can be rebutted under certain conditions. But then the warrant would not properly connect the data or premises to the claim or conclusion. Hence, for the connection to be adequate, there must be a presumption that these conditions of rebuttal do not hold in this case or that they are in turn rebutted or defeated. As we indicated in (1991), such statements could be incorporated into an argument as counterrebutting premises (see pp. 161–5). But such premises might very well be basic premises in these arguments and thus the adequacy of the connections presuppose their acceptability. Hence, answering the question of connection adequacy appears to presuppose that we have an answer to the question of basic premise acceptability.

Given our strategy of thinking of arguments involving basic premises accepted on propositional evidence as extendable to arguments where all the basic premises are accepted in the basic way or constitute basic beliefs, we have seen that we could present an account of basic premise acceptability without raising the question of connection adequacy. To give a full picture of epistemic casuistry we must raise that question, as indeed we must to give a full account of argument cogency. But the questions of connection adequacy and basic premise acceptability are distinct. "Sufficient unto the day is the evil thereof." The work of this day has proved quite sufficient and is now finished.

Notes

Chapter 1

1. This statement requires a caveat. Whereas for Descartes, it appears that the will is always involved in any assent we may make to a proposition and thus the question of acceptance always arises, for Locke, assent to propositions that are certain is automatic. We assent to them of their own force, without any act of will. But such propositions are still acceptable in the sense that assenting to them or accepting them is in no way counter to epistemic duty.

2. Wellman actually entertains seven arguments in all, but evaluating the others involves issues that would take us too far afield at this point.

3. For further development of these views on modal words or modalities, see our (1991), Chapter 5, and (1983), Sections IV and V.

4. For two of the points in this paragraph, we are indebted to Johnson (1990), which contains further critique of Hamblin's position. See especially pp. 284–5.

5. See Wellman (1971, pp. 147–8) for more on infinite regresses and an explanation of why this regress is vicious.

6. It is not clear from Grennan's account whether a statement with probability $2/3$ is likely true or probably true or a statement with probability $5/6$ is probably true or to be counted true.

7. We should note that for Grennan these probability measures are means to arrive at an overall judgment of argument cogency to be expressed in English. Arguments can overall provide weak, moderate, or strong support for their conclusions. Support strength is a function of premise probability and inference strength. Going from English evaluations to arithmetic expressions gives us an easy way of combining the values. For details, see (1987).

8. Our discussion of the senses of probability is heavily indebted to Nolt's account.

9. *Rationality: A Philosophical Inquiry into the Nature and the Rationale of Reason* by Nicholas Rescher (1988). Reprinted by permission of Oxford University Press.

Chapter 2

1. Ilbert attributes the quoted passage to Sir James Stephen.
2. Ullmann-Margalit cites Jones's text on the law of evidence as the source of this quote.
3. This does not imply that the Anglo-American system lacks any rationale for the way it assigns presumption and burden of proof. Assigning the burden of proof to the prosecution gives that side the weightier task. The prosecution must actually establish its case. It is sufficient for the defense to expose flaws in the prosecution's argument. But, as Walton points out in (1988, p. 244), this is perfectly appropriate where one regards the conviction of an innocent person as a greater injustice than letting a guilty person go free.
4. Indeed, in the course of this essay we shall develop a non-relativist account of presumption and how presumptions are allocated. In this we differ from Pinto in (1984), who questions whether there are objective, participant-independent principles of presumption.
5. We say that *principally* a dialogical situation will have two or more participants. This does not rule out that a dialogue could be internalized, with one person assuming various roles in an interior conversation.
6. For a discussion that emphasizes the challenger or listener perspective in developing a normative account of argumentation, see Heysse (1991).
7. Govier makes this point in (1987, pp. 283–4).

Chapter 3

1. *Rationality: A Philosophical Inquiry into the Nature and the Rationale of Reason* by Nicholas Rescher (1988). Reprinted by permission of Oxford University Press.
2. *Rationality: A Philosophical Inquiry into the Nature and the Rationale of Reason* by Nicholas Rescher (1988). Reprinted by permission of Oxford University Press. We may agree that there is a presumption for beliefs arrived at by consulting such sources as reference works or various instruments without regarding such beliefs as perceptual or purely perceptual. Rather, they involve relying on what is called *institutional testimony*. See Chapter 10, pp. 296–7 and section 10.
3. *Rationality: A Philosophical Inquiry into the Nature and the Rationale of Reason* by Nicholas Rescher (1988). Reprinted by permission of Oxford University Press.
4. One might object that I may have formed the belief by being appeared to in a manner that I have learned or taken to be a sign of the presence of a tree. Suppose upon entering my office, I am appeared to in the manner of a green dot with an arrow on it pointing outside my window. Suppose I have learned that such green dots are signs of the presence of trees, the tree being in the direction of the arrow on the dot. I form the belief that there is a tree outside my window. Now, although visual evidence is involved here, I have formed a belief that there is a tree outside my window without being appeared to in that manner. But where is the cognitive malfunction? We reply that there is no apparent cognitive malfunction here, but the belief that there

is a tree outside my window is not formed exclusively on the basis of untutored visual experience. I have learned to interpret experience in a certain way and this is part of the cognitive mechanism producing my belief. If we confine ourselves to beliefs based just on visual experience, as we may suppose is the case here, or extend our example to suppose that we were not appeared to in any manner signifying a tree, then it would seem our point stands.

5. This is not propositional evidence. Being aware that one is appeared to treely is not the same as accepting the experiential proposition, "I am now appeared to treely," from which a perceptual belief might be inferred. Rather, the appearance constitutes evidence for the basic belief that there is a tree in front of me.

6. This contrasts with Clarke's subjective definition. See 1989, p. 79.

7. Clarke refers to the latter as the *opportunity costs*. See 1989, p. 79.

8. For a discussion of why defining cost with respect to objective intrinsic disvalue rather than subjective aversion does not affect the possibility of our making intuitive judgments of the degree of cost, see our (2003, pp. 23–25).

9. For further discussion of this point, see (Freeman 2003, pp. 25–26).

10. This is what Reid calls reflection. See Beanblossom and Lehrer (1983, p. 153).

11. To play, obviously, on the title of Alston's paper, "An Internalist Externalism" (1988).

Chapter 4

1. These accounts appear in (Plantinga 1993a, pp. 7–8).

2. For Peirce, a judgment is a conscious representation to ourselves that we have a belief, where a belief is "a cerebral habit of the highest kind, which will determine what we do in fancy as well as what we do in action" (1955, p. 130).

3. As we noted in Chapter 3 (see note 11).

4. This corrects our position in (1996), where we argued that J_{eg} was too narrow, that a belief could be acceptable yet not justified according to J_{eg}. Our argument there was based on an inappropriately strict reading of certain characterizations Alston gives of an adequate ground. For Alston, S's believing that p on an adequate ground "implies that the believer is in a strong epistemic position in believing that p, i.e., that there is something about the way in which he believes that p that renders it at least likely that the belief is true" (1985, p. 81). Now it is easy to imagine situations that are not typical. Suppose there is no tree in front of me. I am appeared to treely because of some holographic projection which is highly realistic. Now I have no knowledge, justified belief, or awareness that the cause of why I am being appeared to treely is a holographic image. Nothing in my awareness suggests any reason to override the apparent adequacy of my experience to ground my belief that there is a tree in front of me. My situation is phenomenally or phenomenologically the same as if my experience of the tree were actually caused by a tree. There is a presumption from my point of view that there is a tree in front of me. Now can we say that, because of this environmental

anomaly, I do not possess adequate grounds for my belief that there is a tree in front of me, that the belief was formed in a way that is not objectively reliable? This does not follow. I am appeared to in a certain way, am aware of a certain visual presentation, and usually when I am appeared to this way, the perceptual beliefs I form on this basis are veridical. Perception is an objectively reliable belief-generating mechanism. As Alston has pointed out in a private communication to me, "even though the visual appearance is due to a holographic projection, the subject has an objectively adequate ground for the belief that there is a tree before her. I say this on the assumption that it is generally true of that subject that when she believes, or would believe, a tree to be before her on the basis of a visual presentation like this, the beliefs are, or would be, usually correct." Where an anomaly is operating in a given situation to affect the reliability of a given belief-generating mechanism, where there are no reasons to recognize the anomaly's operation, this fact does not render the grounds on which the mechanism operates inadequate.

Chapter 5

1. We note that Sproule says that interpretations principally raise issues of definition. Whatever value this may have heuristically, for our epistemological purposes we find it entirely inadequate as a theoretical account of what interpretations are or how they differ from descriptions. We also believe that it really does not do justice to Sproule's understanding of interpretation. We discuss these issues fully below. See pp. 105–7.

2. In (1998), Secor indicates that she now agrees with the arguability of facts.

3. As Plantinga puts it, "Reason is the faculty whereby we learn of what is possible and necessary" (1993b, p. 105).

4. Some may object that there are noncontingent or necessary evaluative statements, for example, Ross's principles of *prima facie* duty, which he regarded as synthetic *a priori*. Is the general or universal statement "Promises ought *prima facie* to be kept" a contingent statement? Given our analyses in Sections 9.3, 9.4, and 9.5, we regard these statements as not alethically logically necessary and so as contingent. However, we do allow that in another sense of necessity, a generalization of causal necessity that we develop in Chapter 8, principles of *prima facie* duty have a necessity.

5. For an extended discussion of the causal modality, see Burks (1951) and our discussion of causal and nomic necessity in Chapter 8.

6. For this example, we are indebted to Nagel (1961, p. 19).

7. We intend this characterization to include truth-functional compounds of interpretations. For a discussion of why such compounds are themselves interpretations, see Chapter 8.

8. We discuss explicitly how receiving testimony is a special case of taking someone's word in Section 10.2.

9. On the basis of this theory, Myers following Jung developed the Myers-Briggs Type Indicator used in psychological testing.

Chapter 6

1. Compare the discussion in Quine (1961b, pp. 22–23).
2. Compare the discussion in Bradley and Swartz (1979, pp. 240–1) to which we are heavily indebted here.
3. As is well-known, for Quine, the class of logical truths comprises just tautologies and first-order logical truths. From his point of view, the alleged class of analytic statements can be exhaustively subdivided into the formal logical and semantic truths.
4. *The Right and the Good* by W. D. Ross (1930). By permission of Oxford University Press.

Chapter 7

1. See pp. 49–50.
2. For our argument that it is not properly justified, see pp. 18–79.
3. This view is in essential agreement with Plantinga's position in (1993b, pp. 75–77).

Chapter 8

1. See (Nagel 1961, pp. 324–35) for a discussion of five senses of "chance" illustrating the distinction between absolute and relative chance and showing that chance does not introduce some further type of explanation.
2. Personal causal generalizations can be expressed through subjunctive conditionals involving some probabilistic modality. For example, "If the cultural upbringing of a person were to foster intense hatred towards tyrants and participating in the death of the tyrant were open to that person, then it would be likely that the person would participate in the death of the tyrant."
3. The material is presented in (Burks 1951, pp. 377–8).
4. Here "Ex," "Dx" obviously symbolize "x is a beam of electrons moving in a vacuum perpendicular to a magnetic field," "x is deflected," and "a" is an individual constant.
5. Not every ascription of intention is a dispositional statement, however. As Aune points out, there can be occurrent as opposed to dispositional intentions. If one resolves to perform a certain act in a certain situation, one's occurrent act of resolving "counts as a special case of intending – namely, intending as an immediate consequence of deliberation or choice" (see Aune 1967, p. 200).
6. Compare Taylor's discussion of plurality of causes in (1967, p. 63).
7. Sproule identifies one further type of interpretation – humor. Here again, although this marks a rhetorically powerful technique, it introduces no new type of interpretive statement in the logical sense. To point out facts, especially facts about one's opponent, which may be humorous is a matter of simple description, while to point out causal or dispositional consequences that are ridiculous, or to point out a significance that is funny, is not to go beyond the types of interpretation we have already catalogued.

8. Kornblith discusses this empirical evidence in (1993, pp. 100–05).
9. These are problems with the positive reliability of covariation detection. Kornblith points out that there are also problems with negative reliability. However, in assessing the reliability of a belief-generating mechanism, positive reliability is the issue. To fail to generate a belief that covariation is present when it is, is not to generate a false belief that covariation is absent.
10. Kornblith does not reply to this problem.
11. Plantinga also endorses this point. See (1993b, p. 75).
12. See Section 7.2, pp. 136–7.
13. These are Searle's normal input and output conditions. See (1969, p. 53).
14. Thus, the second condition for declaratives is exactly the same as Searle's second condition for promising.
15. Conditions 3–7 parallel Searle's conditions 5–9 for promising and are directly adapted from Searle's formulation. See (1969, pp. 59–61).
16. See pp. 164–5.
17. This clause is necessary. One might come to believe "It is not the case both that if John were hurt, he would run away and if John were hurt he would not run away" without coming to believe that either conjunct were false. But here the conjuncts are logically incompatible, as long as it is nomically possible that John could get hurt.
18. See p. 154 for the truth-conditions for this conditional.
19. See pp. 177–8.
20. These are reviewed in Nagel (1961, pp. 52–56).
21. In discussing a parallel example, Nagel concedes this point. See (1961, pp. 68–69).
22. See Nagel (1961, p. 71) for a specific example.
23. See Nagel's discussion of the nature of nomic universality in (1961, pp. 56–67).

Chapter 9

1. *The Right and the Good* by W. D. Ross (1930). By permission of Oxford University Press.
2. *The Right and the Good* by W. D. Ross (1930). By permission of Oxford University Press.
3. See Harrison (1967, pp. 71–72) for a contrast of these two views and decisive considerations against ethical logicism.
4. See abstract for Section 8 in (1986, p. 73).
5. Compare the discussion in Audi (1997, p. 44).
6. *The Right and the Good* by W. D. Ross (1930). By permission of Oxford University Press.
7. *The Right and the Good* by W. D. Ross (1930). By permission of Oxford University Press.
8. *The Right and the Good* by W. D. Ross (1930). By permission of Oxford University Press.
9. *The Right and the Good* by W. D. Ross (1930). By permission of Oxford University Press.

10. *The Right and the Good* by W. D. Ross (1930). By permission of Oxford University Press.
11. *The Right and the Good* by W. D. Ross (1930). By permission of Oxford University Press.
12. We are presuming the reader will grant some form of the correspondence theory of truth.
13. *The Right and the Good* by W. D. Ross (1930). By permission of Oxford University Press.
14. *The Right and the Good* by W. D. Ross (1930). By permission of Oxford University Press.
15. *The Right and the Good* by W. D. Ross (1930). By permission of Oxford University Press.
16. *The Right and the Good* by W. D. Ross (1930). By permission of Oxford University Press.
17. *The Right and the Good* by W. D. Ross (1930). By permission of Oxford University Press.
18. *The Right and the Good* by W. D. Ross (1930). By permission of Oxford University Press.
19. *The Right and the Good* by W. D. Ross (1930). By permission of Oxford University Press.
20. *The Right and the Good* by W. D. Ross (1930). By permission of Oxford University Press.
21. *The Right and the Good* by W. D. Ross (1930). By permission of Oxford University Press.
22. *The Right and the Good* by W. D. Ross (1930). By permission of Oxford University Press.
23. Ross is skeptical that humans ever desire to do the wrong *qua* wrong or to bring about some particular evil, although he believes that humans do desire to inflict pain on others. Hence, we expect Ross would be skeptical that there are the associated commitments. However this may be as a matter of empirical fact, it is not logically impossible that there be such evil commitments and thus that the desires in accord with them share their moral badness.
24. *The Right and the Good* by W. D. Ross (1930). By permission of Oxford University Press.
25. See references in (1993, p. 45).

Chapter 10

1. *Testimony: A Philosophical Study* by C. A. J. Coady (1992). By permission of Oxford University Press.
2. *Testimony: A Philosophical Study* by C. A. J.Coady (1992). By permission of Oxford University Press.
3. *Testimony: A Philosophical Study* by C. A. J. Coady (1992). By permission of Oxford University Press.
4. *Testimony: A Philosophical Study* by C. A. J. Coady (1992). By permission of Oxford University Press.

5. This understanding might be explicated through Searle's speech act theory. See p. 197.
6. *Testimony: A Philosophical Study* by C. A. J. Coady (1992). By permission of Oxford University Press.
7. *Testimony: A Philosophical Study* by C. A. J. Coady (1992). By permission of Oxford University Press.
8. *Testimony: A Philosophical Study* by C. A. J. Coady (1992). By permission of Oxford University Press.
9. This representation is adapted from (Coady 1992, p. 211). Here "a," "b," "c," ... "n" name witnesses or testifiers in a chain, "p" is a propositional variable, each superscript, $1 \leq m \leq n$, represents a sequence of m primes, where each prime ($'$) represents some modification of the statement to which it is adjoined, "$\Rightarrow$" represents that some experience of p is the input on the basis of which a makes his testimony. Finally "$\rightarrow$" represents the transmission relation.
10. Compare Coady's diagram (4) (1992, p. 212).
11. *Testimony: A Philosophical Study* by C. A. J. Coady (1992). By permission of Oxford University Press.
12. *Testimony: A Philosophical Study* by C. A. J. Coady (1992). By permission of Oxford University Press.
13. Example (7) appears in Govier (1985, p. 81).
14. This argument is basically a generalization of Moore's argument for taking common sense propositions as basic premises in philosophy. See Govier (1981, p. 31).
15. For a further discussion of slanting, see Freeman (1993, pp. 11–15).

Chapter 11

1. For a fanciful example, see Plantinga (1993b, p. 108).
2. These statements are numbered (1), (3), (4) respectively in Section 7.1.
3. *Testimony: A Philosophical Study* by C. A. J. Coady (1992). By permission of Oxford University Press.
4. *Testimony: A Philosophical Study* by C. A. J. Coady (1992). By permission of Oxford University Press.
5. *Testimony: A Philosophical Study* by C. A. J. Coady (1992). By permission of Oxford University Press.
6. Coady presents this example in (1992, pp. 180–1).
7. See p. 299 and p. 301.
8. We are here excluding certain interpretations, such as negations of interpretations, which can come to be believed through descriptive mechanisms.
9. For our discussion of what this involves, see Section. 8.8.

Chapter 12

1. Here we mean argument macrostructure as characterized in our (1991), how the various statements constituting an argument fit together.

2. "Pyrrho" by Philip P. Hallie. From *Encyclopedia of Philosophy* 7, Macmillan Reference USA, © 1967, Macmillan Reference USA. Reprinted by permission of the Gale Group.
3. BonJour is using "basic belief" as we use "properly basic belief."
4. *The Right and the Good* by W. D. Ross (1930). By permission of Oxford University Press.

References

Alston, William. 1967. "Motives and Motivation." *The Encyclopedia of Philosophy* **5**: 399–409. New York: Macmillan Publishing Company and The Free Press.

Alston, William. 1983. "What's Wrong With Immediate Knowledge?" *Synthese* **55**: 73–95.

Alston, William. 1985. "Concepts of Epistemic Justification." *Monist* **68**: 57–89.

Alston, William. 1988. "An Internalist Externalism." *Synthese* **74**: 265–83.

Audi, Robert. 1997. *Moral Knowledge and Ethical Character.* New York and Oxford: Oxford University Press.

Aune, Bruce. 1967. "Intention." *The Encyclopedia of Philosophy* **4**: 198–201. New York: Macmillan Publishing Company and The Free Press.

Beanblossom, Ronald E. 1983. Introduction to *Thomas Reid's Inquiry and Essays*: ix–lvii. Indianapolis: Hackett Publishing Company.

Beanblossom, Ronald E, and Keith Lehrer, eds. 1983. *Thomas Reid's Inquiry and Essays.* Indianapolis: Hackett Publishing Company.

Beardsley, Monroe C. 1975. *Thinking Straight: Principles of Reasoning for Readers and Writers* 4th ed. Englewood Cliffs, NJ: Prentice Hall.

Blair, J. Anthony. 1986. "Acceptability as the Criterion of Premise Adequacy in Arguments." Unpublished manuscript.

Blair, J. Anthony. 1995. "Premiss Adequacy," in Frans H. van Eemeren, Rob Grootendorst, J. Anthony Blair, and Charles A. Willard, eds., *Analysis and Evaluation: Proceedings of the Third ISSA Conference on Argumentation* **2**: 191–202. Amsterdam: Sic Sat.

Blair, J. Anthony, and Ralph H. Johnson. 1987. "Argumentation as Dialectical." *Argumentation* **1**: 41–56.

BonJour, Laurence. 1978. "Can Empirical Knowledge Have a Foundation?" *American Philosophical Quarterly* **15**: 1–13.

BonJour, Laurence. 1985. *The Structure of Empirical Knowledge.* Cambridge, MA: Harvard University Press.

Bradley, Raymond, and Norman Swartz. 1979. *Possible Worlds: An Introduction to Logic and Its Philosophy.* Indianapolis: Hackett Publishing Company.

Broad, C. D. 1952. "Some Reflections on Moral-Sense Theories in Ethics." in Wilfrid Sellars and John Hospers, eds. *Readings in Ethical Theory*. New York: Appleton-Century-Crofts.

Burks, Arthun W. 1951. "The Logic of Causal Propositions." *Mind* **60**: 363–82.

Carnap, Rudolf. 1947. *Meaning and Necessity: A Study in Semantics and Modal Logic*. Chicago: University of Chicago Press.

Cederblom, Jerry, and David Paulsen. 1988. "Making Reasonable Decisions as an Amateur in a World of Experts," in Trudy Govier, ed. *Selected Issues in Logic and Communication*. Belmont, CA: Wadsworth Publishing Company.

Clarke, D. S., Jr. 1989. *Rational Acceptance and Purpose: An Outline of a Pragmatist Epistemology*. Totowa, NJ: Rowman & Littlefield Publishers.

Coady, C. A. J. 1992. *Testimony: A Philosophical Study*. Oxford: Clarendon Press.

Cohen, L. Jonathan. 1986. *The Dialogue of Reason: An Analysis of Analytical Philosophy*. Oxford: Clarendon Press.

Cohen, L. Jonathan. 1992. *An Essay on Belief and Acceptance*. Oxford: Clarendon Press.

Conee, Earl. 1988. "The Basic Nature of Epistemic Justification." *Monist* **71**: 389–404.

Damasio, Antonio R. 1994. *Descartes' Error: Emotion, Reason, and the Human Brain*. New York: G. P. Putnam.

Daniels, Charles B., and James B. Freeman. 1980. "An Analysis of the Subjunctive Conditional." *Notre Dame Journal of Formal Logic* **21**: 639–55.

Descartes, Rene. 1960. *Discourse on Method* and *Meditations*. Indianapolis and New York: Bobbs-Merrill.

Fahnestock, Jeanne, and Marie Secor. 1982. *A Rhetoric of Argument*. New York: Random House.

Feldman, Richard, and Earl Conee. 1985. "Evidentialism." *Philosophical Studies* **48**: 15–34.

Firth, Roderick. 1978. "Are Epistemic Concepts Reducible to Ethical Concepts?" in A. Goldman and J. Kim, eds., *Values and Morals*: 215–29. Dordrecht: D. Reidel Publishing.

Fisher, Alec. 2000. "Informal Logic and Its Implications for Philosophy." *Informal Logic* **20**: 109–15.

Fogelin, Robert J. 1982. *Understanding Arguments: An Introduction to Informal Logic* 2nd ed. New York: Harcourt Brace & Company.

Frankena, William K. 1973. *Ethics* 2nd ed. Englewood Cliffs, NJ: Prentice Hall.

Freeman, James B. 1983. "Logical Form, Probability Interpretations, and the Inductive/Deductive Distinction." *Informal Logic Newsletter* **5**: 2–10.

Freeman, James B. 1991. *Dialectics and the Macrostructure of Arguments*. Berlin and New York: Foris Publications.

Freeman, James B. 1993. *Thinking Logically: Basic Concepts for Reasoning* 2nd ed. Englewood Cliffs, NJ: Prentice Hall.

Freeman, James B. 1996. "Epistemic Justification and Premise Acceptability." *Argumentation* **10**: 59–68.

Freeman, James B. 2000. "What Types of Statements Are There?" *Argumentation* **14**: 135–57.

Freeman, James B. 2003. "The Pragmatic Dimension of Premise Acceptability," in Frans H. van Eemeren, J. Anthony Blair, Charles Willard, and A. Francisca Snoeck-Henkemans, eds., *Anyone Who Has a View: Theoretical Contributions to the Study of Argumentation*: 17–26. Dordrecht: Kluwer Academic Publishers. 17–26.

Gettier, Edmund L. 1963. "Is Justified True Belief Knowledge?" *Analysis* **23**: 121–3.

Govier, Trudy. 1981. "Theory, Common Sense, and Certainty." *Metaphilosophy* **12**: 31–46.

Govier, Trudy. 1985. *A Practical Study of Argument*. Belmont, CA: Wadsworth Publishing Company.

Govier, Trudy. 1987. *Problems in Argument Analysis and Evaluation*. Dordrecht and Providence: Foris Publications.

Grennan, Wayne. 1984. *Argument Evaluation*. Lanham, MD: University Press of America.

Grennan, Wayne. 1987. "A 'Logical Audit' Scheme for Argument Evaluation," in Frans H. van Eemeren, Rob Grootendorst, J. Anthony Blair, and Charles A. Willard, eds., *Argumentation: Analysis and Practices: Proceedings of the Conference on Argumentation 1986*: 17–24. Dordrecht and Providence: Foris Publications.

Hallie, Philip P. 1967. "Pyrrho." *Encyclopedia of Philosophy* **7**: 36–37, New York: Macmillan Publishing Company and The Free Press.

Hamblin, C. L. 1970. *Fallacies*. London: Methuen & Co. Ltd.

Harrison, Jonathan. 1967. "Ethical Objectivism." *Encyclopedia of Philosophy* **3**: 71–75, New York: Macmillan Publishing Company and The Free Press.

Heysse, T. 1991. "Truth and a Theory of Argumentation," in Frans H. van Eemeren, Rob Grootendorst, J. Anthony Blair, and Charles A. Wlllard, eds., *Proceedings of the Second International Conference on Argumentation*: 84–91. Amsterdam: International Society for the Study of Argumentation.

Hitchcock, David. 1985. "Enthymematic Arguments." *Informal Logic* **7**: 83–97.

Hume, David. 1875. *Essays: Moral, Political and Literary* **2**. London: Longmans, Green.

Hume, David. 1888. *A Treatise of Human Nature*. Oxford: Clarendon Press.

Johnson, Ralph H. 1990. "Acceptance is Not Enough: A Critique of Hamblin." *Philosophy and Rhetoric* **23**: 271–87.

Jung, C. G. 1944. *Psychological Types or The Psychology of Individuation*. New York: Harcourt, Brace and Company.

Kornblith, Hilary. 1993. *Inductive Inference and Its Natural Ground: An Essay in Naturalistic Epistemology*. Cambridge, MA: MIT Press.

Kruger, Arthur N. 1975. "The Nature of Controversial Statements." *Philosophy & Rhetoric* **8**: 137–58.

Kuhn, Thomas S. 1970. *The Structure of Scientific Revolutions* 2nd ed. Chicago: University of Chicago Press.

Laplace, Pierre Marquis de. 1951. *A Philosophical Essay on Probabilities*. New York: Dover Publications.

Leblanc, Hugues and William A. Wisdom. 1976. *Deductive Logic* 2nd ed. Boston: Allyn and Bacon.

Lehrer, Keith. 1989. *Thomas Reid*. London and New York: Routledge.

Lennox, James G. 1992. "Philosophy of Biology," in Merrilee H. Salmon, John Earman, Clark Glymour, James G. Lennox, Peter Machamer, J. E. Mc Guire, John D. Norton, Wesley C. Salmon, and Kenneth F. Schaffner, *Introduction to the Philosophy of Science*: 269–309. Englewood Cliffs, NJ: Prentice Hall.

Locke, John. 1961. *An Essay Concerning Human Understanding*. London: J. M. Dent.

MacLagan, W. G. 1960a. "Respect for Persons as a Moral Principle – I." *Philosophy* **35**: 193–217.

MacLagan, W. G. 1960b. "Respect for Persons as a Moral Principle – II." *Philosophy* **35**: 280–305.

McKeon, Richard, ed. 1941. *The Basic Works of Aristotle*. New York: Random House.

Medin, Douglas L. 1989. "Concepts and Conceptual Structure." *American Psychologist* **44**: 1469–81.

Medin, Douglas L., and Andrew Ortony. 1989. "Comments on Part I: Psychological Essentialism," in S. Vosniadou and A. Ortony, eds., *Similarity and Analogical Reasoning*: 179–95. Cambridge: Cambridge University Press.

Meilaender, Gilbert C. 1991. *Faith and Faithfulness: Basic Themes in Christian Ethics*. Notre Dame and London: University of Notre Dame Press.

Moore, Brooke Noel, and Richard Parker. 1986. *Critical Thinking: Evaluating Claims and Arguments in Everyday Life*. Palo Alto, CA: Mayfield Publishing Company.

Moore, George Edward. 1903. *Principia Ethica*. Cambridge: Cambridge University Press.

Myers, Isabel Briggs. 1980. *Introduction to Type* 3rd ed. Palo Alto, CA: Consulting Psychologists Press.

Nagel, Ernest. 1961. *The Structure of Science: Problems in the Logic of Scientific Explanation*. New York: Harcourt, Brace, & Company.

Nolt, John Eric. 1984. *Informal Logic: Possible Worlds and Imagination*. New York: McGraw-Hill.

Paton, H. J. 1948. *The Moral Law: Kant's Groundwork of the Metaphysic of Morals*. London: Hutchinson University Library.

Peirce, Charles S. 1955. *Philosophical Writings of Peirce*. New York: Dover Publications.

Perelman, C., and L. Olbrechts-Tyteca. 1969. *The New Rhetoric: A Treatise on Argumentation*. Notre Dame and London: University of Notre Dame Press.

Pinto, R. C. 1984. "Dialectic and the Structure of Argument." *Informal Logic* **6**: 16–20.

Plantinga, Alvin. 1993a. *Warrant: The Current Debate*. New York: Oxford University Press.

Plantinga, Alvin. 1993b. *Warrant and Proper Function*. New York: Oxford University Press.

Popkin, Richard H. 1967. "Skepticism." *Encyclopedia of Philosophy* **7**: 449–61. New York: Macmillan Publishing Company and The Free Press.

Quine, Willard van Orman. 1961. "Two Dogmas of Empiricism," in *From a Logical Point of View* 2nd ed.: 20–46. New York: Harper Torchbooks.

Quine, Willard van Orman. 1969. *Ontological Relativity and Other Essays*. New York: Columbia University Press.

Quine, Willard van Orman. 1970. *Philosophy of Logic*. Englewood Cliffs, NJ: Prentice Hall.

Quine, Willard van Orman, and J. S. Ullian. 1978. *The Web of Belief* 2nd ed. New York: Random House.

Quinton, Anthony. 1967. "The *A Priori* and the Analytic," in P. F. Strawson, ed., *Philosophical Logic*: 107–28. Oxford: Oxford University Press.

Randall, John Herman, Jr. 1960. *Aristotle*. New York: Columbia University Press.

Raphael, D. Daiches. 1947. *The Moral Sense*. London: Oxford University Press.

Rescher, Nicholas. 1977a. *Dialectics: A Controversy-Oriented Approach to the Theory of Knowledge*. Albany: State University of New York Press.

Rescher, Nicholas. 1977b. *Methodological Pragmatism*. New York: New York University Press.

Rescher, Nicholas. 1988. *Rationality: A Philosophical Inquiry into the Nature and the Rationale of Reason*. Oxford: Clarendon Press.

Ross, W. D. 1930. *The Right and the Good*. Oxford: The Clarendon Press.

Ryle, Gilbert. 1949. *The Concept of Mind*. New York: Barnes and Noble.

Searle, John R. 1969. *Speech Acts: An Essay in the Philosophy of Language*. Cambridge: Cambridge University Press.

Searle, John R. 1979. *Expression and Meaning: Studies in the Theory of Speech Acts*. Cambridge: Cambridge University Press.

Secor, Marie. 1998. "Response to Freeman," in Hans V. Hansen, Christopher W. Tindale, and Athena V. Colman, eds., *Argumentation & Rhetoric*. St. Catharines, Canada: Ontario Society for the Study of Argumentation.

Skagestad, Peter. 1981. *The Road of Inquiry: Charles Peirce's Pragmatic Realism*. New York: Columbia University Press.

Skyrms, Brian. 1986. *Choice and Chance: An Introduction to Inductive Logic* 3rd ed. Belmont, CA: Wadsworth Publishing Company.

Smith, Adam. 1976. *The Theory of Moral Sentiments*. Oxford: Clarendon Press.

Sprague, Elmer. 1967. "Moral Sense." *Encyclopedia of Philosophy* 5: 385–7. New York: Macmillan Publishing Company and The Free Press.

Sproule, J. Michael. 1976. "The Psychological Burden of Proof: On the Evolutionary Development of Richard Whately's Theory of Presumption." *Communication Monographs* **43**: 115–29.

Sproule, J. Michael. 1980. *Argument: Language and Its Influence*. New York: McGraw-Hill.

Stevenson, Charles L. 1944. *Ethics and Language*. New Haven, CT, and London: Yale University Press.

Stough, Charlotte L. 1969. *Greek Skepticism: A Study in Epistemology*. Berkeley and Los Angeles: University of California Press.

Swinburne, Richard. 1996. *Is There a God?* Oxford and New York: Oxford University Press.

Thomas, Stephen Naylor. 1991. *Argument Evaluation*. Tampa, FL: Worthington Publishing Company.

Toulmin, Stephen. 1958. *The Uses of Argument*. Cambridge: Cambridge University Press.

Ullmann-Margalit, Edna. 1983. "On Presumption." *The Journal of Philosophy* **80**: 143–63.

Walton, Douglas N. 1988. "Burden of Proof." *Argumentation* **2**: 233–54.

Wellman, Carl. 1971. *Challenge and Response: Justification in Ethics.* Carbondale and Edwardsville: Southern Illinois University Press.

Whatley, Richard. 1968. "Presumption and Burden of Proof," in Jerry Anderson and Paul J. Dovre, eds. 1968. *Readings in Argumentation*: 26–29. Boston: Allyn and Bacon.

Wilson, James Q. 1993. *The Moral Sense.* New York: The Free Press.

Index

401